Native Chicago

NATIVE

EDITED BY

CHICAGO

TERRY STRAUS AND GRANT P. ARNDT

ISBN: 0-9663371-9-0

© 1998 Native Chicago. All rights revert back to contributors.

Proceeds from the sale of this book benefit Chicago American Indian Organizations.

For ordering information, contact the Master of Arts Program in Social Science at the University of Chicago.

Cover design by Eugene Pine.

Frontispiece image: detail, ancient trails and waterways. Illinois State Historical Library.

Printed by McNaughton & Gunn Inc.

⊚ The paper used in this publication meets the minimum requirements of the American National Standard for Information Sciences—Permanence of Paper for Printed Library Materials, ANSI Z39.48-1992.

CONTENTS

Introduction / ix
Terry Straus

Part I: Communal Roots

SECTION ONE: PREHISTORY

Preface: An Archaeology of the Soul, and
Weeping Greetings and Dancing the Calumet / 3
Robert L. Hall
Native Americans in the Chicago Area / 23
Ed Lace

SECTION TWO: EARLY CHICAGO

The Founding Fathers / 31
Jacqueline Peterson
Founding Mothers / 67
Terry Straus
Father Pinet and the Mission of the Guardian Angel / 78
Penelope Berlet
Red and Black Slaves in the Illinois Territory / 82
Jerry Lewis
Kickapoos and Black Seminoles of Northern Mexico / 87
John Hobgood

SECTION THREE: 20TH CENTURY CHICAGO

Native American Citizenship and Voting Rights in Illinois:
A Native American Womanist's Perspective / 97
Karen Strong
Relocation's Imagined Landscape and the Rise of
Chicago's Native American Community / 114
Grant P. Arndt
Relocation / 128
Ed Goodvoice

Excerpt from a Photoessay on Chicago Elders / 146
Edward E. Goodvoice, as told to Nora Lloyd
The History of the American Indian Center Princess / 148
Debra Valentino
The Chicago Indian Village, 1970 / 155
Natalia Wilson

Part II: Contemporary Life

SECTION ONE: ORGANIZATIONS

Native American Organizations in the Chicago Community / 165

The Chicago American Indian Community / 167
David Beck
Challenges and Changes in Indian Child Welfare / 182
Ingrid Wagner
NARA, the Center of Indian Community in Portland, Oregon / 196
Richard King
The Nation in the City / 201
*Grant P. Arndt, with information provided by
Demetrio Abangan, Jennifer Jones, and John Dall*

SECTION TWO: HERITAGE AND HISTORY

Coming Home / 209
Clare Farrell
The Schingoethe Center of Native American Cultures / 219
Donna Bachman

SECTION THREE: HEALTH

The Healing Circle / 227
Sara Boskowitz
American Indian Cultures Deteriorating From Within / 235
Tim Vermillion

SECTION FOUR: THE ARTS

Eugene Pine, Artist / 245
Terry Straus
First Voice / 248
AIEDA
Red Path Theater / 250
Ed Two Rivers
Poems and Drawings / 252
Jeanne LaTraille
Friends, Kings, and Princess • Chicago Streets • The Last Kiss / 260
Mark LaRoque

The Clown's Dance / 262
Alice Azure
Saturday Night Special / 272
Ed Two Rivers

SECTION FIVE: PEOPLE

Chicago Native American Demographic Profile / 279
AIEDA
The Contested Minority Status of American Indians in Chicago / 286
Marisa Westerveldt
Indian or Not? / 294
Lisa Ortiz
Culturally Intact Heroines / 300
Karen Strong
Canadian Islanders in Chicago / 305
Agnes Wagosh
Coming Around Again / 311
Mary Jacobs
Dr. Robert Beck: Reconnecting / 318
Terry Straus

INTRODUCTION

The concept and format of *Native Chicago* grew out of a prior volume, *Indians of the Chicago Area* (NAES College Press: 1990). In the eight years since the publication of that earlier volume, our colleagues in the social sciences have only just begun to recognize the ethnographic importance of urban Indian communities: published resources are still few and far between. Meanwhile, Indian people in Chicago have continued the critical and continuous work of creating intertribal community and identity: new ideas, new organizations, new stories have become part of community history and experience. Community is, of course, an ongoing process served by reflection and representation. There is always more to learn, more to do, more to tell. The hardest part of editing this volume was determining when and how to stop.

Editorial policy for *Native Chicago* was to accept and include any contribution which focused on the Chicago Indian community and was received by the publication deadline: content was not otherwise screened. Knowing well that those with the greatest knowledge of community process and history are community members themselves, we sent letters to the directors of every Chicago Indian organization, describing the volume and inviting contributions from community members. University of Chicago students, Indian and non-Indian, working in the community, were also invited to contribute. Three previously published articles were specifically solicited for the volume.

The organization of *Native Chicago* emerged from the articles themselves. Much to the chagrin of Mike Brehm, layout editor, the table of contents was the last editorial project rather than the first. Having learned from the experience of my valued friend and colleague, Tim Buckley, and from a long-ago reprimand by Inez Dennison, I have carefully avoided editorial explanation, interpretation, and/or footnoting. Having struggled with adequate three line representations of individual contributors in "about the author" sections, I have omitted such a section here, albeit with some misgivings. Most of you who read *Native Chicago* will know at least one contributor, and therefore can locate and learn about the others.

Terry Straus
July, 1998

PART I
COMMUNAL ROOTS

SECTION ONE
PREHISTORY

Preface: An Archaeology of the Soul, and
Weeping Greetings and Dancing the Calumet
ROBERT L. HALL
3

Native Americans in the Chicago Area
ED LACE
23

Robert L. Hall

Preface: An Archaeology of the Soul, *and* Weeping Greetings and Dancing the Calumet[1]

PREFACE

For 150 years and more museums have been collecting, curating, and exhibiting objects of material culture of the North American Indians. For 150 years and more scholars have been recording the languages, beliefs, and practices of the North American Indians. As a subfield of anthropology, archaeology has sought to straddle both lines of endeavor, using the evidence of the material culture of the past to reconstruct what it could of the social, political, and economic life in America before European contact. The motivation for all this activity has included some element of pure curiosity at all levels of concern, whether it be simply "to see what's there" or to pursue some more grandly defined programs envisioned by their authors to further the aims of social science.

Archaeology in particular has come under criticism from within and without. Beginning with Walter Taylor's 1948 *Study of Archaeology* archaeologists have become especially introspective, examining the theoretical basis for what it is they do as archaeologists. This has culminated in the 1990s with consideration of the question of whether it is really possible to know the past at all. Is our view of the past forever condemned to be merely a backward projection of the present, biased in this or that direction by special interests? For their part, American Indians have mounted their own criticism of anthropology, beginning with activities of the American Indian Movement (AIM) directed at stopping archaeological field projects and continuing with the broader-based campaign to reclaim Indian skeletons, sacred objects, and objects of tribal patrimony from museums.

It is an irony lost upon many that material objects of tribal patrimony often exist as such precisely because they did once become part of a museum collection. The objects of the three Sacred Tents of the Omaha are a case in point. There was a time a little over a century ago when tribal leaders were becoming very concerned over the fate of these objects. Care of the items was traditionally delegated to a line of hereditary keepers, but as the keepers advanced in years, no one was appearing to assume their roles. The objects were so sacred that only qualified persons could even touch them. The leaders were becoming reconciled to the conclusion that the objects would have to be buried with their keepers. Some of the sacred objects had already been buried when Francis La Flesche, the son of a former principal chief of the Omahas, negotiated the transfer of the Sacred Pole to Harvard's Peabody Museum of Archaeology and Ethnology, where it has remained until recently repatriated to the Omahas.

Much the same situation holds for Indian intellectual property. Contrary to much popular and even some scholarly opinion, Indian property rights were well defined. A man might know every word of a song by heart yet be neither allowed nor willing to sing it himself unless he had purchased or earned the right along set guidelines. A person who repeated a sacred story to which he was not entitled was more than a literary thief subject to angry words and actions from his fellow tribesmen; he faced the prospect of supernatural retribution as well. So it was that many custodians of tribal tradition faced a dilemma their ancestors could not have anticipated—whether to make the words of the sacred literature known to outsiders or to allow those words to follow them into the grave. And so it came to pass, for instance, that the guardian of the Sacred White Buffalo Hide transferred his knowledge to Francis La Flesche in 1898.

La Flesche's life work became the recording of the oral traditions of the Osage tribe, a tribe whose language was closely akin to Omaha, of which La Flesche was a native speaker. What would we have lost if La Flesche had not pursued this task? What would the Osage have lost if La Flesche had not pursued this task? Margot Liberty estimates that a complete record of the War Rites and other ceremonies of the Osage—Osage language text, English literal translation, and English free translation of the songs and speeches for all kinship divisions of the tribe—would have occupied about forty thousand pages of print or fifty to eighty volumes, five hundred to eight hundred pages each, of the large size of the *Annual Report of the Bureau of American Ethnology*. And this would be for the Osage alone! Most of this has already been lost, of course. La Flesche was able to obtain and publish only a small representative sample in his lifetime, little more than 5 percent of the total Osage ceremonial record. The heart of this remarkable record has happily been made accessible to a wide readership in the form of a volume of La Flesche's writings edited by Garrick Bailey.[2]

Granting, for argument, that there are redeeming social benefits to Indians for the avid collecting policies of museums and ethnographers through the past century and a half, what are they? Museums can only exhibit so many objects, and the rest too often reside in cabinets as unstudied study collections. Much of the great body of textual materials published for the Osage and many other tribes remains unanalyzed. What purpose can it serve now that it has been saved? Just such a question was posed to his class by one of my former anthropology professors almost fifty years ago.

Professor C. W. M. Hart assigned my class the term paper topic of judging the usefulness of the many volumes of ethnographic "texts" gathered during the formative years of American anthropology by its pioneers. I was not then able to come up with any special insights into the question on the grand scale that it was proposed, although I did find a personal satisfaction in reading Leonard Bloomfield's *Menomini Texts*, one of the important contributors to which I discovered to be Jerome Lawe, a Menominee who had married the niece of my great-grandmother, who was Stockbridge Mohican. I knew well the families of Jerome's son Raymond and daughter Lizzie Lawe Worden and bought a copy of the volume to give to Raymond, who was fluent in Menominee.

Menomini Texts also contained stories related by Valentine Satterlee, one a version of the tale telling how he had tricked the anthropologists Alanson Skinner and Samuel Barrett into eating the beating heart of a giant snapping turtle. That was a story I had heard part of from my grandmother. I showed my grandmother the volume and she told me how one day Leonard Bloomfield overheard two Menominees in Keshena talking to each other in Menominee, one casting his eyes toward the University of Chicago linguist and asking in Menominee, "Who is that guy that's been hanging around here?" The friend shrugged and replied, "I don't know him," after which Bloomfield interjected jokingly, in their own language and much to their astonishment, "Why, I'm a Menominee, of course."

Nostalgia and literary value aside, it was twenty-five years before I really came to appreciate the utility of such texts. I found that texts were valuable for discovering mental associations between otherwise discrete classes of phenomena, associations that provided clues to patterns of thought and belief that might otherwise escape attention. [*An Archaeology of the Soul*] is a summation of much of the work that I began during the seventies exploring the resources of preserved traditions. Important parts were inspired by "experimental archaeology," and much was inspired by objects in museum collections that I found to contain some feature that posed a riddle to me. I discovered that there was culture history to be extracted from museum collections and ethnographic records that I had not before even dreamed the existence of. I gradually redirected my career away from conventional scientific field archaeology toward a more humanistic, noninvasive archaeology emphasizing Native American spirituality. Because of the particular concern of this book for matters of the spirit, I have chosen the title *An Archaeology of the Soul*.

The use of the word "archaeology" in my title is quite appropriate, because the book is not based so much upon fieldwork among contemporary Indian groups as upon records culled from the published literature—archaeological, ethnographic, and historical—which are, for the most part, buried and inaccessible to the average reader for reasons of distance or time. One of the longstanding criticisms of anthropologists by Indians has been the perception that anthropologists see their clientele as other anthropologists rather than the very Indians who provided their source material. This was true enough during the formative years of anthropology in the decades before and after the turn of the past century. It is much less true today. An anthropologist would have to be extremely naive today to think that his or her publications would not be discussed critically by a concerned and informed Native American readership, and such readers are quite actively seeking out the older literature for assistance in discovering aspects of their Indian identities.

As the Lakota anthropologist Bea Medicine has observed, Indian participation in such revitalized rituals as the Sun Dance "transcends tribal affiliation and previous belief orientation" in that Ojibwas may today participate in the Sun Dance of their traditional Lakota enemies, or Canadian Micmacs from New Brunswick may feel "obliged to regain an Indian identity by making a pilgrimage to Pine Ridge."[3] In the early sixties I was invited to participate in a Memorial Day service at Greenwood, South Dakota, of the Native American Church during which the ritual was conducted in the tipi of a visiting Omaha delegation rather than in the wooden meeting house of the resident Yanktons, and the peyote was utilized in the minced form customary for the Yanktons rather than in the whole-button form preferred by the Omahas. More recently, I have participated in a sweat lodge ceremony in Texas led by an Apache instructed in South Dakota and attended by several Maya Indians, in which the fiercely hot and steamy interior of the lodge was incensed by the mingled odors of local kinnikinnick and Guatemalan copal gum, a virtual celebration of eclecticism in a revitalized ritual.

Mixing of this kind has certainly been accelerated and expanded by the efficiency of modern transportation and by the sharing of widely spoken languages, but I do not feel that diffusion and reintegration of elements should be considered to be a purely modern phenomenon. With this in mind I have selected Calumet ceremonialism as a theme around which to relate such seemingly unrelated phenomena as the Morning Star sacrifice of the Skiri Pawnees, the worship of Xipe Totec in Mesoamerica, the relationship of the sacred pipes to spearthrowers, and the cosmology of the Aztec calendar stone. What I am promoting amounts to a doctrine of uniformitarianism for cultural processes today and in the past akin to geological uniformitarianism that teaches that the processes of erosion and sedimentation observable today can explain the geology of continents in

Round-stemmed calumet as used in a Calumet ceremony of the Pawnee Hako type, after Fletcher [and Murie] (1904, pl. 87) and Skinner (1926, pl. 37), revised from Hall (1977, fig. 2c). Not to scale.

ancient times—hardly a unique approach, only uniquely applied. Sharing was an important cultural process in the past, as it is today. My contribution has been the insights that come from the pancontinental, deep-time perspectives of the archaeologist, complementing but not diminishing the contributions of investigators working intensively in a single contemporary community.

My hope is that this work will be seen as a resource facilitating a broader recognition of the continent-wide roots of many varieties of American Indian religious experience, much as the European rediscovery of classic Mediterranean civilization contributed new themes to contemporary art, philosophy, and literature. While this may be presumptuous for me as an individual, it is not so as a programmatic initiative with the potential of helping to give directions to a generation seeking ways in which to discover or express its Indianness.

WEEPING GREETINGS AND DANCING THE CALUMET

After Jean Nicolet, the first European to describe the upper Midwest was Pierre d'Esprit, Sieur de Radisson, whose travels took him and Medard Chouart, Sieur des Groseilliers, to several parts of Wisconsin, Minnesota, and neighboring territory. Groseilliers was the adventurer senior in experience and undoubtedly the leader, but it was his brother-in-law Radisson who left a written record of their travels and hence Radisson whose name is now honored by an international chain of luxury hotels and Radisson whose character in the film *Hudson's Bay* was, as I remember, played by the lean and handsome, Academy Award–winning actor Paul Muni, and Groseilliers's character who was the overweight comic companion.[4] Groseilliers's misfortune is something that the explorer Louis Jolliet could sympathize with. Returning from his 1673 journey of discovery on the Mississippi River it was Jolliet's journal that was lost in a canoe accident and his companion Jacques Marquette's journal that survived, and it is therefore Marquette's words that we remember.

Radisson's description of his and Groseilliers's experiences in northwestern Wisconsin in the years 1658–60 includes incidents worthy of repeating because of what they tell us of Indian customs and the etiquette of intergroup relationships. Four days south of Chequamegon Bay on Lake Superior Radisson and Groseilliers arrived at a village of Ottawas living there as refugees from the Iroquois wars. These Ottawas were on Dakota lands as guests of the Santee or Eastern Dakotas. As Radisson tells it, he explained that certain presents they gave to the Ottawas were for the purpose of assuring that Radisson and his companion would be remembered and spoken of for a hundred years if no other Frenchmen came among them and were as generous, which they thought unlikely.

One present was a kettle to be used by the Indians for calling their friends to the Feast of the Dead that was made each seven years, Radisson wrote, to renew friendships.[5] Two hatchets were given to encourage the young men to make their strength known to others, to protect their wives, and to show themselves to be men by knocking in the heads of their enemies. Six knives were given to show that the French were great and mighty friends and allies of the Indians, and a sword blade was given to show that the French were masters of peace and war, willing to help their allies and destroy their enemies. Sundry awls, combs, needles, red paint, mirrors, brass rings, bells, beads, and other objects were given to signify that the Indians would always be under the protection of the French and to assure that the Indians would remember the French favorably in later years.[6]

COUNCILS OF WELCOME

Following this, Radisson and Groseilliers were called to a council of welcome, to a feast of friendship, and then to a welcoming dance. Before the dance, it was necessary to "mourn for ye deceased." The dance that then followed served "to forgett all sorrow."[7] A very similar sequence of mourning and rejoicing was reported two centuries later by the artist George Catlin when arriving among the Iowas:

This peculiar dance is given to a stranger, or strangers, whom [the Iowas] are decided to welcome in their village; and out of respect to the person or persons to whom they are expressing this welcome, the musicians and all the spectators rise upon their feet while it is being danced.

The song is at first a lament for some friend, or friends, who are dead or gone away, and ends in gay and lively and cheerful step, whilst they are announcing that the friend to whom they are addressing it is received into the place which has been left.[8]

While at the Ottawa village a delegation of Dakotas arrived. These Dakotas stripped Radisson and Groseilliers naked and redressed them in buffalo and beaver skin garments. After this the Dakotas honored the Frenchmen with a weeping greeting, crying over their heads until they were wet, then offering them their pipes to smoke, and finally "perfuming" the French and their weapons with smoke from their pipes, not from common pipes but "pipes of peace and of the warrs, that they pull out but very seldom, when there is occasion for heaven and earth."[9]

The pipe was not an ordinary pipe but a calumet-pipe with a bowl of "a red stone, as bigge as a fist and as long as a hand." The stem was five feet long and as thick as a thumb. To it was tied the tail of an eagle painted with several colors and opened like a fan. On the top of the wooden pipe stem were the feathers of ducks and other birds.[10]

When Radisson and Groseilliers returned to Montreal in 1660, others learned that the way was open and the opportunity available for other Frenchmen to travel west into the area of Lakes Superior and Michigan. A peace negotiated in 1667 between the French and the Iroquois allowed many bands of refugee Indians to return from hiding and settle at locations in Wisconsin more easily accessible to traders. Green Bay became a center of fur trading operations in the west. The first Frenchman to take advantage of the trading opportunities at Green Bay was Nicolas Perrot. While in the Lake Superior area in 1667 Perrot was invited by the Potawatomis settled on Green Bay to visit them, which he did in 1668. He arrived while many of the local Indians were away with a flotilla of canoes bringing furs to Montreal, challenging the monopoly claimed by the Ottawas for trading directly with the French at Montreal. At Green Bay Perrot was received with almost the same awe and honors as Jean Nicolet had been accorded thirty-four years earlier when Nicolet visited the tribes of the area.[11]

In the late fall of 1669 Father Claude Allouez became the first missionary to reach Green Bay. Arriving on December 2, the feast day of St. Francois Xavier, Allouez named his mission for the day and the saint. On April 16, 1670, he left the bay, traveling up the Fox and Wolf Rivers, to visit the village of the Outagamie or Fox Indians. While portaging up the

Fox River on April 19, Allouez reports, the edge of the sun began to darken at noon and continued to darken until a third of the sun's disk was hidden by the moon. He says the eclipse lasted until two o'clock. This was a remarkably accurate description of the event. We can calculate that for Allouez's location near Appleton, Wisconsin, the sun began to disappear at exactly eight minutes before noon, that 32 percent of the face of the sun was eclipsed at the maximum, and that the eclipse ended at ten minutes before two in the afternoon.[12] Five days later Allouez arrived at the village of the Outagamies where he was received by crowds who had come to see the manitou or powerful spirit that was visiting them. True, the first Frenchmen to be seen in each area may often have been regarded as manitous, but it cannot have hurt Allouez's public relations to have arrived within days of a marvelous event.

The winter of 1685–86 found Nicolas Perrot quartered in a fort he built at Trempaleau, Wisconsin, on the Mississippi River. There he was visited by a delegation of Iowas who honored Perrot, as the Dakotas had favored Radisson and Groseilliers a generation earlier, with a weeping greeting, approaching Perrot "weeping hot tears, which they let fall into their hands along with saliva, and with other filth which issued from their noses, with which they rubbed the heads, faces, and garments of the French; all these caresses made their stomachs revolt."[13] Several days later Perrot visited the Iowas in their own village nine leagues away and there:

> Twenty prominent men presented the calumet to Perrot, and carried him upon a buffalo-skin into the cabin of the chief, who walked at the head of the procession. When they had taken their places on the mat, this chief began to weep over Perrot's head, bathing it with his tears, and with the moisture that dripped from his mouth and nose; and those who carried the guest did the same to him. . . . Never in the world were seen greater weepers than those people; their approach is accompanied by tears, and their adieu is the same.[14]

After a winter hunt for beavers to trade with the French a party of Iowas returned to Perrot's fort. Perrot traveled with them to their village and there received the complete honors of a Calumet ceremony:

> [Perrot] sat down on a handsome buffalo-skin, and three Ayoes stood behind him who held his body; meanwhile other persons sang, holding calumets in their hands, and keeping these in motion to the cadence of their songs. . . . They told him that they were going to pass the rest of the winter in hunting beaver, hoping to go in the spring to visit him at his fort; and at the same time *they chose him, by the calumet which they left with him, for the chief of all the tribe.*[15]

This was the ceremony of the Calumet of the Captain which did not in fact make Perrot the chief of the Iowas except in a symbolic sense. We know now that it meant that Perrot was being received as a reincarnation of a dead chief, much as George Catlin was welcomed by the Iowas of a much later generation by being received in the place of someone absent or mourned (above). The unusual weeping greeting that so disgusted the French very likely related in part to the same idea.

Wailing was a part of mortuary rites quite widely and among the Dakota, Iowa, Caddo, and Kiowa, to name just a few. The ritual of greeting included wailing, if not always the actual shedding of tears. The anthropologist James Mooney was told by the Kiowas of the southern Plains that they greeted friends this way after a long absence "because his coming reminded them of those who had died since his last appearance."[16] Precisely the same interpretation of their "welcome of tears" was given to the anthropologist Charles Wagley when he revisited the Tapirape Indians of Brazil after an absence because, they said, this traditional welcome "mixes emotions of joy at seeing an old friend with the sadness of the memory of those who died during the interim. Both the sadness and the joy are expressed ritually by crying."[17]

The comparison between the Brazilian greeting and that offered to Nicolas Perrot can be extended if one merely substitutes a cotton hammock or hanging bed for the buffalo skin on which Perrot was carried by the Iowas before their version of the welcome of tears. Wagley introduces his book *Welcome of Tears* with these descriptions from the period of 1556–1665:

> The traveler must sit down in a cotton bed hanging in the air and wait quietly for a while. Soon afterwards women appear, surround the hammock, squat on the ground and, covering their eyes with their hands, cry. With their tears they welcome the visitor whom they profusely praise.[18]

> When a visitor enters their home, they honor him by crying. As soon as he arrives, the visitor is seated in a hammock; and without speaking, the wife, her daughters and friends sit around him, with lowered heads, touching him with their hands; they begin to cry loudly and with an abundance of tears.[19]

> When any of them or their foreign friends arrive, they immediately offer him a cotton hammock. The women gather around the visitor and with their hands covering their eyes and grasping him by the legs, they begin to cry with shrieks and marvelous exclamations. This is one of the strongest signs of courtesy that they can show their friends.[20]

THE VULNERABLE HOST

The weeping greeting was actually more of an honor than it would seem because Indians did not lightly allow strangers to acquire tears, saliva, sweat, or other bodily effluvia that could be used for the purpose of black magic or witchcraft. The principle can be found worldwide among peoples who believe in magic. In his autobiography Louis Leakey explained that as a baby he was spat upon by members of the local Kikuyu tribe in Africa—as an honor! Leakey related the practice to another Kikuyu practice of spitting into the palm of one's hand before offering the hand to another in a greeting. The idea is that if you want to show your friendship to someone or to honor an influential person or "a stranger to whom you wish to show respect or humility," you offer that person your hand with your spit on it, thus transferring to the other person the magical means to make you vulnerable and put you at his mercy.[21]

We can believe that in their own minds, the Iowas or Dakotas who allowed their tears to flow on the French were making themselves vulnerable to the French even beyond the range of their firearms. In so-called contagious magic it was believed that an object such as a lock of hair or a driblet of saliva forever retained a mystical connection or contact (hence "contagious" magic) with the person who was the source and that any action directed to that object would affect the person equally.[22] Under other circumstances an Indian might hide his saliva after spitting so that he would not be injured by anything that his enemies could do with the saliva. One army officer in the Southwest noticed that Indians off the reservation took pains to spit only in their blankets.[23] Clyde Kluckhohn has described the Navajo belief that a sorcerer intent on harming someone may obtain a nail clipping or a snip of hair or a bit of ground soaked in the urine of the intended victim, bury the object with a shred of flesh from a decaying corpse or a sliver of lightning-struck wood, and then recite a spell setting the number of days to pass after which the victim will die.[24]

The principle of vulnerability that I see in operation in the weeping greeting is recognizable even in our everyday greetings and symbolic acts of friendship. The friendly clinking together of drinking glasses was originally accompanied by a sloshing together of their contents to give assurance that none was poisoned. Offering the open hand in a handshake was originally a demonstration that the hand contained no weapon. The military hand salute survives from a time when warriors fought in armor; a friendly greeting included the raising of the visor of the iron helmet that enclosed the head. A warship entering a friendly harbor fired a cannon salute to show that its cannons were now empty.

The offering of a calumet-pipe to a stranger may relate in some part to the same principle of vulnerability because a calumet-pipe was more than just a sacred smoking pipe. The round-stemmed calumet, such as that used in the Calumet ceremony proper, was a symbolic arrow. In that sense the offering of a calumet-pipe was equivalent to the offering of an arrow in greeting, and Indians did, in fact, rather widely offer arrows in greeting. While on the Gulf Coast in 1528 the Spanish explorer Alvar Nunez Cabeza de Vaca was given a gift of arrows as "a pledge of friendship" or "in token of friendship."[25] The Manahoac Indians of Virginia presented

Captain John Smith with a quiver of arrows when the English and Manahoacs made their first friendly contact in 1608.[26]

That part of the calumet-pipe that was most sacred was the long feathered stem or calumet proper rather than the stone pipe bowl, and this has led to some confusion. In popular English usage today a calumet is any highly decorated Indian pipe with a long wooden stem. The word "calumet" is not of Indian but of French origin. *Calumet* was the regional variation in Normandy of the literary French word *chalumet* derived from Old French *chalemel* and ultimately from the Low Latin diminutive *calamellus* of Latin *calamus* "reed."[27] These French words signified a tube, reed, pipe, or shepherd's flute. I say "calumet-pipe'" when I am talking about the combination of long stem and bowl but "calumet" when I am talking about the long stem by itself. In his study of sacred pipes Jordan Paper uses the term "sacred pipe" to refer to the whole class of pipes with detachable long stems.[28]

DANCING THE CALUMET

Calumet pipes may be divided into round-stemmed and flat-stemmed varieties. The round-stemmed calumets included those that explicitly symbolized arrows and that were used in the calumet ceremonies patterned on the Pawnee Hako ceremony.[29] The flat-stemmed calumet-pipes were commonly tribal and clan pipes, certainly equally sacred but with a different history and function. They symbolized the corporate identity of a group. I derive the flat-stemmed calumet-pipe from an inferred practice two to three thousand years ago of using a flat-stemmed atlatl or spearthrower of the single-hole variety as a holder for a cane (i.e., American bamboo) or stone tube pipe. The flat-stemmed calumet was always used in combination with a bowl as a calumet-pipe. The round-stemmed calumet was commonly used without the bowl in ceremonies and often was not even perforated. One other long-stemmed pipe had an even more complex history. That with a round, disk-shaped, red pipestone bowl originally represented a ceremonial club or "mace," as archaeologists have called it, which itself was of a form derived from that of a spearthrower of the twin-fingerloop variety.

Calumet ceremonialism involving visitors might be limited to the ritual offering of smoke to six directions—east, west, north, south, sky, and earth—plus the passing of the pipe from hand to hand and from mouth to mouth for smoking. The complete ceremony included the Calumet Dance, which was a choreographed mock battle scene, plus the ritual adoption of the honored guest, which in earlier years served to symbolically reincarnate someone prominent among the honored dead. The historical relationship of the ceremony to mourning was evident in some early historical accounts of calumet ceremonialism but was not explicit in nineteenth- and twentieth-century ethnographic descriptions of ceremonies such as the Hako.

Before his mission to the Indians at Green Bay Father Allouez had traveled in 1665 to Chequamegon Bay on the southern shore of Lake Superior, where among Indians of many other tribes he had met some of the Illinois nation who there had a village hundreds of miles north of their home territory. These Illinois told Allouez that out of fear of the Iroquois others of their tribesmen had taken refuge west of a great river they called Mesipi. This was the first recorded knowledge of the Mississippi River by that name.[30] It would have to be from these Illinois visitors to Lake Superior that Allouez learned in the period of 1665–67 of the Calumet Dance:

> [The Illinois] practice a kind of dance, quite peculiar to themselves, which they call "the dance of the tobacco-pipe." It is executed thus: they prepare a great pipe, which they deck with plumes, and put [it] in the middle of the room, with a sort of veneration. One of the company rises, begins to dance, and then yields his place to another, and this one to a third; and thus they dance in succession, one after another, and not all together.
>
> One would take this dance for a pantomime ballet; and it is executed to the beating of a drum. The performer makes war in rhythmic time, preparing his arms, attiring himself, running, discovering the foe, raising the cry, slaying the enemy, removing his scalp, and returning home with a song of victory—and all with an astonishing exactness, promptitude and agility.
>
> After they have all danced, one after the other, around the pipe, it is taken and offered to the chief man in the whole assembly, for him to smoke; then to another, and so in succession to all. This ceremony resembles in its significance the French custom of drinking, several out of the same glass; but in addition, the pipe is left in the keeping of the most honored man, as a sacred trust, and a sure pledge of the peace and union that will ever subsist among them as long as it shall remain in that person's hands.[31]

Vernon Kinietz years ago noticed the similarity between the Calumet Dance as described above and the Discovery Dance, which was often performed in connection with the mourning of a warrior in the Midwest.[32] The "discovery" part of the Discovery Dance referred to the discovery of the enemy during the course of the raid dramatized in the dance. The Discovery Dance and adoption each figured in the mourning of the dead and in the full Calumet ceremony.

The first European to leave a written account of the upper Mississippi River was Father Jacques Marquette, who accompanied Louis Jolliet on his exploration of the Mississippi in 1673. The discoverer of the lower Mississippi River was Hernando de Soto. De Soto came upon the Mississippi in 1541, but it fell to others to actually describe the river. De Soto died and was buried in the Mississippi in 1542.

Jolliet and Marquette began their expedition at St. Ignace, Michigan, on May 17, 1673, accompanied only by five Canadian voyageurs—Pierre Moreau, Jean Plattier, Jean Tiberge, Jacques Largillier, and an unnamed youth.[33] Canoeing along the west shore of Green Bay several days later they met the Menominees, who tried to dissuade them from traveling down the Mississippi. The inhabitants of the area were warlike and unmerciful, they said, and the river full of dangerous places and horrible monsters that could devour men and canoes together. One was supposed to be a demon who could be heard from a great distance.

Continuing beyond Lake Winnebago the Frenchmen visited the Mascouten village on the upper Fox River. This village was inhabited also by the Miamis and Kickapoos. All three peoples were living in Wisconsin as refugees from their own territory in northeastern Illinois and northern Indiana from which they had fled to remove themselves from the reach of Iroquois war parties. On June 10 Jolliet and Marquette left the Mascouten village with two Miamis as guides who escorted them up the Fox River as far as the portage trail to the Wisconsin River. Once afloat on the Wisconsin they saw no more Indians for days. On June 17 they entered the Mississippi River, "with a joy that I cannot express," wrote Marquette.[34]

Several days later they observed that turkeys and "wild cattle" (buffalo) had begun to replace the kinds of wild game that had been familiar in Wisconsin. On June 25 they notice a trail at the water's edge leading inland. With a courage that it is hard today to imagine, Jolliet and Marquette left the others of their party with their two canoes and followed the trail two leagues inland until they reached a community of three villages of the Illinois. This was a stroke of luck because Marquette had a familiarity with the Illinois language, which he had taken pains to acquire from an Illinois slave he had met at Chequamegon Bay in 1669. Marquette had prepared himself well for just such an opportunity as he was now taking advantage of.[35]

Arriving at the first village Jolliet and Marquette made their presence known to the Illinois who assigned four tribal elders to greet the strangers. Two of the Illinois men carried tobacco-pipes elaborately decorated with feathers, which they raised to the sun as if offering the pipes to the sun to smoke. The Indians identified themselves as Illinois and offered their pipes to the Frenchmen to smoke. Later, the Frenchmen received an invitation to visit the paramount chief of the Illinois in a neighboring village of three hundred lodges, and they did so. There the chief gave the visitors a small slave boy and a calumet as gifts and treated them to an enormous four-course feast of corn, fish, dog, and buffalo. The Europeans declined to partake of the cooked dog as politely as they could. The next day Jolliet and Marquette were escorted back to their canoes by nearly six hundred Indians. The brevity of the visit was balanced by the wealth of information that Marquette included in his journal on the customs of the Illinois:

> There remains no more, except to speak of the Calumet. There is nothing more mysterious or more respected among them. Less honor is paid to the

Crowns and scepters of Kings than the savages bestow upon this. It seems to be the god of peace and of war, the Arbiter of life and death. It has but to be carried upon one's person, and displayed, to enable one to walk safely through the midst of Enemies—who, in the hottest of the Fight, lay down Their arms when it is shown. For that reason, the Illinois gave me one, to serve as a safeguard among all the Nations through whom I had to pass during my voyage.

There is a Calumet for peace, and one for war, which are distinguished solely by the Color of the feathers with which they are adorned; Red is a sign of war. They also use it to put an end to Their disputes, to strengthen Their alliances, and to speak to Strangers. It is fashioned from a red stone, polished like marble, and bored in such a manner that one end serves as a receptacle for the tobacco, while the other end fits into the stem; this is a stick two feet long, as thick as an ordinary cane, and bored through the middle. It is ornamented with the heads and necks of various birds, whose plummage is very beautiful. To these they also add large feathers,—red, green and other colors,—wherewith the whole is adorned. They have a great regard for it because they look upon it as the calumet of the Sun; and, in fact, they offer it to the latter to smoke when they wish to obtain a calm, or rain, or fine weather. . . .

The Calumet dance, which is very famous among these peoples, is performed solely for important reasons; sometimes to strengthen peace, or to unite themselves for some great war; at other times, for public rejoicing. Sometimes they thus do honor to a Nation who are invited to be present; sometimes it is danced at the reception of some important personage, as if they wished to give him the diversion of a Ball or a Comedy. . . . A large mat of rushes. . . . serves as a carpet upon which to place with honor the God of the person who gives the Dance; for each has his own god, which they call their Manitou. This is a serpent, a bird, or other similar thing, of which they have dreamed while sleeping, and in which they place all their confidence for the success of their war, their fishing, and their hunting. Near this Manitou, and at its right, is placed the Calumet in honor of which the feast is given; and all around it a sort of trophy is made, and the weapons used by the warriors of the Nations are spread, namely: clubs, war-hatchets, bows, quivers, and arrows.

Everything being thus arranged, and the hour of the Dance drawing near, those who have been appointed to sing take the most honorable places under the branches; these are men and women who are gifted with the best voices, and who sing together in perfect harmony. Afterward, all come to take their seats in a circle under the branches; but each one, on arriving, must salute the Manitou. This he does by inhaling the smoke, and blowing it from his mouth upon the Manitou, as if he were offering to it incense. Every one, at the outset, takes the Calumet in a respectful manner, and, supporting it with both hands, causes it to dance in cadence, keeping good time with the air of the songs. He makes it execute many differing figures; sometimes he shows it to the whole assembly, turning himself from one side to the other. After that, he who is to begin the Dance appears in the middle of the assembly, and at once continues this. Sometimes he offers it to the sun, as if he wished the latter to smoke it; sometimes he inclines it toward the earth; again, he makes it spread its wings, as if about to fly; at other times, he puts it near the mouths of those present, that they may smoke. The whole is done in cadence; and this is, as it were, the first Scene of the Ballet.

The second consists of a Combat, carried on to the sound of a kind of drum, which succeeds the songs, or even unites with them, harmonizing very well together. The Dancer makes a sign to some warrior to come to take the arms which lie upon the mat, and invites him to fight to the sound of the drums. The latter approaches, takes up the bow and arrows, and the war-hatchet, and begins the duel with the other, whose sole defense is the Calumet. This spectacle is very pleasing, especially as all is done in cadence; for one attacks, the other defends himself; one strikes blows, the other parries them; one takes to flight, the other pursues; and then he who was fleeing faces about, and causes his adversary to flee. This is done so well—with slow and measured steps, and to the rhythmic sound of the voices and drums—that it might pass for a very fine opening of a Ballet in France.

The third Scene consists of a lofty Discourse, delivered by him who holds the Calumet; for, when the Combat is ended without bloodshed, he recounts the battles at which he has been present, the victories that he has won, the names of the Nations, the places, and the Captives whom he has made. And, to reward him, he who presides at the Dance makes him a present of a fine robe of Beaver-skins, or some other article. Then, having received it, he hands the Calumet to another, the latter to a third, and so on with all the other, until every one has done his duty; then the President presents the Calumet itself to the Nation that has been invited to the Ceremony, as a token of the everlasting peace that is to exist between the two peoples.[36]

Somewhere in Arkansas, Jolliet and Marquette reached a relocated village of the Mitchigamea branch of the Illinois. Like the Moingwena, Peoria, Kaskaskia, Tamaroa, and Cahokia—all branches of the Illinois Nation—the Mitchigamea feared attack from the League of the Iroquois. It was the Peoria-Illinois that Jolliet and Marquette had encountered on June 25 in their villages near the mouth of the Des Moines River in what is now Clark County, Missouri, many days travel by foot west of their homes on the Illinois River.[37] The Illinois did not have light, bark canoes like the northern Indians that could be easily portaged from stream to stream. While among the Peoria Marquette must have been told about the Moingwena-Illinois living farther inland on the river now named for them, the Des Moines, because that is where they appear on Marquette's map. The Mitchigamea are shown on the west side of the Mississippi River just upstream from the Arkansas River.

The sighting of Jolliet and Marquette's bark canoes created an alarm in the Mitchigamea village. Warriors armed themselves with bows and arrows, tomahawks, warclubs, and shields and prepared to attack the small party of Frenchmen from the shore and on water. Warriors scrambled into heavy wooden dugout canoes made from large logs and paddled themselves into positions upstream and downstream from the strangers. One warrior hurled his club at the intruders, but it sailed by without striking anyone, and all the while Marquette was anxiously holding high the sacred calumet without effect.

Finally, some older men standing on the shore recognized the calumet in Marquette's hands. They shouted to the young men who were positioning themselves to attack the canoes, and the attack was checked. Two of these elders then approached the canoes and threw their own bows and arrows at the feet of the Frenchmen, "as if . . . to reassure us," Marquette says.[38] The showing of the calumet by Marquette had generated a response from the Mitchigamea that was tantamount to a gift of arrows. The display of the calumet—the symbolic arrow—was returned in kind, and tensions were relaxed.

At the Mitchigamea village Jolliet and Marquette heard of another and larger village eight or ten leagues farther down the Mississippi. This was the village of the Arkansa or Quapaw tribe. By now the presence of the strange travelers on the river was known and their peaceful intentions clear. A half-league from the Quapaw town two canoes came out, in one of which was a leader who stood upright holding his own calumet in view and who then smoked with the Frenchmen. Once in the town they learned that they were within only days of the sea. At this point Jolliet and Marquette came to fear that they would fall into the hands of the Spanish if they continued farther, and they decided to return to Canada. They had accomplished their purpose: they had satisfied themselves that the Mississippi flowed into the Gulf of Mexico. They would have jeopardized their ability to report their findings if they had traveled among Indians who might turn them over to the Spanish. The chief of the Quapaws danced the calumet for the visitors and made them a present of it.

Jolliet and Marquette began their return journey on July 17, 1673, and arrived back at the mouth of Green Bay by the end of September. They traveled this time by a somewhat different route. They followed the Illinois and Des Plaines Rivers to a portage to the Chicago River and thence northward along the west shore of Lake Michigan. While still on the Illinois River near present-day Utica, Illinois, across from Starved Rock, they visited a village of seventy-four lodges of the Kaskaskia-Illinois and Father Marquette left them with his promise to return soon to establish a mission. Marquette did keep his promise.

Marquette began his trip a year later to return to the Kaskaskias, but he was too ill to travel beyond the Chicago River. He wintered at the future site of Chicago until March 29, 1675, when he set out once more for the Kaskaskia town. There Marquette established the Mission of the Conception in a ceremony that lasted from Maundy Thursday, April 11, until Easter Sunday, April 14, 1675, but he knew he could not stay. He was too weak and close to death. On Monday he received a long line of his new Indian followers while lying on his bed and promised them that if he could not return someone else would to continue the mission.[39]

Marquette was placed on a buffalo robe held taut by young men who carried him to his canoe. Near midnight on May 18, 1675, Father Jacques Marquette died and was buried in a grave at the mouth of the Marquette River near present-day Ludington, Michigan. Two years later his bones were returned to St. Ignace in a birch-bark box and reburied in the floor of the chapel. In 1705 the Jesuits were obliged to leave St. Ignace, but before leaving they burned the chapel over Marquette's grave.[40]

There was no later Catholic religious presence at the site of the St. Ignace mission until 1873. In that year a priest was again stationed at the location of the former mission, and to the new priest, almost two hundred years after Marquette's reburial, "some ancient Ottawas told the legend of a great priest who had been buried near the inlet now known as East Moran Bay."[41] The site of the burned mission chapel was discovered and below a fire-reddened floor strewn with ashes, charcoal, and rusting nails was found a pit containing only scraps of birch-bark. The grave was empty, opened years earlier, but eighteen fragments of human bone found next to the crude crypt were collected and saved. These relics are preserved in the Jesuit university in Milwaukee, Wisconsin, that keeps Marquette's name alive.

Notes

1. From *An Archaeology of the Soul: North American Indian Belief and Ritual.* Copyright 1997 by the Board of Trustees of the University of Illinois. Used with the permission of the University of Illinois Press.

2. Bailey 1995; Liberty 1978, 52.

3. Medicine 1981, 281.

4. Medard Chouart, Sieur des Groseilliers, was married to Marguerite, the half-sister of Pierre d'Esprit, Sieur de Radisson. Groseilliers arrived in Canada in 1641 and Radisson, ten years later. Radisson wrote an account of their travels in English for the purpose of interesting King Charles II in sponsoring a fur-trading venture with posts on Hudson's Bay. The bay was accessible to the English by sea, and trading there did not interest French authorities. A manuscript of the account was discovered in 1750 among others being used as wrapping paper by London shopkeepers. In 1670 Charles II did grant a charter for what became the Hudson's Bay Company, still doing business after more than three centuries.

5. The Feast of the Dead was a ceremony found among the Hurons, who were non-League Iroquoians, and their Algonquian neighbors to the west, such as the Ojibwas and Nipissings. The ceremony was held at intervals of about seven years and rotated among villages. It was an occasion for the reburial of the dead from many villages in a common grave and was used to confirm continuing friendly intergroup relationships. See, for example, Hickerson 1960.

6. Radisson 1888, 76-77.

7. Ibid., 77.

8. Skinner 1915, 700-701.

9. Radisson 1888, 83.

10. Ibid., 83.

11. Kellogg 1925, 123. Through the present century it has been widely believed that Jean Nicolet traveled through the Great Lakes until arriving in 1634 among the Winnebago Indians at or near their traditional village on the east shore of Green Bay in Wisconsin. As archaeological knowledge of Wisconsin has become more refined, however, the archaeology has become increasingly difficult to reconcile with the idea of a Green Bay landfall for Nicolet.

It is currently believed possible: (a) that the Winnebago, as known today, are the survivors of a population that until the fifteenth century occupied much of southern Wisconsin and northern Illinois but which had diminished by 1634 to much smaller numbers occupying a territory south of Chicago, represented by the distribution of the Huber culture (a phase of Oneota culture); (b) that it was in this southern Cook County, Illinois, location where Nicolet actually found the Winnebago in 1634; and (c) that the traditional Green Bay village was the location where the Winnebago reorganized their independent tribal life after a period of captivity following a devastating defeat around 1640 by the Illinois, who then moved into the former Winnebago territory in Illinois, where the Illinois were found in 1673 by Jacques Marquette and Louis Jolliet (Hall 1995b). This interpretation finds support in new knowledge of the archaeological identity of the Illinois that suggest that the Illinois had a much shallower history of occupation in Illinois than previously believed and were more likely indigenous to a location in or near the Lake Erie basin than that of Lake Michigan.

12. Hall 1995a; *Jesuit Relations* 54:217; *Wisconsin Historical Collections (WHC)* 16:68. A bronze combination sundial and compass was found in 1902 at Point Sable on Green Bay that dates to Allouez's time (Hall 1993b, 25-26; *WHC* 16:opposite 64). The mile of shore between Point Sable and Red Banks to the north contains evidence of several Indian occupations, at least one believed to date to the late seventeenth century (Hall 1993b; Hall 1995b).

13. La Potherie 1911-1912, 368.

14. Ibid., 368-369.

15. Ibid., 369-370; emphasis added.

16. Swanton 1946, 722-733.

17. Wagley 1977, 238.

18. Ibid., vii, citing Jean de Lery, *Le Voyage au Bresil, 1556-1557* (1st ed., 1578), 1927 edition, 258.

19. Wagley 1977, vii, citing Fernan Cardim, *Tratado da Terra e Gente do Brasil em 1665*, describing the Tupinamba.

20. Wagley 1977, vii, citing Abbeville n.d., describing the Tupinamba.

21. Leakey 1973, 5-6.

22. This is not a characteristic of "primitive" reasoning but of the way the brains of all humans are organized. To learn about the underlying principle involved see Frazer (1935, 1:174-214), Hall (1977, 500-502), and Jakobson and Halle (1971).

23. Bergen 1899, 19.

24. Kluckhohn 1944, 18.

25. Nunez Cabeza de Vaca 1871, 66; Nunez Cabeza de Vaca 1904, 56.

26. Bushnell 1935, 5.

27. Hewitt 1907, 191.

28. Paper 1988, 88.

29. Fletcher [and Murie] 1904.

30. *Jesuit Relations* 51:47, 53; Kellogg 1925, 154.

31. *Wisconsin Historical Collections* 16:57-58; paragraphing added.

32. Kinietz 1940, 195.

33. Hamilton 1970a, 117; Hamilton 1970b, 47.

34. *Jesuit Relations* 59:106-107.
35. Hamilton 1970a, 161.
36. *Jesuit Relations* 59:129-137.
37. Two of the three Peoria villages mentioned by Marquette have recently been discovered and are the subject of test excavations, one by Larry Grantham of the Missouri Division of State Parks and another by Kathy Ehrhardt of New York University in collaboration with Lawrence Conrad of Western Illinois University. It had previously been thought that these villages were located near Toolesboro, Iowa.
38. *Jesuit Relations* 59:150-151.
39. Ibid., 185-191.
40. Hamilton 1970a, 48, 146-150; Hamilton 1970b, 74-77; *Jesuit Relations* 59:201-205.
41. Hamilton 1970a, 189-195, 196.

BIBLIOGRAPHY

Bailey, Garrick. *The Osage and the Invisible World, from the Works of Francis La Flesche.* Norman: University of Oklahoma Press, 1995.

Bergen, Fanny D. "Animal and Plant Lore." *American Folk-Lore Society Memoirs, vol. 7.* Reprint. Kraus Reprint: New York, 1969.

Bushnell, David I., Jr. "The Manahoac Tribes in Virginia, 1608." *Smithsonian Miscellaneous Collections 94.* 1935.

Fletcher, Alice, and James R. Murie. "The Hako, a Pawnee Ceremony." *Twenty-Second Annual Report of the Bureau of American Ethnology.* 1904.

Frazer, James George. *The Magic Arts and the Evolution of Kings.* New York: Macmillan, 1935.

Hall, Robert L. "An Anthropocentric Perspective for Eastern United States Prehistory." *American Antiquity 42.* 1977.

Hall, Robert L. "Red Banks, Oneota, and the Winnebago: Views from a Distant Rock." *Wisconsin Archeologist.* 1933.

Hall, Robert L. " 'The Open Door Recognizes a Window of Opportunity' and Other Tales of Suns Turned Black." Paper presented at the Midwestern Archaeological Conference, Beloit College, Beloit, Wisconsin, 1995.

Hall, Robert L. "Relating the Big Fish and the Big Stone: The Archaeological Identity and Habitat of the Winnebago in 1634." *Oneota Archaeology: Past, Present and Future.* 1995.

Hamilton, Rafael N., S. J. *Marquette's Explorations: The Narratives Reexamined.* Madison: University of Wisconsin Press, 1970.

Hamilton, Rafael N., S. J. *Father Marquette.* Grand Rapids: William B. Eerdmans, 1970.

Hewitt, J. N. B. "The Calumet." *Bureau of American Ethnology Bulletin 30.* 1907.

Hickerson, Harold. "The Feast of the Dead Among the Seventeenth Century Algonkians of the Upper Great Lakes." *American Anthropologist 62.* 1960.

Jakobson, Roman, and Morris Halle. *Fundamentals of Language.* 3rd ed. The Hague: Mouton, 1971.

Jesuit Relations. Cleveland: Burrows Brothers, 1896-1901.

Kellogg, Louise Phelps. *The French Regime in Wisconsin and the Northwest.* Madison: State Historical Society of Wisconsin, 1925.

Kinietz, W. Vernon. *The Indians of the Western Great Lakes 1615-1760.* Ann Arbor: University of Michigan Press, 1940.

Kluckhohn, Clyde. "Navaho Witchcraft." *Papers of the Peabody Museum of American Archaeology and Ethnology, Harvard University 22.* 1944.

La Potherie, Claude Charles Le Roy, Sieur De Bacqueville. "History of the Savage Peoples who are Allies of New France." *The Indian Tribes of the Upper Mississippi Valley and Region of the Great Lakes.* Cleveland: Arthur H. Clark, 1911-1912.

Leakey, Louis S. B. *White African*. New York: Ballantine Books, 1973.

Liberty, Margot. "The Northern Cheyenne Sun Dance and the Opening of the Sacred Medicine Hat 1959." *Plains Anthropologist*. 1967.

Liberty, Margot. "Francis La Flesche: The Osage Odyssey." *American Indian Intellectuals, 1976 Proceedings of the American Ethnological Society*. St. Paul: West, 1978.

Medicine, Beatrice. "Native American Resistance to Integration: Contemporary Confrontations and Religious Revitalization." *Plains Anthropologist 26*. 1981.

Nunez Cabeza de Vaca, Alvar. *Relation of Alvar Nunez Cabeza de Vaca*. New York. 1966.

Nunez Cabeza de Vaca, Alvar. *The Journey of Alvar Nunez Cabeza de Vaca, and His Companions from Florida to the Pacific, 1528-1536*. New York: Allerton, 1964.

Paper, Jordan. *Offering Smoke: The Sacred Pipe and Native American Religion*. Moscow: University of Idaho Press, 1988.

Radisson, Pierre d'Esprit, Sieur de. "Radisson and Groseilliers in Wisconsin." *Wisconsin Historical Collections*. 1888.

Skinner, Alanson B. "Societies of the Ioway, Kansa, and Ponca Indians." *Anthropological Papers of the American Museum of Natural History 11*. 1915.

Swanton, John R. "The Indians of the Southeastern United States." *Bureau of American Ethnology Bulletin 137*. 1946.

Wagley, Charles. Welcome of Tears: The Tapirape Indians of Central Brazil. New York: Oxford University Press, 1977.

"Collections of the State Historical Society of Wisconsin." *Wisconsin Historical Collections*. 1855-1915.

Ed Lace

Native Americans in the Chicago Area

Before the coming of the French to Green Bay in 1634, Indians had already lived in the Chicago area for more than ten thousand years. From evidence found in numerous campsites and villages, archeologists recognize several cultures, somewhat overlapping in time. Generally, we cannot be certain whether the newer ones evolved from preceding ones, or if fresh ideas, customs and crafts were brought in from surrounding areas. But it seems clear that increase in trade and leisure time with the growth of agriculture greatly influenced change in later cultures.

Twenty thousand years ago the Wisconsin advance of the continental glacier covered most of the northern half of Illinois. This was the last major advance of the Ice Age. Nothing is known of any human occupation preceding this time. The amount of frozen water in the continental glaciers lowered the level of the world's oceans by about 300 feet. This created a broad land connection between Alaska and Siberia allowing animals and their predators to move from one continent to another. It is possible that some persons could have come by other means at other times, and that there was movement back and forth, but most anthropologists believe that early humans came to the Americas across the land bridge described above.

Immigrants who came down the West Coast 20,000 years ago may have continued into Central and South America. The Chicago area remained covered with ice for another 4,000 years. The first indication of humans in this area comes from two worked pieces of elk antler, one from a Dyer, Indiana bog, and one from a bog near Woodstock, Illinois. These two artifacts give us a radiocarbon date of approximately 12,000 B.C. Both of these artifacts suggest that humans were here just after the glacier began its last retreat and the Valparaiso terminal moraine was formed.

The melt-water of the Valparaiso ice would become the future Lake Michigan.

Our first citizens were the wandering Paleo-Indians. We know little of their culture because their artifacts (the objects they made) are seldom found in our region. When they are found, it is generally on sites inland of the Calumet Beach. This tells us that they were here at a time when present Lake Michigan was 40 feet deeper than now, prior to 8000 B.C. We would not expect to find Paleo-Indian sites east or north of the Calumet Beach because the lake was there at this time.

Paleo-Indian culture is identified by beautiful fluted spear points. Known as Clovis style, these unusual points were used to kill mega fauna such as the woolly mammoth of the prairie and the mastodon of the forest. Both of these pachyderms were present in Chicago at prairie, forest, and glacier edge. Sometime prior to 8000 B.C., as the great glaciers melted and retreated northward, the human population followed the elephants into central Michigan and Wisconsin. In the greater Chicago region this was as far north as these animals and Paleo-Indian people roamed.

These early people lived in small family groups, hunting the mastodon with their beautifully fluted flint spearheads. Since their giant quarry followed the northward advance of the evergreen forests in the wake of the melting glacier, the Paleo-Indians early wandered out of the Chicago region and are not recorded in later time.

Their place is taken by people representing the Archaic culture, which appeared about 8000 B.C. and lasted 7,000 years. The great cultural advance of this period was the manufacture and use of such tools as the axe, adz, and gouge. Archaic campsites also yield many grinding stones, used to process foods gathered from local trees and plants. Rare indications of temporary shelters have been found. The Archaic copper culture around Lake Superior represents the earliest example of metal-working in the world, but it is still a Stone Age culture, since the metal was not smelted. The Archaic people led a nomadic life hunting and gathering native flora and fauna. The Archaic people probably migrated with the bison, the elk, and even the birds. Their large side-notched spear and knife points are common and the carbonized remains at their camp-sites indicate what plants were gathered as foods. More than 7,000 years ago these people found and used copper to make weapons and tools. They were some of the earliest metal-workers in the world.

Then came the Woodland people, so called because they lived in the wooded parts of their area. Agriculture became important to their lives as did the art of pottery making. Farming of any kind required staying in one place for extended periods of time. Thus permanent and semi-permanent dwellings were built and villages formed.

The Early Woodland people—2500 to 500 B.C.—brought the important art of pottery making to Chicago, with characteristic grit-tempered clay. They are also responsible for erecting small houses and for the use of burial mounds. They began the practice of agriculture on a small scale—the first important step in environmental control. Trade with other Native American groups was also important to the Early Woodland culture and increased in the Middle Woodland period beginning about 2,500 years ago.

The Middle Woodland Indians reached a cultural peak in social activity, arts, and crafts. This is due to the increase in leisure afforded by an agricultural economy. The remarkable Hopewell Indians or mound builders are part of this culture. Their burial mounds contain superbly artistic pottery and naturalistic stone figurines, recognizable as people, specific birds, etc. Extensive trade was carried on with distant groups. Their campsites and burial mounds reveal mica from the East, copper from the North, sea shells and alligator teeth from the Gulf coast. This trade must have greatly influenced the improved techniques and designs of artists and craftsmen. This culture lasted 1,300 years, until 1200 A.D.

Previous to the Middle Woodland period Native Americans used spears and spear throwers called atl-atls. The use of bows and arrows began with Middle Woodland people. More sophisticated weapons meant greater success in hunting. The coming of maize (corn) from the southwest provided a more varied and nutritious diet. Life expectancy increased, but due to more starch in the diet so did dental caries.

After 800 or 900 A.D., there was an abrupt decline in culture. In this Late Woodland period, effigy mounds, some in the shape of long, undulating reptiles, were built. These required enormous amounts of material and time for their construction and are thought to have religious significance.

The Mississippian culture is so called because of the large villages found along the rivers in the Eastern United States. Village sites in the Chicago region show that long, oval houses covered with bark mats probably served several families. Some villages evidently had populations of hundreds, and such relatively permanent locales were possible because of the dominance of agriculture. Hoes of flint, bone, and shell are found, along with milling stones for grinding flour. Hunting and fishing were, of course, added sources of food.

Extensive garbage pits and kitchen middens give detailed information about the diet of the Mississippians. Shells of mussels, clams, and snails occur with the bones of fish, birds, reptiles, and mammals. The mammals included squirrels, deer, elk, and bison. The birds included turkeys, cranes, ducks, and geese. There is also charred evidence or corn cobs, nut shells, and other foods. Pottery was made in a variety of forms, together with other clay items, such as smoking pipes, beads, and effigies. Most of this pottery was tempered with crushed shell, providing one method of identifying the culture sites.

There were two separate groups of Mississippian which at times seem to intermingle. One group made a pottery tempered with black grit. The other group, sometimes called the Oneota, made pottery tempered with shell. All of these later cultures had trails that connected throughout North America. The main highways were the rivers, and canoes were the major mode of transportation. Birch-bark canoes were used in the north but birch was not common in Chicago and dugout canoes were built instead.

Real roads came in historic times along with horses and wagons. The so-called Indian "trail trees" in the area seem to be all of an age consistent with the last Indians who may have shaped them more than 150 years ago. It is thought that the trees may point to such important features as portages, fords, or springs.

The Indians of the agricultural groups need four essentials for location of villages. First was a source of water, preferably a spring which ran all year. Second was a source of food such as deer, ducks, fish, and mussels. Third was tillable soil, which could be found on the floodplain of the river. Last and very important was a reliable fuel supply. When the nearby forest was used up the village had to move.

An important trade and subsistence item was salt. Salt springs at Starved Rock and Thornton became the focus of many archeological sites.

The historical period began with the coming of the French to Green Bay. Archaeological evidence indicates contact between the French and Indians of the Chicago area about that time. Official contact took place with the coming of Marquette and Jolliet in 1673 and the explorations of La Salle a few years later.

Marquette's journal indicates that the Kaskaskia Indians were met at Starved Rock and that the Miami Indians were in the Chicago area. Even at this early date the explorers recommended the digging of a canal to join the Illinois River to Lake Michigan.

Under pressure by the English, depredations by the Iroquois in the French-claimed areas soon forced the Potawatami into the Chicago region and pushed the Miami southeast into Indiana. Later, warlike pressure forced the Chippewa of Wisconsin and the Ottawa of Michigan to move into that area. They joined with the Potawatomi and this group called themselves Three Fires.

The year 1803 marked the construction of Fort Dearborn by the United States to protect white settlers and the future canal route. Joining with the British during the War of 1812, local Indians burned the fort and killed many Americans. The fort was later rebuilt and peace was maintained until the time of the Black Hawk War in 1832. Settlers at a trading post on the Chicago River were killed but most warlike activity occurred in northwestern Illinois and southwestern Wisconsin.

The Treaty of Chicago in 1833 forced the Native Americans to move to Iowa. Later they moved to a reservation near Independence, Kansas, where descendents still live. Some people of mixed blood were given land grants in northeastern Illinois. Examples include the Robinson and Caldwell reserves.

Today there are probably more American Indians living in the area than ever lived here before. They represent tribal affiliations from throughout North America and even from Central and South America. The story continues.

Anyone doing excavation in the Chicago area may come upon an Indian site. The information from such areas should be recorded by experts before it is destroyed forever. Under no circumstances should inexperienced persons be allowed to dig simply to acquire a few arrowheads; the valuable information contained is destroyed by the excavations and must be recorded carefully. We strongly urge that you notify the Chicago Academy of Sciences, Chicago Natural History Museum, or Illinois Archeological Survey.

PART I

COMMUNAL ROOTS

SECTION TWO
EARLY CHICAGO

The Founding Fathers
JACQUELINE PETERSON
31

Founding Mothers
TERRY STRAUS
67

Father Pinet and the Mission of the Guardian Angel
PENELOPE BERLET
78

Red and Black Slaves in the Illinois Territory
JERRY LEWIS
82

Kickapoos and Black Seminoles of Northern Mexico
JOHN HOBGOOD
87

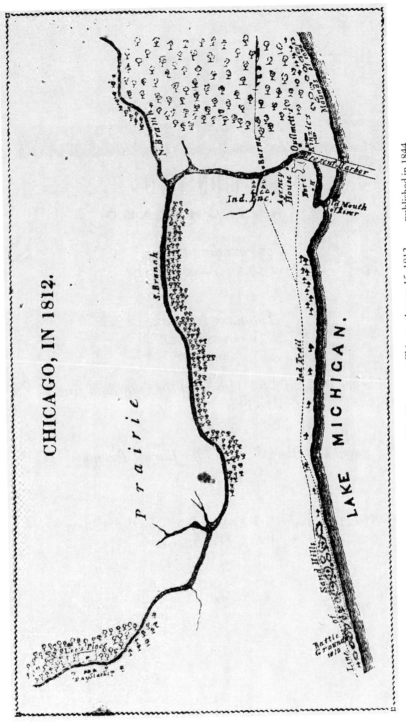

CHICAGO, IN 1812.

Prairie

N. Branch

S. Branch

Burns

Ind. Enc.

Agency House

Fort

Kinzies

Present Harbor

Old Mouth of River

Ind. Trail

LAKE MICHIGAN.

Sand Hills

Battle Ground 1812

Line of March

Lee's Place

Hardscrabble

From Mrs. Juliette A. Kinzie's The narrative of the Massacre at Chicago, August 15, 1812, . . . , published in 1844.

Jacqueline Peterson

The Founding Fathers*

The Absorption of French-Indian Chicago, 1816–1837

Author's Note: This chapter derives from research initially begun under the supervision of the late Professor Gilbert Osofsky at the University of Illinois at Chicago Circle. It owes much to his inspiration and is written in his honor.

> *If we write histories of the way in which heterogeneous people arrived on a frontier, come to form themselves into a community . . . we shall be writing something complementary to histories of disintegration. We shall be writing the history of becoming whole.*
> —Robert Redfield, *The Little Community*

I

> *Have you built your ship of death, O have you? O build your ship of death, for you will need it. And die the death, the long and painful death that lies between the old self and the new.*
> —D. H. Lawrence, "The Ship of Death"

Riding from the east toward Chicago, a visitor today can see, even in bright midday, the hulking steel mills of Gary burning miles off in the distance. Orange and black clouds hang heavy in the sky as if to warn of some terrible pestilence. Travelers grimly lock themselves in airtight spaces away from the stench of sulphur, and hurry by.

Rising with the Chicago Skyway bridge, the traveler wonders what kind of unheavenly vision William B. Ogden, early nineteenth-century industrialist and railroad maker, could have had. A century after him, the corroded assemblage of steel girders, rail tracks, foundries, breweries, and

*Reprinted from Holli, Melvin and Pete D. A. Jones (ed). Ethnic Chicago: A Multi-Cultural Portrait. Eerdman Publishing, 1995, with permission of the author and Eerdman Publishing Company.

shipping cranes fans out below the bridge like a giant black erector set devastated in a fiery holocaust. Humans do not easily belong here. Beyond, the curve of the bridge is Wolf Lake. The vision is startling, for there in the midst of angry waste and decay—and Wolf Lake itself is an industrial sewage dump—is a scene that has eluded time: the grassy marshes, frozen in winter, which swell and flood the lowlands in spring; the shallow lakes and ponds broken only by narrow glacial or man-made ridges; the stunted scrub oak, poplar, and pines; the reed-covered banks lying low in the water so that a canoe need only be pushed up a foot or two to rest on the shore. It is all there, except for the stillness and the wild rice of the marshes.[1]

This neglected landscape is what Chicago must have looked like as late as 1833. It was an inhospitable spot. Its sloughs defied the cart and buggy: "No Bottom" signs marked much of what was later to become a bastion of straight-laced skyscrapers; ladies "calling" in long silk dresses were often seen wading barefoot in the knee-deep mud. Only canoes or hollowed-out scows made their way with ease across the wet grasslands or wound a path through the wild rice blanketing the Chicago River's branches and streams.[2]

The desolation of the unbroken prairie stretching to the south as far as the eye could reach—as far as Springfield—inspired dread and, only occasionally, admiration. The interminable vista reduced people to miniature stature. The gnawing loneliness did not come from a lack of human company; it came rather from the land, a terrain that took nothing in halfway measure.[3]

Old settlers, army scouts, fur trappers, and the Indians before them waited in the silent heat of summer for the brown prairie grasses to burst into flame in the momentary blaze of fusion of sun and horizon. They listened on white winter nights to the thunder of a nor'easter lashing and breaking the frozen piles on the shore and sending the ice-clogged waters of the Chicago River scurrying backward to ravage its tributary banks. Wolves howled at the shore, and weeks without sun or moon made the inhabitants as blind men whose only guide was the sound of the wind.[4]

It would later occur to easterners that a way to shut out the lonesome vastness was to reshape the landscape. These town builders, less innovative than in need of psychological fortification, laid the imprint of a grid for city streets and in so doing cut through hill, stream, and forest, drained scores of marshes, raised buildings a full story above lake level, and absorbed a population of more than 4,000 within four short years of incorporation (1833–37), whose members filled the more subtle fortresses of judicial, political, religious, and social organization.[5] The master planners had conceived a blueprint for the systematic production of civilization. But it was unnatural; it could have been anywhere.

Its place name was *Checagou*, and that, at least, we owe to its earliest inhabitants. Archaeological diggings at the end of the nineteenth century indicated that prior to the European invasion there were at least twenty-one major Indian villages in Chicago's environs, all located on waterways: the Chicago River and its branches, the Des Plaines, the DuPage, the Calumet, and the lakeshore. In early historic times, the rolling Illinois and Wabash country was held by bands of the Miami and Illinois tribal confederations. The Miami maintained permanent summer residence at Chicago, where native women planted, harvested, and stored maize, squash, and beans. Miami hunters tracked the southern Illinois plains in search of buffalo. In spring and summer whole bands gathered to construct fresh mat-covered houses, to kindle a new fire for the coming year, to attend clan feasts, and to open and bless the sacred medicine bundles. By winter the Miami and the Illinois split into family hunting units to farm the waterways for muskrat and beaver.[6]

The Miami tribe was one of nine major Great Lakes Indian groups that developed, between 1600 and 1760, a distinctive tribal identity and culture. They numbered only 4,000 on the eve of the great white migration, a scant percentage of the approximately 100,000 natives who occupied the region. Living far to the north on the upper shores of Lake Michigan and Lake Superior, the numerically dominant Ojibway (25,000–30,000), adventurers and nomadic hunters, were to become the prototypes for the white fur traders. To the South, along the western shore of Lake Michigan, camped the semi-nomadic Fox, Sauks, Winnebago, and the Menomini wild rice gatherers. Along the eastern shore lived the farming-hunting Potawatomi and the highly structured urban communities of the Huron and Ottawa farmers. At the bottom bowl of the lake were the Miami and the Illinois tribes.[7]

The wide range of Indian cultural variation that developed in the years 1600 to 1760 is indicative of a stabilizing geographic and ecological order, although a reverse effect was already in motion by the end of that period.[8] Tribes with a relatively static population, a value system ranking leisure above energy expenditure, and a subsistence economy had little need to wander further out beyond the boundaries marking economic survival, except in years of famine or natural catastrophe. The tribal world, a primarily "spiritual" entity, overlay—in fact, was identical with—the geographic area necessary for subsistence. The tribal worldview was centripetal and cyclical—inward-turning and bent to the symbiotic balance of nature's resources.

Each Great Lakes tribe claimed in seeming perpetuity its own loosely defined territorial domain. No one was foolish enough to think that he might, individually, hold title over the land; but tribes and kin hunting units did, through years of tradition, "own" the lands they occupied. Their boundaries were by and large respected. Warfare was a manifestation of tribal honor or of personal revenge, not of geographical or territorial conquest. There was no reason to obtain more territory.

The arrival of the European fur trade, particularly in its Anglo-Saxon phase, had a profound effect on the Indian conception of time and spatial integrity. All the land, even regions of which the Great Lakes tribes had neither heard nor seen, was said to "belong" to Frenchmen and Englishmen. The natives must have thought them vain, these God-like white men who set their linear-progressive stamp on times and places as yet unknown and who vied with one another for the "protection" of their "primitive" wards. Europeans had no respect for the cyclical stores of nature; nor did they respect the spiritual knowledge of the "savage". They scoffed at the notion that nature's vicissitudes were personally directed—for good or for evil—toward humans. Natural phenomena were to be understood and then controlled.

Perhaps—although current research signals otherwise—the native momentarily accepted the "superior" notion that a land which had seemed only comfortably to support a population ratio of one per square mile was suddenly limitless in its abundance. Indeed, for the Indian hunter the land was not without limits, and the diminishing herds of elk, caribou, and deer led the natives, already increasingly dependent on European material culture, away from the maize fields into the vast stretches of forest and finally onto the trails of the white fur-trader. These trails, long used by Indian messengers, heavy with wampum and running to announce war, death, birth, or high council, had never been avenues of ingress. They crossed boundaries never surveyed, but which ensured the integrity of distinct tribal cultures. With the coming of the fur trade, the ancient roads became highways of destruction.[9]

Competition for hunting grounds and trade routes had by 1800 despoiled most of the diversity and autonomy of the Great Lakes tribes. Early nineteenth-century residents of and visitors to Chicago regarded their Indian neighbors as little more than stray dogs—vermin-infested scavengers. These were, of course, insensitive observers; but a direct result of the fur traffic had indeed been the emergence between 1760 and 1800, of a pan-Indian culture in the Lakes region, one that mimicked the peripatetic, band-oriented Chippewa social structure and depended heavily on imported trade goods. The art of pottery making was lost around 1780. Maize cultivation, once an activity central to the unity of village life, was now carried on primarily for white consumption. Ironically, years of famine brought on by the depletion in game reserves found Chicago-area Potawatomi buying back at grossly inflated prices corn meal that they had earlier cultivated.[10]

The rapid transition to a fur-trading culture by all of the Great Lakes tribes was propelled by a mistaken supposition that a white-Indian alliance might prove reciprocally enriching. Unfortunately, the disintegration of stable and coexisting tribal structures was the necessary price of the formation of a new social order. Tribal disintegration, even in its earliest stages, had devastating consequences. The tearing of a social fabric woven by oral tradition left the individual native defenseless in the face of a more sophisticated technology. Indian magic lost face to the gun.

The importation of European goods and foodstuffs destroyed the meaningful division of labor between the sexes. Potters, weavers, basketmakers, stoneworkers, and planters lost their occupations and status rank. Time, once the gentle discipline behind seasons, duties, and things spiritual, became an albatross. Intricate patterns of consanguineous and affineal recognition and avoidance were destroyed by intermarriage with whites, who refused to "avoid" certain relatives, tantamount to incest. Acceptance of "half-blood" chiefs confused, fragmented, and ultimately defused the potency of clan identification. Above all, the never-ending search for peltry broke up villages and kin groupings and clouded recognition of tribal boundaries. The result was prolonged intertribal war.[11]

Ancient runners' trails from the north, south, and east crossed at Chicago. With the establishment of fur-trading centers at St. Louis, Green Bay, Detroit, Fort Wayne, and Sandusky, the Miami and Illinois saw their hunting grounds invaded from three sides. From the north and west came the Sauk, Fox, and Kickapoo, and from the east marauding Iroquois bands. By the time Fort Dearborn was first built in 1803, the Miami had largely been driven toward the Wabash Valley.[12]

The Potawatomi were already bending under white influence. Earlier habitation near Detroit and Green Bay had exposed their members to intimate contact with French and British traders. Considerable intermarriage had occurred: dark-skinned daughters of mixed marriages were often trained and educated in French-Canadian homes, while sons were encouraged to enter the trade with their fathers. Signs of a metal age were everywhere: elaborate silver breastplates, crosses, earbobs, and crescent-shaped gorgets; iron spear- and arrowheads; copper cooking utensils; copper studs ornamenting the avenging end of tribal war clubs; and finely crafted tomahawks and hatchets.[13]

The influence of educated mixed-bloods within the tribe increased out of all proportion to their actual numbers. By 1833, on the eve of Potawatomi removal, a fair number of mixed-blood leaders had assumed, by American appointment, "chiefly" status. Such "chiefs" and their followers eventually came into the villages to live side by side with British and French traders, sharing food, equipment, and advice. They built one-or two-room log and bark huts, and they took on the trappings of European civilization in language, dress, and material wealth. Their social movement between white and Indian lifestyles seems to have been fluid, and their services were at least temporarily needed—as buffers between

Ancient runners' trails and waterways met at Fort Dearborn (Chicago). Courtesy of the Illinois State Historical Library.

antagonistic cultures.[14] The majority of Potawatomi, meanwhile, still camped in band villages along streams and rivers. Their mat-covered, dome-shaped wigwams did not impinge on the landscape but followed its curves and hollows, forming a loose circle on high, level ground. They retained the language of their ancestors, the traditional religious beliefs, the tribal authority, and the social structure. However, their lives, like those of their mixed-blood leaders, had been irreparably altered: they had become part of a larger community.[15]

No member of the fur-trade world—either white or native—escaped the anguish dealt by the extinction of "the occupation" and the transition to a highly organized and stratified society launched by the Yankee invasion of the Old Northwest. Most white traders were neither prosperous nor urban in outlook. Rather, they blended into the pan-Indian culture developing in the Great Lakes region, learning Ojibway, the *lingua franca* of the trade, as their Indian counterparts learned a French *patois*. They adopted many of the customs and habits of the tribes with whom they wintered. They too were the victims of lavishly financed entrepreneurial ventures emanating from New York and Montreal, which culminated in a regionwide monopoly between 1811 and 1834 that was led by John Jacob Astor's American Fur Company.[16] When Astor's profits dipped sharply between 1828 and 1834, he merely sold his Great Lakes holdings and moved the trade beyond the Mississippi. His white and Indian employees—clerks, traders, *voyageurs*, and *engages*—were left behind to stagger into the new world rising from the east.

Traditionally, the lower Great Lakes fur trade has been divided into pre-Astor entrepreneurial and post-Astor monopoly phases. That division implies that, prior to the formation of the American Fur Company, access to the trade was open to anyone with gumption, and that profitable competition was carried on by small French-Canadian, British, and mixed-blood traders throughout the region. However, this does not appear to have been the case. Few people of little means realized profits from the fur trade; most lived barely above the subsistence level and were perpetually in debt to supply agencies at Detroit, Montreal, or Michilimackinac. In collusion with British investors, Astor's Southwest Fur Company held a virtual monopoly over the Chicago region prior to the War of 1812, which forced his British partners to sell their American interests. A reorganized "American" Fur Company (AFC) was the result.

What actual competition existed prior to the AFC consisted of eastern capitalists who supplied local middlemen traders through their personal agents at Detroit and Michilimackinac. Such high-level competition survived throughout the Astor regime. The Detroit houses of Conant & Mack and William Brewster financed the ventures of two of the most successful traders in the Chicago area between 1820 and 1828.[17] The local traders themselves were never able to compete successfully. They lacked both capital and the respect of their employers. Despite a wealth of field experience, such men were regularly refused promotion to the inner executive chambers of the great trading houses. Most seriously, prices of pelts and trade goods were fixed in the East and abroad.[18]

The Chicago of 1816 to 1834 was thus a community of such middlemen traders and their employees—clerks, *voyageurs*, and *engages* of French, British, American, Indian, and mixed extraction. They existed for the most part under the aegis of the AFC. Their work, social aspirations, and group solidarity revolved around the profit-and-loss ledger kept by Astor's chief assistants at Michilimackinac, Ramsay Crooks and Robert Stuart, and the annual trek to the "great house" on that island. Thus, in the following discussion of early Chicago lifeways, one must not forget the hidden specter of a ruling class looking sternly down Lake Michigan from its storehouse at Mackinac. Entrance to this ruling class was closed to local men. The exclusion of Chicago residents between 1816 and 1834 meant that they were already accustomed to taking orders from outsiders when the eastern speculators arrived. It also meant that the natural instinct of men to acquire status, dignity, and personal gain would exercise itself in other spheres. This was as true for the Potawatomi as for the British, French-Canadian, and "metis" employees of the trade.

The multiracial settlement of the early 1800s at Chicago was no utopian paradise. Exchanges between Indian and white culture had produced an ordering of financial and social status, though perhaps less sophisticated than that of the eastern newcomers. Slander, theft, moral outrage, extravagant competition, hints of petty squabbling, and even murder marked the social lives of the old settlers. But those lives were also marked by the security of clan; a tenuous kind of racial harmony; an easy, enveloping spirit that gathered in the entire village; and a peaceful, irreverent disdain for "progress."

II

The earth keeps some vibration going. There in your heart, and that is you. And if the people find you can fiddle, Why fiddle you must, for all your life.
—Edgar Lee Masters, "Fiddler Jones"

Chicago, on the eve of the Fort Dearborn garrison's second coming in 1816, lay fallow, as it had lain for centuries, awaiting the imperceptible retreat of Lake Michigan's glacial waters to dry out its sandy bottom. Riders on horseback, skirting the sand dunes of the lower bowl of the lake, must have been struck, as they took the northward curve, with the notion that they were treading on ground already claimed. Such men were not geologists, but when they saw the blue mist veiling the high hill in the distance, they named it Blue Island. This mound and its less auspicious neighbor, Stony Island, were by some chance of nature built of sturdier bedrock than the surrounding terrain. The mounds had been spared the leveling scrape of the last glacier. And when American soldiers arrived in 1816, the triple arms of the Chicago River still embraced much of the land for six months of the year.[19]

The lifeways of Chicago's early nineteenth-century inhabitants were of necessity waterways. A liquid boundary arc stretched from Wilmette (Ouillmette) at the northern lakeshore, down the north branch of the Chicago River to Wolf Point, following the river's south branch to what became 35th Street, and then cutting across to the southern lakeshore. Within this arc were scattered at least fifteen families whose lives were interdependent—united by blood, occupational survival, common values, and the river. As if by instinct, residents set their log and bark cabins and barns on the high bank and let their lives lean to the current. Such houses rarely had more than one or two rooms and fewer windows, but their inhabitants chose, without need of plat, the level ground, and placed their doors toward the river road and the yellow sundown prairie.

The human landscape was as careless as the meandering river, but was not without design. A respect for space and the needs of field and stable kept households apart; but there was another meaning to the sprawl. Long before a greedy state legislature—anticipating an Illinois-Michigan Canal—put Chicago on the map, and lots, streets, and ward boundaries were platted, the settlement had its geographic divisions. In addition to the Yankee garrison ensconced on the south bank of the main river branch, four other kin groups or clans had claimed their "turf": the British (Mc)Kinzies and their southern relatives Clybourne and Hall on the north side; the French-Indian Ouillmette, Beaubien, and LaFramboise families on the far north, west, and south sides.

So dispersed was the settlement that it was impossible for the eye to encompass it in a single sweeping glance from the fort's blockhouse, which occupied the highest ground. To an outsider "accustomed to the comforting spectacle of shelters huddled together", Chicago seemed hardly to exist at all. United States Army Engineer William H. Keating recorded "but a few huts, inhabited by a miserable race of men, scarcely equal to the Indians from whom they are descended . . . [whose] log or bark houses are low, filthy and disgusting." Yet the town probably had a stable population of more than 150 outside the garrison prior to 1831. By its own enduring admission, it was a community.[20]

The view to the south of the fort covered a wide grassy plain that stretched for several miles beyond the garrison's orchards and corn fields at the foot of the stockade. A half mile down the lakeshore lay several scattered shanties used by the fort and the American Fur Company and a commodious, though jerrybuilt house occupied by Jean Baptiste Beaubien, AFC agent, and his mixed-blood family. To the west the plain was interrupted by a thin stand of trees lining the south branch of the river. Hidden among the timber was an establishment called Hardscrabble.[21]

The name Hardscrabble, perhaps derived from limestone outcroppings in the vicinity, is suggestive of a single farm but actually included at least ten cabins, a major house and post, and sleeping quarters for *voyageurs* spread out along the river bank. Title to this establishment, as to almost every other dwelling in the community, was obscure. Located at the entrance to Mud Lake, the spring portage route to the Des Plaines, Illinois, and Mississippi rivers, Hardscrabble rivaled Beaubien's cabin at the lakefront as a trading location. While Beaubien, as well as AFC agents before him, had the advantage of intercepting the first shipments of trade goods from Detroit and Michilimackinac in late summer, the traders at Hardscrabble were the first to see the Niteaux returning heavy with pelts in the spring.

Although Hardscrabble was most consistently occupied by the LaFramboise clan and other mixed-blood traders like Alexander Robinson, it became from time to time the seat of serious competition with the AFC. Prior to being bought out by Astor in 1824, John Crafts, representing Conant & Mack of Detroit, conducted his business there. Afterward, when Crafts had taken over the lakefront store for the AFC, William H.

Wallace of Detroit traded at Hardscrabble until his death in 1827. Antoine Ouillmette, whose home and trading store hugged the lakeshore ten miles north of the principal settlement, also had a connection with the place. Wallace was paying him rent in 1827.[22]

"Improvements" at Chicago lacked the value easterners would later assign to them. Lots and houses were swapped for as little as a cord of wood and a pair of moccasins, or changed hands as the casual winnings off a fast pony or a shrewd card game. Residents almost never registered their property at the early Wayne and Crawford county seats. Their rudely fashioned cabins did not weather the winds or the damp, and the thatched or bark-shingled roofs inevitably invited fire. Like the portable wigwams of their Indian neighbors, such houses had little material worth. But, that is not to say that the early residents did not value permanence and stability; rather, their sense of community was not embodied in a tidy row of whitewashed domiciles legally bound and named.[23]

The "Kinzie mansion" was an exception. Although the Kinzie title is still unrecovered, presumably the house on the north bank opposite the fort was the same property that Jean Baptiste Point du Sable registered and sold in 1800 to Jean Lalime, post interpreter and Kinzie's rival. Lalime resided in the house prior to 1804, when the vituperative redbeard Kinzie arrived and immediately took firm possession.[24]

By 1831 the family had abandoned the mansion to a tenant postmaster. Perched on a sandhill, it had seen fifty years of storm and drift and seemed impatient to slide into the river. In its heyday, the house had been an impressive example of the French *habitant* architecture of the Mississippi Valley, the *poteaux en terre*. It had five rooms—a spacious salon with a small room off each corner—and a wide piazza running the length of the river side. Behind it were stables, a bakehouse, huts for employees, and, characteristically, a garden and orchard fenced by a palisade. Although presumably similar to other dwellings in the vicinity, the Kinzie mansion was certainly the largest—and the only house with a palisade.[25]

Smaller homes of similar construction were indiscriminately lumped with "log cabins" by early travelers. However, the typical American "log cabin" of Swedish-Finnish origin was formed of logs set horizontally, with a fireplace at one end of the building. Cabins of this style were not unknown at Chicago, but prior to 1820 they were vastly outnumbered by houses of a primitive French-Canadian design, the *pieux en terre*, whose origins probably owe something to the Huron longhouse.[26] Typically, the French-Canadian dwelling was constructed of roughhewn logs set vertically into a trench and chinked with grass and mud mortar. The thatched or shingled roof was peaked high to facilitate runoff, the fireplace sat astride the roof's center. Ordinarily, the logs were covered with bark slabs, but when the timber was clean-shaven and whitewashed, the structure took on the appearance of stone or frame. It is not surprising that Mark

John Kinzie— "Father of Chicago."
Courtesy of the Chicago Historical
Society.

Beaubien's "pretentious" two-story, blue-shuttered tavern, the Sauganash, was mistaken for a New England frame house. There is no evidence, however, that the *I* frame, with its central hall, preceded the Yankee influx of 1833.[27]

Fanning out beyond the "mansion," the numerous members of the Kinzie clan populated the wooded sloughs along the north bank and east of the north branch of the Chicago River. The north side was barely habitable: a dense growth of trees, knee-deep in water, choked out the sunlight, and the bogs were unfit for cultivation. When William B. Ogden's brother-in-law purchased the better part of the "Kinzie Addition" on speculation in the early 1830s, he was forced to initiate an extensive drainage program to render it fit for settlement. Yet from the very beginning this gloomy marsh spelled status, as did the Kinzie name.[28]

Viewed variously as the "father of Chicago" and as a common horse thief, Kinzie in fantasy obscures Kinzie in fact. A British subject and native of the Grosse Pointe district of Detroit, John Kinzie entered the fur trade early, after developing a fair skill as a silversmith. Ruthlessly ambitious, he soon wormed his way into the Detroit circle of merchant agents and found a patron for his Sandusky, Maumee, and St. Joseph trading "adventures." He apparently realized the potential value of territory in advance of the line of settlement. In 1795, he, his half-brother Thomas Forsyth, and other Detroit entrepreneurs almost succeeded in a conspiracy to grab title to Indian lands in Michigan and Indiana before General Anthony Wayne could finalize the Treaty of Greenville.[29]

Between 1804 and 1812, Kinzie at Chicago and Forsyth at Peoria together carved out a small empire in northern Illinois. Kinzie was unquestionably the most powerful man at Chicago during this period, outranking even the garrison officers, who were humbled monthly by

Mark Beaubien "kept
tavern like hell." Photo-
graph by Charles D.
Mosher, courtesy of
the Chicago Historical
Society.

Kinzie currency advanced to cover their overdue military pay. Most of the
French-Indian inhabitants—the Mirandeaus, Ouillmettes, LaFramboises,
and Robinsons—worked for Kinzie and Forsyth during these years,
although it might well be a mistake to label them simply *voyageurs* or
engages. At least one mixed-blood, Captain Billy Caldwell, son of an Irish
officer and a Mohawk mother, served as clerk, a position of some responsibility.[30] But whatever the aspirations of local residents, guile, intimida-
tion, and the soporific effects of British rum were devices Kinzie used to
ensure that renegade trappers thought twice before embarking for Detroit
to strike a separate bargain for their beaver pelts. Kinzie's recorded malev-
olence is limited to the murder of Jean Lalime in 1812, but hints of other
threats abound.[31]

Despite Kinzie's local influence, he never escaped the pecuniary grasp
of the Detroit merchants. Caught in the vast financial octopus that spread
its tentacles to Montreal, London, and as far as Peking, Kinzie owed his
livelihood to George McDougall, supply agent at Detroit, who in turn
made his commission off trade goods sold by Forsyth and Richardson in
Montreal. After he was imprisoned following the Fort Dearborn Massacre in 1812 because of his British sympathies, Kinzie's credit collapsed,
and he was forced to sell all his real property. His debt to George
McDougall alone was a hefty $22,000.[32]

When the second Fort Dearborn garrison returned to rebuild the post in 1816, an aging Kinzie followed. The wrath of the Potawatomi had been aimed at the Americans; thus the "Kinzie mansion," Hardscrabble, J. B. Beaubien's house on the southern lakeshore, and other assorted cabins stood unchanged. Even the scattered remains of the massacred whites, left to rot on the beach, had settled comfortably into temporary sandy graves. The bleached bones seemed ominous, and the garrison hastily shoved them into wooden coffins and dropped them into higher ground. But for John Kinzie it was a homecoming.

Time had been a visitor. The Kinzie family reclaimed its place on the north bank, but John never recovered his former status. The fort, more self-assured after the recent United States victory, had little need for a quarrelsome old trader whose past allegiances were suspect. Still, from a Yankee perspective, a Britisher was more comely than a Frenchman; before his death in 1828, Kinzie did manage to wangle brief appointments as interpreter and subagent (the latter a gratuity extended by his Indian agent son-in-law).[33]

The American Fur Company took him more seriously. An established trader, well known among the Potawatomi and mixed-blood *voyageurs*, Kinzie was viewed by Ramsay Crooks at Michilimackinac as the new company's key to the consolidation of the Illinois country. Yet, Kinzie failed to meet Crooks's expectations: although he was reinforced by a second AFC trader, J. B. Beaubien, Kinzie's efforts to overwhelm the competition at Chicago were in vain. In desperation, Astor bought out his competitor's agent, John Crafts, and turned control of the Chicago trade over to him. After Crafts's death in 1825, Kinzie again assumed control, with Beaubien retaining one-third share. The Creole Beaubien, who had an Indian wife, received short shrift at the hands of Ramsay Crooks and Robert Stuart at the big house: he was treated as a perpetual "second" man, even though his lines of connection with the mixed-blood trappers ran deeper than Kinzie's. When Kinzie died, Astor, plagued by a diminishing return, sold his Illinois interests to Gurdon Hubbard, the American Fur Company agent on the Wabash.[34]

The Chicago settlement in Kinzie's day was dependent to a man on the fur trade. The social hierarchy, therefore, tended to coincide with rank in the occupation, at least in the eyes of the Detroit and Michilimackinac suppliers. The Kinzie family stood at the top of the social pyramid, closely followed by the Beaubiens, and then the mixed-blood families of LaFramboise, Ouillmette, Mirandeau, Billy Caldwell, and Alexander Robinson. The Indian *engages* and hunters occupied the base—or so the Kinzies would have said. Whether their version of the community structure was accurate, however, was largely unimportant. The subtle mechanisms that draw human beings together are for the most part unspoken; the sum of individual visions that converge to form a collective consciousness is never large enough to explain the whole. The view from the bottom of the social pyramid would no doubt have been considerably different. The Beaubiens and LaFramboises were well-loved by the Potawatomi; and Billy Caldwell and Alexander Robinson carried political weight within the local bands.[35]

With the ebb of "the occupation," the struggle for power and position began anew. The Kinzies would quite naturally choose to align with the fort: the Yankee garrison was the self-styled "bringer of civilization," and the Kinzies had always felt culturally superior to their French Creole and Indian neighbors. They had paid the bad debts of their Indian employees and sheltered numerous children of the Ouillmette and Mirandeau lines, who, while serving as maids and stable boys, were given the opportunity to observe Anglo-Saxon manners and virtues. Still, a turn to the fort was a sharp shift in allegiance: the garrison had always seemed alien, an intrusion on the measured rhythm of the Chicago community.[36]

At some imperceptible point around 1820, however, the fort merged with the community to become for a brief period its ruling class. Why the inhabitants of Chicago allowed this to happen is unknown. It may have been the unconscious drift of a people who had lost their moorings. Direction had always floated down from Detroit or Mackinac, and when—simultaneously—Ramsay Crooks began to pack his bags and the fur boats came home empty, residents panicked. The paternal symbolism of the fort became, at that point, too obvious to resist. Union with the fort took two forms. For most of Chicago's inhabitants it was a simple matter of making the best use of the fort's presence. A garrison at the northern mouth of a new state would mean the influx of people (though in numbers more vast than the enterprising Beaubiens ever imagined). Overnight, a number of trading cabins were hastily converted to taverns, hostelries, and food-supply stores.[37]

The Kinzies beat a more direct path. Treating the garrison like a territorial clan, they marched through the front gate and brought home as relatives the highest ranking officials. Kinzie's elder son, John Harris, married Connecticut-born Juliette Magill, niece of the government Indian agent, Alexander Wolcott; his daughters Ellen Marion and Maria Indiana married Alexander Wolcott and Captain (later General) David Hunter, respectively; and his younger son, Robert Allen, married Gwinthlean Whistler, daughter of the commandant of the fort. As added insurance, both John Harris and Robert Allen became Army officers. These were calculated moves to retain status, and they succeeded. The family's prestige had been on the wane between 1816 and 1828, but in the eyes of the first Yankee arrivals in 1832–33, Kinzie was once again the foremost name in Chicago.[38]

Juliette Magill Kinzie was aware of that fact when, on a gray winter night in 1831, she first stood with her new husband on the threshold of

Elijah Wentworth's trading store and sometime inn at Wolf Point and looked down the main branch of the river flowing eastward toward Lake Michigan. To her right she could make out the silhouette of the two bastions of Fort Dearborn nestled in the elbow of the river's sharp bend to the south; to her left, directly across the river from the fort, was the old Kinzie home hidden somewhere in the darkness among the sand hills. It was Juliette's initial visit, but she already knew her place.[39]

A few hours earlier, on the last leg of a three-day journey on horseback, she and her husband, John Harris Kinzie, and their company of French-Canadian employees and guides had stumbled up the frozen bank of the Des Plaines River to warm themselves in front of Bernardus Laughton's fireplace. Mrs. Kinzie was shocked to find a stove and carpet in the middle of the Illinois wilderness. However, her hostess, Mrs. Laughton, was not comforted by such accoutrements of civilization. Like so many women—and men—set adrift on the prairie, she waited nervously, with her arms tightly folded, for the westward advance of her "Eastern family" to catch up.[40]

Mrs. Kinzie had more romantic illusions, born in part of her husband's success as an Indian agent at Fort Winnebago and his unusual apprenticeship to Robert Stuart at Michilimackinac, and in part by her own sense of *noblesse oblige*. Although she had never been to Chicago, she understood her rank in the social order. With the old trader Kinzie gone, she and John Harris Kinzie were the acknowledged leaders of the clan. In view of their Anglo-Saxon ancestry, they presumably were the leaders of the community as well.[41]

A different Kinzie kin group had begun to trickle into the north side as early as 1816: this was a bastard southern line fathered during the American Revolution by the elder John Kinzie; the mother was a young white woman who had been an Indian captive. Juliette Kinzie and other family historians chose to ignore it. However, its importance for early town development was great indeed, and its numbers, even if unacknowledged, served to reinforce the hegemony of the Kinzie name. The anxious adoption of Yankee values by John Kinzie's legitimate second crop of children must be given a fair share of the credit for the testy snubbing, feuding, and in-house squabbling that marked the relations of the two branches between 1816 and 1833. Unofficial marriages and separations were common enough in unorganized territory, and children of different mothers were usually united without stigma or anguish. When threatened by outside competition or family death, the two sets of Kinzie children could act as a unit, but the alliance was tenuous and easily broken.

In the late 1770s, John Kinzie and a trading companion, Alexander Clark, had either ransomed or been "given" two Giles County, Virginia girls whom Tecumseh's Shawnees had captured in a raid. Margaret and Elizabeth Mackenzie set up housekeeping with John Kinzie and Alexander Clark near Sandusky, and over the next decade John Kinzie had three children: James, William, and Elizabeth. Clark fathered a son, whom he named John Kinzie Clark for his friend.[42]

After the Revolution, the Mackenzie girls' father, hearing of his daughters' residence at Detroit, rode north to fetch them and their children. For whatever cause—a brutish John Kinzie, a distaste for the northern frontier, or the fear of reprisal due their British husbands—Elizabeth and Margaret fled to Virginia with their children and in short order married Jonas Clybourne and Benjamin Hall, respectively, also of Giles County.[43] As early as 1816, however, a renegade James Kinzie had sought out his natural father and was trading in Chicago. Kinzie apparently took his son in and treated him kindly. His wife Eleanor undoubtedly harbored reservations: as the eldest Kinzie, James threatened the succession rights of her sons, John Harris and his younger brother, Robert Allen. Ironically, in terms of native habits and inclinations, James was the obvious inheritor of John Kinzie's prairie domain. While Kinzie's daughters were acquiring polish at schools in Detroit and the East, and John and Robert were clerking for the AFC, James and his father worked the trade, chased wolves, raced horses, and got roaring drunk together. Had the rowdy old man lived until 1833, he might well have been a source of embarrassment to his own "refined" children. As it turned out, John Kinzie became a legend; James became the embarrassment.[44]

The southern contingent of the Kinzie clan kept arriving. Word from James of fertile land and a burgeoning Illinois population brought his sister Elizabeth and his mother's and aunt's new families, the Halls and Clybournes. Others who came included John Kinzie Clark (thenceforth known as "Indian Clark"); the Caldwells, relatives of the Halls; and the Virginia-bred Miller brothers, one of whom married Elizabeth Kinzie. By 1829 they were at least twenty strong, too large a population to ignore.[45]

The southerners introduced a diversity of occupations unknown in early Chicago, breaking down the monolithic clutch of the fur trade several years before the easterners brought their crockery and sewing needles. The first attempts were at tavern-keeping, but by 1829 the southern members of the Kinzie clan were also engaged in butchering, tanning, intensive farming, ferrying, and blacksmithing. In addition, it seems clear that the Halls and Clybournes operated a still, Kentucky whiskey having replaced British rum as the liquid staple after 1812. The entire group built their log cabins on the east side of the north branch, running from the forks up to Rolling Meadows, and they settled in, in an uneasy harmony with their northside relatives and neighbors.[46]

The territorial space in which all families met—both occupationally and socially—was Wolf Point, a sort of "free zone." Located on the western, prairie side of the juncture between the two river branches, the Point was about midway between Hardscrabble and Clybourne's cattle yard at

Rolling Meadows. A natural intersection, it served for nearly twenty years as the hub of village life—the scene of frolicking, trade, religion, education, and politics.

The Potawatomi were camping there after 1816, and they did not bother to move when stores and cabins were erected. By 1820, the LaFramboise brothers, mixed-blood "chiefs" Alexander Robinson and Billy Caldwell, and James Kinzie were operating out of trading huts at the Point. Shortly thereafter, James Kinzie built the Wolf Tavern and the Green Tree Tavern, which sported a false second-story front and a gallery, because Kinzie said he "wanted a white man's house." By 1828 the itinerant Methodist preachers Jesse Walker and William See were exhorting audiences weekly in a meetinghouse that was also used irregularly as a school for Chicago's French-Indian children.[47]

That same year Mark Beaubien, younger brother of Jean Baptiste Beaubien, was running a tavern that was later expanded into the famed "Sauganash," named for Billy Caldwell, on the bank opposite the Point to the south. Archibald Clybourne and Sam Miller also managed a tavern on the riverbank to the north. A few years later, David Hall and Robert Kinzie erected their own trading stores at the Point; and Miller and Hall's tannery operated to the north of Miller's tavern. By 1832 the Point was a bustling paradise of exotica. Races and accents mingled freely, as if the mere place had momentarily destroyed the compartments in people's minds and the territorial divisions of the town.[48] Next to survival, "frolicking" was the major preoccupation of the town. No one expected to make a fast buck; that heady prospect had not yet presented itself. Instead, winter and summer, residents spent a part of their day and uncounted evenings at the Point, swapping tales, playing at cards, racing on foot or horseback, trading, dancing, and flying high on corn "likker," rum, and French brandy. Social class and clan affiliation had no bearing here: it was physical prowess, a witty tongue, or a graceful step that brought people into community.

Full-blooded Indian employees of the Kinzies, who were barred from the dinner table, could hold the whole village captive by the gymnastic fluidity of the Discovery Dance at Wolf Point. The French-Indian Beaubien and LaFramboise girls, who had the gayest feet on earth, found admiring partners among the Virginia farmers, who were just as willing as they to dance until dawn. Whiskey was the official solvent. Everyone—even the women—drank, often from the same bottle. It probably was not only the "dissipated" Indians who camped out on the prairie; Virginia boys, too, hitched their ponies and rolled in the long grass to sleep off a night's hilarity. No wonder easterners and ministers were shocked to find a people so ignorant of the healthful, refreshing qualities of water. Liquor was a "problem" all over the state—over the whole region, for that matter.[49]

Perhaps whiskey was seen as a device to break down the barriers between strangers who seemed to have little in common. Or its fantasy-producing properties may have lent a rosier cast to otherwise gray and frightened lives, going nowhere but into the grave. Outwardly, liquor was called a tonic, a body-builder, and a daily necessity for many frontiersmen. That Mark Beaubien's tavern, the Sauganash, was the focal point of the community, therefore, should not seem odd. Its opening in 1826 coincided with several important changes. A declining fur trade threatened the occupational security of many of Chicago's earliest residents, and the population was suddenly growing: the Clybournes, Halls, Galloways, Scotts, Sees, more Mirandeaus, and John K. Clark had already arrived; and the full-grown children of the first families—the Kinzies and Beaubiens—were returning from school and looking for mates.

There was more to the convergence at Beaubien's place than social need. There were, after all, other taverns: Barney Laughton's on the "Aux Plaines," for example, was a favorite resort of the younger Kinzies. And since hospitality was a primary avenue to status, there was always a drinking circle at John Kinzie's, at Hardscrabble, and at J. B. Beaubien's house at the lakeshore. But Mark Beaubien, at a pivotal juncture in Chicago's history, offered more: entertainment and a defiant middle finger to the world.[50]

Beaubien joked that he "kept tavern like hell," and he evidently did. From 1826 until 1835, several years after the Yankee flood, when Mark tried a new venture, the Beaubien house was bursting its seams nightly. The Sauganash boarded and lodged upwards of twenty or thirty travelers and single townsmen at a time; by 1834 meals and blankets were being served in shifts. No one complained. After his bustling, round wife, the former Monique Nadeau, had cleared the table, Mark commenced the show. He played the fiddle like a madman, and full-blooded Potawatomi, French Creoles, Yankees, and Virginians could not keep from dancing.[51]

Dancing was a principal amusement among French *habitants*, and it became, next to drinking, the most significant community-binding ritual at Chicago. Everyone came and everyone danced. Besides the graceful French-Canadian cotillions, residents learned southern reels, the athletic War and Discovery dances, and the sedate social dances of the Potawatomi. There was hardly a man in Chicago in 1832 who did not know how to paint his body, decorate his hair with eagle feathers, and leap in frenzied exultation, terrorizing effete easterners. When town dances were formalized and limited by invitation in the 1830s, they were called *wabanos* or Grand Wa-ba-nos, a reference to an Indian medicine society noted for its all-night revelries. The name retained the native flavor. But something had changed: the Potawatomi and most of the mixed-bloods were noticeably absent from the guest lists.[52]

Mark Beaubien liked everyone, and the feeling was mutual. Among the

Dancing was a principal amusement among the French *habitants;* next to drinking, it was the most important community-binding ritual in Chicago. Drawing courtesy of the Illinois State Historical Library.

Yankee reminiscences of Chicago's early years, the stories about Mark are the most poignant—filled with memories of handsome Creole charm, mirth, and abundant kindness to Indians and Yankees alike. His first loves were fiddle playing, horse racing at the Point (or later across a rickety bridge erected in front of the Sauganash in 1831, which he was supposed to be "tending" as toll collector), and propagation. The most prolific man in town, he fathered twenty-three children, many of them named after early settlers he esteemed. He gave away to friends valuable lots he had purchased when the first Michigan-Illinois Canal lands were platted and sold. The only land he apparently possessed when Chicago was incorporated as a city in 1837 was a sixty-four-acre tract at the mouth of the Calumet River, which the Indians had given to "their good friend Mark Beaubien" in the 1833 cession.[53]

The Sauganash was more than a watering hole and ballroom; it also saw its share of the meetings of the Chicago Debating Society (J. B. Beaubien presiding in 1831) and of local politics, seen in the chartering of the town. Chicago's incorporation in 1837 was largely a response to outside interest in the Canal and the downstate need for a local county seat. The village had certainly been large enough to incorporate earlier, but it had evidently not occurred to residents to legalize their community status. However, the early settlers were not unmindful of politics and government: when the area was still part of Peoria County between 1825 and 1831, Chicago men, particularly the Virginians, had avidly sought political office.[54]

Prior to 1827, when the Chicago precinct was organized, all offices were appointive. The commissioners at Peoria gave preference to the men of rank in Chicago, but they also appointed men who appeared eager for position. Old John Kinzie and Jean Baptiste Beaubien were made justices of the peace in 1825 (Alexander Wolcott replaced the deceased Kinzie in 1828), and the southern newcomers Archibald Clybourne and John K. Clark received the nod for constable in 1825 and 1827. Local notables also recommended Billy Caldwell's appointment as justice of the peace, and he was installed on April 18, 1826.[55] Until 1828, J. B. Beaubien, John Kinzie, and Alexander Wolcott, the Indian agent, presided as election judges. James Kinzie later replaced his deceased father in that office. The job of election clerk was in fact that of messenger (the trip to and from Peoria with the voting returns paid $16.00), and that office went to John K. Clark in 1825; Alexander Robinson and Henley Clybourne for the two years following; and the Reverend Jesse Walker in 1832.[56]

A surprisingly large turnout participated in nine elections between 1825 and 1831. Thirty-five men registered in the first general election in 1826; thirty-three in 1828; and thirty-two in 1830. Nearly all of the available Kinzies (Canadian and southern) participated, as did most of the French Creole and mixed-blood men of the south and west sides. No political preference emerged during these three elections. The most obvious comment that can be made of the returns is that the village voted with the fort.[57]

Beginning in 1828, however, local elections were of a different species. Chicagoans took a provincial view of politics, and when the candidates were familiar, a high-spirited campaign ensued. The election in 1830 to replace Wolcott as justice of the peace, for instance, drew fifty-six voters. The southerners clamored for office. In 1828, Henley Clybourne was elected constable, along with David Hunter; together they represented the Kinzie clan and the fort. Archibald Clybourne tried unsuccessfully in 1828 and 1830 to win election as justice of the peace; and in 1832 he ran as an Independent for Congress, losing to the Democratic candidate from Jacksonville. But in 1828 he did manage to win appointment, along with Samuel Miller, as trustee for the school section land sale and as treasurer of the First Court of Cook County Commissioners. James Kinzie was elected first sheriff of Cook County in 1831, but in 1832 he was beaten by Stephen Forbes, a Yankee schoolteacher.[58]

Despite the small trickle of Yankees into Chicago up to 1832, Forbes's election was the first clear indication that Chicago's old settlers were about to lose the control they had exerted over their own political destinies. The

experiment in political and occupational independence had been too brief
to test whether Chicagoans could flourish apace with the rest of the state,
under their own leadership. Their confusion and fear of autonomy was
still manifest in 1833: when given the opportunity to elect a president of
the town trustees, they chose Thomas J. V. Owen, the government Indian agent. A month later, as United States commissioner, Owen concluded a land cession treaty between the united Potawatomi, Ottawa, and
Chippewa nations and the government that in effect disfranchised half of
Chicago's residents. J. B. Beaubien's mixed-blood son Madore was a member of Owen's Board of Town Trustees in 1833, and John H. Kinzie was
elected president in 1834. Thereafter, not one old settler held a position
of importance in town or city government. Early residents simply could
not compete with the horde of Yankees who descended on the prairie village between 1832 and 1836.[59]

The problem was not one of wits. Early Chicago settlers placed a surprisingly high value on education. Despite the historical impression that
Yankees brought to a spiritually and educationally impoverished hinter-
land a fully developed cultural matrix, the cornerstone of which was the
school, Chicago residents were already remarkably well educated, though
somewhat less than godly. Perhaps because Chicago was in many ways an
extension of urban Detroit (Kinzie and the Beaubien brothers were raised
in the same Grosse Pointe district), many of the early settlers were more
enlightened than their rural counterparts downstate. However, the southern branch of the Kinzie clan certainly lacked literary and scientific polish. No poets, orators, or physicians rose from their ranks. The most
prominent Virginian was the lay Methodist exhorter William See, who
flapped his long blacksmith arms like a scarecrow when he preached and
ended his delivery with something between a curtsy and a bow. See organized the first church meeting at the Point, but he always became so entangled in the web of his own scattered thoughts that he failed to bring many
sinners to Christ.[60]

Bereft of formal religion until 1833, the Catholic French Creoles and
mixed-bloods and the Episcopal Kinzies turned to the secular world.
They packed their sons and daughters off to Detroit boarding and finishing schools or to Isaac McCoy's Indian mission school at Niles, Michigan.
The Kinzie family connection was presumably with Mrs. Pattinson's
establishment at Detroit, since John Kinzie, desperately in debt in 1815,
had sold his Grosse Pointe farm to Mrs. Pattinson's husband. Kinzie's
legal sons both attended school in Detroit, and his daughters went on to
college in Middletown, Connecticut.[61] Some of the LaFramboise children studied in Detroit, as did the daughters of the Beaubien brothers.
Madore and Charles Henry Beaubien, Jean Baptiste's sons by his first
marriage to an Ottawa woman, after a stint at McCoy's Indian school,
were sent to Hamilton College and Princeton, respectively. Captain Billy

Caldwell, son of a British army officer, was highly literate, an eloquent speaker, and received a Catholic education at Detroit.[62]

Periodically, the early settlers tried to induce private tutors to come to Chicago. Most of these attempts were ill-fated. Family tutoring was a common means of working one's way west or locating a husband, and most teachers did not last the year. Female teachers, paid by the town as late as 1837, still had to be recruited semiannually. The Kinzies and Beaubiens turned to family members: for example, John Harris Kinzie first studied under his father's half brother, Robert Forsyth, and when Charles Henry Beaubien returned from Princeton, he ran a school at home for the Beaubien-LaFramboise children.[63]

The first Yankee schoolteacher arrived unsolicited in 1830. A native of Vermont, Stephen Forbes was received with a mixture of apprehension and curiosity by those who had met his sister, the priggish Mrs. Laughton. Yet there was dire need for his services: the Beaubien and LaFramboise roosts were bursting. Forbes taught in the Beaubien house for a year and then quit to become sheriff. Perhaps he disliked his clientele; the pupils were overwhelmingly of mixed blood. The southerners did not send their offspring to Forbes' school; in fact, there is no indication that children on the north branch received any education at all until the town school districts were formed in 1837.[64]

In 1832, Thomas Watkins taught in the meeting-house at the Point. His pupils, again, were largely French-Indian, although a growing number of Yankee families sent their children there. Watkins apparently also agreed to take full-blooded Indian children into the school. Billy Caldwell, convinced that literacy was a key to native survival, offered to pay the tuition of any Potawatomi child who would wear European clothing. None accepted this offer.[65]

The year 1833 was pivotal in the annals of Chicago religion and education, as it was in almost every other sphere. The return of the Fort Dearborn garrison during the Black Hawk War of 1832 brought an eastern Presbyterian minister, the Reverend Jeremiah Porter, and a schoolmarm from Michilimackinac with dreams of a female academy. Chicago's ungodliness scandalized Porter, but he quickly formed a church group around a coterie of eastern arrivals of 1831-32 and members of the garrison. Porter's group was not so much pious or devout as it was conscious of a need for formality. Porter shared the meetinghouse at the Point with the Methodists for a brief time, but the congregation pushed for a separate church building. Porter's first communion was embellished with the use of Major Wilcox's silver service. The new six-hundred-dollar church opened its doors six months later. Unfortunately, women filled out the congregation while their men caused "a wanton abuse of the holy day by . . . sin[ning] against dear light and abus[ing] divine compassion and love."

On that communion Sunday, enterprising Yankee males were busy unloading two vessels in the new harbor.[66]

The Methodists still operated at the Point, reinforced in 1831 and 1833 by the Reverends Stephen Beggs and Jesse Walker, both southerners. By 1834 a revivalistic spirit produced a host of new members, primarily of southern origin, who erected a church on the north side. At the time, it seemed a logical place to build, since most of the Kinzie-Clybourne-Hall clan had settled on the north branch. However, it was not long before the Methodists felt "outclassed" by the wealthy Yankees settling in Ogden's improved "Kinzie's addition. " The congregation bodily moved its church across the river in 1836 to the area just west of the fort, Chicago's new "free zone."[67]

Although Baptists, Catholics, and Episcopalians each established a church in 1833, religion exerted little control over the everyday social and moral lives of most residents. An exception was the devout collection of Episcopalian Methodists who met at the home of Mark Noble on Thursday evenings for prayer and discussion. The group organized the first Sunday School in 1832, which was interdenominational in character.[68] Noble's enthusiastic followers represented in their piety and temperance the only persons in town—with the possible exception of some of Porter's "highfalutin" Presbyterians—who resisted the understandably attractive urge to accommodate themselves to the casual transcultural lifestyle around them. They did not join Beaubien's Debating Society; nor did they frequent the favorite haunts of early residents, the Sauganash and Laughton's Tavern. Instead, they performed charitable acts, nourished the school system and church attendance, and, though books were scarce, promoted an interest in literature. Mark Noble carried his entire library to the Sunday School wrapped in his pocket handkerchief, and his own timber built the Methodists' northside chapel. Arthur Bronson, east coast financier and cohort of William B. Ogden, was so impressed with Noble's endeavors that he shipped one hundred free books to the school.[69]

Eighteen thirty-three was a time of ambivalence and guarded optimism. The population had doubled since 1831. There was talk of a canal, of pre-emption, of a land cession, and of the official incorporation of Chicago as a county seat—with all the legal and social trappings. But no one was sure any of this would come about. Lots in the emerging central business district on the south side, formed by the sale of the township's school section, were still going for as little as $200 and were traded away with nonchalance. The Yankee influx had been gradual, so gradual that one easterner's assimilation into the lifeways of the older settlers was accomplished before his next potential ally against the reigning social order arrived.[70]

Hamilton-educated, the mixed blood Madore Beaubien was one of Chicago's "golden young-sters." Courtesy of the State Historical Society of Wisconsin.

The Yankee influence was felt in institutional ways: churches and classi-cal academies; ordinances for fire, garbage disposal, vagrant cattle, shoot-ing, and horse-racing; and lawyers predominating among the arrivals of 1833. But the more subtle matrix of social habits and relations had not been significantly altered. Hospitality (rather than privacy and exclusivity), essential to the native French Creole, and southern prestige systems, was still an unspoken requirement. Personal antagonisms that might generate complex patterns of avoidance in private life were inappropriate when the community gathered to act out its wholeness. There were no "private" par-ties. One's home, more than just a compartment for the family and one's prejudices, displayed the extent of one's generosity. A spacious house, able to fit the whole crowd under its rafters, was a distinct social attribute.[71]

The first Yankees did not build spacious homes; in fact, most rented back rooms or boarded at the Sauganash or at one of James Kinzie's tav-erns. In a way, they became adopted relatives who danced, drank, and caroused until dawn, and sometimes through the following day with the rest. Eastern visitors were startled to see dark-skinned maidens with bead-ed leggings under their black stroud dresses jigging with army officers, and genteel ladies twirling on the arms of southern hayseeds. All under the merry auspices of Mark Beaubien and his fiddle.[72]

Wolf-hunting, horse-racing, card-sharking, and shooting matches were still in vogue, although mostly removed beyond the town limits. Army officers and later "pillars of the city" met weekly—on Wednesday morning—at the Sauganash for a bracer, before heading out over the wolf-bedeviled prairie with Hamilton-educated Madore Beaubien, in brilliant headdress, whooping at the forefront. Rev. Jeremiah Porter noticed, to his chagrin, that there were as many Yankees as French-Canadians gambling at cards on the Sabbath (a reputable Sunday pastime for French *habitants*). French *carioles* raced across the ice in winter, and those who lacked a sleigh built their own rude version from timber cut on the north side. Ice-skating by moonlight was a favorite community activity, concluded, as usual, by a rowdy warming at the Sauganash.[73]

Chicago residents did not need holidays to celebrate. However, New Year's Eve warranted something spectacular, particularly for the French-Canadians. In the early years, the *Guignolee* and the *Reveillon* enlivened New Year's festivities all over the territory. Around 1833, Madore Beaubien and the "boys" fitted up the garrison's sizable skow with runners and made the rounds of village houses, adding sleigh party revelers at each stop. By the end of the evening the excitement was so out of hand that the group completely broke up a local tavern. The next morning, the "boys" paid $800 in damages without blinking an eye.[74]

There was something frenetic about the village scene. An unhoped-for material prosperity was in the wind, and residents rocked nervously on their heels—waiting. But there was also the scent of death. Black Hawk was defeated. His people, pushed into the turbulent Mississippi, had fallen like straw before the American scythe. Stragglers on the shore were dying of starvation or at the hands of the Sioux. What were white folks to do? What was anyone to do, in 1833, but wait?[75]

III

. . . If lost to honor and to pride Thou wilt become the white man's bride Then go within the strong armed wall Partake the pomp of brilliant hall And wreath above thy maiden brow The sparkling gems to which they bow.
—"The Muse of the Forest," written for *The Chicago Democrat*, February 18, 1834

Chicago's future was secured by the tail end of the summer of 1833. The town received its corporate seal, elected its first set of trustees, and let it be known that the school section was to be auctioned off in order to raise funds for civic improvements, notably a courthouse. Settlers were notified of their pre-emption rights, and there was a dash—at least by some—to register their homesteads. The united Potawatomi, Chippewa, and

Ottawa nation ceded all its land east of the Mississippi in exchange for 5,000,000 acres of promised soil west of the Missouri.*[76]

The year 1833 began with a sigh of relief. The Indian war was over, and the cholera that left a hundred army graves on the south bank had spent its malignancy in the winter freeze. General Scott's remaining troops were on their way east to spread the news about a lush green wilderness in Wisconsin and northern Illinois. Food, rationed during the Black Hawk scare, was once more in adequate supply. People got back to the normal business of running their small industries and drinking it up at Beaubien's.[77]

But it was not quite the same. The Yankee stream continued, increasing its breadth and current. The newcomers were primarily young men, single and ambitious, whose main goal in life was not to amass great wealth (although many would change their minds when given the opportunity), but to find a place that suited them and their talents, a place with which to grow. Chicago was not the first stop for many, nor the last for a few. The majority probably agreed, however, that Chicago was an advantageous place in which to settle during the 1830s. All occupational classes were arriving. Whereas the 1831-32 migration had seen a lopsided preponderance of merchants and a few professionals, 1833 witnessed a flock of lawyers and tradesmen who anticipated a growing urban center.[78]

In small numbers the New Englanders seemed to have been assimilated. Yet one by one they added cement to a structurally different worldview. Linear progress, historians would later call it: the belief that the future was only attainable by cheating the present, by conserving time, currency, energy, and emotion, and by walking a straight line. The Indians did not think people's lives should be bottled up like so much stale spring water. Nor did the French or the southerners (or Old John Kinzie when he lived). The Indians thought rather that the circle was the more natural version of things. The sun was round, the year was round, and if a hill was round, what sense did it make to cut a straight line through it?

Nineteenth-century Yankees, obsessed with their rightness, could not wean the native and his French sympathizer away from such notions. The simultaneous disappearance of the French, the Canadian *metis*, and the Indian from Illinois indicates a similarity in worldview and survival technique not generally granted significance. The lack of Yankee initiative among *habitants* of the Mississippi valley may be traced to more than an enslaving land system. The New Englanders had more success with the Kinzies and their southern kinsmen, though the latter had difficulty adjusting to Yankee aloofness and smug moralism as the years passed.[79]

The transition seemed relatively simple in 1833. Many of the town elders were dead: Francis LaFramboise, John Kinzie, Benjamin Hall, and Alexander Wolcott. Young men remained but, like their Yankee counterparts, most were under thirty-five, and a fair share of those were under twenty-five. Before the horde of speculators arrived briefly in 1833 for the sale of the school section, and came to stay during the Illinois-Michigan Canal sales of 1835, Chicago was a town of "boys."

There was something innocent, almost naive, about the young men's optimism. Robert Allen Kinzie, John Kinzie's youngest son, pre-empted 160 acres on the north bank, but rejected an opportunity to register land at the Point because the family would never use all they had acquired. Early in 1833, while on an eastern buying trip for his trading store, the same young man was flabbergasted when he was offered $20,000—by a shrewder judge of land values than he, Mr. Arthur Bronson—for his tract of swamp. In 1835, Bronson sold the acreage to his silent partner, Samuel Butler, for $100,000. In late summer of the same year, William B. Ogden, newly arrived to dispose of his brother-in-law's property, sold one-third of the property for the same amount. Ogden was not impressed at the time. But Robert Allen Kinzie was: his family might have been millionaires had they known.[80]

Mark Beaubien, only thirty-three and one of the "boys" himself, continued to pack travelers into the Sauganash, putting up curtains as sleeping partitions. When they laid out the town in 1831, his tavern sat in the middle of the street. "Didn't expect no town," he said, and the ease with which he continued to give away his lots suggests that he didn't care if it came.[81] Madore Beaubien took a Yankee partner, John Boyer, and married his daughter. The store foundered, but Madore had a high time selling fancy vests, hats, and laces to his Indian friends while the venture lasted. Like his uncle Mark, he sold his lots too early to share in any of the wealth. And he lost his Yankee wife. The second time around, Madore married a Potawatomi woman.[82]

The southerners expanded their cattle raising, butchering, and tanning operation at Rolling Meadows and cashed in on the eastern demand for beef. The newly dredged harbor, begun in 1833, turned meatpacking into Chicago's most profitable business in the 1830s, with the exception of platting and selling 11 paper towns." Archibald Clybourne, the man probably least admired by the old settlers, was easily the most successful in the later city. This negative relationship held true for John H. Kinzie as well, who retained his former prestige as leader of the north side's first family until his death, even though he proved a financial lightweight.[83]

Chicago's French-Indian families and Kinzie's employees appeared to resent his growing air of condescension. Even in the early years, when Kinzie was Indian agent at Fort Winnebago, the habitually sly, joking French-Canadian *engages* referred to him as "Quinze Nez." Creole *voyageurs* made an art of the French-English double entendre: they called the Judge of Probate, for example, "Le juge trop bete." Always sniffing for a way up, Kinzie did not fool his employees. Worse yet was Kinzie's romance-stricken wife, who reveled in her husband's noble attention to the poor "savage."[84]

The route an old settler had to take to rise in the increasingly eastern social milieu, and the amount of selling out that had to occur, is best illustrated by Kinzie's use of his wife's illusions. During the 1830s easterners in Chicago took a fancy to the finer aspects of Indian culture. Yankees were not particularly interested in seeing the display firsthand, but they welcomed Kinzie's tales of the wilderness, his rendition of sacred Potawatomi legend, his war paint, and his mock stag dance. Incredibly, he was so brash as to take an Indian show (in which he was the principal star) to the 1834-35 state legislature at Jacksonville for the purpose of "delighting" the delegates into passing a bill funding the proposed canal which was to cross land more or less taken from the Indians only a year earlier. Madore Beaubien must have burned down to his toes.[85]

The unmarried Yankee men lived together at the several boarding houses in a manner akin to rival fraternities. They gave in for the most part to the wilder ways of the young early settlers. John Wentworth, one of the "boys" for a time, and later mayor, claimed that he had never seen so much smoking and drinking. He found that the early churches also resembled fraternities, and he urged all of his friends to attend the Baptist services, where the best crowd gathered. The more contemplative Yankees, not so much averse to as timid about the drinking and shouting, were seated nightly in one or the other dry goods store playing checkers. Such games provided a political forum for the numerous young lawyers in town, who immediately swept novice officerholders like James Kinzie, Madore Beaubien, and Samuel Miller off their feet and out the governmental door.[86]

Aside from politics, there was still a healthy rapport among the young men in 1833. The Yankees relished a horse race as much as the early residents, and Mark Beaubien's daughters, as well as the dapper gentleman himself, drew the Yankees in as if magnetized. The old territorial divisions of the town were in a state of confusion, and new lines of class and race demarcation had not yet been drawn. Nearly all the Yankees lived on the near south side, the "free zone" which had replaced the Point as the central community meeting place. The boarding houses provided a kind of protective limbo, around which the bewildering array of conflicting values dashed but did not affect the people's lives. They were in the eye of the storm, and Mark Beaubien was Peter Pan. The "boys" were never going to grow up.[87]

The town found its adulthood abruptly and painfully. In early September 1833, the newly elected president of the town board, Robert C. V. Owen, called a grand council of the chiefs and headmen of the united Indian nations to discuss treaty arrangements for their removal west of the Mississippi. Owen, acting in his capacity as United States government commissioner, opened the proceedings by explaining to the assembly that he had heard that they wished to sell their lands. This was a blatant untruth. But the Indians unfortunately had no precedent for supposing that they would be allowed to keep their territory, even if they chose to. They deliberated.[88]

The 5,000 men, women, and children took their time, however, spending nearly three weeks at Chicago. They camped along the lakeshore and at the Point and enlarged their already mammoth debts to the local white traders, Robert Allen Kinzie among them. The bulk of the traffic was in liquor—alcohol enough to put them all in a drunken stupor for a week. Tipsy families wept together beside their tents, and in the sober morning there was still the wailing. [89]

On September 26 the treaty was concluded. Under a spacious open shed, specially constructed on the north side of the river for the occasion, the officers and spectators gathered. The chiefs did not arrive until the sun was red in the sky, and again they delayed while two old chiefs, wobbling with whiskey, made incoherent rebuttals. Then they signed. The commissioners sat with the sundown blaze in their faces, appearing, ironically, as brothers of the men they were herding away. Facing east, the Indians huddled in darkness.[90]

The spectacle rocked the inner heart of the town. Yankees were horrified at so pagan and slovenly a group; sympathy gave way to disgust. "Halfbreeds" who had been raised as part of the community shunned their previous friends. By order of the court in 1834, Justice of the Peace Beaubien publicly posted a "no trespassing" sign at Hardscrabble. White traders, new and old, hustled the sales while they could and then went home to estimate the amount of indebtedness the tribe had accumulated. The treaty allotted $150,000 to settle past liens, but the final settlement was $175,000. Undoubtedly many traders inflated the sum due; it seems that every white man in Chicago got a slice. The American Fur Company received an outrageous $20,000. The various members of the Kinzie family, including some of the Forsyths, received the next largest payment.[91]

In addition to the land west of the Missouri and the allotment to collectors, the treaty provided for cash payment in lieu of reservations, which was requested by innumerable "mixed-bloods" who wished to remain in Chicago. However, only three applicants' reservations were granted; the rest were given a pittance, ranging downward from $1800. A hungry Kinzie family again received a sizable grant, far exceeding the sums distributed among the French-Indians. The fourth and fifth clauses of the treaty provided for a twenty-year annual payment of $14,000, and $100,000 in goods to be distributed after ratification.[92] Goods worth $65,000 were presented to the nation on October 4. In preparation, the traders had ordered vast stores of whiskey (one trader alone asked for fifteen barrels). Fortunately, a prevailing south wind hindered ship passage up the river, and the traders were forced to content themselves with selling the supply on hand, as well as overpriced trinkets, blankets, knives, and so forth.[93]

It was a black Sunday. Worshipers did the only thing respectable people knew how to do: they hid within their churches from the drunken shouting, wailing, and fleecing. And they prayed. An old Indian stood playing a jew's-harp at the Reverend Jeremiah Porter's door, unaware that he was interrupting a religious service. When the payment was concluded, high winds and a driving rain sent the traders fleeing back into their cabins. The Indians went back to their camp at the Aux Plaines with $30,000 in silver. Porter thought that someone's prayer had been answered.[94]

In the months to come, the numerous mixed-blood residents of Chicago wrenched their hearts over whether to remove with their Potawatomi kinsmen or stay. Many wanted to remain: the sacred ground in which their grandfathers were buried meant more to people of native extraction than to the Yankees who were about to gain the territory. But the breach was irreparable. Indians and mixed-blood settlers willing to forgive were treated like some ghastly sore, too horrible to look at. The sore would not heal. It festered because the source of the disease was inside the Yankee eye. In time the Indian became the real evil in people's minds.[95]

Typical of the educated "mixed-bloods," Madore Beaubien was no fool. One of Chicago's "golden youngsters," he had wanted his share of power. Years later, as he wasted away on a reservation in Kansas, he explained that he had yearned for recognition in the white world. Denied that, he sought prestige within the tribe. Beaubien and most of his cohorts joined the local Potawatomi bands in 1835. Painted in the colors of death, they made their final turn through the streets already covering the ancient trails and fields, dancing their way out of the Americans' vision, their shrieks sticking in the Americans' ears.[96]

In 1835 the land sales—and one of the most incredible heights of speculative fancy the West had ever seen—began. Chicago was again a one-horse town. Everyone dealt in lots. But the land bore a stigma: by 1838 the majority of Chicago's newer residents, as well as a few old ones who had managed to keep their heads long enough to see the six-figure totals, were bankrupt.[97]

It would be easy to suggest that William B. Ogden was elected the first mayor of Chicago, incorporated in 1837, because wealth was the measure of power. However, it seems just as likely that residents could not stand to face someone more familiar in their midst. New blood, clean blood, a new family, a new community might root and bloom in the desecrated land and make it whole once more.

NOTES

1. Earliest descriptions of the Chicago Portage, with its frozen marshes and floods, are those of Marquette, Joliet, and La Salle, 1674-1682. See A. T. Andreas, *History of Chicago, From the Earliest Period to the Present Time* (Chicago, 1884), 1, 44-45. Later descriptions can be found in Henry Rowe Schoolcraft, "A Journey up the Illinois River in 1821," in Milo M.

Quaife, ed., *Pictures of Illinois One Hundred Years Ago* (Chicago, 1918), pp. 120-121; Gurdon Hubbard, "Recollections of First Year," Gurdon Hubbard Papers, Chicago Historical Society; Charles Cleaver, *Early Chicago Reminiscences* (Chicago, 1882), pp. 28, 30, 46; Edwin O. Gale, *Early Chicago and Vicinity* (Chicago, 1902), p. 105; Colbee C. Benton, in Paul Angle, ed., *Prairie State: Impressions of Illinois* (Chicago, 1968), p. 114; Bessie Louise Pierce, *A History of Chicago, 1673-1848* (New York, 1937), pp. 6-12.

2. Cleaver, pp. 28-29; Andreas, p. 192; "Remarks of Hon. George Bates," *Michigan Historical Collections*, 40 vols. (Lansing, 1877-1929), 11, 180-181.

3. William H. Keating was one of the more outspoken critics of Chicago as a site for future settlement. See his *Narrative of an Expedition to the Source of St. Peter's River, Lake Winnepeek, Lake of the Woods, etc. Performed in the Year 1823* . . . (London, 1825),1, 162-163, 165-166. For more favorable comments, see James Herrington to Jacob Herrington, Chicago, January 27, 1831, in Alphabetical File: James Herrington, Chicago Historical Society; "Recollections of First Year," p. 20; Charles Butler journal, Friday, August 2, 1833, in Letter File: Charles Butler, Chicago Historical Society; Benton, *A Visitor to Chicago in Indian Days*, Paul M. Angle and James R. Getz, eds. (Chicago, 1957), p. 76; Andreas, p. 129. Charlotte Erickson's "The British Immigration in the Old Northwest, 1815-1860," in David M. Ellis, ed., *The Frontier in American Development* (Ithaca, N.Y., 1969), is an interesting study of the British exception to the American farmer's aversion to prairie living during this period.

4. Gale, pp. 105-106; Cleaver, p. 28; Andreas, p. 207. Wolves were numerous on Chicago's north side as late as 1834.

5. See Cleaver, p. 30, for description of street drainage and building raising. Population estimates for the years 1833-1837 vary somewhat: Andreas claimed that the town grew from 200 in 1833 to 4,000 in 1837 (p. 142); a visitor's estimate in 1833 was 350, as cited in Angle, p. 64. Pierce (p. 14) lists 3,989 whites and 77 blacks in 1837.

6. See the Augustus Dilg Collection and the Albert Scharf Papers, Chicago Historical Society. See also Andreas, Ch. 1, and Louis Deliette, "Memoir Concerning the Illinois Country," Theodore C. Pease and Raymond C. Werner, eds., *Collections of the Illinois State Historical Library*, XXIII, French Series 1 (1934) (a copy signed "DeGannes" is in the Edward Everett Ayer Collection, Newberry Library Chicago); Hiram Beckwith, *The Illinois and Indiana Indians* (Chicago, 1884), pp. 99-117; Raymond E. Hauser, "An Ethnohistory of the Illinois Indian Tribe, 1673-1832" (Ph.D. diss., Northern Illinois University, 1973).

7. For geographic movement and settlement patterns of the Great Lakes tribes, see George Quimby, *Indians in the Upper Great Lakes Region, 11,000 B. C. to A. D. 1809* (Chicago, 1960) and James E. Fitting and Charles Cleland, "Late Prehistoric Settlement Patterns in the Upper Great Lakes," *Ethnohistory*, XVI (1969), 289-302. For cultural variations, see W. Vernon Kinietz, *The Indians of the Western Great Lakes, 1615-1760* (Occasional Contributions from the Museum of Anthropology of the University of Michigan, No. 10, 1940; reprinted by University of Michigan Press, 1965).

8. Quimby, p. 110.

9. *Ibid.*, pp. 109-115. The 1600-1760 estimated population density of the Great Lakes tribes of one per square mile assumes that Great Lakes peoples were subsistence farmers as well as hunters during this period. A growing literature concerns the impact of the fur trade upon Indian society: see, most recently, Calvin Martin, "The European impact on the Culture of a Northeastern Algonquian Tribe: An Ecological Interpretation," *William and Mary Quarterly*, XXXI, Set. 1 (1974), 3-26.

10. Quimby, pp. 147-151. See also Quimby, *Indian Culture and European Trade Goods* (Madison, Wis., 1966); Harold Hickerson, *The Chippewa and Their Neighbors: A Study in Ethnohistory* (New York, 1970); Felix M. Keesing, "The Menomini Indians of Wisconsin," *Memoirs of the American Philosophical Society*, X (1939); and Arthur J. Ray, *Indians in the Fur Trade: Their Role as Trappers, Hunters, and Middlemen in the Lands Southwest of Hudson Bay 1660-1870* (Toronto, 1974).

11. Quimby, *Indians in the Upper Great Lakes*, pp. 151 and *passim*. That traditional

authority was threatened is indicated by the tribal attempt to integrate British and American fathers into the patrilineal clan structure. Britishers were made members of a new clan, "the Lion," and Americans, "the Eagle."

12. Andreas, pp. 34-45; James A. Clifton, *The Prairie People: Continuity and Change in Potawatomi Indian Culture, 1665-1965* (Lawrence, Kan., 1977); Erminie Wheeler-Voegelin and David B. Stone, *Indians of Illinois and Northwestern Indiana* (New York, 1974).

13. Quimby, pp. 147-15 1; John Kinzie Papers and Accounts, Chicago Historical Society; the Chicago Historical Society's collection of material artifacts, particularly the Fort Dearborn display; Arthur Woodward, *The Denominators of the Fur Trade* (Pasadena, Cal., 1970), pp. 22-23, and passim.

14. Madore Beaubien Papers, Beaubien Family Papers (including information on Chief Alexander Robinson) and Billy Caldwell Papers, Chicago Historical Society. See also Jacqueline Peterson "'Ethnogenesis: Metis Development and Influence in the Great Lakes Region, 1690-1836" (Ph.D. diss., University of Illinois, Chicago Circle, 1977).

15. Juliette Kinzie, *Wau-bun, The Early Days in the Northwest* (Chicago, 1932), pp. 193-194; Beaubien, Family Papers, Chicago Historical Society.

16. John Kinzie Papers and Accounts, Chicago Historical Society; "Recollections of First Year," Gurdon S. Hubbard Papers; American Fur Company Papers, Letter Books, Chicago Historical Society; John Jacob Astor to Ramsay Crooks, New York, Mar. 17, 1817, in *Collections of the State Historical Society of Wisconsin* (Madison, 1854-193 1), XIX, 45 1. See also Gordon Charles Davidson, *The Northwest Company* (New York, 1918); David Lavender, *The Fist in the Wilderness* (Garden City, N.Y., 1964); John D. Haeger, "The American Fur Company and the Chicago of 1812-1835," *Journal of the Illinois State Historical Society* (Summer 1968), 117-139.

17. Account Books, American Fur Company Papers, Chicago Historical Society. Details of the estates of the American Fur Company's competition at Chicago, William Wallace and John Crafts, are given in Ernest B. East's "Contributions to Chicago History from Peoria County Records: Part 1, *Journal of the Illinois State Historical Society* (Mar.-Dec. 1938), 197-207. See especially Robert Stuart to John Crafts, Aug. 20, 1824; Mar. 2, 1825; Aug. 26, 1824, American Fur Company Papers, Chicago Historical Society.

18. John Kinzie Papers and Accounts, Chicago Historical Society; Robert Stuart to Astor, Sep. 12, 1825, American Fur Company Papers, Chicago Historical Society.

19. Quimby, pp. 1-20. In 1800, most of the land at Chicago was free of water at least half of the year. The lake continues to recede.

20. Cleaver, pp. 15-16; Juliette Kinzie, pp. 205-211; Keating, pp. 165-166.

21. Juliette Kinzie, pp. 209-211; Benton in Paul Angle, *Prairie State*, pp. 112-114; Surgeon John Cooper's description in James Grant Wilson Papers, Chicago Historical Society; Captain John Whistler, 1808, Fort Dearborn Papers, Chicago Historical Society.

22. Robert Stuart to John Kinzie, Oct. 22, 1825, American Fur Company Papers, Chicago Historical Society; Juliette Kinzie, p. 215; testimony of Mary Galloway, wife of Archibald Clybourne, in Andreas, *History of Chicago*, p. 103; Ernest B. East, "The Inhabitants of Chicago, 1825-1831," *Journal of the Illinois State Historical Society* (1944), 155.

23. Keating, in Angle, p. 84; Marshall Smelser, "Material Customs in the Territory of Illinois," *Journal of the Illinois State Historical Society* (Apr. 1936), 17; Andreas, p. 134; Beaubien Family Papers, Chicago Historical Society; "Beaubiens of Chicago," NIS in Frank Gordon Beaubien Papers, Chicago Historical Society.

24. Information concerning Jean Baptiste Point du Sable is elusive. For a brief sketch, see Lyman Draper interview with Robert Forsyth in Lyman S. Draper manuscripts, XXII (1868), 104, Wisconsin Historical Society, Madison, Wisconsin. See also Milo M. Quaife, *Checagou* (Chicago, 1933), p. 90; Pierce, *A History of Chicago*, p. 13; William C. Smith to James May, Fort Dearborn, Dec. 9, 1803, William C. Smith Papers, Chicago Historical Society; "Beaubiens of Chicago," Frank Gordon Beaubien Papers, Chicago Historical Society. The Wayne County records at Detroit, Michigan, show the sale of du Sable's house to

Lahme, as well as several Indian grants of land to Kinzie at Detroit. Pierre Menard claimed to have purchased a tract of land on the north bank of the Chicago River from an "Indian" named Bonhomme and later sold it to the Kinzies for $50. No houses are mentioned in these transactions.

25. Juliette Kinzie, p. 210. There is a drawing in the Augustus Dilg Collection, Chicago Historical Society, of the old Kinzie house which fairly matches Mrs. Kinzie's description. See also John Wentworth, *Early Chicago* (Chicago, 1876), p. 23, and Elizabeth Therese Baird, "Reminiscence Of Early Days on Mackinac Island, "*Collections of the State Historical Society of Wisconsin*, XIV, 25. For a description of the 11 *poteaux en terre* of the lower Illinois country, see John Reynolds, *The Pioneer History of Illinois* (Belleville, Ill., 1852), pp. 30-31.

26. Smelser, pp. 18-19; John McDermott, ed., *The French in the Mississippi Valley* (Urbana, 1965), pp. 26-40. For a description of "half-breed" housing, see John H. Fonda in *Collections of the State Historical Society of Wisconsin*, v. 232; Peterson, op. cit., Ch. 5.

27. Jane F. Babson, "The Architecture of Early Illinois Forts," *Journal of the Illinois State Historical Society* (Spring 1968), 9-40; Fred Kniffer, "Folk Housing: Key to Diffusion," *Annals of the Association of American Geographers* (Dec. 1965); interview by Milo M. Quaife of Emily (Beaubien) LeBeau, Aug. 3, 1911, in Emily LeBeau Papers, Chicago Historical Society.

28. "The water lay 6 inches to 9 inches deep the year round," according to Cleaver, p. 30. See also "William B. Ogden," *Fergus Historical Series*, No. 17 (Chicago, 1882), 45; Benton in Angle, p. 114; Quaife, *Checagou*, p. 78.

29. John Kinzie Papers and Accounts, Chicago Historical Society, F. Clever Bald, *Detroit's First American Decade, 1796-1805* (Ann Arbor, 1948), p. 12. See also Eleanor Lytle Kinzie Gordon, *John Kinzie, the Father of Chicago: A Sketch* (1910). This inflated family history suggests that Kinzie lived in New York City and ran off to Quebec to learn a silversmith's trade, a plausible though unsubstantiated story.

30. John Kinzie Papers and Accounts; Quaife, p. 95; Pierce, p. 21; Lyman S. Draper Manuscripts, S, XXII (1868), 102, Wisconsin Historical Society, Madison, Wisconsin; Clifton, "Captain Billy Caldwell."

31. Surgeon John Cooper of the first garrison at Fort Dearborn said that Kinzie was a man of "ungovernable temper" who had bitter quarrels with people. Cooper also charged Kinzie with Lalime's murder. See the James Grant Wilson Papers, Chicago Historical Society See also *Hyde Park-Kenwood Voices*, 111, No. 8 (1960), in John Kinzie Papers; Matthew Irwin to William Eustis, Chicago, July 3, 1812, in Lewis Cass Papers, 11, Clements Library, Ann Arbor, Michigan.

32. Bald, p. 76; John Kinzie Papers and Accounts.

33. John Kinzie Papers and Accounts; Andreas, pp. 90-91; Lewis Cass to John Calhoun, Jan. 9, 1819, Lewis Cass Papers, Burton Historical Collection, Detroit Public Library.

34. John Kinzie Papers and Accounts; Robert Stuart to Astor, Sept. 12, 1825, American Fur Company Papers; Robert Stuart to J. B. Beaubien, Sept. 11, 1825, American Fur Company Papers; Gurdon Hubbard, Jan. 2, 1828, Gurdon S. Hubbard Papers.

35. Conway, p. 405 and *passim*; Charles J. Kappler, ed., *Indian Affairs. Law and Treaties* (Washington, D.C., 1904),11,402-404; James R. Clifton, "Captain Billy Caldwell: The Reconstruction of an Abused identity," paper read at the American Historical Association meetings, Dec. 1976, Washington, D.C.

36. Eleanor L. K. Gordon, *John Kinzie, Father of Chicago*, p. 28; John Kinzie Papers and Accounts; Ramsay Crooks to John Kinzie, Oct, 29, 1819, and Aug. 11, 1819, and Robert Stuart to Kinzie, 1826-1827, in American Fur Company Papers.

37. Between 1829 and 1830 alone, prominent Chicagoans Archibald Clybourne, Samuel Miller, Archibald Caldwell, Mark Beaubien, Alexander Robinson, and Russell Heacock were licensed to keep tavern. See Ernest East, "Contributions to Chicago History from Peoria County Records," Part II, *Journal of the Illinois State Historical Society* (1938), 328-329; "Beaubiens of Chicago," Frank Gordon Beaubien Papers, Chicago Historical Society.

38. Kinzie Family Papers; Gale, p. 125.

39. Juliette Kinzie, p. 209.

40. *Ibid.*, p. 205.

41. See Keating in Angle, *Prairie State*, pp. 84-86. Mrs. Kinzie's *Wau-bun*, while an important historical document, is unfortunately skewed to favor the family's social aspirations.

42. Juliette Kinzie Papers, Chicago Historical Society; Eleanor L. K. Gordon, pp. 6-7. Trader Clark's first name is listed variously as John and Alexander. Mrs. Kinzie omitted this branch of the Kinzie family in her *Wau-Bun.*

43. Gordon, *loc. cit.*; Andreas, pp. 101-102.

44. Andreas, p. 100; John Kinzie Papers; Robert Stuart to John Crafts, Mar. 2, 1825, American Fur Company Papers.

45. Andreas, pp. 100-102; Wentworth, *Early Chicago*, Supplemental Notes, pp. 34-35.

46. East, "Contributions," Part 11, 329-331, 336-339; East, "The Inhabitants of Chicago, 1825-1831," *passim.*

47. The canal section, platted and sold in 1831, held the only lots on the market when the Eastern speculators began to arrive in 1833. Its location, the central loop, gave it a speculative advantage over areas further away from the new harbor. The Kinzie family did not pre-empt the Point, and it went to southerners who did not have a flair for exciting the Eastern interest. See Andreas, pp. 111, 130-132; also Gale, p. 54.

48. Mark Beaubien Papers, Chicago Historical Society; Andreas, pp. 106, 288-289.

49. For the *habitant* dancing tradition, see John Reynolds, *The Pioneer History of Illinois*, Pp. 52-53. Cleaver, *Early Chicago Reminiscences*, pp. 5-12; John H. Kinzie Papers; "John Dean Caton Recollections," *Reception to the Settlers of Chicago Prior to 1840, by the Calumet Club of Chicago, Tuesday evening May 27, 1879* (Chicago, 1879), 36-37. For a discussion of the liquor problem, see Marshall Smelser, pp. 11-13; Thomas Forsyth to General William Clark, Peoria, Apr. 9, 1824, Thomas Forsyth Papers, Folder 2, Missouri Historical Society, St. Louis, Missouri.

50. Juliette Kinzie, p. 205; Beaubien Family Papers.

51. "John Wentworth's Recollections," Calumet Club, pp. 42, 48; Cleaver, p. 13. Beaubien's tavern was only 16 by 24 feet, yet in 1833-34, forty people were being boarded in shifts. No one knows how many people actually slept there in a given evening.

52. "John Wentworth's Recollections," Calumet Club, pp. 49, 71. In the winter of 1835-36, prominent Easterners and the Kinzies built the Lake House on the North Side. Gale said, "They ain't going to call it no tavern," and Cleaver said there was a joke circulating that no one worth less than $10,000 would be allowed to stay there. Weekly dancing parties were held there by invitation only. At least some of the French Creoles were being included: there is an 1843 dance ticket in the Beaubien Family Papers requesting the company of the "misses Beaubien. See also "Beaubiens of Chicago," Frank Gordon Beaubien Papers; Gale, p. 118.

53. On the Beaubien farm at Grosse Pointe, see Bald, p. 35. Beaubien was early Chicago's most colorful character, according to most easterners' recollections. He is mentioned in nearly every old settler's reminiscences, especially in Gale, Cleaver, the John Wentworth Papers, Chicago Historical Society, and "Sketch of Hon. J. Young Scammon," *Chicago Magazine*, Mar. 1857, reprinted in *Fergus Historical Series*, No. 5 (Chicago, 1876). See "Beaubiens of Chicago," Frank Gordon Beaubien Papers and Beaubien Family Papers, for particulars, and Andreas (p. 107) for a physical description: "His favorite dress on 'great occasions' was a swallow-tail coat with brass buttons . . . . He was in his glory at a horse-race."

54. Andreas, pp. 85, 174; East, "Contributions," Part 1, pp. 191-197.

55. East, "Contributions," Part I, pp. 191-197; Wentworth, *Early Chicago*, p. 41.

56. *Ibid.*

57. See Jean Baptiste Beaubien Papers for original voting lists; "Beaubiens of Chicago," Frank, Gordon Beaubien Papers; Andreas, pp. 600-602.

58. Andreas, p. 602; East, "The Inhabitants of Chicago," *passim.*

59. Regarding the first Board of Trustees, see Andreas, pp. 174-175; *Chicago Democrat* (Dec. 10, 1833).

60. John Kinzie Papers, Madore Beaubien Papers, and Beaubien Family Papers; for a vivid description of Rev. See, see Juliette Kinzie, p. 216.

61. For a description of private schools in Detroit, see Bald, pp. 88-91; Beaubien Family Papers.

62. "The Beaubiens of Chicago," Frank Gordon Beaubien Papers; Madore Beaubien and Billy Caldwell Papers; Clifton, "Captain Billy Caldwell."

63. John Kinzie Papers; Madore Beaubien, 1881 and 1882 letters, Madore Beaubien Papers; Andreas, pp. 204-209.

64. Andreas, p. 205; Mary Ann Hubbard, *Family Memories* (printed for private circulation, 1912), p. 68.

65. Andreas, p. 205; letter from John Watkins in Calumet Club, pp. 73-74.

66. Andreas, pp. 299-301; Rev. Jeremiah Porter, *Early Chicago's Religious History* (Chicago, 1881), pp. 54-58.

67. Andreas, pp. 288-289; Gale, p. 60.

68. Andreas, p. 289; Porter, pp. 56-57.

69. Gale, p. 60; Andreas, p. 289.

70. Andreas, pp. 174, 111-124; Beaubien Family Papers.

71. Andreas, pp. 132-133; *Chicago Democrat*, Nov. 26, 1833; Wentworth, *Early Chicago*, pp. 39-40.

72. John Wentworth to Lydia Wentworth, Nov. 10, 1836, John Wentworth Papers, Chicago Historical Society; Madore Beaubien Papers; Harriet Martineau, in *Reminiscences of Early Chicago* (Chicago, 1912), p. 30; Cleaver, p. 27.

73. Charles Fenno Hoffman, in *Reminiscences of Early Chicago*, pp. 21-22; Beaubien Family Papers; Porter, p. 78; Cleaver, pp. 5, 12. According to Cleaver, large hunts of over 100 men were still being held in 1834. He describes improvised sleighs built by setting crockery crates filled with hay on two young saplings shaved at the end to create runners. See Reynolds, p. 229, for the French Creole habit of cardplaying on Sunday.

74. Cleaver, p. 12. For descriptions of the *Guignolee* and other French customs transplanted in the Illinois country, see Natalia Maree Belting, *Kaskaskia Under the French Regime*, Illinois Studies in the Social Sciences, XXIX, No. 3 (Urbana, 1948); J. M. Carriere, *Life and Customs in the French Villages of the Old Illinois Country* (Report of the Canadian Historical Association, 1939).

75. See Andreas, pp. 267-271, for a treatment of Chicago's role in the Black Hawk War; interview with Madore Beaubien, *Chicago Times*, May 16, 1882, in "Beaubiens of Chicago," p. 39, Frank Gordon Beaubien Papers.

*A surprising number of French-Indians and non-Indian husbands went west with the Potawatomi. Over half of the registered voters between 1828 and 1830 were, or were thought to be, in Indian country during the 1850s.

76. Andreas, pp. 122-128, 174-175; Kappler, ed., pp. 402-403; Charles Royce, *Indian Land Cessions in the United States*, 18th Annual Report of the Bureau of American Ethnology (Washington, 1899), pp. 750-751; Anselm J. Gerwing, "The Chicago Indian Treaty of 1833," *Journal of the Illinois State Historical Society* (1964); Wentworth, *Early Chicago*, pp. 39-40.

77. Andreas, pp. 120-121; "Biography of Thomas Church," *Fergus Historical Series*, No. 5 (Chicago, 1876), p. 42.

78. Andreas, pp. 131-133. See Daniel Elazar, *Cities of the Prairie* (New York, 1970), pp. 153-180, for Illinois migration streams; "List of Settlers of Chicago Who Came Between January, 1831, and December, 1836," in Rufus Blanchard, *Discovery and Conquest of the Northwest, with the History of Chicago* (Wheaton, 1879), pp. 424-433.

79. See Madore Beaubien Papers. Mark Beaubien spoke of the affinity of French Creoles for the Potawatomi and Potawatomi culture on his deathbed, in "Beaubiens of Chicago," Frank Gordon Beaubien Papers.

80. Andreas, pp. 130-131; Kinzie Family Papers; "William B. Ogden," *Fergus Historical*

Series, No. 17 (Chicago, 1882); "John Dean Caton Recollections," Calumet Club, p. 35; John Wentworth to Lydia Wentworth, Nov. 10, 1836, John Wentworth Papers.

81. Beaubien Family Papers; "Beaubiens of Chicago," Frank Gordon Beaubien Papers.

82. Beaubien Family Papers; store inventory, Madore Beaubien Papers.

83. Andreas, p. 103.

84. Juliette Kinzie, pp. 227-229.

85. John Harris Kinzie Papers, 1833-1837, Chicago Historical Society; Harriet Martineau, *Reminiscences of Early Chicago,* p. 32; Martineau, "Strange Early Days," *Annals of Chicago,* IX (Chicago, 1876).

86. Cleaver, pp. 13, 24; Gale, p. 122; John Wentworth to Lydia Wentworth, Nov. 10, 1836, in John Wentworth Papers.

87. Cleaver, p. 27.

88. Andreas, pp. 122-125.

89. *Ibid.,* p. 123; Charles Latrobe, *A Rambler in North America* (London, 1836), pp. 201, 207, 210-211.

90. Andreas, p. 124; Latrobe, pp. 213-214. For the influence of mixed-bloods in Potawatomi politics and the treaty of 1833, see miscellaneous fragment, n.d., Alphabetical File: James Herrington, Chicago Historical Society; Frank R. Grover, *Antoine Ouilmette* (Evanston, 1908), pp. 12-16; Conway, pp. 410-418; Clifton, "Captain Billy Caldwell."

91. Andreas, pp. 126-128; Porter, pp. 71-73; *Chicago Democrat* (Dec. 10, 1833).

92. Andreas, pp. 126-128; Kappler, ed., pp. 402-410.

93. Porter, pp. 73-74.

94. *Ibid.*

95. Gale, p. 154; Madore Beaubien Papers.

96. In his old age, Madore Beaubien said that he wanted his children to honor his name and lamented the fact that Chicago had not remembered him. See interview in *Chicago Times,* May 16, 1882, in "Beaubiens of Chicago," Frank Gordon Beaubien Papers. See also John Dean Caton, *The Last of the Illinois and a Sketch of the Pottawatomie* (Chicago, 1876), pp. 26-30; Wentworth, *Early Chicago,* pp. 35-36.

97. Pierce, pp. 57-69. See also John D. Haeger, *Men and Money: The Urban Frontier at Green Bay, 1815-1840* (Mt. Pleasant, Mich.: Clarke Historical Library, Central Michigan University, 1970) for a comparable takeover by Eastern speculators of another fur-trading town.

Terry Straus

Founding Mothers

Indian Women in Early Chicago

The documentary history of Chicago begins with its missionaries, explorers, and fur traders in the last quarter of the seventeenth century. The "discovery" of Chicago was actually an accident and a disappointment: under the auspices of Count Frontenac of New France, Jolliet was looking for the famed Mississippi River and its promise of a water-route to the Gulf (Quaife 1933 :8). Père Marquette had been hoping to do missionary work among the Illinois Indians for some while, even learning something of the local language from an Illini Indian captive among the Ottawa near the mission at Chequamegon. Ill health forced him to camp on the north branch of the Chicago River at first, but he later made his way to what is now Damen Avenue and the South Branch, where a monument marks his mission. When Marquette arrived, there were already some fur traders among the Illini people (Quaife1933: 13).

Chicago became a secondary fur trade center, a "meeting ground" for people at the meeting of the two great waterways (the Great Lakes-St. Lawrence-Atlantic and the Illinois-Mississippi-Gulf systems). In the fur trade, Indian women were active agents of social and economic change. European voyageurs and fur traders were men, usually unattached men, who came to America because it offered both freedom from European establishment and economic opportunity. At that time, all of America was "Indian Country," and the only women in Indian country, of course, were Indian women. Indian women frequently developed marital partnerships with white traders and became "an integral part of fur-trade society" (Van Kirk 1980: 75).

Such unions are generally represented as the result of European (especially French) policy to secure Indian political and commercial support. The picture is one of predatory white male traders who came swooping down on poor, unprepared, and unsuspecting Indian women who were, of course, overwhelmed and overtaken. This view, however, ignores and demeans the intelligence and purposefulness of those Indian women. "Indeed, some Indian women took the initiative in securing fur-trade husbands and sought to make the most of the opportunities offered by this new role move" (idem). Indian women, as always, actively sought to improve life circumstances for themselves and their families: the fur-trade offered vast possibilities for such improvements and those possibilities were not lost upon them.

The initial unions between Indian women and white fur traders led to "half-breed" offspring who then replaced their Indian mothers as "people in-between." By the mid-18th century, there was a large mixed-blood population in North America. White fur trader fathers sought unions for their mixed-blood daughters with incoming white traders or with the mixed-blood sons of their colleagues. By the beginning of the nineteenth century, more white women had begun to come into the New World, making unions with Indian women less common. An 1806 ruling by the Northwest Company acknowledging informal marriages with white women and rejecting marriages with full-blood Indian women encouraged this tendency. However, the mixed-blood Indian woman was still considered stronger, more capable, and better suited to fur trade life than the newly arrived European white woman (Van Kirk 1980: 195). While it is certainly true that the status and power of Indian women in fur trade society declined as the trade itself declined, the women of early Chicago were part of the trade at perhaps its highest point, and their roles within it were acknowledged by their contemporaries if not by later historians.

Not surprisingly, documentary records of early Chicago focused on the men who were the traders, trappers, and tavern owners, and rarely on the women. We know very little of the women—Indian, white, or mixed. This imbalance in history is particularly problematic here as full-and mixed-blood Indian women played such key roles in the fur trade economy, polity, and society that characterized the early city. It is clear that women were very much present in the early days of the city, and that most of those women were full-or mixed-blood Indian women.

The names of only a very few Indian women are still remembered: Monee and Watseka have towns named after them; Victoire Pothier and Jane Miranda received reservations in the 1829 Prairie Du Chien Treaty. With these four, Archange Chevalier Ouilmette serves as a reminder that Indian women were not just occasional visitors but absolutely essential participants in the robust inter-ethnic society of early Chicago.

Archange was born in Michigan to a French Canadian fur trader named Francois Chevalier and a Potawatomi woman whose name, as is commonly the case, was unrecorded. Her mother may have been the "chopa" listed in church records in Council Bluffs, Iowa (Hussey 1996:2) where the family lived after Removal. Archange may have had a brother named Petrus. A woman identified as her sister (though we do not know if this was a blood sister) married Pierre Bulbona, a French trader, and had a large family. Bulbona's cabin was on the Peoria and Galena road, where a timber grove was named after him. His cabin was a double cabin: half as living space, half to store trade goods. A celebration at the cabin after the marriage of their daughter was allegedly attended by Zachariah Taylor and Jefferson Davis (Mastson 1989:75).

Like her "sister," and in some sense replicating the marriage of her parents, Archange married a French fur trader, Antoine Ouilmette. Ouilmette arrived in Chicago in 1790 and became the first white man to settle permanently there; his home stood about where the Tribune Tower stands today. A Frenchman, he was described by Moses Morgan, who helped reconstruct Ft. Dearborn, as a "medium-sized, half-starved Indian" (Quaife 1933:1790). He became a guide for travelers and traders, transporting them across the approximately 30 mile portage from the lake to the forks of the Illinois, using oxen to pull the boats and goods. Archange assisted him in his work as a guide through the portage, in trading for the American Fur Company and later for John Kinzie. Like other Indian and mixed-blood women, she knew the terrain, knew the portage route and its problem spots, knew how to set trap lines and dress hides; she also knew the fur trade customs of Chicago, as they had borrowed much from their Indian precursors (Hussey 1996). Her knowledge, her ability to communicate with and relate to Indian hunters and trappers, and her physical labor made her an essential part of Ouilmette's endeavor. They also found in each other "good companions;" and their marriage lasted a lifetime (Hussey 1996:3).

Archange Ouilmette and her children were granted a reservation in the 1829 treaty as well: "2 sections for herself and her children on Lake Michigan, south of and adjoining the boundary of the cession herein made by the Indians . . . to the U.S." Nine hundred acres of this 1,200 acre reservation are now a Chicago suburb bearing her married name, spelled as "Wilmette"; the remaining 300 are part of north Evanston. Archange may also have been granted a reservation on the Kankakee River in the 1833 treaty, held jointly with her sister, in compensation for losses in the 1812 Fort Dearborn conflict: some of her sister's family was said to be living there fifty years later (Matson 1989:73). It has been suggested that Archange received her treaty land(s) on behalf of her husband: he could not receive such land because he was not Indian and not party to the negotiations. However, it seems equally and, in fact, more likely that the reservation was granted to her upon her own merits, resulting from her involvement in the fur trade community and her reputation and recognition within that community. Other reservations granted to women in the same treaty support this interpretation. It should be remembered that at this point in American history, women were not landholders: it was partly this which excluded them from the right to vote. This makes it all the more significant that three Indian women received individual reservations in 1829, at the very beginnings of the new city. This is about the same as the number of men receiving reservations in the 1829 treaty (Billy Caldwell, Alexander Robinson, Claude LaFramboise within the city, Beaubien and Aptakisic outside of it)! Clearly, the residents of the new city acknowledged the critical presence and contribution of Indian women.

Archange Ouilmette and her children lived on their 1829 reservation. After the 1833 treaty of Chicago and consequent removal of Potawatomis from the area, and following a dispute regarding the theft of lumber from her property, she and her children moved to Council Bluffs, Iowa, to join their Indian relatives who had removed there. This was the common history of others receiving reservations. Much of the land once held by these individuals is now held by the Cook County Forest Preserve District. The continuing good relationships sustained by Archange Ouilmette, Jane Miranda, and Victoire Pothier, with their Potawatomi kin is affirmed by their ultimate removal to those Potawatomi communities. Characterized by some contemporary Indians as "sell-outs" who aided whites to the detriment of native people, those who received reservations were not thought of in that way by their own people.

A few specific names are known of the Potawatomi people who developed and built the early city. It should be remembered, however, that most of the Potawatomis did not live in the confines of what was later to become the city of Chicago: most continued to camp along the streams and rivers, some in quite large villages, until (and for that matter, *after*) the 1833 treaty and subsequent removal. Those who did live in the city continued to connect with their families in such camps and villages, perhaps not unlike present-day residents of the city.

The Indian and mixed-blood presence in the early city is affirmed by this none-too-positive description given by William Keating, a University of Pennsylvania mineralogist who visited the city in 1823: "The village presents no cheering prospects, as, notwithstanding its antiquity, it consists of but few huts, inhabited by a miserable race of men, scarcely equal to the Indians from whom they are descended (Schnedler 1933:24)." In the inter-ethnic, inter-racial mix of early Chicago, Anglo European culture had no special privilege. Although we have tended to view Indian-white marriage as inevitably resulting in the assimilation of the Indian spouse, it has finally begun to dawn on us that it is at least as likely for the reverse to occur (see especially Brenda K. Manvelito's University of Arizona Ph.D). In the context of the fur trade, it was even more likely for the reverse to occur. White fur traders, alone in a new land, adopted many of the customs and concepts of the tribes with whom they wintered. The fur trade culture that developed in the Great Lakes area is generally thought of as a pan-Indian overlay on a Chippewa base. Such was the background and lifeway of the people who built and lived in the early city. Saturday nights at the Sauganash, Mark Beaubien's tavern and the center of social life in the early city—the same tavern where the elite Chicago Debating Society met—included feathers and drums and "wobanos" or Indian dancing.

Jean Baptiste Point duSable, a Black man and the first permanent non-Indian resident of the Chicago area, was a fur trader. He was said by a grandson to have escaped slavery in Kentucky and come to live in an Indian village on the Des Plaines River, where he married a Potawatomi Indian woman and raised several mixed-blood Indian children. Later, he built a cabin at the mouth of the Chicago River, across from the fort. Three other cabins were soon built in this central area, all belonging to French fur traders with Potawatomi or half-breed Potawatomi wives: Pierre LeMay, Louis Petite, and Antoine Ouilmette (Quaife 1935: 88). DuSable's establishment was a bustling locus of fur trade activity. His relations with his wife's people remained strong. He may well have learned Ojibwa as the lingua franca of his trade, and it is clear that he participated in the local Indian fur trade community. In 1800, when he sold his business, he moved to East Peoria with a group of Potawatomis. Du Sable sold his house to a French trader named LeMai, but the property became John Kinzie's.

John Kinzie was a British fur trader formerly of Detroit. He was certainly the leading citizen of Chicago in the beginning of the nineteenth century. He came to Chicago in 1804, with the Fort Dearborn troops. He traded with the Potawatomi and worked at the fort (which consistently drew traders and storekeepers as well as troops to the area). His home, the class house in town, stood where du Sable's cabin had been. His household included Jeffrey Nash, a Black slave, and two Potawatomi Indian women, Victoire Pothier and Jane Miranda. Jeffrey Nash had been purchased in 1803 in Detroit, where slavery was fairly common. In Chicago, Nash became a contract laborer (an indentured servant, really)—not, apparently, because Kinzie and his partner opposed slavery but because they did not realize the flexibility of the 1789 Northwest Ordinance outlawing slavery in the Northwest Territories. Kinzie's partner in his early years in Chicago was his half-brother, Thomas Forsythe of Peoria. Kinzie's status was the result of his position in the broader fur trade hierarchy, especially his relation with suppliers in Detroit and Michilimackinac, the centers of American Fur Company trade (Peterson 1995, 43). Although distinguished in status and power, he was fully a member of the fur trade society and dependent upon it for his continued success. Most of the French-Indian residents of the early city worked for Kinzie at one time or another: Mirandeau, the Ouilmettes, the LaFramboises and the Robinsons; Billy Caldwell served as his clerk. These mixed blood men and their families were powerful and respected in the early city, sitting just below Kinzie on the local social pyramid. Many of the families lived in the

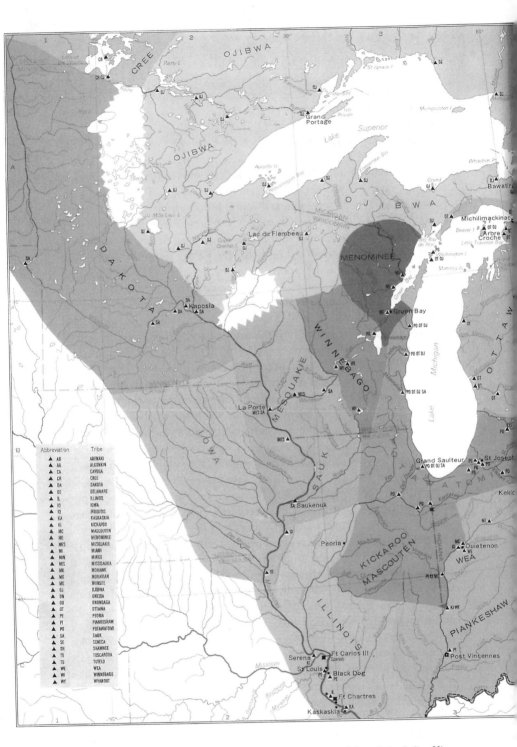

Indian Villages and Tribal Distribution c. 1768. From Tanner Helen, *Areas of Great Lakes Indian History*. University of Oklahoma Press. 1989 Reprinted with permission of the University of Oklahoma Press.

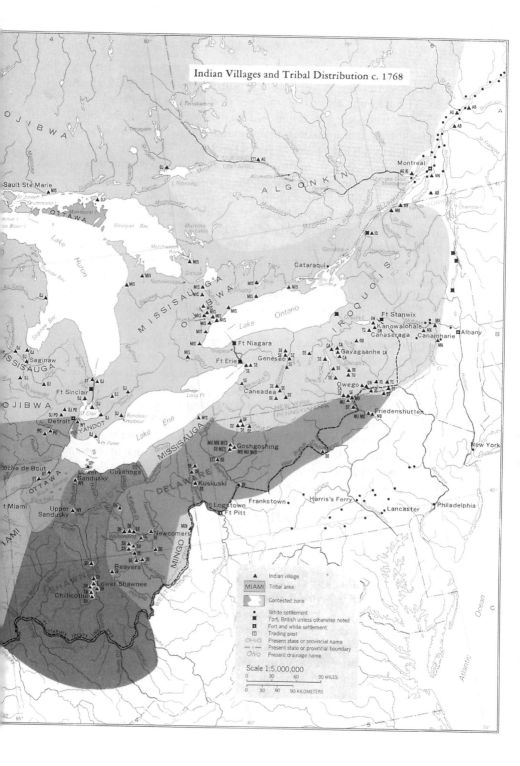

Indian Villages and Tribal Distribution c. 1768

Legend:

▲ Indian village
MIAMI Tribal area
(contested zone) Contested zone
• White settlement
■ Fort, British unless otherwise noted
⊞ Fort and white settlement
⊡ Trading post
OHIO Present state or provincial name
— ·· — Present state or provincial boundary
Ohio Present drainage name

Scale 1:5,000,000

0   30   60   90 MILES
0 30 60 90 KILOMETERS

area then called "Hardscrabble" (today, Bridgeport) where they were the first to contact the *engages* and *voyageurs* returning in the spring (Peterson 1995). The area was also sometimes referred to as "Lee's Place" after Charles Lee who built two cabins and established a farm on the south branch of the river, four miles from its mouth. Lee and most of his family were killed in the 1812 Fort Dearborn conflict.

Jean Baptiste Beaubien, an American Fur Company agent married to a Potawatomi woman, established another powerful family in the early city. Their mixed-blood Potawatomi daughter became the First Lady of Milwaukee, married to Mayor Juneau, the first mayor of that neighboring town. His younger brother, Mark, built and ran the Sauganash, named after the successful half-breed trader, Billy Caldwell. His mixed-blood son, Madore, was a prominent political leader in the Chicago community who served on the town's first Board of Trustees. The defeat of the half-breed Madore Beaubien by William Ogden in the first mayoral election in 1837 signaled the end to the old social order and power structure of the new city.

The prominent Indian people in early historic Chicago were Potawatomi people, and Potawatomi people signed the treaties that ceded the land that became present day Chicago (see map on pages 72-3). However, the Potawatomi were only one of many Indian groups to occupy the Chicago area. There were other native people, other Indian women, in the Chicago area, long before the eighteenth century when their fur trade experience made the newly arrived Potawatomis dominant. More than 6,000 prehistoric and historic sites in the Chicago area represent each of the four basic archaeological periods recognized in North America: Paleo-Indian, Archaic, Woodland, and Mississippian (see Lace article). Illini people, the early historic peoples of the Chicago area, either replaced or were continuous with the Woodlands mound builders. Cahokia, Kaskaskia, Tamaroa, and later Michagamea and Peoria of the Algonquian speaking Illini confederacy pursued a variegated lifeway that included hunting and planting as well as wild rice harvesting. In Illini camps and villages, women were the agriculturists and the potters; the men roamed widely into the southern prairies, hunting the prairie buffalo and other animals (Miller, 1990). When pottery and, later, beadwork, was exchanged between villages, it fell to the women to accept or reject, to encourage or deny such exchanges. When new people came to the village, it was the women who were reliably there to incorporate and enculturate them. Long before the fur trade, Indian women found themselves at the crossroads of cultures. Women were traders and producers of valued trade items. With the primary responsibility for the welfare of their children in their hands, these Indian women likely embraced new ideas, new ways of doing things, new opportunities for themselves and their children, just as later Indian women did in the context of the fur trade. While gender was an important determi-

nant of role in these communities, women's roles were probably more flexible than those of men. Men, after all, were required to leave the camp:
when they were away, the women at home assumed their domestic duties
and camp roles, becoming situational hunters, warriors, leaders. They
moved the camps with the seasons, between their fields and the camps in
resource areas and their large (sometimes hundreds of lodges) summer villages (Miller 1990:82), deciding where and with whom to live and determining relations with their neighbors.

The Miami, later Algonquian residents of the area, and the associated
Piankeshaw and Wea people, followed a similar lifeway (Miller 1990). A
band of Miami arrived in Chicago around 1690 (Quaife 1933:23), when
they moved to avoid conflict with the Iroquois. Others joined them and
soon there were two Miami villages where the city would later stand. The
Miami and Illini people were displaced from the area by the Potawatomi
and related Chippewa and Ottawa. The 1763 Treaty of Paris ending the
"French and Indian War" was a factor in encouraging Ottawa and
Chippewa movement into the area: the pro-French Ottawa moved near
the French fort in Ottawa, Illinois, when the British took over Detroit
(Tanner 1989:19). The arrival of these new groups displaced the Miami
proper towards the Wabash River valley where they remain today (Peterson 1995:23). However, the displacement of residents due to the arrival of
the People of the Three Fires should not be exaggerated: certainly, some
Illini and Miami people joined new camps and villages and remained in
the immediate area. The Potawatomi, with whom we began, became
politically dominant in regard to relations with the European and later
American peoples, but they were a new group in what was already a socially and culturally diverse area. Early fur-trade Chicago, dominated by men
born to and married to Indian women, gave way to rapid development in
the second quarter of the nineteenth century.

The Erie Canal had opened in 1825, opening a new Great Lakes water
route to Chicago from the east: in 1823, "the whole annual shipment of
the trade on the lake did not exceed the cargo of 5 or 6 schooners . . . the
dangers attending the navigation of the lake and the scarcity of harbors
along the shore (being) . . . a serious obstacle for increase of commercial
importance of Chicago" (Keating in Schnedler 1993, 24). The plotting of
the route for an Illinois and Michigan Canal allowing access to the Mississippi River thus confirmed Chicago as a central hub in American trade
and business. "It was a canal rather than a railroad that put Chicago on the
map as a city and brought its first boom" (Schnedler, 26). And boom it did.
In 1830, when the first official census was taken in the city, the enumerat-
ed population was 50 and $100 was the highest price paid in the initial
auction of lots in the one square kilometer that was the original plotted
city (Cronin 1991). By 1833, with the Removal of Potawatomis and the
incorporation of the city, Chicago had already begun to attract the atten-

tion of those higher up in the commercial establishment, people in Detroit, for example, who saw the great growth potential in the city's location. In the 1830s, Chicago experienced "the most intense land speculation in American history" (Cronon 1991). By 1836, the highest auction price per plot had increased to $100,000 and the population of the city was enumerated at 3,265. This was also the year in which the Fort was demobilized as the "Indian threat" was considered to have evaporated (Pacyga 1986, 3). Within the next year, Chicago already supported 17 lawyers— "lawyers and litigation were another sign of developing urbanization" — due to real estate and land speculation (idem). The great influx of land speculators and other business people in the 1830s displaced the true "Founding Fathers" and changed the character and control of the city. We know that Indian people continued to live in the city and its environs, though most left to join relatives in other communities; we know that the expansion of the city depended upon Indian lumber and Indian labor, but we have little record of those Indian people. For about 60 years, until the period of the World's Columbian Exposition in 1893, there is a discontinuity in the historical record of Indian people in the Chicago area.

What is clear of the city before its incorporation by the new "Yankee" establishment is that it was a vibrant, multi-ethnic community in which Indian women, especially Potawatomi Indian women, figured prominently. Indian women were the wives and the mothers of the majority of men who populated and controlled the city until 1833. Indian women were also workers and landholders here, unusual in the history of earlier, eastern cities. Indian women, nameless by fault of history, were central participants in the fur trade economy that fueled the initial growth and development of the city. In this important sense, it must be argued that Indian women were the Founding Mothers of the city, the women who took the initiative to become involved in the fur trade, the women who were able to make transitions and reinvent themselves and their communities, marrying fur traders and raising children well enough versed in the ways of both worlds to build and become early Chicago as it grew outside the fort. These Founding Mothers, moreover, followed a long tradition in the Chicago area of Indian women who monitored and managed the opportunities presented by their multi-ethnic social environment.

BIBLIOGRAPHY

Cronon, William. *Nature's Metropolis: Chicago and the Great West*. New York: WW Norton, 1991.

Hussey, Virginia. *Archange Ouilmette*. Evanston Historical Society, 1996.

Manuelito, Brenda K. *Land and Lifeway in the Chicago Area: Chicago and the Illinois-Miami* in Straus, T. Indians of the Chicago Area. Chicago: NAES College Press, 1990.

Matson, N. *Memories of Shaubena*. Chicago: DB Cooke and Company, 1878; reprinted by Rand McNally and Co., Chicago, 1989.

Miller, Jay. *Land and Lifeway in the Chicago Area: Chicago and the Illinois-Miami* in Straus, T. Indians of the Chicago Area. Chicago: NAES College Press, 1990.

Pacyga, Dominic and Ellen Skerrett. *Chicago: City of Neighborhoods*. Chicago: Loyola University Press, 1986.

Peterson, Jacqueline. *Founding Fathers: The Absorption of French-Indian Chicago, 1816-1837* in Holli and Jones (eds.) Ethnic Chicago. WB Eerdman, 1995.

Quaife, Milo M. *Checagou: 1673-1835*. Chicago: University of Chicago Press, 1933.

Schnedler, Jack *Chicago*. Oakland: Fodor's Travel Publications, 1993.

Tanner, Helen. *Atlas of Great Lakes Indian History*. Norman: University of Oklahoma Press, 1989.

VanKirk, Sylvia. *Many Tender Ties*. Norman: University of Oklahoma Press, 1980.

Penelope Berlet

Father Pinet and the Mission of the Guardian Angel

"The annals of this Illinois county, like most of New France, cannot be written without paying some measure of respect to the Jesuit fathers of that era who have given us much of its history in the Jesuit " (Grover).

In Winnetka, at the top of a hill, 400 yards from the Metra Station at Winnetka Avenue, is a marker that reads:

"Indian village site. Unearthed relics and testimony of early settlers indicated that this ridge throughout its length was a frequent campsite of Potawatomie Indians and antecedent tribes."

Across Ridge Road is another sign that reads:

"INDIAN HILL CLUB. MEMBERS ONLY."

Between these two signs is an interesting and controversial story.

The Potawatomi Indians mentioned in the first sign were one of the People of the Three Fires: Potawatomie, Odawa, and Chippewa (Edmund). The Potawatomi, Odawa and Chippewa migrated westward to the area of the Great Lakes from homelands near the Saint Lawrence River. The westward movement was at least partly due to their participation in the European fur trade: as the more easterly lands were depleted of fur trade game, those whose livelihood had come to depend upon the trade moved westward in search of game. Potawatomi village sites are located throughout the Chicago area (see Lace article in this volume), and Potawatomi people were living in the area until the final, 1833, treaty of Chicago by which they relinquished their last lands here. After the 1833 Treaty, many moved west of the Mississippi or up into Wisconsin. By the time the village of Winnetka developed, the Potawatomie had relinquished all right to their lands in the Chicago area.

The "antecedent tribes" noted in the first sign were, first, people of the Illini Confederacy, the first Indian people described in the area, the people associated with the famous site near the confluence of the Illinois, Missouri, and Mississippi Rivers at Cahokia. Later, the Miami people moved into the area, only to be later replaced by the Potawatomi. Evidence of human habitation on the sand ridge where the marker is found goes back for thousands of years and through several different cultural groups or complexes. The ridge itself was selected as a habitation site because it was high ground and also had a good supply of water from a nearby spring, water that did not freeze in the winter because it was constantly flowing. The ridge, created by the glaciers, was a geological as well as a cultural meeting ground: it was also the water system divide. While most archaeological materials from the ridge are associated with Potawatomie, there is also evidence of the earlier populations.

Winnetka became a town in the end of nineteenth century. In December, 1912, residents established the Winnetka Country Club, renamed "Indian Hill Club" in March 1914 as the club was not formerly within the boundary of incorporated Winnetka and the membership was not exclusively of Winnetka residents (Schalgetter 1998). In 1914, the Indian Hill Club was founded by some of the town's more prominent settlers. In the grounds work and landscaping of the golf course of the new club, a variety of artifacts were inadvertently discovered. Edward S. Rogers of the ground committee collected "more than a bushel of implements and arrow and spearheads while walking over the course" (Indian Hill Club History, 11). These artifacts were on exhibit in the club and eventually were stored in the basement of the new clubhouse, but disappeared sometime in the early 1940s. It is possible that some of those artifacts, including both pottery and copper pieces, are now held by the Mitchell Museum of the American Indian in Evanston.

Indian habitation of the property owned by the club was well known to local Winnetka residents. The high area in the northeast section of the property was known to have been used as a lookout and signal point—thus the name "Indian Hill." The amount and the nature of the archaeological material discovered in the site suggested to Rogers that the site was different from the average village site in the area, and he surmised that it was the location of Father Pinet's Guardian Angel Mission. Rogers located the village along the trail on the sand ridge that extended north from the Chicago River to Green Bay and later became Green Bay Road (Indian Hill Club History, 12). A later article by Charles Farmer in a local newspaper (The Winnetka Talk, July 15, 1948), noted that the trail trees in the area pointed to the location of the site on the Indian Hill Golf Club and that Fr. Pinet and his group would probably have followed the trees as they sought a site for their new mission.

Rogers's hypothesis found support in the earlier conclusions of Frank

R. Grover, Vice President of the Evanston Historical Society. In his 1916 talk at the Evanston Historical Society, he argued that the Mission of the Guardian Angel, founded by Father Pierre Francois Pinet, had been located on a sand ridge near the south end of the Indian Hill Club, somewhere around the eleventh green and twelfth tee.

Father Pierre Francois Pinet himself was born in 1661 in Limoges, France. In 1694, he became a missionary and was sent to Mackinac to provide services to the Indian people there. In 1696, he was sent to work among the Miami Indian people in Chicago. Two Miami villages are reported from that time, one on the main river and one on the south branch (Quaife 1933, 23). Although Fr. Marquette had been the first white man to reside in the Chicago area, arriving more than twenty years earlier, Fr. Pinet was generally thought to have been Chicago's first resident clergyman (ibid).

While Fr. Pinet himself was "a man of deeds and not words," and "left no record" (Grover, 1916: 6, 16), in 1698, Fr. Jean Francois Saint Cosme has provided some information. Forced by a storm to land their canoes in the area of present day Wilmette, Fr. Cosme and his companions and guides were welcomed at the mission by Fr. Pinet. Saint-Cosme wrote of the mission, "Their house is built on the bank of a small lake, having a lake on one side and a fine prairie on the other. The Indian village is of over one hundred and fifty cabins, and one leg (3 miles) on the river. There is another village almost as large. They are both of the Miamis" (Indian Hill Club History, 12).

Grover draws on Fr. Cosme's description, in conjunction to the topography of the north shore at the time, in placing the mission "at the site of a former Indian village in the vicinity of Indian Hill Golf Grounds and on the bank of the then Skokie Lake, or on the bank of the North Branch of the Chicago River near the Skokie for which this river was the outlet" (ibid., 16–17).

Between 1907, when Grover first advanced this claim, and 1916 when he gave the cited lecture, he had received "both compliment and criticism" for his assertion. Many doubted the North Shore location of the mission, placing it near the river in Chicago instead. In the 1930s, the Illinois Catholic Historical Society took exception to the Grover-Rogers theory and placed a memorial tablet in the Builders' Building then on the corner of LaSalle and Wacker Drives in downtown Chicago to mark the site of Pinet's mission. This analysis conforms with other reports, especially from French Catholic mission records, which place Pinet "on the bank of the main river on the northern border of the city's loop" (Quaife 1933: 24). In fact, when Fr. Pinet returned to the mission again in 1698, after being temporarily recalled by Count Frontenac, he reported that some 150 cabins stood on the main river where the mission was located.

Father Pinet left the Guardian Angel Mission again two years later, in

1700, to join the St. Francis mission near St. Louis and establish the first permanent white settlement at Cahokia and Kaskaskia. For awhile, the Guardian Angel Mission was continued by Fr. Jean Mermet, but he did not stay long at the Guardian Angel mission, either, and it was abandoned later in the same year (Grover 1916, 16).

The Winnetka sign, today, claims only the "Indian Village Site" and does not mention the Angel Guardian Mission. The records of the Indian Hill Club, however, attest to the belief among Club members that Fr. Pinet's mission was located on Club property. It seems possible, with all the movement of missionaries into and out of the area, and the short length of stay of both Fr. Pinet and Fr. Mermet, that some other or adjunct mission or missionary activity might have been focused on the land south of the signal hill on the Indian Hill golf course.

BIBLIOGRAPHY

The First Evanstonians. A paper read before a joint meeting of the Chicago Historical Society and the Evanston Historical Society in the Chicago Historical Society Building, 1916 by Frank Grover, (Vice-)?President of the Evanston Society.

Indian Hill, the First 75 Years: 1914-1989. A publication of the Club.

The Early History of Illinois from Its Discovery by the French in 1673 Until Its Cession to Great Britain in 1763, Including the Narrative of Marquette's Discovery of the Mississippi, Sydney Breese, E.B. Meyer and Company, Chicago: 1884.

The Jesuit Relations and Allied Documents. Reuben Gold Thwaites. Pageant Book Company. New York, 1959.

The Potawatomies, Keepers of the Fire. R. Dave Edmunds. University of Oklahoma Press: Norman, 1978.

"Do Trail Trees Point to the Site of Pinet's Mission?" Charles R. Farmer, Jr. In *The Winnetka Talk,* July 15, 1948.

Quaife, Milo M. *Chegagou: 1673-1835.* University of Chicago Press. 1933.

Schlagetter, Dave; Grounds Director, Indian Hill Club; telephone interview, May 1988.

Jerry Lewis

Red and Black Slaves in the Illinois Territory

Colonial French settlement in Illinois centered in Kaskaskia, Cahokia, and Prairie du Rocher. Kaskaskia was the earliest, settled around 1720, in what had been an Indian town. The French in these settlements kept both Indian and African slaves (church records of birth, baptism, and marriage from these towns are a good source of information on the colonial populations). In 1763, at the end of the French and Indian War, the French ceded their lands to Britain. Fifteen years later, the Americans won Kaskaskia and Cahokia from the British.

George Rogers Clark (1752–1818) led the American attack on the British at Kaskaskia and Cahokia in 1777–78. His success in these battles was once considered crucial to American acquisition of old Northwest Territory. When the Revolutionary War ended in 1783, Clark was rewarded for his actions by being made a member of the board of commissioners of the new Illinois Territory. This American "hero" acknowledged "red and black slavery" in the area and called for even greater restrictions on the slaves in the following proclamation, first in French, with the English translation following:

Proclamation by George R. Clark, December 24, 1778.
George Rogers Clark Ecuyer Colonel Commandant la partie or entale des Illinois et ses dependences &c.

Sur les plaintes qui nous ont été addressées par les differens habitans de cette rive, par leurs requêtes qui nous a été presentée le vingt deux du Current, tendante a ce qu'il nous plut remedier aux desordres, abus et Brigandages qui durent depuis Long-temps, causée par le trop grande liberté dont jouisse les Eclaves rouges et noirs, qui les Empechent de Vanquer[?] aux differens ouvrages aux quels leurs maitres les Employent qui causent la perte totale de cette colonie, nous En consequence des susdittes plaintes et pour maintenir le bon ordre dans toute l' Etendue de ce pais il nous a Plut ordonner et ordonnons ce qui suit sçavoir.

I. Deffendons et faisons trés Expresse inhibition a toute Personnes de quelque qualité quelles puissent être de vendre ou faire donner ou traitter aucune Liqueurs enyvrant sous quelque pretexte que se soit et En quelque petite où grande quantité que se puisse être, aux Esclaves rouges et noirs sous peine de vingt Piastres Demande pour la premier fois et du double s'il recide dont le Denonciateur en recevera la moitié.

2. Deffendons a toutes personnes de cette rive de pretter où Loüir Gratuitement a aucun Esclaves rouges où noirs leurs maison où Batiments même leurs cours pour y danser après le soleil couché où la nuit pour y festiner où y faire des assemblées nocturnes sous peine de Quarante Piastres demande Pour la premiere fois et du double s'il recidive dont le denunciateur En recevera la moitié. cependant n'Entendons pas Empecher Que les ·dits Esclaves rouges où noirs prennent leur recreation Les dimanches où fêtes a danser moyennant que se soit le jour seulement et que les dits Esclaves soyent Pourvü d'un Parmi [sic] signé de leur maitre pour cet Effet pour lors toutes Personnes pourront leurs Louer où pretter leur maison Pour y danser dans le jours sans aucune gêne.

3. Deffendons pour prevenir les vols et lareins des Esclaves rouges où Noirs a tous Esclaves de sortir de la maison où cours de leurs maitre après la retraitte Battue a moins quils ne soyent pourvu d'un parmi signé de leur dit maitre qui ne leur sera accordé que dans le Cas de necessité qui ne pourra leur servir que pour une fois, ceux qui En sortiront sans être muni dudit parmis apprès la retraitte Battue seront fustigé au depens de leur maitre En place publique de trente neuf coups de foüet, Pareillement celui qui ira d'un village à l'autre sans être muni d'un parmis de son maitre subira le meme chatiment et s'il recidive il sera doublement Puni et toujours au depends de son maitre.

4. Enfin deffendons a toutes personnes d'achepter où Echanger avec les dits Esclaves rouges où noirs aucunes denrées cochons ou bois ni autre que se puisse être sans que les dits Esclaves ne soyent munis d'un parmis de leurs maitre pour vendre où Echanger les dittes denrées et ce sous peines d'une amende arbitraire par les contreveneurs a notre presente proclamation.

5. Enjoignons a tous capitaines officiers de milices et autres Particuliers de tenir la main a L'Execution de la presente Proclamation et a tous Blancs d'arreter les Esclaves rouges où noirs qu'ils remontreront dans les rües de chaque village de cette rive apres la retraitte Battue où huit heurs, Pareillement les Esclaves qui se trouveront dans des cabannes d'autres Esclaves, que celles de son maitre après la ratraitte battue où huit heures du soir seront aussi arreté et fustigé de trente neuf coups de foü En place publique et au depends de son maitre et celui qui arretera un ou Plusieurs Esclaves après

la retraitte Battue où huit heures du soir soit dans la rue où dans une cabanne qui ne sera pas la demeure de l'Esclave, recevera que [*sic*] Piastre sur le charge du maitre au quel appartiendra Vesclave qui aura été arreté par chaque tête.

6. Sera notre presente proclamation affichée a la porte de chaque Eglise des village de cette rive pour que personnes n'en puisse ignorer.

Donné au fort Clark sous le sceau de nos armes et le seing de notre secretaire le 24me Xbre 1778.

Signé Jean Girault

Par Monseigneur signé G R Clark

Carbonneaux, Greffier

ENGLISH TRANSLATION

Proclamation by George R. Clark, December 24, 1778.

George Rogers Clark Esquire, commanding the eastern part of Illinois and its dependences, etc.

On Account of the Complaints, which have been addressed to us by several inhabitants of this bank through their petitions, presented to us the twenty-second of the current month, in which they beg us to remedy the disorders, abuses, and brigandage of so long duration, that has been caused, by the too great liberty enjoyed by the red and black slaves, a liberty that prevents them from accomplishing the different pieces of work in which their masters employ them, and is thus causing the total loss of this colony: in consequence of the aforesaid complaints and in order to maintain good order in the whole extent of this country, it has pleased us to ordain and we do ordain what follows: to wit,

1. We forbid and prohibit very expressly all persons of whatsoever quality they may be from selling to, causing to be given to, or trading with the red and black slaves any intoxicating liquors under any pretext whatsoever and in any quantity, little or big, under penalty of twenty *piastres* fine for the first offense and of double, if it is repeated; of which fine the accuser shall receive half.

2. We forbid all persons living on this bank to lend or rent gratuitously to any red or black slaves their house, buildings, and courts, after sunset or for the night, for the purpose of dancing, feasting, or holding nocturnal assemblies therein, under penalty of forty *piastres* fine for the first offence and of double, if it is repeated; of which fine the accuser shall receive half. We do not intend, however, to prevent the said red or black slaves from taking their recreation in dancing on Sundays and feast days; provided it is during the day time, and the said slaves are furnished with a permit signed by their masters to the effect that all persons can rent or lend them their houses for the purpose of dancing without restraint during the day.

3. In order to prevent thefts and robberies by red and black slaves, we forbid them to go out of the house or court of their masters after tattoo is beaten unless they are provided with a permit signed by their said master, and this shall be granted them only in case of necessity and can be used only once. Those who shall go out after tattoo is beaten, without being furnished with the said permit, shall in a public place be given thirty-nine strokes of the whip at the expense of their masters. Likewise he who shall go from one village to another without being furnished with a permit from his master shall suffer the same chastisement; and if it is repeated, he shall be punished with twice the number of strokes, always at the expense of his master.

4. Finally we forbid all persons to buy from, or exchange with, the said red or black slaves any goods, commodities, pigs, wood, or other things whatsoever, unless the said slaves are furnished with a permit from their Masters to sell or exchange the said commodities; and this under penalty of an arbitrary fine payable by the transgressors of this our present proclamation.

5. We enjoin all captains, officers of the militia, and other individuals to enforce the execution of the present proclamation, and all white men to arrest the red or black slaves whom they shall meet in the streets of each village of this bank after tattoo is beaten or eight o'clock in the evening; and likewise the slaves who shall be found after the beating of tattoo or eight o'clock in the evening in the cabins of other slaves than those of their master shall be also arrested and, in a public place, beaten with thirty-nine strokes of the whip at the expense of their masters; and he who shall arrest one or several slaves, after the beating of tattoo or eight o'clock in the evening, either in the street or in a cabin which is not the dwelling place of the slave, shall receive [que?] *piastres* for each slave who shall be arrested, at the charge of the master to whom the slave shall belong.

6. Our present proclamation shall be posted on the door of each church of the villages of this bank so that no person can be ignorant thereof.

Given at Fort Clark under the seal of our coat of arms and the signature of our secretary, December 24, 1778,

by Monseigneur (signed) G. R. Clark.

(Signed) Jean Girault.

Carbonneaux, Clerk.

This document is reproduced from the Illinois Historical Society's Kaskaskia Records: 1778–1790. It was part of the display for Native American Indian History Month at South Suburban College where I work. I brought Tim, my ten-year-old, tribally enrolled grandson to the exhibit. He had learned about George Rogers Clark in school. He had not, of course, learned about slavery in Illinois/Indiana or about Clark's support of it. I offered him a copy to take to his teacher, but he thought it would be too upsetting to contradict the image of Clark as a hero and the assumptions that slavery was always of Africans and that it had no part in the history of Indiana or Illinois. I don't have much to do with the writing of textbooks at this time of my life, but I want my grandson to have an education which includes balanced materials to study. Access to primary materials such as the 1778 proclamation of George Rogers Clark allows for that kind of balance. For Tim and for others of the next generation, I have included it here.

When Congress established the Old Northwest Territory, it outlawed slavery in general, but permitted the old French to retain their Indian and African slaves. George Rogers Clark himself led an ill-fated attack on the Wabash Tribe in 1786, during which his troops mutinied. Clark was subsequently charged with a number of improprieties stretching back to his Revolutionary War campaigns. Congress subsequently revoked his commission in Illinois. This ruined him financially, and Clark spent the last decades of his life attempting to recoup his fortunes and regain his reputation.

John Hobgood

Kickapoos and Black Seminoles of Northern Mexico
Guardians of the Rio Bravo Borderlands

Author's Note: I wish to thank Dr. Ignacio Bernal, former Director of the National Museum of Anthropology, for helping me to make use of the diplomatic archives in Mexico and to Eduardo Corona for copying the archival material. I thank the Research Committee of Chicago State University for the faculty grant used to conduct this research. This paper discusses migration of the Black Seminole and the Kickapoo Indians from Indian Territory to Northern Mexico, a process that began in 1849–1850.

In the middle of the nineteenth century, a colony of Indians and Blacks developed in northern Mexico. Among the Indian people who emigrated voluntarily to Mexico were Kickapoo formerly from the Illinois area. Descendants of those original emigrants still live in Mexico today.

In 1768, more than 2,000 Kickapoo and Mascouten lived in central Illinois and Indiana, south of the Potawatomi. The Kickapoo ceded their entire holdings, some 13,000,000 acres, in the Edwardsville Treaty of 1819. Thereafter, they became widely dispersed due to a complicated sequence of migration, settlement, and removal. Many removed to the appointed reservation on the Osage River in southwestern Missouri; other moved to the White River also in Missouri. In 1833, the Missouri Kickapoo were removed again, this time, to Kansas. Some Kickapoo split off from the Missouri group and traveled as far south as Texas to join relatives already living there. At least 600 and perhaps all of the remaining 1,000 Kickapoo remained in the Illinois-Indiana area, living in villages along the Illinois, Wabash and Vermillion Rivers, not far from Chicago. One village of 15 to 20 lodges was located west, on the Mississippi River, south of Saukenuk (Tanner 1987, 139).

Since at least 1775, a community of Kickapoo had lived in the area that later became Texas, occupying a Spanish land grant in exchange for serving Charles III of Spain by protecting the area from southern Plains raiders. In February, 1778, the Kickapoo chief traveled to Louisiana to be presented with a silver medal for this work. This arrangement ended abruptly with the Louisiana purchase in 1803, but the community of Texas Kickapoo remained, numbering around 800 in 1824. They were later joined by several hundred from the Kansas Kickapoo and they were at first allowed to remain after Texas became independent of Mexico (1836). In the Texas war of independence, however, most of the Kickapoo backed Mexico. The Texans later retaliated in 1839 by expelling them from the area. Many Texas Kickapoo migrated to Indian Territory, then settling in central Oklahoma, where they were later joined by a group of Kansas Kickapoo under the prophet Kenukuk. Other Kickapoo exiled from Texas joined with a group of Seminoles and traveled to Mexico in 1850, sustaining their alliance with Mexico and seeking to develop a relationship with the Mexican government similar to what their fathers had had with the Spanish government when Mexico had been "New Spain" (Kehoe 1981, 301).

The Seminole group they joined included Black Seminoles who had been removed from Florida to the Creek Nation in Indian Territory after the Third Seminole War. In Indian Territory, Creeks and Seminoles disagreed about the treatment of Black Seminoles. In 1850, a Seminole chief by the name of Coacochee or Wildcat entered the controversy between the Seminole and the Creek Indians over the fate of the Black Seminoles. Wildcat was the son of King Philip, one of the Florida chiefs. Already during the Seminole wars in Florida, he seemed to have been a man of some influence among both Indians and Blacks.

Wildcat quickly gained great influence among the Seminoles and Seminole Blacks by proposing that they migrate to Mexico. The fact that Mexico had abolished slavery under Hildago in 1810 (with the death penalty imposed for keeping slaves) and continued to take a strong stand against slavery was a compelling reason for Seminole Blacks to migrate to the Mexican Republic. Wildcat proposed the development of a Mexican colony of North American Indians and Blacks. He allied himself with the Black leaders, Gopher John and Jimmey Bowlegs, and formed a scouting party that included Blacks, Seminoles, Creeks, and Cherokees to contact Mexican authorities and to scout out the area of possible settlement. As word of a plan to migrate to Mexico spread, seven or eight hundred Seminoles from the east as well as plains Indians from the Lipans, Wacos, and Karakawa tribes joined Wildcat's command.

The Kickapoo people from Illinois who joined Wildcat's group in 1849–50 had traveled on notarized "safe conduct" passes from Chicago's own Fort Dearborn, signed by Major William Whittles on September 28, 1832. The same passes are used today by their descendants when they cross the border at Eagle Pass into America. Other Mexican Kickapoos travel on a parolee card similar to those carried by Cuban refugees, except that their "nationality" is listed as Kickapoo.

In 1850, a delegation of Kickapoo and Seminole under Wildcat went to see President Herrera in Mexico City. At that meeting, they received a land grant in exchange for border protection. They received four sites near Morelos, Coahuila, where they became Mexican citizens (Ritzenthaler, 19).

Wildcat, representing the allied Seminoles, Black Seminoles, and Kickapoos, was assigned approximately 70,000 acres. The grant stipulated that "the new colonies were to obey the authorities and laws of the republic, maintain harmonious relations with nations friendly to Mexico; prevent, by all means possible, the Comanches and other barbarous tribe from continuing their raiding through the area; pursue and punish them; refrain from any commerce with these tribes; and maintain the best possible relations with the citizens of the United States" (Latore [note 53] 1991, 365).

The Kickapoo people sustained a very significant additional clause in the agreement, which states ". . . although the Kickapoos, Seminoles, Mascogan Negroes and other Indians who may come to Mexico must subject themselves to the laws of the country, it is not demanded of them to change their habits and customs" (Latore [note 54] 1991, 14).

For various reasons, including protection from slave raids, the particular homelands were shifted. Today the tract occupied by the Mexican Kickapoos is in Naciemento, near Muzquiz in the state of Coahuila.

The Kickapoo community in Mexico grew with the later (1862) addition of some 250 Kickapoo from Indian Territory who emigrated from the U.S. to avoid engagement in the Civil War and to escape the disruption of the reservation due to the 1862 treaty which opened the reservation to railroad construction and routing. In 1864, they petitioned for permanent residence and a grant of land. In 1866, they were granted land near Naciemento, land formerly occupied by Seminoles. In 1937, ten thousand acres of land from the adjoining La Mariposa ranch were added to their holding.

Letters between Washington, D.C., and Mexico City, as well as correspondence between various border posts on the Mexican frontier (found in the Diplomatic Archives in Mexico City under the heading "Indios Barbaros") throw much light on Mexico's positive attitude towards the immigration of Native American tribes that were originally from the Southeastern United States and from the American Midwest. Wildcat's colony became an integral part of the system of defense for frontier Mexico. Comanche and Apache hostility to Wildcat's proposed colony developed because the plains Indians realized that Mexico wished to create a presidio or fortified town out of Wildcat's colony to serve as a Rio Grande buffer for the Mexican settlements otherwise prey to their raids. Several groups of Seminole Blacks attempting to join Wildcat and Gopher John in Mexico were massacred by Comanche war parties. One Captain March, who inquired as to the cause of the Comanche hostility to the Blacks, was told "that it was because they were slaves to the Creeks and that the Indians were so sorry for them that they killed them to send them to a better world and release them from the Fretters of bondage" (Foreman 1985 261–266); but the real Comanche motive was clear.

More than one tribe considered the advantages of moving out of the jurisdiction of the United States. When the American Congress and the Dawes Commission countered the Five Civilized Tribes' attempt to create the state of Sequoyah out of Indian Territory by including Indian Territory in the new state of Oklahoma, all of the Five Civilized Tribes turned their eyes toward Mexico. The Cherokee met with President Diaz in an earnest but unsuccessful attempt to continue their tribal existence by relocating in northern Mexico. Eventually due to the efforts of the government of the United States, the Five Civilized Tribes stayed in Oklahoma; but the remarkable settlement founded by Wildcat, Gopher John Jimmy Bowlegs is still a part of the Mexican American border culture today.

The United States, of course, opposed the emigration and settlement. A petulant note from the American Minister urged the Mexicans to expel the Indians and Black Seminoles from Mexico:

Sir,
    I have the honor to acknowledge the receipt of your Excellency's note of the 19th instant, in which you make reply to my note of the 9th. of May last in which under instructions from the Secretary of State, the United States communicated to your excellency the difficulties and opposition, which the Commissioner encountered in his efforts to effect the return of the Kickapoo and other Indians to the United States.
[signed by]
His Excellency
J.M. Lafragua
Minister of Foreign Affairs
Mexico
([Mexican Diplomatic Archives Ex. H/ 242.7 (72:73) 24.] Actos de Tribus barbaras Substraidas No. 165 Julio 10-1875. –traduscido Legation of the United States. Mexico June 24. 1875)

THE AMERICAN RESPONSE FOLLOWS FROM
JOHN FOSTER, AMERICAN MINISTER:

I will without delay transmit a copy of your excellency's note to the Department of State at Washington for the information of my government and embrace this opportunity to express my gratification for the efforts that your government and of the Mexican States, where these Indians are located, to remove any obstacle that may present itself whenever their removal is again attempted.

While I have no desire to enter in detail upon a discussion of your Excellency's note, I deem it proper to make brief reference to one or two of the points presented by you. The Government of the United States has for many years made itself responsible for the support, education and care of these Indians, whose guardian it is, and they have been placed on special reservations and put under the supervision of the official agents and the army of the government. During our late civil war, the Indians took advantage of the temporary suspension of the authority of the United States to abandon their reservations and come into this Republic without the consent, and contrary to the policy of the Government of Mexico, at a time when its power was also partially suspended by the war of European intervention.

In view of this state of affairs, I have tried to express the conviction that Your Excellency's government erred in deciding that it could not require these Indians to return to their reservations. Under the circumstances they could only be considered as refugees from the authority of the government of the United States, and in the spirit of international cooperation should have again been returned to the territory of the United States.

Your Excellency seems to find the cause, if not a palliation for the opposition manifested to the mission of the commissions, in the bitter language and harsh judgment expressed by the newspapers of Texas against the inhabitants of the Mexican frontier. It is not strange that public opinion in Texas is unfavorable to the justice and honesty of the Mexican authorities and people of the Rio Grande frontier, when it is remembered that the citizens of Texas have been the prey for years, of raiding bands of outlaws from Mexico; that they have witnessed the murder of their kindred, the burning of their houses, and the plunder of their property by organized bands of Mexicans, publicly reported to be instigated and equipped, many of them, by a General of the Mexican Army; that these bands find friends in Mexico, where their plunder is disposed of; and that no punishment is inflicted upon them by the authorities. It may not be unnatural that harsh measures are advocated in Texas urging counter invasions and reprisals, and in view of the inability or indifference of the federal government of Mexico, that there are found individuals and even a newspaper which advocates the placing of that region under the authority of the United States.

Your Excellency will please to receive the renewed assurances of my most distinguished consideration.

John W. Foster

The border culture discussed by Foster needs to be examined in greater detail. The fact that an important branch of the underground railroad led south into free Mexico is barely mentioned in the general histories.

The Mackenzie Raid an (officially) unauthorized foray into Mexico without the consent of the Mexican government to round up the troublesome Kickapoo in March of 1873 and carry them off to Indian Territory is well documented (Latore 1991, 22). The warm support of the Mexican government for the Kickapoo and the Black Muscogees is significant in the light of the nineteenth century race relations. Understandably the Mexicans were irritated by military incursions to kidnap Indians. The demands of the governor of Texas to President Hayes that northern Mexico should be placed under United States jurisdiction were certainly not calculated to win friends and influence people in the Republic of Mexico. From the President of the Republic down to the people of Muzquiz Coahuila, support for the Indians was almost universal.

It is worth citing some of the diplomatic exchanges verbatim to give a better idea of this conflict. The Diaz regime stands out at this time for its vigorous defense of Mexican sovereignty and citizenship, regardless of race or national origin.

The Mexican response to a prior communication by John W. Foster is very significant:

Sir,

This communication sent without comment by Mr. LaFragua has prevented me from answering the note sent by Your Excellency on the 24th of June in which I communicate to Your Excellency what has been transmitted by the department of State in Washington in the note dated the 19th of this month concerning the response dictated by the government of Mexico to avoid difficulties in removing the Kickapoo Indians to their old reservations in the United States.

Your Excellency, it would be good to give you several explanations concerning one or two points in the American note referred to, without going into great detail in this discussion.

Today with the concurrence of the President (President Diaz) who has been informed of the facts to give an answer to Your Excellency:

According to Your Excellency the government of the United States has for many years been responsible for the maintenance, education, and care of these Indians and the government is their tutor.

That these Indians have been placed in special reserves under the vigilance of official Indian agents and the army of the government. That these Indians abandoned their reservations taking advantage of the temporary incapacity of the United States during the Civil War in order to come to Mexican territory. That the Indians came without the permission of and against the policies of the Mexican government while it also was rendered powerless during the war of European intervention.

This statement implies that Your Excellency believes that the government of Mexico is in error, in deciding that the United States cannot oblige these Indians to return to their reservations. You assert that they can only be considered as refugees escaping the authority of the United States, and that they should be returned to you in the spirit of international courtesy.

Later Your Excellency states that you have found the cause, now that the commission sent to urge the Indians to return to the United States has been unsuccessful. Of the very violent and bitter language of the Texan Newspapers against the inhabitants of the Mexican Frontier, and that you do not find it strange that public opinion in Texas exhibits an unfavorable opinion of Mexican honor and equity and of the people of the Frontier of the Rio Grande. And that after all it should be remembered that the citizens of Texas have for years been the victims of great abuses and crimes that Your Excellency refers to in a general way and that you blame Mexican individuals who are not chastised by the authorities.

Because of this Your Excellency finds the excitement and clamor for reprisals to be only natural in view of the inaction and indifference of the Mexican government, and some individuals are even found who argue that the whole region be put under the political authority of the United Sates.

Considering your first point relative to the obligation the government of the United States has of imposing itself as tutor of the Indians and to provide for their education and substance, something that the government of Mexico has not taken the trouble to investigate or understand, for the simple reason that no independent state recognizes nor should recognize another independent state within its borders. We claim the right of the government to act if it is not against international relations and obligations contracted reciprocally because of international treaties that Mexico has celebrated with the United States. In the treaty of extradition agreed to by both republics there is no mention of whole tribes of people only of individuals from both nations who have committed specific offenses for which they can be reclaimed according to the stipulations of the treaty. *On the other hand Your Excellency knows that the laws of Mexico do not make any distinction between races, and that regardless of social class or nationality if a person is in Mexican Territory he is under the protection of these same laws except in those cases where, in the government's judgment (which is never arbitrary and always relies on the facts to justify its judgments) expulsion is recommended. If one or more strangers are expelled it is because it is known that they are disturbing public order. In consequence the Indians like any other class of men that inhabit Mexico, are subject to its laws and just as the government can chastise those who break the law, also we have to respect in the law the guarantees that the constitution gives to the inhabitants of the Republic. Therefore the government of Mexico has not committed an error in deciding that it cannot force these Indians to return to their reservations . . .*

(Ex. H/ 242.7 (72:73) 24. Actos de Tribus barbaras Substraidas No. 165 Ministerio de Relaciones Exteriores Mexico 30 de Abril 1875)

It is good to know that Mexico could really stand up for human rights on at least some occasions during the Diaz regime. The Kickapoo people continue to benefit from the strong stance of the Mexican government.

BIBLIOGRAPHY

Foreman, Grant. *The Five Civilized Tribes*. Norman, Oklahoma: University of Oklahoma Press, 1985.

Kehoe, Alice. *North American Indians: A Contemporary Account*. Englewood Cliffs, New Jersey: Prentice Hall, 1981.

Latore, Felipe and Delores. *The Mexican Kickapoo Indians*. Austin, Texas: University of Texas Press, 1976.

Ritzenthaler, Robt. E. *The Mexican Kickapoo Indians*. Milwaukee Public Museum Publications in Anthropology 2. Milwaukee, 1956.

Tanner, Helen. *Atlas of Great Lakes Indian History*. Norman, Oklahoma: University of Oklahoma Press, 1987.

PART I
COMMUNAL ROOTS

SECTION THREE
20TH CENTURY CHICAGO

Native American Citizenship and Voting Rights in Illinois
KAREN STRONG
97

*Relocation's Imagined Landscape and the Rise of
Chicago's Native American Community*
GRANT P. ARNDT
114

Relocation
ED GOODVOICE
128

Excerpt from a Photoessay on Chicago Elders
EDWARD E. GOODVOICE,
AS TOLD TO NORA LLOYD
146

The History of the American Indian Center Princess
DEBRA VALENTINO
148

The Chicago Indian Village, 1970
NATALIA WILSON
155

Karen Strong

Native American Citizenship and Voting Rights in Illinois

A Native Womanist's Perspective

INTRODUCTION

This paper presents an overview of trading standards and land ownership in the history of the state of Illinois. It will explain why it took an act (1924) of Congress to make Native Americans born within the territorial limits of the United States, citizens. Native American citizenship rights were first usurped through a domination of trading and land issues by European royal authority, and later, through the land ownership framework established by the United States federal government. Then, an examination of the treaty and trading issues will follow. All of these issues disenfranchised Native women's citizenship and rights. Finally, I will look at some recent developments.

LAND AND LEADERSHIP

Robert A. Williams Jr. offered a bleak description of immigrant concern for Native American land ownership. Recognizing the open greed of the immigrants for land ownership in the New World, he states,

> Few legislative bodies in American history have so mired themselves in corrupted self-interest parading as principle as did the Revolutionary-era American Continental Congress. (Williams 1990, 288)

The Congressional debate lasted ten years. If the Articles of Confederation would secure control of the West, then the Native American land grants would be affirmed and validated. Either the states "landed" by British colonial charter or the central government would supervise the process of land acquisition and distribution of the frontier. This would directly affect Illinois country.

One powerful trading syndicate had delegates participating in this debate: the Illinois-Wabash Company. The Illinois-Wabash Company was formed by the traders William Murray and Louis Viviat, whose land speculations hinged upon the outcome of this debate. On 11 June 1773, Murray tested Captain Hugh Lord, commander of the English garrison at Fort Gage, within the lands of the Kaskaskia by purchasing land directly from the Kaskaskia Nation. Lord was under strict orders to enforce the Proclamation of 1763, which prohibited Native American land sales to colonial speculators. However, Murray challenged this order with the *Camden-Yorke* opinion, which claimed, "that His Majesty's subjects were at liberty to purchase whatever quantity of lands they chose of Indians. . ." (*Camden-Yorke Opinion*, Mogul Case, 1757). Murray threatened suit against Lord, as a military officer who violated his "English liberties." Lord allowed the purchase, but would not allow settlement, which was clearly forbidden. Thus, on 5 July 1773, Murray paid $24,000.00 for land at the junction of the Ohio and Mississippi Rivers, and the junction of the Illinois and Mississippi Rivers. Viviat purchased lands on the upper Ohio from the Piankeshaw in 1775. Eventually, the debate around this land purchase lead to a Supreme Court decision, *Johnson V. McIntosh*. (21 U.S. (8 Wheat) 543, 21 U.S.573).

Chief Justice John Marshall's opinion concerning the sole right of acquiring land from Native Americans in 1823 recognizes the Doctrine of Discovery. This *post hoc* legal rationalization offered a compromise on the frontier lands debate and vested superior title of frontier Native American lands to the United States government. This interpretation of the law brokered the term "for the public good," which did not include Native peoples. This was the permission most patriots needed to deal for Native American lands in earnest. Thus, the disenfranchisement of Native American land ownership was a legal compromise to substantiate claims for land ownership by others prominently placed. An examination of the disenfranchisement of trading standards happened next.

UNDERSTANDING TRADING STANDARDS

The Illinois tribes met by the French trader La Salle west of the St. Lawrence River and Lake Huron are the "Ciscas, Chaoens, Peoria, Kaskaskia, Moigoana, Taponero, Coiracoentanon, Chinkoa, Chepoisessea, Maroa, Koackia, Tamaroa, and the Michigamea" (La Salle 1634, 2, 201). The French traders wanted to extend their trade into Illinois country in order to connect their Canadian trade with their Louisiana trade.

The French documented their interior trade route, therefore their right of discovery, through their annual reports. La Salle reported that the Illinois tribes were attacked by the Iroquois in 1655. A counterattack ensued. This intertribal war ended in 1667. La Salle began to realize the importance of knowing the exact head count of his new trading partners and began a head count of the Illinois tribes. During 1657 and 1659, he reported the tribal population to be larger at this time than any other period. La Salle counted 60 villages with 20,000 Natives at the Illinois and Mississippi Rivers (Coulin 1958, 5). The depopulation of the Illinois tribes through trading and land ownership disputes with European and other tribal nations began soon after this first head count.

In 1666 the first Jesuit mission was established at the confluence of the Illinois and Mississippi Rivers. The Jesuits began to teach the Illinois Native Americans the important French legal concepts of male ownership and voting rights. The absence of a centralized system of political authority was frustrating to the French, who called the leaders of the tribes of Illinois "captains," "principal men," or "chiefs" until 1765 (Hauser 1973, 275, 278). The French refused to recognize the Illinois tribal councils, which included Native American women. The French made an effort to define these positions and clarify leadership according to their own conception of it. This was important because of the strategic military potential that Illinois country held: Illinois was viewed as a keystone connecting the French empire between Canada and Louisiana.

Leadership among the Illinois tribes was closer to a subtribal village council than a proper European centralized system. The council was the primary agency for deliberating important issues. Any decisions required a collective action. Consensus was the only uniform procedure among these tribal people. Consensus did not necessarily have to be among the men of the tribe. Any woman, with clear reasoning, was allowed to speak. Women were among the voting citizenry of tribes.

This was not a novel concept. For example, women were traditional leaders among the Iroquois Nation. The political concept of the Tree of Peace shared by the Iroquois Nations was proposed by a Haudenosaunee woman named Hikonsaseh, Mother of Nations (Barreiro 1988, 68). She proposed the concept of democracy to the Iroquois councils, bringing peace to the Six Nations after a trading trip to Illinois country. The harmony brought about by this peace was only shattered by broken treaties, including the Treaty of 1874 mentioned earlier.

When Iroquois lands were being divided among the immigrant land owners, the Iroquois began to battle with the frontier tribes for land as the Iroquois were being pushed further west. The Kaskaskia were welcoming of other tribes, but inter-tribal conflict from the east continued. In 1680 the Iroquois attacked the Kaskaskia. La Salle gathered his native allies around Fort St. Louis in 1683. He counted 3,880 warriors from the Illinois, Wea, Piankasha, Shawnee, Abnaki, and Miami Nations (Coulin, 1958, 16). These forces were collectively successful over the Iroquois from 1683 to 1684. However, the price was deemed too high. By 1690 only the Illinois tribes were left at Kaskaskia. The Cahokia village was attacked by the Shawnee and the Chickasaw Nations, causing a split from Canadian and Louisiana trade with the French.

The Treaty of Halston with the British colonies later known as the United States was signed by the Potawatomi, Mascoutens, Sauk, Foxes, Winnebago, and Miami Nations in 1701. Illinois country was a valuable trade route with crossroads from all directions as long as peace was maintained. Native American nations claimed and received protection of one more powerful. This treaty recognized their right to self-government and pledged the faith of the colonial duty of protection.

The French chose not to recognize Native American women as traders and Native American women faced open discrimination in the trade community. Often Native American women began initial trading efforts intertribally and with the European traders. Sylvia Van Kirk documented in her book *Many Tender Ties: Women in Fur-Trade Society, 1670–1870* (1980) how Native American women would begin trading for knives and pots, later leading to trading for foodstuffs. This did not encourage long term agreements. Thus, the traders began to trade with the men, introducing liquor as a continued need. The French knew men away from home would sample and follow the abuse of alcohol modeled by the traders. The French traders eventually began to marry Native American women. The French traders brought in the Jesuits to establish finishing schools for the daughters of the traders. Often tribal women and mixed-race women were allowed to enroll, and were taught a woman's place in European society along with literacy, rhetoric, and mathematics. Thus, the independence allowed within the tribal perspective was extinguished as an unnecessary virtue in the Jesuit missions.

Purposeful disenfranchisement in this way, helped to win half the battle by excluding the Native American woman's voice for centuries. Native American women were to be seen and not heard until invited to speak. Native American women have quietly endured for a long time, in spite of the fact that Illinois tribal women outnumbered the men.

Intertribal warfare in the area continued until Pontiac formed his confederacy in 1763. At this time the French relinquished Illinois country in the Treaty of Paris. The Illinois prairie was left to the English traders, who were planning to purchase land from the Illinois tribes in order to dominate the land.

Randolph C. Downes's *Council Fires on the Upper Ohio: A Narrative of Indian Affairs in the Upper Ohio Valley until 1795* discusses how the English established trade discourse with Native American men. Downes offers a detailed account of Native American political discourse preempted by the need for individual signers, documented by Clarence Walworth Alvord in his editions of *Cahokia Records, 1778–1790* and *Kaskaskia Records, 1778–1790*.

Trade and politics were closely linked in the Illinois Country. (See for example: *A Guide to the History of Illinois*, ed. John Hoffmen, Greenwood Press, Westport, Conn., 1991, p.41. *History of the Conspiracy of Pontiac*, Francis Parkman, Boston, 1851. 'The Famous Hair Buyer General': Henry Hamilton, George Rogers Clark, and the American Indian," *Indiana Magazine of History*, Bernard W. Sheehan, 79, March 1983.) A privileged class dominated the dispossession of the Native American trade and land (Pease and Pease 1929). Insider politics made those in touch with Illinois affairs wealthy men. Other men continued this practice one hundred years later. The insider political strategy was openly misused again and again.

Passage of the Northwest Ordinance (1787) by the Continental Congress resolved one important trade issue. The ordinance stated that: "The utmost good faith" shall be shown to the Indians, their property "shall never be taken from them without their consent"; and, "they shall never be invaded or disturbed, unless in just and lawful wars authorized by Congress" (The Northwest Ordinance 1787). The Ordinance was upheld when the Continental Congress chose not to provide federal troops for the war between the Creek Nation and the state of Georgia nor allow the state to purchase land from the Creeks. Native American land was one step closer to the federal policy called "Manifest Destiny."

THE UNITED STATES TREATY PERIOD

When the United States Constitution (1789) was adopted, Article I, Section 3, Clause 3 authorized Congress to regulate "commerce . . . with the Indian tribes." Article II, Section 2, Clause 2 empowered the President to make treaties, including Indian treaties, with the consent of the Senate. Thus, a legal definition for land sale was established. The federal government recognized the status of chief, captain, or warrior as the designated signer for these land sales. This definitely disenfranchised those tribal groups who were matrilineally oriented in terms of ownership, such as the Miami. (A detailed description is offered in Otis Louis Miller's doctoral dissertation, "Indian-White Relations in Illinois Country, 1789-1818," St. Louis University, 1972.)

Congress created the War Department in 7 Aug 1789 and assigned to it the duties to suppress Native American hostilities and regulate Indian-white trade. The first Congress also passed the 1790 Indian Trade and Intercourse Act. No sale of Native American lands was valid without United States authority. The Act was extended in 1793, 1796, 1802, 1817, 1822, and 1834. Indian country was nationally recognized as restricted land. Trade was regulated. Liquor was prohibited. Federal standards for crimes between the races were set into a federal code. Like the French, the United States promoted education and civilization, and also continued to exclude Native American women from political discourse.

General Anthony Wayne's victory at Fallen Timbers caused the British and their Native American allies to leave certain western posts in 1794. The Treaty of Greenville of 1795 ceded strategic areas in the Old Northwest Territory. Thus, the British had vacated Illinois Country. Since the French traders had left thirty-one years before, the Americans needed to deal with the French government concerning land ownership. The United States government decided to solidify their trade relationships with Indian Country before approaching France. The Peace Treaty of 1795 between the United States and the Wyandots, Delawares, Shawnees, Ottawas, Chippewas, Potawatomies, Miamis, Eel Rivers, Weas, Kickapoos, Piankeshaws, and Kaskaskias was part of this effort. The first seven tribes received a thousand dollars each, the remaining tribes received five hundred dollars each to relinquish, cede, and confirm to the United States all land within the following boundaries:

"Beginning at the confluence of the Ohio and Mississippi rivers; thence up the Ohio, to the mouth of Saline Creek, about twelve miles below the mouth of the Wabash; thence along the dividing ridge between the waters of said creek and the Wabash, to the general dividing ridge between the waters which fall into the Wabash and those which fall into the Kaskaskia river; thence along the said ridge until it reaches the waters which fall into the Illinois river; thence a direct line to the confluence of the Kankakee and Maple rivers; thence down the Illinois river, to its confluence with the Mississippi, and down the latter to the beginning. (Peace Treaty of 1795, Kappler, 39-45; 7 Stat. 49-54)

The signers also agreed to peacefully hunt, allow free passage by land and water to the people of the United States. All other treaties were considered null and void upon signing this treaty.

The 1796 Indian Trading House Act, (Indian Trading House Act, U.S. Apr. 1796, c. 13 1 Stat. 452) began what was called the trading factory era. This act established a trade agreement with the United States government, which was viewed as a government-owned national franchise. A flurry of treaty-making was about to begin. In 1803 the Louisiana Purchase between France and the United States was consummated. The acquisition of Florida was negotiated from 1812 to 1819. These land purchases from France doubled the size of the United States, and gave birth to "Manifest Destiny" (Holt and Forrester 1990).

The Illinois nations recognized by the treaties were the Kaskaskia Nation, the Piankashaw Nation, the Kickapoo Nation, the Potawatomi Nation, the Miami Nation, the Wyandot Nation, the Peoria Nation, the Mitchigamea Nation, the Cahokia Nation, the Tamarao Nation, the Wea Nation, the Shawnee Nation, the Eel Rivers Nation, the Sacs Nation and the Foxes Nation. Thus, fifteen of the twenty-two indigenous tribes of

Illinois Country were federally recognized by treaty. The Chinko, the Chepoussa, the Moingwena, the Amonokoa, and the Ocansa (Hauser 1973, 420), were no longer living as singular tribal nations when the treaty-signing began. Altogether sixty-nine treaties were signed concerning Illinois Country during the Treaty era from 1778 to 1867, which is 18.8 percent of all treaties signed with the United States. Nineteen treaties were signed by the Potawatomi tribal members and fifteen by the Shawnee tribal members alone before a general consensus was reached.

Some tribal nations negotiated for federal resolution of tribally-specific issues. The Kickapoos signed eleven treaties, negotiating for all prior treaties to be recognized and confirmed, intruders on the reservation to be restrained, and protection acknowledged by the United States government. The Piankashaws signed eight, requesting hostilities to be forgiven and forgotten, perpetual peace and friendship declared, protection promised against other tribes, a reservation established, and hunting rights on the ceded lands. The Kaskaskias signed six, with 350 acres set aside for a reservation near the town of Kaskaskia.

This multitude of treaties were signed because no permanent homes, tribal organization, or territorial limits existed for these tribal nations. Often factions of tribal nations signed treaties, tribal members who were actually hunting parties, maple sugar harvesters, huckleberry pickers, those fleeing epidemics, or followers of a rival chief or medicine man. Even friends of the nation and those recently married into a nation, both of whom did not understand the tribal language fully, had signed without understanding what was signed. This was compounded by administrators who knew little of the history of these nations. Thus, this compendia of treaties were eventually negotiated into a general consensus (Foreman, Russell and Russell 1946, 14).

The 1803 Treaty between the Eel Rivers, the Wyandot, Piankeshaw, and Kaskaskia Nations, the tribes of the Kickapoos, and the United States allowed these tribes to continue to live and hunt on the ceded land in the same manner they had hitherto done.

The 1809 Delaware Treaty included Kickapoo tribal members. A Kickapoo treaty included Piankashaw tribal members. A Kaskaskia treaty also included Piankashaw tribal members. This was not considered unusual since these tribes intermarried, held longstanding informal trade agreements, and shared hunting and harvesting grounds peacefully. However, both tribal groups were unwilling to hold a general consensus with these treaties.

Shawnee Chief Tecumseh attempted to explain the occupancy issue to William Henry Harrison at Vincennes, 12 Aug 1810, "Any sale not made by all is not valid" (Drake 1841, 617–18). He meant all tribes who use the land must agree to sell. Tecumseh also explained further that

All red men have equal rights to the unoccupied land. The right of occupancy is as good in one place as in another. There cannot to two occupations in the same place. The first excludes all others. It is not so in hunting or traveling; for there the same ground will serve many, as they may follow each other all day; but the camp is stationary, and that is occupancy. It belongs to the first who sits down on his blanket or skins, which he has thrown upon the ground, and till he leaves it no other has a right (Drake 1841, 617–18)

Tecumseh meant that all who shared this land shall decide upon a permanent camp site to be recognized as a permanent place for their respective tribal groups. Plus, each tribe wanted to continue to hunt and travel on the ceded land.

Territorial Acts, such as Illinois, (1813) prohibited trade with the Kaskaskia, Illinois, (1814) concerned retaliation upon hostile Indians, and prohibited the sale of liquor to the Kaskaskia (Coleman 1979, 238–42). These acts muddied the waters of who was responsible, the federal government or the territorial governor, since the territorial governors signed territorial agreements. The federal government wanted to clarify the responsibility issue.

An 1818 treaty with the Peoria, Kaskaskia, Mitchigamia, Cahokia, and Tamarois was signed to hereby relinquish, cede, and confirm to the United States all the land within the same boundaries presented in the Peace Treaty of 1795. Once again, the Kaskaskias signed, this time with different tribal nations concerning the exact same piece of land quoted in the 1795 treaty. Thus, the federal government established authority over territorial attempts at governing Illinois Country.

The words in these treaties have been unchallenged and unchanged since their signing. For example, the Peoria Treaty of 1818 states:

ART. 3 And the said Peoria Tribe do hereby engage to refrain from making war, or giving any insult or offense, to any other Indian tribe, or to any foreign nation, without first having obtained the approbation and consent of the United States. (*Treaties Between The U.S. and the Indians 1778-1837.* Kraus Reprint Co., Millwood, N.Y., 1975)

Thus, one Peoria tribal treaty ensures that Peoria tribal members shall not do or say anything insulting or offensive to any person from another tribe or country without requesting permission from the United States government to do so first.

These treaties were negotiated in an attempt to clear the land ownership disputes that began with French, Spanish, Dutch, and British citizens who came into Illinois country for many reasons. The Illinois tribes needed protection from the warring factions of these nations as well as the American immigrants and impending tribal emigrants being pushed west from the east. The treaties were to resolve these land ownership disputes in order to clear Illinois country for immigrant ownership. However, the emigrants did not wait for the American military to complete the treaty process. As a result, many of the treaties signed were broken, further embedding the land ownership disputes. The tribes recognized these treaties as being null and void, further muddying a war-torn territory. Even the words of Shawnee Chief Blue Jacket at Greenville could not help settle matters when he said:

> Now send forth your speeches to all our brethren far around us, and let us unite to seek for that which shall be for our eternal welfare; and unite ourselves in a band of perpetual brotherhood. (Moquin and Van Doren 1995, 132)

The tribal groups continued to oppose the American treaty agreements. Meanwhile, the emigrants were requesting protection as well.

The embedding of the land ownership disputes with the slow legal remedies of the circuit courts established in the territories caused the tide of immigrants to support "a growing sentiment for removal of the Indians from that region" (Foreman, Russell, and Russell 1972, 19). The 23 July 1814 Treaty with the Wyandots, Delawares, Shawnee, Seneca, and Miami was signed, as an agreement of peace and friendship. (*American State Papers*, "Indian Affairs," I, 836) The treaty council started with possible removal discourse. However, the Eel River, Wea, Potawatomi, Ottawa, and Kickapoo left the old 1795 treaty campsite, refusing to enter this discussion. Thus, a peace treaty was signed in order to continue the good faith agreement status.

Treaties resolved the embedded land ownership disputes by establishing the United States federal government as the primary co-signer of all treaty agreements and stabilized trading standards by nationalizing all trade agreements. Since the federal government was responsible, the state contracts were null and void. Federal authority was clear. The federal government began to push for statehood within the Northwest Territory. The immigrants living in Illinois supported Illinois statehood as well.

ILLINOIS STATEHOOD, REMOVAL, AND VOTING RIGHTS

In 1812, Congress abandoned the freeholding requirement and gave the vote to any adult male who resided in the [Illinois] Territory a year and had paid a state or county tax (Cornelius 1972, 12). Convention delegates continued this policy. Indiana, New Hampshire, Georgia, Maryland, and South Carolina earlier established this form of male suffrage. Aliens were allowed to vote and hold office; Blacks and women were denied suffrage. The compromise on the slavery article guaranteed both that Illinois would be a free state and the existing property rights would be protected (Cornelius 1972, 16). The wording of the Illinois Bill of Rights was largely taken from the Ohio, Kentucky, Tennessee and Indiana constitutions, with little thought given to changes in these basic statements of individual rights (Cornelius 1972, 16–17). This federal action to establish another freehold state was directly intended to curb southern influence in Illinois.

The state of Illinois has been called the back door for the South. Long before Ray Bial documented trails within the Underground Railroad (1990) or the freedman migrations into the cities of the Midwest began, Southern influence was present in Illinois. The Illinois State Voting Act (*Shepard's Acts and Cases by Popular Names, Federal & State*, Shepard's McGraw-Hill, Inc., Colorado Springs, Oct 1992, Government Documents) and the South Carolina State Voting Act, (*The Constitution of South Carolina*, Ed. David Duncan Wallace, 342.7572,1895) appear to be one and the same document except for the titles. The Illinois state legislators may have other clear connections through primary resources to the South regarding voting rights, citizenship, and literacy as these issues pertain to segregation and integration.

Other politicians certainly were pressing their own ideas into the arena. For example, as Governor of the Michigan Territory, Lewis Cass called for reform of Native American relations. His initial policy goal was to sever all Native ties to the British. He preferred negotiation, but was willing to use force if necessary (Prucha 1981, 81). The end of British trade with Native Americans was not enough for Lewis Cass. He wanted the British to leave altogether.

By 1812, the land issue disputes with the British, Dutch, Spanish, and French made any simple solution impossible, leading to the War of 1812. During federal legislation to raise troops for this war, Congress directed two million acres of Illinois land surveyed into townships, sections, and quartersections, made available as "military lands" by the Sauk and Fox Treaty of 1804 (Kappler 74–77, 7 Stat.84–87). The Potawatomi challenged this. Earlier treaties did not resolve these issues. President Madison submitted a treaty, 26 December 1815 (Kappler 1 17–18, 7 Stat. 131–33), which ended all hostilities with the tribes. The Treaty of 4 Jan 1819 (Kappler, 145–55;7 Stat. 160–70) stated the abandonment of fealty to Great Britain, and announced loyalty to the United States by the Wyandots, Delawares, Shawnee, Seneca, Miami, Potawatomi of Illinois River, Piankshaw, Tetoni, Sioux, Yancton, Maha, Kickapoo, Chippewa, Ottawa, Great and Little Osage, the Sauk of Missouri River, Foxes, Iowa, and Kansas.

The federal attempt with the Trade and Intercourse Act and the Trading House Act did not resolve continued conflict with the increased westward emigration of tribes from east of the Mississippi. There were not enough Circuit Courts within the Territory to resolve the local disputes between the European immigrants and the indigenous tribes. One of the first acts of the state legislature was an attempt to improve the administration of justice. Illinois' three federal circuit court judges were absent from their duties for long periods of time. (See for example: Francis S. Philbrick, ea., *The Laws of Indiana Territory, 1801-1809, Collections of the Illinois State Library* Springfield, 1930; introduction in Philbrick, et al, *Laws of Illinois Territory 1809-1818*; Clarence Alvord, *The Illinois Country, 1673-1818*, Chicago, Loyola University Press Reprint Series, 1965, Solon S. Buck, *Illinois in 1818*, 2d ed. rev, Urbana, University of Illinois Press, 1967, originally published as the introductory volume of The Centennial History of Illinois)

President Monroe inaugurated removal of the Illinois tribes. The Piankshaws were removed by General Clark. In his letter to the Secretary of War, 27 March 1819, ("Clark Papers," Kansas Historical Society, Letter Book, 2-3, p. 81) General Clark relayed the Piankshaw request for monetary assistance since the 180 souls left their field plots, which they had cultivated for centuries on the Waubashaw River. They had no resources or skills to begin the new life on the Missouri River. The agreements with the next tribes showed more concern.

The negotiations within the 25 September 1818 treaty (Kappler 165-66, 7 Stat. 181–83) offered the Peoria, Kaskaskia, Michigamea, Cahokia, and Tamaroa tribes furnished horses and boats for transport as well as provisions to be removed to an undesignated place on the Missouri River, without military escort. The remaining tribes did not leave as easily. The Kickapoo, Potawatomi, Delawares, and Shawnee were split in negotiations and general consensus did not leave as planned. Many were sick and starving. Also, these tribes were not welcomed by indigenous tribal groups within the removal sites.

Even though the Delaware negotiations were fair, the theft of the best horses and supplies by white immigrants in 1820 stopped their removal. The Delawares were sick and hungry, and stopped to plant corn, which was killed by an early frost. They requested more supplies (Foreman 1936, 36). Compounding the difficulties of removal were traders who were selling alcohol to the travelers. Similar experiences were happening to the Ottawa, Shawnees, and Senecas. By 1835 a total of 251 Seneca from Sandusky and 211 of the Seneca and Shawneee band had been moved to the tract between the western boundary of Missouri and the eastern boundary of the Cherokee Nation (Doc., I, 399 Doc., II 869, "Clark Papers to Superintendent of Indian Affairs, [Kansas Historical Society]). Therefore, honest federal negotiations were often exploited by private citizens, negating any attempt at fair interactions.

Treaties with the Potawatomi began in 1803 and continued until 1833. The last treaty signed resulted in the surrender of eastern Illinois, from the eastern border to the Kankakee River, including the southeast corner of Cook County, most of Iroquois County, and parts of Ford and Vermilion Counties. In the same time period, President Jackson was elected, supporting the removal of all tribes to western territories. Thus the push for the removal of all tribes was renewed. Removal of the Potawatomi began through the 27 Oct 1832 Treaty at Tippecanoe River for an annuity of $15,000 for twelve years, $42,000 in goods, payment of debts to traders, a schedule of which was attached to the treaty, amounting to $20,721; and the sum of $2,000 for the education of the Potawatomi youth. Those Potawatomi warriors who fought with the Americans in the Black Hawk War were also identified and reimbursed at this time. The removal of Potawatomi was limited to 68. Although 140 agreed to go, only 68 were ready when Lewis H. Sands left Logansport. The removal was aborted at Fort Leavenworth since a cholera epidemic was reported in St. Louis.

Removal was again attempted in 1836. This time 497 Potawatomi began the journey, with 50 dropping out, then 160 left the travel party. The remaining 287 were counted at Council Bluffs agency. The next year, 151 were taken west to Missouri. The first forced march began, 4 September 1838, with General John Tipton in command.

> When all was in readiness, this gruesome procession, nearly three miles long, like a funeral procession, which in reality it was, started on its final journey. (Kappler 372–75, 7 Stat. 399–403)

William Polk, the official recorder, wrote that 20 of the troops deserted the first day, stealing 20 of the 296 horses upon leaving the command. Later, 167 contracted malaria, but the march pressed forward to their destination. Even an anticipated Mormon attack did not slow the march. (Father Petit, "Trail of Death," *Indiana Magazine of History*, XXI, 315, p.99) The Potawatomi refer to this removal as the March of Death (Tipton 1838, 437–40). Tipton was reprimanded for spending too much money on militiamen or "volunteers" in order to keep the march moving. However, staying within indigenous campsites would have encouraged more hostile interaction with immigrants.

These removals were not simple operations. A military escort was necessary to keep white people from stealing horses and goods, selling alcohol to those willing to buy, and to avert the travelers from epidemics within the communities they were passing through. Those in command had no authority to stop people from delaying whenever they chose to stop for whatever reason. By 1839, most tribes had been removed west of the Missouri River. These removals were by no means complete. Pockets of tribal people were left scattered throughout the territory.

The inapplicability of the old laws to new circumstances plagued the commissioners of Indian affairs. Commissioner George W. Manypenny negotiated nine treaties during 1853–54. One 1854 treaty negotiation was with the Kaskaskia, Peoria, Piankshaw, and Wea. Another was with the

Miami. He lamented that speculation and desire for choice lands caused many to entirely overlook the rights of the aboriginal inhabitants. The updated Trade and Intercourse Act of 1834 (U.S., June 30, 1834, c. 161, 4 Stat. 729, Shepard's, 1992, p. 147) and the Trading House Act of 1806 (U.S., Apr. 21, 1806, c. 48, 2 Stat. 402, Shepard's ,1992, p. 147) were not protecting Native Americans and their property. Between 1829 and 1851, 86 ratified treaties were signed in the Old Northwest Territory.

The embedded unresolved disputes eventually led to the Indian Removal Act, another federal legislative action demonstrating federal authority over these issues. During removal efforts, another issue arose. Christian leaders agreed civilizing the Native American population might assist or even diminish these disputes.

The passage of a civilization bill was promoted by Thomas L. McKenney. On the lecture circuit, he claimed Indians were Asiatic in origin and had migrated to the New World by way of the Bering Strait (*Memoirs, Official and Personal; With Sketches of Travels among the Northern and Southern Indians*, 2 vols. in 1 (New York: Pain and Burgess, 1846), p. 15). This statement was debated openly, since Native Americans were not considered to be descendants of Adam and Eve. McKenney requested petitions from around the country in support of a Congressional appropriation of $10,000.00 for educating Native Americans. Baptist and Quaker Churches answered his call, including churches from Illinois (File HR 15A-G6.2, Petitions and Memorial Relating to Indian Affairs, Received by the House of Representatives, RG 233, NA). The civilization bill became law (U.S. Congress, House, *Journal*, 15th song. 2d. sees., Serial 16, 18 January 1819, p.188). Considering perception was that "the Indian was an irremediable savage, impossible to civilize" (Prucha 1981, 182–83), McKenney was a persuasive speaker. Even Thomas Jefferson professed mankind passed through stages of society, from savagism to barbarism and on to civilization (Jefferson to William Ludlow, September 6, 1824, *The Writings of Thomas Jefferson.*, ed. Andrew A. Lipscomb, 20 vols. (Washington: Thomas Jefferson Memorial Association, 1903-1904), 16: 74-75). However, by 1868, the racist rhetoric was seen as unreasonable. Nathaniel G. Taylor, Commissioner of Indian Affairs, was lauding the Five Civilized Tribes for their accomplishments in education (Report of the Commissioner of Indian Affairs, 1868, in *House Executive Document* no. 1, 40th Cong., 3d. sess. ser. 1366, ppl. 476-477). Unfortunately, the promise of Native Americans becoming good citizens did not stop those who wanted to continue to break up Native American land holdings.

The Railroad Incorporation Act of 1872 (P.A. 1971–2, p. 625, approved and eff. March 1, 1872, IL Rev. Stat. 1991, p. 2108. *House Report* no. 63, 40–2, serial 1358, in *Congressional Globe*, 40th song. 2d sess. (June 18, 1868), 3256–3257) was another insider trade development which allowed five or more persons to become an incorporated company for the purpose of constructing and operating any railroad in the state of Illinois. The corporation was authorized and empowered to purchase, own, or operate and maintain any railroad. All the powers and privileges of sale or deed of trust belonged to this corporation. Originally, one Illinois citizen and his Harvard classmates from Kentucky, South Carolina, and Tennessee lobbied for this act in Chicago. H. Craig Miner's *The Corporation and the Indian* (1988) documents this account from the regional national archives. Miner claims many corporations began by borrowing from this trust, then defaulting on the loan. Thus, land from both Native American land holdings and white citizen holdings were taken for the public good in order to build railroad tracks through Illinois. The monies held in trust were used again to start corporations. What happened in Illinois occurred around the nation. This is but one example of the continued effort to break up Native American land holdings.

On March 2, 1887, an act to grant the right of way through Indian Country to the Chicago, Kansas, and Nebraska Railway was passed (24 Stat. 446, Kappler, Vol. 1, Ch 319, p. 250). Another act offered passage into Oklahoma (June 27,1890, 26 Stat., 181, Kappler, Vol. 1, Ch 633, p. 358). Another act the next year extended passage to Chickasaw Station (February 28, 1893, 27 Stat. 495, Kappler, Vol. 1, Ch.175, p. 475). Thus, railroad construction cut a swath through Indian Country.

Another federal act continued to narrow the land holdings of Native Americans. The Allotment Act effectively broke up Native American lands. This act gave every Native American 160 acres of land to individually own. Every eighteen-year-old received an allotment. The surplus land was sold to the public. This was another windfall for those who could afford to buy this land when it was sold. After twenty-five years, land held in trust would be fee-patented to individuals. The allotees were to become citizens of the United States, subject to state criminal and civil law. This act has inevitably led to checkerboarded land ownership throughout Indian Country.

In Illinois, an act passed March 2, 1889, called the United Peoria and Miamies, Indian Territory Sale of Surplus Lands, provided a per capita and a payment for services to the delegates or officers of said tribes (Vol. 25, p. 1014, Fifty-Seventh Congress, Sess. 1. Ch 888, 190). Land sales were a persistent paradox to the acceptance of Native Americans as citizens of the states where they resided.

The Land Grant Forfeiture Act (U.S. Code 1988 Title 43 section 904 et seq. 912, 940. Sept. 29,1890, c.1040, 26 Stat. 496) was passed to further clarify railroad construction through the states. Other acts were passed in Illinois concerning sales, title registration, and land trust as well. Native-owned land could soon be individually owned. By 1905 Claire O'Connell Coulin identified 195 Piankashaw, Kaskaskia, Wea, and Peoria living within Illinois. These, she claimed, were mostly half-breeds (*A Chrono-*

logical Outline of IL Indians, College of Education, University of Illinois, 1958, p. 56). The 1906 Dawes Act (U.S. Statutes at Large, 34: 182-183) extended the Americanizing citizenship process, as did the Lacey Act of 1907 (U.S. Statutes at Large, 34: 1221-1222). Guardianship continued. Cases in other states confirmed this form of federal protection in the rental of lands, the sale of resources grown on these lands, including the sale of liquor.

The Fourteenth Amendment offered suffrage to Blacks. Congress determined that since tribes did not ratify this amendment, tribes did not accept this amendment, and could not become citizens without tribal expressed consent (Senate Report no. 268, "Effect of the Fourteenth Amendment upon Indian Tribes," 1, 41st Congress, 3rd Session [1870]). Illinois State Repeal's Act of 1913, approved June 26, 1913, was in force July 1, 1913. Senate Bill No. 125, approved April 29, 1921, gave full suffrage to women. The fifty-second state legislature offered suffrage to all but Native tribal members by 1921. Generations of Native Americans were perceived as incapable of carrying out the duties of citizenship that all others were exercising.

Under the Act of November 6, 1919, (41 Stat. 350) Indian men who enlisted in the armed forces to fight in World War II could become citizens.

In 1921 Donald Sutherland was hired to lobby Congress for full citizenship rights for Alaska Natives. The Alaska Native Brotherhood, a social organization started by Presbyterian students who were Alaska natives attending Sheldon Jackson at Sitka, Alaska, in 1912, wanted voting and land ownership rights for the Tlingit, Haida, and Tsimshian Nations. Donald Sutherland decided to push for citizenship for all Native Americans since he could not think of a good reason to exclude other tribal nations. Thus, June 2, 1924, the American Indian Citizenship Act (H.R. 6355, 43 Stat. 253, Kappler, Vol. 4. Ch 233, p. 420) was passed. All non-citizen Indians born within the territorial limits of the United States were granted citizenship.

Indigenous tribal people accepted U.S. citizenship in 1924, but it was not until 1997 that tribal citizenship received an organizational presence in the state of Illinois with the opening of the Ho-Chunk tribal office in Chicago. The Kickapoo bought land at Le Roy, Ilinois, originally known as the site of their grand village. The Kickapoo danced in Illinois for the first time since 1819 at a pow-wow they hosted at Le Roy, Illinois, May 30-31, 1998. The indigenous tribes are returning to Illinois country. This was possible because in 1995, displaced Native Americans, and indigenous tribal nations began negotiating a constitution and by-laws for a tribal coalition called the American Indian Council of Illinois. These Native people want to organize to support native issues in contemporary society. The confederation of tribal peoples within Illinois may offer the political support needed to garner federal and state monies necessary to serve their respective communities. These people realize that individually, native people have no say in how they are to be served. Their individual voices counted 33,500 in 1995. (Illinois State Census 1995) This is a 50 percent increase of displaced Native Americans within the last five years. As a confederation, one voice may be heard.

CONCLUSION

Tribal citizenship and voting rights for Native Americans in Illinois have come full circle. When Native Americans have the authority to govern, all tribal members can vote. In Illinois, through the American Indian Council, general consensus among all Indian members including native women has brought to issue the repatriation of the 12,000 human remains identified by mandate of the Native American Graves Protection and Repatriation Act (1990), a statewide foster parent program as a minimum standard for placement of Native American children identified by the Indian Child Welfare Act (1978), and three requests to the Illinois State Board of Education to suggest a list of authentic children's books about Native Americans be distributed to the public schools, to suggest Indian mascots within the public schools be dropped, and to establish a Native American Advisory Board for the Governor's office. (American Indian Council of Illinois meeting minutes, September 27, 1997)

BIBLIOGRAPHY

A Guide to the History of Illinois. John Hoffmen, ed. Conneticut: Greenwood Press, 1991.
American State Papers. Indian Affairs. I, 836.
Camden-Yorke Opinion, Mogul Case, 1757.
Clark Papers. Kansas Historical Society.
Cornelius, Janet. *Constitution Making in Illinois.* Illinois: University of Illinois, 1972.
Coulin, Claire O'Connell. *A Chronological Outline of Illinois Indians.* 1958.
Drake, Samuel G. *Biography and History of the Indians of North America.* Massachusettes: 1841.
Forman, Grant. *Indians and Pioneers.* Oklahoma: University of Oklahoma, 1936.
Foreman, Grant, Russell and Russell. *The Last Trek of the Indians.* New York: 1946.
Great Documents in American Indian History. Wayne Moquin and Charles Van Doren, ed. New York: De Capo Press, 1995.
Hauser, Raymond E. *An Ethnohistory of the Illinois Indian Tribe.* Illinois: Northern Illinois University, 1973.
Holt, H. Barry and Gary Forrester. *Digest of American Indian Law.* Colorado: Fred B. Rothman & Co., 1990
Indian Trading House Act. Stat. 452, 1796.
Journal. U.S. Congress, House. 15th song, 2nd session. Jan. 1819.
Laws of the Colonial and State Governments, Relating to Indians & Indian Affairs from 1633 to 1831 Inclusive: With an Appendix Containing the Proceedings of the Congress of the Confederation & the Laws of the Congress from 1800 to 1830. Earl M. Coleman, pub. New York: 1979.
Memoirs, Official and Personal; With Sketches of Travels among the Northern and Southern Indians. New York: Pain and Burgess, 1846.

Miller, Otis Louis. *Indian-White Relations in Illinois Country, 1789-1818.* 1972.

Parkman, Francis. *History of the Conspiracy of Pontiac.* Boston: 1851.

Pease, T. C. and M. J. Pease. *George Rogers Clark and the Revolution in Illinois, 1763-1787: A Sesquicentennial Memorial.* 1929.

Petit, Father. *Trail of Death. Indiana Magazine of History.* XXI.

Prucha, Francis Paul. *Indian Policy in the United States: Historical Essays.* Nebraska: University of Nebraska Press, 1981.

Shepard's Acts and Cases by Popular Names, Federal & State. Government Documents. Colorado: Shepard's McGraw-Hill, 1992.

The Constitution of South Carolina. 342.7572, 1895.

The Constitution of the United States. Article I, Sec. 3, Clause 3. Article II, Sec. 2, Clause 2. 1789.

The Northwest Ordinance, 1787.

The Roots of American Democracy. Jose Barreiro, ed. 1988.

The Writings of Thomas Jefferson. Andrew A. Lipscomb, ed. 1903-1904.

Tipton, General. *Annual Report of the Secretary of War, Report of the Commissioner of Indian Affairs.* 1838.

Treaties Between the U.S. and the Indians 1778-1837. New York: Kraus Reprint Co., 1975.

Sheehan, Bernard W. 'The Famous Hair Buyer General': Henry Hamilton, George Rogers Clark, and the American Indian. *Indiana Magazine of History.* P. 79, March. 1983.

Van Kirk, Sylvia. *Many Tender Ties.* Norman, University of Oklahoma Press. 1980

Williams, Robert A., Jr. *The American Indian in Western Legal Thought: The Discourses of Conquest.* 1990.

Grant P. Arndt

Relocation's Imagined Landscape and the Rise of Chicago's Native American Community

During the 1950s, the Bureau of Indian Affairs (BIA) used images of Native American life in the United States to justify federal initiatives to terminate Native American tribes as federally recognized entities and to relocate many of the residents of Native American communities to cities. Throughout the media, the BIA and its supporters assembled images into an imagined version of the American landscape upon which they could map American Indian movement to cities as a transformative journey from backward, dissolute reservations to cities depicted as factories turning out upstanding, hard-working American citizens. In this article, I reconstruct the imagined landscape that the BIA used to try to lure Native Americans to Chicago. Drawing on the archival record, I show how, ironically, it trapped the BIA into unwittingly supporting the creation of the American Indian Center, which soon became a platform from which Chicago Indians could challenge the imagined landscape of Relocation and the federal Indian policies that it was used to justify.

The images of Relocation's imagined landscape were not new. For hundreds of years the city and the rural countryside had been imagined as two distinct parts of the social world, opposed in lifestyle and in moral worth (see Williams 1975 for some British examples, Cronon 1991 for American). Although up through the early part of the twentieth century, the country was traditionally deemed to occupy the morally superior position in relation to the city, this was never the case when the country was "Indian Country." The central image of the BIA's imagined landscape was that of Indian reservations as "slums." They were held to be simultaneously places of pre-civilized disorder and yet decayed and corrupted by all the ills of American society. As reserves of negative imagery, reservations were conceived of as un-healthy, un-modern, and un-American places with an irresistible influence over human beings, making or keeping their

Indian residents backward, diseased, and profligate. Journalist Carl Rowan produced vivid examples of this construction of Indian reservations in a 1957 series of articles for the *Minneapolis Star-Tribune*. The articles were republished in the *Chicago Sun-Times* the same year as "Indian's Lot: Silent Misery"(May 12); "Indian is Wed to Poverty and Despair" (May 13): "An Indian Mother Fights to Subsist on $118 a Month" (May 14); "Tell of Indian Girls Poverty on Reservation" (May 15); "Why Indian Doesn't Fit In; He Lives in Past" (May 16); "How Society can Help Solve Plight of Indian" (May 17)). Rowan used the Mille Lacs Chippewa Reservation in Minnesota as a metonymic example of "Indian Country'," describing how its 500 Indians " . . . seine minnows, scrub resort floors and drink beer by summer, pick wild rice and drink beer by fall, chase deer, rabbits , squirrels and doles for the needy by winter" (May 13). At Red Lake, another Chippewa reservation in northern Minnesota, Rowan found some of his most potent images of the decay on the reservations:

> You leave the car and walk through the trees to a cabin, looking for the leader of one of Red Lake's political factions. A pan of dead fish is in the yard. A bony black puppy shivers at the cabin door. The windows are broken and the screen has been pushed through the door on which you rap but get no response. Peeking in, you see three children stir on a cot. Then a woman crawls from under the covers. As she opens the door a stifling stench oozes out. One child's dirty drawers hang to her knees, another's face is a mask of sores. (May 13)

Rowan found Native American voices to confirm his portrait of the problems caused by Indian reservations. In Minnesota a young woman confided that she hoped she was not forced to return to White Earth (another Ojibwa reservation): "If I go back, I'll only get in trouble again," she explained. "There is nothing to do there but go to a beer tavern or park in the woods with a boy"(May 15). Elsewhere Rowan showed just what does await the Native American who returns to his or her reservation. On the Standing Rock reservation, Rowan "renew[ed] an old acquaintance" with Josephine Kelly, "the first Indian girl to graduate from Carlisle." He found her

> sitting in an old wooden chair, a coal scuttle between her feet, a pasteboard box in her lap, picking wild grapes for jelly and jam she hoped would sustain her through the bitter winter. The wind sang as it danced though the tin on the roof, rattling the cardboard covering the hole in the wall, shaking the carton of milk that sat in the "refrigerator" (the north window) and ruffling a lock of Mrs. Kelly's long gray hair. (May 13)

Mrs. Kelly became the embodiment of the geographical miasma Rowan perceived on the reservations:

The pride was gone from the voice of this woman who served four terms as head of her tribal council until she got too deeply involved in a losing fight against the federal Bureau of Indian Affairs. "I know what it is to have been well off, and now I know what it means to be hopelessly poor," she said. "The Indian is so miserable and hard-up these says, and the situation is getting worse." (May 13)

Rowan concludes by stating that "I saw nothing on any reservation that gave me even a remote hope that the Indian can become a healthy, self-respecting citizen living in the bleak isolation of these desolate forests and prairies" (May 17). Luckily, Rowan had a map that outlined the journey through the imaginary landscape of relocation. If American Indians on reservations were "lost in modern American," a few "notable exceptions" had, in his words, "cut tribal ties and discovered they can make their way in the mainstream of American life." This message of assimilation was one of the oldest American responses to the problem of the American Indian, and during the era of Termination and Relocation it returned to the forefront of public rhetoric (and provoked a critical response from Native Americans, as will be discussed below).

If Rowan portrayed reservations as the nadir of the American landscape, other articles in the mainstream press of the time helped chart the journey Native Americans were to undertake. In a *Reader's Digest*

article entitled "The Indian Trail to Success" (1950), Louis R. Bruce described how he overcame common feelings of persecution as an Indian by "leaving the blanket" to attend boarding school, then college, and finally start a career as a salesman at a New York City men's clothing store. Bruce was not alone. Readers of the *Chicago Tribune* learned early in 1952 that

Indians were "flocking" to their city for a "wampum hunt":

Under a new program, instituted this year, more than 500 American Indians have been brought here from reservations where living conditions and employment opportunities are poor, where the lands are submarginal, and where an Indian can stalk little to live on. They are finding Chicago good hunting grounds and are taking to big city life in a heap big way ... finding jobs as machinists, stenographers, hospital aids, shipping clerks, welders, warehouse workers, and construction laborers (Fitzpatrick 1952)

Politically inspired imagery is most effective with those who can least challenge its version of reality, and if journalists like Rowan and others mapped relocation for non-Indian audiences by depicting the horrors of the reservations, the city as other pole of the Native American journey emerged most vividly in BIA publicity material aimed at potential Native American participants in the program. One striking example is found in an article published in the Fort Berthold Indian Agency paper in 1953 (in the files of the Robert Reitz Papers at NAES College Tribal Research Center). The article's text surrounds an illustration of a Native American on horseback standing at a crossroads with a sign pointing to icons of the four cities where the BIA had relocation offices: Chicago, Denver, Salt Lake City, and Los Angeles. All the cities are represented by images of modern industrial society: bridges, mines, and ports. Chicago, the most popular destination, was represented by the image of a factory, with smokestacks belching out smoke.

Within the year, the Chicago relocation office was sending more posters to Fort Berthold to advertise the program's success. One poster proudly announced that "329 steady jobs were found for Indians in Chicago in the past six months." The posters depicted the city iconically as a skyscraper (containing the relocation office) and an employer at a desk, connected by a phone cord, surrounding images of jobs and workers representing the range of employment possibilities in Chicago.

Drawings from *Working Our Way*, Fort Berthold Agency News Bulleten, October 30, 1953, vol. 4, number 10. Reitz Papers.

Other Indians were shown films of Chicago produced by the Chicago Chamber of Commerce. As one later recalled:

> Only the most favorable aspects of the city were shown. The high Buildings, the beaches, and the parks were shown, not the slums or elevated trains. New homes were shown and the family was told that they could own one within a few years. (Arends 1958:69)

Early relocatees quickly became figures in the imagined landscape. A "Mr. Charley" described how the BIA had had him record a tape for Indians on the reservation, depicting his successful relocation to the city.

> Pictures were taken of him working at a job he did not have. People on the reservation knew that he had wanted to be a meat cutter so he was photographed in a butcher shop with a meat saw even though he had never worked there. (Arends 1958, 54 note 5)

A more famous early relocatee was used to model the journey of the imagined landscape in propaganda designed for a wider audience. In May of 1952, the Chicago BIA office relocated Ira Hamilton Hayes, famous Pima veteran of WWII's battle of Iwo Jima. Hayes had been the object of a widespread publicity campaign after the war, which had made him a celebrity, and had contributed to his problem of readjustment to rural life on the Pima Reservation (see Fixico 1986). A May 19, 1952, photo in the *Sun-Times* showed Hayes arriving in Chicago. He was greeted by Indians in full regalia, with a caption informing the reader that "jobless, he found work as machine shop trainee before the day was over."

Although Hayes soon left the city, and returned to a tragic end in Arizona, the ideology of the transformative urban journey remained. Ironically, the ideology faced its first major challenge only with the emergence of a group of truly "cosmopolitan Indians" who had a long, if tenuous, relationship with the BIA relocation program.

* * * *

The Relocation Program started out in Chicago narrowly focused on getting Native Americans jobs in the city. In the opening months of the field office in Chicago, the Relocation worker Mary Nan Gamble contacted twelve state employment offices in Wisconsin, Illinois, and Indiana to cultivate their help in contacting employers and in screening future relocatees (Archives of the Chicago Relocation Office[CRO]) (January 1952). She also contacted area employers directly, including Republic Steel, the Sunbeam corporation, U.S. Steel, Carnegie Steel, Hansell-Elcock, Ullrich Plumbing, Mattison Machinery, Curtiss Candy, Inland Steel, and Linberg Engineering Company. Several companies expressed a willingness to hire Indians on a test basis, and Rockford, Illinois, companies submitted orders for machine tool workers. In January of 1952, Gamble went to the Great Lakes consolidated Bureau of Indian Affairs agency to interview prospective relocatees for jobs with Republic Steel and Hansell-Elcock Foundry.

Eight men were selected and, after a delay in obtaining the funding need-ed for their transportation, they arrived in the city in February of 1952.

Soon after the arrival of the first relocatees in Chicago, the Relocation office began to experience problems. Caseworkers sent back frequent reports to the main office in Washington, D.C., describing the problems they were encountering with relocatees. Of the first crop of relocatees, one of the men selected for an apprenticeship at Republic Steel was found to be "industrially blind in one eye" and was refused employment. Anoth-er man decided after two weeks to join the Marines, then returned to the office days later broke and uncertain about his plans and another place-ment had to be arranged. Such problems would mount in the coming months. The BIA invariably saw such situations as problem of adjustment, and early on Gamble suggested more thorough screening of prospective relocatees, with refusal of relocation as a "disciplinary action" for those who "failed to measure up" (CRO, January 1952).

By April of 1952, the program found that of 82 individuals who had been placed, 21 had "failed to adjust to the program." The report also dis-cussed the "uncontrolled drinking on the part of a rather large minority of relocatees," reflecting "conditions that are presumably of long stand-ing." The Relocation Office opined that "unpredictable complications" of relocation were creating many of the adjustment problems of relocatees that necessitated interventions by the office.

> The need for community help on social adjustment remains great. We are certain that a goodly percentage of those relocatees who have dropped out or failed did so because of confusion and loneliness in a strange environ-ment. (CRO, April 1952)

The office suggested that the use of staff time "to promote communi-ty assistance" and to cultivate the assistance of other Indians in Chicago seemed to offer the best hope for addressing the problems. Even before setting up operations in Chicago, the BIA had begun to work with the local coordinating body for social services, the Metropolitan Welfare Council, to organize a meeting to explore the coordination of Indian groups in Chicago (see Arndt 1998 for an account that explores the devel-opment of post-war organizations in more detail). The project was limit-ed by personal friction between the leaders of Chicago's existing Indian groups (the Indian Council Fire, the Off-the-Street Club and the Amer-ican Indian Lodge) and by Native American "skepticism . . . toward the activities of the BIA" (CRO, April 1952).

In June of 1952, the BIA noted with alarm an "exodus" of relocatees back to the reservation, which almost canceled out the month's place-ments. Although they received assurance that many who had left Chica-go would return, the exodus reinforced the Relocation Office's concern over finding ways to help integrate Native Americans into Chicago. They reflected in their July report that

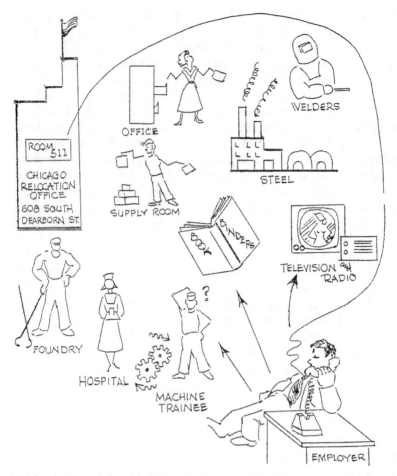

"329 Steady Jobs were found for Indians in Chicago in the last six months. . . ". Flyer produced by Chicago Relocation Office, Bureau of Indian Affairs, 608 South Dearborn St., Chicago, Illinois, September 30, 1954.

> Failure to make an impressive showing . . . [in instilling "habits of self-sufficiency and receptivity to community resources"] by merely continuing to find jobs and housing, will jeopardize the success in Chicago. If our small pilot project is to be convincing as to the merits of the program, we shall have to come up with a convincing success story. (CRO, July 1952)

The Relocation office formed a "Citizen's Advisory Board" in order to "activate community leaders and agencies in behalf of relocatees" (CRO, August 1952). The Citizen's Advisory Board had a series of subcommittees devoted to issues like Family Housing, Social Services, Employment, and Vocational Training. The most important subcommittee, and apparently the most active, was the one concerned with the "leisure-time preoccupations" of Chicago's Native Americans (CRO, August 1952). It soon began to make contact with the leaders of existing organizations, such as Eli Powless, who set up a Bowling League that the Relocation office staff encouraged relocatees to join.

* * * *

As the BIA noticed, when Native Americans left their reservations to come to Chicago they experienced a disjuncture between the images of the city in BIA propaganda and the realities of urban life. Chicago contained challenges and dangers that the BIA had not prepared them to address. Although BIA statistics do not allow an appreciation of how life in the city looked to one of the "maladjusted," letters written by the relocatees themselves give a picture of the problems they faced. In one such letter, a relocatee wrote back to the BIA worker on his reservation to describe his problems in Chicago:

When I got here on Monday June 14th [1952] at 2 p.m. I was like a drifting bark on choppy waters. No one to see to meet us. Had to get help from a Cop and he in turn had Travelers Aid call the Indian Bureau. They send us to Van Buren Hotel. Next day at 8:30 (Tuesday) was when the financial mistakes or troubles started. Instead of the [$]90.00 a week like we agreed in your office I got [$]30.00. [$]16 for rent right off. [$]9 for Eats and what was left I used for car fare . . . . so I just about *hiked out* of *City* just on account of shortage of funds for other necessities . . . . Ive walk'd almost 50 miles trying to save enuff so 2 boys could eat bread. Im on Ohio St. and have to get to work by 6, fast time . . . . Im sweating it out at Sante Fe Section Crew. You should know just about how far it is [from] Ohio Street to Sante Fe Terminal. About 3 mile 1 way & 6 round trip. Ive 2 more weeks till first pay day that why Im—about the allowance I was short changed . . . . by the time you're reading this I may be out on the street. So Mr. Reitz Im asking you to tell them straight and send us some boys money. Main thing is Ive started to sweating it out and with Gods help I hope to stick it out a few pay days, before I go back to my blanket and teepee.(ha) Be cing u & please don't fail me on the request of funds [emphasis in original]. (Reitz Papers)

Others faced similar problems. Insufficient paychecks; unreliable employers; scarce, overpriced housing; and inadequate public transportation caused many to find the transition to the city anything but the edifying journey the BIA had promised. Despite their best efforts, relocatees faced an urban environment that could often be harsh on Native American and non-Native workers alike.

* * * *

In September of 1952, the BIA Citizens Advisory Board subcommittee on "leisure-time occupations" set up recreation centers in cooperation with the Chicago Park District at the Chase Park Field House on the South

Side and at the Ogden Park Field House on the North Side. The recreation centers, known collectively as the American Indian Club, started their activities in early October of 1952 and quickly attracted not just relocatees, but also more established Indian residents of Chicago. Several of these "old-timers" soon acquired leadership positions in the club. The BIA office looked on their participation as signs of a new positive feeling toward the BIA, but relations between the Relocation office and Chicago Indians would prove to be fraught with potential for conflict.

At time of the relocation of Ira Hayes, in the spring of 1953, the American Indian Club had become a successful organization, and several of its powwows had gained wide exposure for Indians in Chicago. Even as Eli Powless (Oneida) a member of the subcommittee of Leisure Time Preoccupations and president of the Indian Council Fire, along with Ione Jeneusse and Betty Maney, were photographed greeting Hayes at Northwestern Station, the American Indian Club and BIA Advisory Board were in the process of creating the American Indian Center.

By this time, the statistics on Relocation were showing improvement. A "population census" in June 1953 found that, of the 1,045 Native Americans relocated, 639 relocatees were still at work in the city, 265 had returned to their reservations, and 141 had left Chicago for non-reservation destinations. The Relocation office found a decrease in return rates for relocatees, from 40 to 25 percent since the beginning of the program. They saw the decrease as "largely due to growth of an Indian community in Chicago and the greater feeling of security on the part of the individual which comes from group identification. Many activities by local Indian organizations including dances, socials, sports and picnics have contributed to this." They predicted more successful adjustment as the field staff gained experience and "an Indian community takes normal roots here. . . ."(June 1953)

The American Indian Center opened in November of 1953. It had no full-time staff, and so Thomas Segundo, former chairman of the Papago tribal council and a student at the University of Chicago (and full-time employee of the Ford Motor Plant), acted as executive director. The Indian Center's programming was minimal, consisting mainly of social activities organized by individual Native Americans or the American Indian Club.

* * * *

By 1955, as the media, both national and local, began to cover the BIA relocation program and profile the existence of Native Americans in urban areas, the Center gained nationwide exposure. In January 1955, *Reader's Digest* featured an article entitled "The Indians are Going to Town" by O. K. and Marjorie Armstrong. The Armstrongs depicted Relocation as a government program designed to help Indians "win back their birthright" and escape the "handicaps" of tradition and prejudice. They described the role of the Indian Centers in Chicago and Los Angeles in providing

a clubhouse with reading rooms, kitchen for refreshments, and recreation
hall . . . . the Chicago all-Tribes American Indian Center sponsors a baseball team[and] . . . . its news sheet, Tom Tom Echoes, keeps all tribes
informed of Indian Doings. Teenager parties are lively affairs. Hearts are
never lonely at the Indian Center. Many romances blossom. (Armstrong
and Armstrong 1955)

Chicago's media were also paying attention to relocation and to the existence of the Center. In September 1955, the Chicago *Sun-Times* profiled
the Center in an article entitled "The Return of the Red Man." The story
presented a humanizing portrait of Chicago's Indian residences, including
the way in which the Center mixed ". . . . Indian traditions and modern
city ways . . . . with surprising results" (Carter 1955). The opening vignette
humorously depicted the (apparently universal) generation gap as manifest at the Center, with teenagers and their elders arguing whether to
spend the evening on traditional tribal dancing or "jitterbugging." A vote
favored traditional dancing, but the article noted that the jitterbuggers
were allowed to practice a bit before the traditional dancing commenced.

Settling into a more serious tone, the article emphasized that the Center was

a spot where Indians in Chicago can turn, not only to have fun and make
friends, but to adjust to a kind of life which in many cases is new and bewildering to them. It fills a need of which many Chicagoans may be unaware.
(Carter, 1955)

The experiences of Center board member Hiawatha Hood and his wife
Louise illustrated the experience of Chicago's relocatees. Hiawatha had
little trouble adapting to life in Chicago because his work in construction
had frequently taken him off the Yavapi reservation in Fort McDowell
Arizona; Louise, like many of the BIA relocatees, had a more difficult
transition. As her husband related, "She didn't tell me then, but every day
after I went to work, she would cry all day . . . . She was lonely. She didn't
know anybody." The Center was credited with making the difference for
Louise Hood and others like her in their adjustment to the city, providing them with social contacts and the support of fellow Native American
residents in Chicago (Carter 1955).

Though the Center had become an important part of the Relocation
program's public image, by 1956 the Center's close formal link with the
Chicago Relocation Office had begun to break down. Local opposition to
the Relocation program was growing among Native Americans and in
January long noticed tensions between Native Americans and the Relocation office erupted into public denunciations. By March, the BIA office
considered the Center's leaders to be " . . . . militant . . . anti-Bureau people . . . ." One of the Center's board members, Dorothy Van De Mark (one
of two non-Indians on the board), wrote an article called "The Raid on

the Reservations" in *Harper's* calling the Chicago Relocation Program a "dumping process." She felt that the federal government, in seeking to terminate its involvement in Indian affairs, was simply trying to depopulate reservations and let the burden of social welfare fall on city service agencies. "The real Indian problems are poverty, ill health, poor education, and economic stagnation. Relocation can solve none of these."

The BIA attempted to stem the negative publicity in Chicago. In June 1956 they sponsored a meeting on the relocated Indians at the Central YMCA that failed to bring about a reconciliation. Throughout the rest of the decade, the BIA office remained estranged from the Chicago Indian community and marginal to local groups working with Native Americans. They had helped Native American leaders to found an organized community in Chicago, but after 1956 they were no longer active parts in the community's growth.

* * * *

By the summer of 1955, attacks on federal Indian policy had become more intense across the nation (Burt 1982, 66). The National Congress of American Indians (NCAI) denounced Federal Indian Policy at its annual meeting and Oliver La Farge of the American Association of Indian Affairs (AAIA) wrote to the White House to denounce the termination policies. A series of articles by Harold Fey in the *Christian Century* led to an awareness of Termination and Relocation among Protestant churchgoers (Burt 1982, 77–78). But just as controversy over the Relocation program grew in the American public, the program was becoming more popular with Native Americans. By 1956, applications for the program were up. The BIA increased funding for Relocation, opening new offices in St. Louis, San Francisco, and San Jose. That same year, funding for the program more than tripled, from $1,016,400 to $3,472,000. Public Law 959, passed in August 1956, provided increased vocational training for Native Americans, and soon this vocational training became part of the Relocation program. (Fixico, 1986:143; Burt 1982:74).

* * * *

By 1957, American Indian Center leadership had not only broken with the BIA, but had self-consciously taken on the task of acting as the public representatives of the Chicago Indian Community (see description in Arends 1958, 96). The publication of Carl Rowan's articles [discussed in the beginning of this chapter] in the Chicago *Sun-Times* served as the opportunity for them to publicly attack the image of Indians and the symbolism of the Relocation program.

Center leaders called a meeting on May 18th to denounce Rowan's articles. One hundred Native Americans attended the four-hour meeting, along with others, such as anthropologist Sol Tax and some of his students from the University of Chicago and journalists from the local papers.

Ira Hayes, an Iwo-Jima flag raiser, being met at the La Salle Street Railroad Station, Chicago, Illinois., 1953. Daily News Collection. Photograph courtesy of the Chicago Historical Society.

Chicago Indians were upset not so much by Rowan's depiction of the terrible conditions they faced on the reservations and in city slums, but by his clear indication that their Indianness was part of their problem, and that, as Indians, they were both helpless and hopeless. Robert Thomas (Cherokee), an assistant in anthropology at the University of Chicago, observed that most people who expressed concern for Native Americans "do not ask what is wrong with the situation the Indian is made to face but what is wrong with the Indian . . . . Anybody knows the solution to the problem is that the Indian way of life should be helped" (Martin 1957). Thomas Segundo dismissed Rowan's charge that Indian culture was a thing of the past; "When Indians are accused of living in the past, it is a misunderstanding and a mis-statement . . . they are simply holding on to the tribal culture." He asked ". . . is there really anything so bad about listening to those old voices of the past[?] They made so much sense. It seems to me that we did fine for 10,000 years until this foreign culture entered. I thought tribal life and the things we learned had a lot to give our people and other people who came to these shores" (ibid.). Thurman Wolf expanded on Segundo's defense of Native American cultures by tracing the problems Native Americans experienced in the city to the white culture they were supposed to emulate, ". . . [the] White man has taught the

Indian to have cocktails before supper . . . I took too many cocktails. I threw Indian ways aside. I did get a job—worked eight hours a day, came home at night and look[ed] at television. That was not enough so I went to our old Indians to find out about more there is to life" (ibid.). Center members also disputed Rowan's depiction of the reservations. Center member Susan Kelly (Sioux) criticized Rowan's portrait of her mother, Josephine Kelly [see above] for obscuring the fact that she had refused to leave the reservation, "because it is the only home she knows [and because] she can help her people there" (ibid.).

* * * *

The Center's criticisms of the Relocation program reveal a new imagined landscape that foreshadows the rise of Native American militancy in the coming decades. Rather than the reservation being disconnected and antithetical to the city, Chicago's Native Americans saw the two realms as interlinked. The economic necessity that brought Native Americans to the city, elevated to the central constitutive principal of Relocation's imagined landscape, was here treated as secondary to cultural and communal solidarity. Underlying this interlinking of the different realms was a reminder of history: non-Indians were reminded that they, not Native Americans, were the foreigners in America, and that the present conditions of reservations and tribal culture were indicative of the ignoble history of invasion and conquest.

The Chicago Indian Center's rebuttal of Rowan and their other public actions also exposed the problems of urban life to public view, offering a critique of the image of the city in the BIA's imagined landscape. They depicted an urban landscape that better matched the experiences of many relocatees. Chicago was far more than just a factory. Though it offered economic betterment, it also contained within it new forms of exploitation and perils not included among the images presented by the Relocation program.

Most importantly, the Center's public actions transformed Native Americans from passive figures in the imagined landscapes of others, into active figures on a new landscape. The ". . . frail old men, weary old women, crying little girls and under nourished little boys" who lived in the past, "wed to poverty and despair" in Rowan's version of the landscape of Relocation, became successful Indians, without having to cut their ties with reservations or with their past. In the words of Thomas Segundo, then the Center's director, "It is a sad mistake to say Indians are a voiceless people. This meeting shows that we have a voice and we are voicing a unified stand" (Martin, 1957). The BIA's Relocation program, which had been designed by the federal government to help finally dismantle reservation communities, had helped Native Americans create a new form of community through which they could take a unified stand on behalf of both their reservation homelands and their lives in urban America. Using the American Indian Center as their platform, Chicago's Native Americans constructed a new imagined landscape, one in which Native Americans living in cities could look to reservations as a sort of homeland, the repository of their traditions and history, and a reminder of Native American autonomy and their unjust treatment by the United States. The move to the city had been transformative, but not in the way that the BIA had expected: the Native Americans who came to Chicago would do much to change the place of Native Americans in America's imagined landscape.

BIBLIOGRAPHY

Arends, Wade B. "A Socio-Cultural Study of the Relocated American Indians in Chicago." [unpublished M.A. paper] The University of Chicago, 1958.

Armstrong, O. K., and Marjorie Armstrong. "The Indians are Going to Town." *Reader's Digest.* January,1955, p. 39-43.

Arndt, Grant P. "Contrary to Our Way of Thinking: The Struggle for an American Indian Center in Chicago." *American Indian Culture and Research Journal.* 1998.

Bain. Howard G. "A Sociological Analysis of the Chicago Skid-Row Lifeway." [unpublished M.A. paper] The University of Chicago, 1950.

Bogue, Donald. J. *Skid Row in American Cities.* Community and Family Study Center, The University of Chicago: Chicago, 1963.

Burt, Larry. *Tribalism in Crisis: Federal Indian Policy, 1953-1961.* University of New Mexico Press: Albuquerque, 1982.

Butler, Raymond V. 'The Bureau of Indian Affairs: Activities Since 1945." AAPSS. *Annals.* 436, March, 1978, p. 50-60.

Bruce, Louis R. "The Indian Trail to Success." *Reader's Digest.* 1950.

Carter, Lucia. "Return of the Red Man, Chicago's 3,500 Indians are making a swift adjustment to city life." *The Chicago Sun-Times,* September 25, 1955.

Chicago Relocation Office. Unpublished archives RG75, BIA Chicago, located at National Archives, Great Lakes Branch, Chicago, Il.

Cronon, William. *Natures Metropolis: Chicago and the Great West,* New York: W. W. Norton. 1991.

Fitzpatrick, Rita. "Indians look to Chicago for Wampum Hunt, 20 Tribes' Members get Paying Jobs." *Chicago Tribune.* December 26, 1952.

Fixico, Donald L. *Termination and Relocation: Federal Indian Policy, 1945-1960.* University of New Mexico Press: Albuquerque, 1986.

Martin, Fletcher. "Indians Protest Portrayal of Misery" *Chicago Sun Times.* May 19, 1957.

Neils, Elaine. M. "The Urbanization of the American Indian and the Federal Program of Relocation Assistance." [unpublished M.A. Paper] The University of Chicago, 1969.

Rowan, Carl. "Indian's Lot: Silent Misery." (May 12); "Indian is Wed to Poverty and Despair." (May 13); "An Indian Mother Fights to Subsist on $118 a Month." (May 14); "Tell of Indian Girl's Poverty on Reservation." (May 15); "Why Indian Doesn't Fit In: He Lives in Past." (May 16); "How Society Can Help Solve Plight of Indian." (May 17). Chicago Sun-Times: 1957.

Reitz papers. Unpublished Archives. NAES College, Chicago, Il.

Van de Mark, Dorothy. "The Raid on the Reservations." *Harper's* Magazine. March, 1956, p. 48-53.

Williams, Raymond. *The Country and the City.* New York: Oxford University Press. 1975 (1973).

Ed Goodvoice

Relocation

Indian Life on Skid Row

INTRODUCTION

During and after World War II, many American Indian people relocated from their reservations to urban areas with the expectation of a better lifestyle than the one they left behind. The government's Relocation program, which started in 1952, provided paid transportation to a city, help finding a job and a place to live, and a small stipend until the first paycheck came in. All of these conditions sounded ideal to many Indians who were eager to begin working and living in the big city. Hopes were raised that perhaps it was now possible to fulfill some of those dreams, dreams of a good job, clothes, and a nice place to live and maybe even a nice shiny car that could someday be driven back to the reservation. Within the first six months, these dreams for life in the city were put on hold. Rent was high and housing was often poor, especially for relocated families with children. The big city with its fast pace and impersonal attitude, among other problems, plagued relocatees. Many became frustrated and discouraged, beginning a downward spiral onto "Skid Row."

I came to Chicago on Relocation, arriving on October 5, 1957, from the Rosebud Sioux Reservation in South Dakota. I was single and 27 years old. I got off the train at the Northwestern Depot on Madison and Canal Streets carrying written directions to the YMCA where all the relocatees were sent. It was cold and windy as I stepped out onto that infamous Skid Row of West Madison Street. Fine powdery snow was falling and blowing about in this place they called the Windy City. Although I had been advised not to by relatives who had been here on Relocation and had returned to the reservation, I immediately headed west when I got out on the street. I did not find an Indian bar or see any Indians. I walked for several blocks on this stormy night, and I stopped in at a bar to have a shot of wine. I was hoping to see an Indian face. No such luck! This was my introduction to West Madison Street.

I finally headed east on Madison Street in what I hoped would be the general direction of the YMCA at 826 South Wabash. I had cab fare, but was content to walk and explore, though few people were on the street. I walked for about two hours. After what seemed like an all night walk, I finally found the YMCA and checked in. This YMCA was where all the Native Americans coming into Chicago on Relocation were housed for the first week or so. Although rooms were rented at a discounted price for Native Americans on the program, I was told that those rooms were all taken and I would have to pay the full price. I was tired, so I was willing to pay the price. The YMCA was to become my home for the next four weeks. Its policies were strict: you had to show your key at the elevator and go directly to the floor on which your room was assigned.

I had arranged for a 7:00 A.M. wake-up call, because I had instructions to report to the Relocation Office, located three blocks from the YMCA at Harrison and Dearborn, at 9:00 A.M. on October 6th. I got up before the wake-up call came because I was anxious and in a hurry to begin my new life in Chicago. I wanted a new lifestyle that would include a good paying job, a nice apartment, and a late model car. When I went out, it was still cold but the snowstorm had passed, and I walked out of the YMCA with my dream. The Conrad Hilton Hotel was located about half a block across the street from YMCA. Beyond this great hotel, I could see Grant Park and, of course, Lake Michigan. The sight of the lake reminded me of my first glimpse of the Pacific Ocean in the early fifties when I was on my way to boot camp in San Diego, California.

Since I had plenty of time before my appointment at the Relocation office, I continued to walk north on Wabash and was surprised to actually see a whole train traveling between buildings on what appeared to be a long railroad bridge. I had no idea that a train also ran underground. I later learned that this was called the elevated train and that part of the route was called the Loop. After retracing my steps back to the YMCA (I did not want to get lost on the first day), I timidly requested directions to the Relocation office from a white man. I use the term "timid" because Indians rarely initiated conversations with a white man. Back on the reservation, when working for a white farmer or rancher, you were a hired hand and you did not talk much.

Since I had three or four dollars left over, I decided to get some breakfast. I found a combination bar and snack shop just off Ninth and State streets. It was only a block or so from the YMCA. A middle-aged, grayhaired, fat but friendly Italian man appeared to be the proprietor and cook. The long counter showed signs of wear, but it was clean. I was greeted with a hearty "Good morning, Chief". I felt the veins go taut in my neck. I looked around at a couple of guys sitting at one of the only two booths that were crowded into the corner of the snack shop. These two guys were Native Americans. I immediately felt a sense of relief as I headed in their direction. I was no longer a stranger in Chicago.

Native Americans do not ordinarily take a direct approach when meeting another Native. However, I was acquainted with one of those guys. He was a Navajo whom I had met on a Skid Row in Los Angeles in the mid-1950's. These two men were already veterans of the Relocation program. They had been in Chicago awhile and had jobs working the temporary Christmas rush at the main post office, loading and unloading bags of mail.

The Navajo, a few years later, was found stabbed to death on an Uptown area beach. The other Native, a Sioux, returned to his reservation in South Dakota. This was a pattern that many Native Americans would follow in the two decades after the 1953 Relocation Act. But I am getting ahead of myself. After a hearty breakfast (sixty cents back in those days) and an almost endless conversation about Relocation and jobs they sent you to, I anxiously said that I had a 9:00 A.M. appointment at the Relocation office.

Words of encouragement followed me out of the door as I began the two-and-a-half-block walk to the office. As I was about to enter the building, I could almost sense the cold and gloomy atmosphere that seems to come with these federally-sponsored programs. I still had visions of being shuffled from one office building to another as had happened while I was back on the reservation in Rosebud, South Dakota.

At five minutes to nine, I knocked on the door marked "Indian Relocation Office." As I entered the reception area, I saw a neatly groomed, attractive Indian woman who greeted me with a smile. I was a little surprised given my earlier visions of cold and gloom: the office and staff appeared professional and competent. My initial impression was a positive one, but now I began to wonder about my own appearance. All the men wore neat slacks, shirts, and ties. I began to feel uncomfortable with the way I was dressed. I had on well-worn cowboy boots with traces of South Dakota mud on them. My jeans and shirt need laundering, or so I was told by the interviewer. I just wanted to disappear. I was told that I would be given a clothing order.

At the end of the day, after the laborious task of being interviewed, answering questions about my background, and filling out numerous forms, I was told to report back the following day at the same time. I would be taken for another interview with a prospective employer. Meanwhile, I was to continue living at the YMCA until other housing arrangements could be made for me. Bus fare and money for meals were to be supplied by the program until I received my first month's paycheck.

I was hired by Continental Can Company as a stock man at an hourly wage of $2.28, which was good money in the 1950's. The money for transportation and food was to be picked up at the office every Friday evening. It was on these Fridays that I began to meet other Native Americans. Some would come right from work, still wearing the grease and grime of the day. Others were relatively clean and sometimes had responsible jobs such as shipping clerk, light machine operators, or loading dock checker. After I had been on my job for approximately three weeks, I was ready to assume the responsibility of paying rent, shopping for food, and most importantly, learning how to manage my own paycheck. All of this was too good to be true, as I was laid off the following month. Many employees were laid off because of inventory prior to the Christmas and New Year's holiday. This was the first of many problems I would encounter on my downward spiral to the skids.

The only thing I could think of at this point was to go back to the Relocation office and inform the staff of the layoff. After a brief interview at the Relocation office, I was given a letter of reference and instructed to report to Readymen, Inc., on North Avenue and Halsted Streets at one p.m. Readymen a daily pay office, played a large role in the lives of Native Americans who had either been laid off or terminated from their jobs. Many of the Native Americans, former Relocation clients, were working out of this daily pay office. Entire families were working out of the Uptown Readymen office. The connection between the Relocation office and Readymen was quite obvious to me.

As I walked into the Readymen office with my letter of reference, I was stared at and sized up by a group of Indians who were standing in one corner of the room. I overheard one asking others in Lakota who I was. The four walls of the room were lined with rough wooden benches. There was loud and boisterous conversation coming from several of the groups of men in the huge room. I had been warned to watch my pockets. The room was crowded with men who were either waiting for a check or waiting for a work ticket on the swing or the midnight shift. Others sat quietly on the bench, staring anxiously at the dispatcher who stood behind an elevated counter that separated the office from the waiting room. These men probably had not received a work ticket for the day. Almost everyone in the room was aware of the cold December weather at this time of the year. You had to keep up with the rent money. Minimum wage was one dollar per hour, and if you failed to get a work ticket, you could be out on the street. After taxes and carfare, an eight-hour check would barely cover living expenses.

The dispatcher began calling out names of some of the men who were either getting a work ticket or a Readymen check. A hush would fall over the crowd when the dispatcher leaned out over the counter with work tickets or checks in his hand. Some of the men would stand right in front of the elevated counter and would be told to step aside for men coming in with signed work tickets from the job site. You could not get paid without a ticket signed by the employer at the job site.

The group of Native Americans continued to laugh and joke with each other in a boisterous manner. They acted like they did not have a care in the world. It was approximately 4:00 P.M. and other Native Americans began to come in with what appeared to be signed work tickets. As each one stepped into the room he would be loudly greeted with, "Here's a live one, he can buy a jug." Like working for Readymen, the use of the jug of wine as a social lubricant was part of the way of life for many Indians who had originally come to Chicago on the Relocation program and ended up on Skid Row. Some were either separated or divorced from loved ones, others just found life on Skid Row more acceptable: there were no social or economic barriers there. About half of the Indians who picked up Readymen checks would end up cruising Skid Row at night.

CAREER PATHS ON SKID ROW

The Indian on Skid Row worked almost every day. In groups of drinking friends, they would find work from the ever increasing number of daily pay offices like Readymen that sprouted up on Skid Row. Some of these offices had lucrative contracts with worksites, paying more than the minimum wage at $1.15 a hour. One site office would send experienced lumber handlers even to the far suburbs to contract whole boxcars loaded with lumber. They would contract a flat rate for board feet unloaded from the boxcar. Each Indian lumber handler wanted a fast and experienced handler to work with. The sooner the box was unloaded, the sooner you got paid, which was a major motivating factor in picking a partner. Since two good Indian lumber handlers could unload a boxcar of lumber in one day at one hundred dollars or more a car, they were considered one of two or three groups of the elite on Skid Row. All Indian lumber handlers tended to drink together and to tell tall stories about how many board-feet of lumber the partners unloaded in an unbelievably short time.

A second group of elites was found among the Indians employed by Readymen, Inc. Not all, but proven groups were consistently invited back to work the various conventions, trade shows, and other city-sponsored events including the Blackhawk and Bulls games as well as the Ice Capades at the Chicago Stadium. Some of the Canadian Indians would tease and joke with famous Bobby Hull of the Chicago Blackhawks, who is also a Canadian.

Readymen, also had special crews made up of Indians living on or near Skid Row to work the trade show expositions that were held at the Palmer House, Conrad Hilton, and the newly built McCormick Place in the early 1960's. These Indians worked alongside the union members such as electricians, carpenters, dock workers, machinery movers, and other highly paid skilled workers whose union wages were sometimes three or four times higher than the going minimum wage paid to the Indians working out of the Readymen office. Local 214 of Teamsters' Union permitted the Readymen crew to load, unload, and move exhibits to halls with a union permit. Although Readymen crews, including the Indians, were relegated to busting freight (unloading heavy crates from tractor trailers), such work was preferable to setting dollies under seven-or eight-hundred-pound crates and pushing them into the exhibition halls. At the very least, you could always sneak a drink while working inside the trailers there at the Hilton Hotel.

This Indian crew was familiar with all the nearest bars and liquor stores in and around the Conrad Hilton. They were referred to as the Hilton crew. They could be depended on to work long hours, especially when one show had to be moved out because another and different show had to be moved in. It was not unusual to work round the clock, go upstairs and sleep for two or three hours, and come back to start on the trailers that were lined up for two blocks, waiting to be unloaded. The crew would routinely work 38, 40, or 42 hours in one shift.

Indians living on Skid Row looked forward to the trade shows because jugs were always available, there were lots of hiding places to stash jugs, and they got plenty of fancy rich food that was left over from the banquet and dinners held by various organizations at the Hilton. Teamsters and machinery movers shared tips with the Readymen crew, so that no one ever ran out of change for more jugs. Lastly, United Exposition paid time and a half for eight hours. The money was great for Indians living on Skid Row and working out of a daily pay office. Most would complete the first eight hours at straight pay and go on time and a half for the rest of the five days allowed by the labor board. With two or three hours of sleep per shift (United Exposition paid for two rooms in the hotel), you could build up a lot of hours and with tips could almost feel rich.

Meanwhile, United Exposition also had an Indian crew working on the same trade show at the Palmer House with the same advantages and rewards. The dock supervisors were, for the most part, ex-Readymen who were hired to work directly for United Expositions. One such boss was an Indian called Big John (not his real name) who was tough on Indians caught drinking or drunk. If you were caught in the act of tipping a jug, or if you were observed making a mad dash to the trailer from the bar across Wabash Avenue, you were immediately assigned to pick up your Readymen work ticket and go home. You were, however, expected to return at 8:00 A.M. the following day or sooner, since the trailers were being unloaded throughout the day and night. It only took about four hours to sober up and the Readymen Indian would be welcomed back on the job. He would be good for another forty hours of working inside the trailers.

Most Indians from the far North Side Readymen office and many non-Indians were not willing to put in long hours and were always ready to go home after completing eight hours. Those Indians living on Skid Row were called crazy by the North Side Indians because they would continuously hustle to get those trade shows in and out on schedule. Bosses liked this. When shows were officially opened to the buying public and during the three or four days scheduled for the event, the Madison Street Indians were off. They would pick up their three-or four-hundred-dollar checks at the Readymen office.

Although few Indians went out on the work trains as gandy-dancers (railroad repair workers), those that did would return to Chicago late in fall and rocking chair (draw railroad unemployment compensation) through the winter months, many joining other Indians on Skid Row.

Life on Skid Row

Readymen paychecks would be cashed at the Barrel House on North Avenue and Halsted Street. There would be hearty laughter, teasing, and boisterous joking while each crew member took his turn buying a round of fifteen cent suds (steins of beer) for his peers. When references were made to "from Madison Street," they were usually voiced in a haughty manner by other Indians. Actually, some of the Indians from Madison Street considered themselves better off because there was no need to cop a front and they were responsible only for themselves. They would tell you that you could survive Skid Row without doing a lick of work. There were the missions, soup lines, Catholic Charities, Salvation Army, and other social service organizations on or near Skid Row. A clean change of clothes was available at most of these missions. You could even shower and shave at city-operated facilities on Madison Street. It was possible to stay neat and clean while living on Skid Row.

After finishing several rounds of suds at the Barrel House, the Indian trade show crews began to break up into smaller groups of drinking buddies. Despite the extra hard-earned cash, they would then buy a jug or two and make the fifteen-block trek back to Madison Street. An Indian working for Readymen would tell you, "I can walk anywhere or carry the stick all night if I have a jug in my pocket." A jug was a powerful companion.

Since these small groups of Indians were dusty, moldy, and considered rich ("live ones") on the street, the first choice was to go to one of the many second-hand stores to buy clean clothes. Then they would check into a flophouse to shower and shave and check out the Indian Bar, the Jack Pot. Once inside the Jack Pot, the Indian trade show crews would be given respect equal to another elite group, the Indian lumber handlers. There was that saying, "Money talks."

Many of the bars at which the Indian lumber handlers drank on Skid

Row, like the restaurants and flophouses, were owned by the same daily pay offices they drew their pay from after unloading the box-cars. To say those Indians were coerced into spending their paycheck at those establishments owned by the "slave market" (daily pay office) is an understatement. Paychecks, in reality, were vouchers good only at the slave market's bar. Meal tickets to be used at the company restaurant were handed out. They also took deductions of a generous fee for transportation and lunch money plus two or three nights at their mice, roach, and greyback (body lice) infested flophouse. The idea was to keep the workers broke and owing money so that they were almost forced to come back and continue to work under the aforementioned circumstances. All the daily pay offices tended to operate in this way.

Since most Indians living on Skid Row had no permanent mailing address, the slave-markets, the American Indian Center and, of course, the Indian bars were only too willing to receive and hold checks. Slave markets and bars were more likely to be the mailing addresses because they were within walking distance and checks could be cashed there, especially at the bars where credit was more easily established. Credit or an advance on a veteran's pension check meant that some veterans signed over their checks to the bar owners and began drinking up the next month's check.

A second-hand store on Skid Row catered to the needs of all gandy-dancers. The owner, who was nicknamed Identity Sam, would extend credit and sometimes cash to gandy-dancers who needed only to show railroad identification cards to earn the credit. In addition, Indian gandy-dancers would bring in boots, jackets, and other winter gear such as ill-conditioned shoes, and winter caps for the price of a jug or two.

THE JACK POT

The Jack Pot was often referred to as the "Indian Bar" by Indians and non-Indians alike. Although the bar had been rumored to be mob controlled, the title to the bar was in the name of the Indian wife who married the Italian owner.

The Jack Pot was known as a place where you could get hustled, jack-rolled, beaten, and thrown bodily out in the street. However, the Jack Pot also had its good points. It was relatively safe for non-Indians and Indians alike if they were known by the Jack Pot crowd. Since most of the Indians who frequented the Jack Pot worked out of Readymen or out of another of the many daily pay offices on Skid Row, they would buy jugs and just hang out at the tables until closing time. Some of the positive things about this bar were that free hot dogs and ham sandwiches were served to all steady customers and complete turkey or chicken dinners were also served on special holidays such as Christmas, Thanksgiving, and Easter Sunday.

As a come-on, a raffle ticket was given for every drink purchased at the bar and winning tickets were worth four dollars at the 9:00 P.M. and 11:00 P.M. drawings. The final drawing was held at 2:00 A.M., closing time. The winning prize was a "take-home half pint" and the lucky winner would jokingly be accused of being in cahoots with the bar owner. A half pint would not last in the bottle gang that would form shortly after closing time. After closing was also a time to be on the lookout for Tuttle and Augie in the police "bum wagon." The police knew most of the heavy drinkers and considered them relatively harmless. If you were caught with a jug, they would direct you to go off the main drag, to get out of sight, and to finish the bottle. Don Eagle, an Indian who took the name of a famous wrestler, would jokingly challenge the detectives to a wrestling match. They would decline, often with a chuckle.

A favorite watering hole of the gandy-dancers, complete with sleeping quarters, was a flophouse located near Identity Sam's store. The bar stools were the only seating available. With the exception of an old juke box, the floor was bare of any of the furniture usually present in Skid Row watering holes. Gallon jugs of wine were placed at intervals on the floor by the gandy-dancers, who gathered there to rehash and trade tall tales about working and living in the different towns and states. It seemed natural to focus in on the drinking environment in some of the small towns where local police might have been especially tough on gandy-dancers. The gandy-dancers were a generous lot: anyone from the street was welcome to take a drink from the jugs on the floor. It was like an open house. An Indian could walk in, take a drink from each of the may jugs on the floor, double clutch on the jug located nearest the Indian gandy-dancers, and walk out the lobby door stoned drunk. The unwritten rule was one from each jug unless you were invited to stick around.

THE BOTTLE GANG

Indians living on Skid Row would continue to develop survival skills and use the resources available in the Skid Row environment. Scoring a jug was a shared goal. A few of the hard-core Indian Skid Row residents would tell you that activities leading up to the scoring of a jug could be almost fun. Three Indians would team up to put into practice the skills that lead up to scoring a jug. One would act as a lookout for the "Dicks" (detectives) in the chosen area, while two others would each take one side of the street and begin to "put the hammer" on every passerby. The slogan was "Don't let anyone pass you by." These two panhandlers competed with one another to see who had the most change at the end of the run. After a three-way split of the change, the Indians would retire to an isolated location, usually a doorway, an alley, or an abandoned building, with a jug. After cracking the bottle of white port and tossing a capful out with

"Here's one for the boys," the drinking would begin. The ritual was common to all drinking Indians living on Skid Row, in respect of those who had passed away.

The drinking of this first jug would begin, and accounts of the success and responses of some of the would-be victims of "the hammer" (panhandling) were recalled with humor. One of the Indians could scarcely believe that a very pretty young woman at a bus stop, despite his smelly, dusty, moldy appearance, gave him a whole five dollar bill, just for the asking. He continued, "I must have really looked pitiful." The joking response, "I wouldn't want to be seen in public with you," was returned from others in the group. There were different styles of putting the hammer on people. One Indian may begin his mission with "Kind sir, can you help out a poor Sioux Indian from South Dakota, trying to get back to the reservation?" This Indian was Winnebago, but was trying, with humor, to put his Sioux buddy on the spot.

The drinking continued with more teasing, laughter and joking, and the stories were becoming taller and taller as one Indian would comment, "The bullshit is getting deeper." After the last round, when the "dead solider" (empty jug) was put to rest, Bull Dog was chosen to make the new run and a parting shot from the other two might be, "Don't let any double-clutchers see you come back here." A double-clutcher was a person who would tip the jug up and drink double, sometimes triple his share of the wine. A double-clutcher was an undesirable member of a bottle gang: his turn was usually last.

Some Indians should be given equal billing with bloodhounds. Whether or not it was a keen sense of smell or their intuitions, these Indians seemed to follow their noses to the most isolated and hidden spots where jugs were present and were being passed around by the bottle gang. Such a person may not have been fully welcome, but was given his turn at the jug. Meanwhile, Bull Dog had returned from making the run. He had been gone beyond reasonable time, or so the other two thought. They had begun to wonder whether Bull Dog had "gone South" (deliberately failed to return to the group). The few Indians who were prone to going South were shunned by all drinking Indians on Skid Row.

Spending the night on Skid Row

At 2:00 a.m. closing time, some Indians would move to a 4:00 a.m. bar to continue drinking. A few would "carry the stick" (walk the street all night). Others would go to favorite places to sleep such as "the Bird Brothers' Hole" under Sangamon Bridge, the parking lot behind the Merchandise Mart, "Indian Docks" near Milwaukee and Des Plaines, or under a huge railroad bridge beneath Halsted, Hubbard, and Green Streets, or in the bushes by the expressways. The Indians usually traveled in twos or threes, as there was a lot of competition for spots to sleep. It was also necessary to take a couple of jugs for the morning after, although a very few Indians would resist taking a drink at night when it was so readily available.

"Indian Docks" was the most popular choice for many Native Americans simply because it was so difficult to climb the steep hill from Milwaukee Avenue near Des Plaines Street to get to the Dock that it was relatively safe from police and other intruders. It was also clean, free of rats, and a good place either to sober up or to continue drinking. It was so difficult to climb up this steep hill that one or two of the Indians who were too drunk to make the climb had to have help. Yes, when the going gets rough, Native Americans living on Skid Row would lend a helping hand, especially if they were drinking partners.

For the most part, all Indians living on Skid Row were close, especially those within a particular drinking group. They tended to help each other out when the need arose. A good example of this cooperation was among the group of Indians who resided under the railroad bridge. Each Indian seemed to know exactly what his task was and would carry it out without thinking twice about it. One Indian would make a sweep of the alleys near factories and along the railroads for firewood. Two or three of the boys would go to the market to forage for vegetables and soup bones. Another one would assign himself the task of hauling the water needed for the soup pot. The soup pot in use was an old five gallon lard can. Many had experienced the hobo jungles throughout the United States and learned from them. Since this railroad bridge was a huge, semi-enclosed structure, there were three other ethnic groups represented here, including a Mexican Indian group, four or five African-Americans and a group of whites. Each group had their own spot or territory staked out with the usual overcoats, blankets and cooking pot. True to the old saying about "honesty among thieves," these drunks respected each other's camps and would not intrude on one another unless they were invited to partake in the soup or to have a drink of wine. They did not steal from each other when one or more of the groups were out for the day.

Another, more exclusive group of Indians hung out east of the expressway near the Harbor Light Salvation Army. These Indians did not work out of any daily pay office but preferred to be "pieced off" by the few from their group who were on the Salvation Army's work program for alcoholics. These few Indians were paid wages by the work programs set up by the Salvation Army. They would take turns getting on the work program and then would share the wages. Other Indians who hung out west of the expressway were not welcomed by this "Sally bunch." They even had their own spot to sleep, drink, or just hang out. It was under the Lake Street Bridge on the east side of the expressway. This spot was neatly arranged with a rug on the dirt floor, well equipped with overcoats and blankets and shelves made from cardboard boxes. One Indian woman and

her younger brother shared this living arrangement as well as the drinking and scouring of jugs. She later died of cirrhosis of the liver and other
physical ailments directly attributed to the drinking environment and
lifestyles.

Trouble with the Law

Drinking on the street, in alleys or doorways, and being locked up in jail
became the accepted lifestyle on Skid Row for most Indians. Small groups
of Indian men and sometimes women (there were four women on the
street then) could be found on a street corner, in an alley or in a doorway,
passing a jug of wine around and seeming to have a good time. There was
always a lot of laughing and joking among the various tribes of Indians.
This kind of a group was called a "bottle gang" by police, who seemed to
know all the hiding places where Indians would drink. Depending on how
much room was left in the paddy wagon or how the policemen felt that
evening, this so called "bottle gang" would more than likely spend the
night in jail. A female, of course, would be excluded by the police, even
though she would usually just join up with another bottle gang down the
street.

It was not unusual for many of the Indians to get arrested for drinking
on the street or becoming too drunk for their own safety. Police in the
paddy wagons and squad cars, including detectives, knew most of the Indians by name and, if you were a favorite, they would sometimes give you a
bottle that had been confiscated from some poor wino. The Indians also
knew the police by name, shift, and route. They also knew how often the
paddy wagon came around a certain block to a bar or an alley. Each
Policeman had a nickname; such as: Cactus Jack and Hook Nose, Tuttle
and Augie (detectives), Mutt and Jeff.

Police brutality was no stranger to the Indian on Skid Row. The most
notorious of the pairs were Cactus Jack and Hook Nose. These two
policemen were the most feared not only by the Indians but by all Skid
Row residents because they seemed to take delight in throwing drunks
headfirst into the paddy wagon after beating them with their nightsticks.
Over the years, a few of the Indians had suffered a broken rib or two. Cactus Jack, especially, seemed to enjoy giving the arrested Indian a couple of
whacks alongside of the head as he was being processed for the Drunk
Tank at the station.

Drunk tank, bull pen, cells, steel bunks, and baloney sandwiches were
all terms that were all too common for Indians living on Skid Row. Over
time, many of us have lost count of the number of times we had been
arrested for being intoxicated. For Indians on Skid Row, going to jail was
an accepted part of life. Drunk tanks and the smaller cells were not too
bad to lie down in during the early part of the evening, but space became a

problem after closing time for the bars on the streets. By this time, you were sober enough to realize that you could no longer lie in peace even it was on a cold steel bunk or the cement floor. Incoming drunks were continually being packed into every inch of space in the bull pen and the cells. Some of the drunks would fall down on top of some poor Indian who was trying to sleep.

Once in the tank, a drunk loudly demanded that I move over to make room for him on the floor. I knew that this kind of arrangement was not going to work with a drunk lying there next to me. I was lucky enough to spot a small space underneath one of the steel bunks. Because I was slender (probably from malnutrition), I was able to slide under this man's steel bunk for protection from the commotion as incoming drunks jockeyed for a place to sit or to lie down. It was not safe to lie out in the open floor. Some drunk, attempting to reach the one commode or washbasin at the back of the cell, would stagger and sometimes fall on top of the now sober men lying on the floor trying to sleep. It was likely that someone in this crowd would become sick, and while attempting to reach the commode, would spray vomit down on those below. It was now 3:00 A.M. and the turnkey (policemen in charge of the drunk tank) would come around to chase everyone into the bull pen. The smaller cells had to be emptied out so that they could be swept, mopped, and hosed down for later use. When the cells became full again, the vicious cycle would continue. Sometimes it was a merciful one for the chronically addicted Indian drunk, especially when it as extremely cold outside. He was safer in jail.

Meanwhile the bull pen was packed so tightly we felt like sardines. At 3:00 A.M. the only prisoners who were still locked up in two or three of the smaller calls were the more serious offenders, who would be taken to court at 26th Street and California at 5:00 A.M. These prisoners were usually charged with: jack-rolling (strong-arm robbery), picking pockets, stealing cars, burglary, and armed holdups at taverns. With a few exceptions, Indians were rarely charged with any of these offenses.

Despite the hangovers, the Indians in the crowded bull pen had maneuvered themselves into a space and were having animated conversation, joking, teasing, and laughing among themselves. As usual, the topic of conversion wasthe jug and if it would be wise to volunteer for janitorial duty at the jail on Monroe and Racine. To work as a janitor meant that no one would be allowed to leave the building until court was terminated upstairs. Sometimes, it was a good idea to volunteer for duty as a janitor because volunteers did not go before the judge. For example, if you showed up in court with a black eye, the judge might give you ten, twenty, or thirty days out in the House of Correction. It was also a good idea to volunteer as janitor because the bull pen became almost intolerable. The odor of unwashed bodies, vomit, urine, and a mixture of stale beer and wine fouled what little was left of the precious air. Arguments and fighting among the drunks sometimes broke out over a tiny space to sit or stand in, or everyone one was trying to get far away from some wino who was painstakingly picking greybacks (body lice) off his vomit-stained shirt or jacket.

The turnkey would call for volunteers to pass out the baloney sandwiches and hot, strong black coffee. He had his favorites, including a few of the Indians, whom he would then let out of the bull pen to begin sweeping down empty cells, cells that still had the signs of drunks spending an uncomfortable night, especially when eight or nine drunks had been packed into two-man cells. After sweeping the empty cells, the Indian volunteers were more or less free to wander around the cell blocks. More baloney sandwiches and coffee were available if you were hungry, but it was very difficult to hold down water, much less a baloney sandwich, when you had a hangover.

It was then time for the sick, sorry, and sober drunks from the bull pens to be sent upstairs to go before the judge. Most judges who sat on the drunk court bench were well known by the Indians and vice versa. The judge would most likely address each Indian with, "Chief, what name are you using this morning? Is it Rainwater or Santa Maria?" Even after years of going up in front of Judge Stein, Kelly, or O'Malley, for example, the drunken Native Americans would use one or more fictitious names of well-known Indians of the past (Crazy Horse, Don Eagle, or Rainwater). The judges were not fooled but would play along. While courtroom proceedings were going on, the Indian volunteer janitors were escorted downstairs to the basement to the police locker rooms to remedy those hangovers. A couple of the more trustworthy Indian drunks were sent on a "run" to Vogt's Wine Shop, which was located around the corner from the police station at Monroe and Racine, to bring back half a gallon of wine. Now the unpleasant task of trying to hold down the first drink became a must for everyone in the group. It was especially difficult when shaking badly because of withdrawal from the drug alcohol. More alcohol was the remedy for that hangover, and the hangover was routinely accepted as a part of the drinking environment by Native Americans living on Skid Row.

Let us not forget about the Native Americans who had elected to go before the presiding judge at Drunk Court. It had been a long night for some of these people, especially if they had been picked up earlier in the evening. The call to the stand before the judge could also be a difficult time. It was not unusual for one or two of these hangover Indians to pull a wing-ding (to have an alcoholic seizure) in front of the judge. When this happens, the seizure victim is a sure bet to be sentenced for a ten day stretch out at the House of Corrections. Cermack Hospital was out there, and the judges who were increasingly aware of alcoholism would ask those with the shakes if they needed to go to the hospital. Others, with mild to moderate hangovers, would be directed to an "A.A." person who was present at the Court session. This "A.A." person was a detective who would take the hungover Indian to his office and give him his medicine (wine or whiskey) to calm him down. There was also a social worker available to those who had had their shoes stolen or were badly in need of a clean shirt. A representative from the Salvation Army (Harbor Light) would hand each one of the now sober men a breakfast ticket that was good for a bowl of oatmeal, a roll, and coffee at the Harbor Light Center.

Since Drunk Court has been cleared of all who were deemed well enough to walk out by the judge, the Indian janitors had the final chore of sweeping and mopping all the second floor, including the holding pen, which was located adjacent to the courtroom. After helping to knock out a half gallon of wine while waiting in the basement, they felt more than ready to complete this final chore and then head to Vogt's for a jug. Vogt's Wine Shop, which was located at 1100 West Adams Street, was a large, family owned liquor store that catered mostly to small tavern operators. The store was half a block long and half a block wide with three warehouses located in the same building. Nearly all the Indians, after being turned loose by the judge, would immediately head to Vogt's, where a quart of cheap wine might have cost fifty cents, a price far out of reach for Indians who have just gotten out of jail, so they might have to settle for a "flat one," a pint. In anticipation of this moment, the Indians had often counted their change and chipped in while still locked up in the cells the previous night. The Indians who were lucky enough to somehow avoid going to jail would come to Vogt's to take advantage of specials and sales. Where else could you buy a fifth of Golden Spur, 21 percent volume, for fifty cents?

Passing around the Golden Spur, the Indians would hang together in a large group, seemingly high in spirits (alcohol induced). There would be three distinct smaller groups within the larger one. The first would be the ones who did not spend the night in jail; the second, the ones who were processed through the court system; the third, the janitors who were well on their way to another drunken episode. It was clearly understood as an unwritten rule that each smaller group member who had chipped in would share the jug with only his own group. All Native Americans went through a ritual when cracking a jug (opening a bottle). When cracking a jug, you should hold the jug firmly in one hand, at a 45 degree angle, and whack the bottom sharply with the heel of the hand in order to jar the seal loose. The cap of the jug was then filled with some of the precious wine and tossed out in the name of former drinking friends who had passed on.

After all means of scoring another jug were exhausted, those Indians who were still relatively sober will go to the Readymen office to try get a work ticket for night work. Others would hang around the store to hustle customers (tavern owners). Mr. Vogt would allow a select few of the Indians to help customers load their cars or trucks for tips. Like the police, the customers also knew the Indians by name and were sometime generous to a fault with their tips. (Remember that a fifth of Golden Spur costs only fifty cents.) Each Indian hustler would make five or ten dollars in two or three hours.

This entire scenario would be repeated almost every day by Indians who gathered at Vogt's not only to score jugs but to "shoot the bull." Shooting the bull would involve conversations about how and where each tramp (Indians would not allow themselves to be called bums) survived the night. Stories were told, for example, about who had been thrown out of the Jack Pot for bringing a foreign jug into the bar. Management demanded that you buy your jugs in the bar you visited. Although opening a bottle of wine in the bar might have been against the law, bartenders seemed to encourage Indians, at least those who could afford it, to buy jugs, sit at a table, and drink until closing time at 2:00 A.M. Over the years, many Indians died while drinking and passing out at those tables. No one at the bar was really surprised when John or Jane Doe, from all appearances sleeping it off, in reality had died from alcoholism.

Escaping from the Skid Row lifestyle

The Salvation Army and other similar treatment programs, including "doing time" out at the House of Corrections, temporarily prolonged the lives of most of the Indians living on Skid Row. Today, however, this writer, who lived on Skid Row for approximately seventeen years, cannot count more than five survivors from that era. Because of excessive drinking, nutritional deficit, and the lack of proper rest, the resistance of the body to many kinds of diseases (tuberculosis, cirrhosis, and others) was lowered.

The Salvation Army had a clinic that took care of the health needs of nearly all the Indians living on Skid Row. A volunteer doctor, two or three nurses, and a paid health advocate attended to the health needs of all Skid Row residents. The health advocate (called Lacy) was the favorite of the Indians who, more often than not, would ask to see Lacy when seeking medical attention for street-related combat wounds. Since a chest x-ray was routine when visiting the clinic, those Indians with active tuberculosis were usually tracked down by the court system, word was sent out through the Indian grapevine on the street, or they were caught at the next visit to the clinic and taken to the Municipal Tuberculosis Sanitarium located on North Pulaski Road. With the development of more advanced tuberculosis medications in the 1960's, it was no longer necessary to be confined to a sanitarium for more than two months, depending on the severity of the case. However, Indians did not like to be confined in a hospital setting and, as a result, would overstay passes. An immediate pickup order was then sent out by the City Board of Health, and those Indians unlucky enough to show up before the judge at Chicago Avenue or Monroe and Racine Drunk Court would be held for transfer back to the tuberculosis sanitarium. Since Skid Row was home to nearly all Indians at the sanitarium, they would invariably go back to Madison Street to continue the former, well-developed lifestyle. They would continue to score jugs, forego proper nutrition, and sleep out under bridges, at Indian docks or in the "hole."

After being discharged from the sanitarium, former patients were required to visit a tuberculosis clinic at Ogden and Taylor Streets and to continue with medications for up to two years as part of the aftercare plan. An important past of the aftercare plan was abstinence, preferably total from all drinking of alcohol. Medications would be rendered useless by the alcohol. Abstention was the most difficult part of the aftercare plan for the Indians living on Skid Row, as their whole lifestyle seemed to revolve around drinking. For the most part, former tuberculosis patients who were relatively successful in completing two years of aftercare would fall off the wagon later from the debilitating disease of alcoholism.

CONCLUSION: DEVELOPMENT OF SKID ROW AND DISPLACEMENT OF SKID ROW RESIDENTS

The Skid Row that I was introduced to as I stepped out of the Northwestern Train depot in October, 1957, has long since been torn down. Economic development, urban renewal, and demolition of favorite watering holes came slowly at first. Since the flophouses were owned by millionaires, they were the first to go. Parking lots and corporate businesses began to spring up on the now-empty lots along Skid Row. By 1977, some stretches of Skid Row resembled the prairie found in my home state of South Dakota. The Indians on Skid Row appeared to be undaunted by all this activity by the now-familiar wrecking ball. Bottle gangs no longer had to go to jail for drunkenness. Instead, they would be transported by bum wagons to Haymarket House, a detox center that began operating in June, 1976. Treatment for alcoholism, not jail, was advocated by American Medical Association. Readymen and other daily pay offices continued to be used as before, detox centers became places to sleep one off, or you could just walk out after the intake process had been completed. By the 1980s, Madison Street had almost ceased to exist as a Skid Row, because of the declining population and urban renewal.

It would be unfair to say "Indians tend to drink to excess to drown any or all problems." After all, the statistics tell us that only about five or six percent of all alcoholics end up on the skids. Today, a small percentage of Indians who had been former residents of Skid Row survived and are now leading useful lives. There are several single Indians and families who have made it to retirement or are leading useful and successful lives after coming to Chicago on Relocation. Others have returned to their reservations.

Single men were mobile and able to go anywhere, especially after layoffs and terminations from employment.

After the many years of living and interacting with Native Americans on Skid Row, I have found that most were comfortable with the environment and lifestyle. Prices on Skid Row were within the reach of a Readymen paycheck. Despite what seemed to be a life of hardship, the tragic deaths of drinking companions, "carrying the stick" (staying on the street all night) and standing in souplines, Skid Row was a sort of home to many Indians who had originally come to Chicago on the infamous federal Relocation program.

This article adapted from the Author's NAES College field project.

Edward E. Goodvoice,
as told to Nora Lloyd

Excerpt from a Photoessay on Chicago Elders

FAMILY LIFE AT ROSEBUD

I was told that since my parents lived approximately mile from the main house, my grandmother, as I was told, took myself and my first cousin and raised both of us. So I grew up with my grandmother.

There were really only two of us—my sister and myself. She's two years younger than I am. She lived with my parents, while my mother's sister's daughter and I were raised by my grandmother, so we lived with her. Those were the days when they had extended families in close proximity.

My grandfather was self-educated so . . . he served as a part-time judge on the reservation. So he spoke fluent English.

My grandmother's sister, who was my great aunt, also had a boy my age. And I can remember when we were really small, we danced at the powwows and we had dance outfits that were all handmade: eagle feathers and beadwork that was done by my grandmother.

I stayed with her [grandmother] until I was about nine years old and then I went to a boarding school because things were starting to become a little bit tough in terms of economics. So my mother decided that I would go to boarding school. So my sister and I ended up in a mission school on Rosebud Reservation. A Catholic mission—St. Francis.

LEARNING ABOUT THE RELOCATION PROGRAM

I decided this was my chance to see if I could do something with my life.

The office was located on the reservation and as a matter of fact it was located in the agency's offices. And I just heard that people go there if they want to leave the reservation and go out to the city looking for a job. In any case, I already knew about Relocation because when I was still in the service they had one in Los Angeles. So I knew what they do. To me it sounded like a pretty good deal because here were people who were gonna

Portrait of Ed Goodvoice, courtesy of Nora Lloyd.

pay for your transportation to a large city anywhere in the United States and help you find a job, pay your rent, and transportation until you got your first paycheck. And I thought that was a pretty good deal.

I thought that I wouldn't stay on the reservation after I got out of the service. And I was happy I did, as one day I would go back to college because I dropped out in the first year. I did go back, many years later.

Debra Valentino

The History of the American
Indian Center Princess

The American Indian Center of Chicago is the oldest urban Indian center in the country. During the Relocation era, a group of Indians and non-Indians who called themselves the Citizens Committee laid the groundwork for the organization: the doors of the old building at 411 North La Salle Street opened on November 1, 1953. The first Director of the Center was Thomas Segundo (Papago); the Center board was elected from the membership of the Center and included: John Willard, president; Babe Begay (Navajo), vice-president; Eli Powless (Oneida), treasurer; Felix Chico (Papago); Daniel Glozne (Cherokee); Hiawatha Hood (Yavapai); Mrs. Elmer B. Luckow (non-Indian); and Ernest Naquayouma (Hopi). For nearly half a century, the American Indian Center has been the most prominent organization in the Chicago Indian community. It has been a meeting place, a place for ceremony and celebration, a place for sports and for academic enrichment, and a place for cultural learning and expression. It has been the point of contact for Indians new to the city and for non-Indians in the city to connect with the Indian community.

For most of those almost 50 years, the annual American Indian Center powwow has brought Indian people from all the different tribal groups in the Chicago area together to renew old friendships and make new ones, share stories, develop common activities and express good feelings in songs and dances. Indian people came to Chicago from as many as 120 different tribal groups and from every area of the country: some came on the Relocation program, some came independently; some came as part of the war effort; some to find stable employment; some had been here long before the war. Their reservations and their life experiences varied tremendously, yet they consistently sought the company of other Indian people. The Indian Center powwow is and has, since its inception, been a critical event in the creation of community among the various Indian people in Chicago, and it occupies a central role in the community oral history.

The American Indian Center powwow has changed and grown a lot over its forty-three year history. As with other powwows around the country, today, it follows the structure, format, and etiquette that have evolved over time in powwows throughout Indian Country. The Grand Entry of dancers is always led by veterans bearing the flags (the American flag, a POW flag, and an American Indian eagle staff are usually present). As the dancers enter the arena according to their category of dance/outfit, under the direction of the arena director, they are led by "Royalty," which includes the local Princess and any visiting Princesses from other communities and organizations. As a "Contest powwow," the American Indian Center powwow encourages the best dancers and drummers from North America to participate and compete: it also, then, provides them the experience of meeting other dancers and of becoming familiar with the Indian community in Chicago. Arts and crafts vendors, now part of most contest powwows, arrive from around the country to display, sell, and trade items from throughout the continent.

The modern powwow has a very long history in Indian communities, but the powwow in its modern form took shape at about the same time that the Indian Center was established. In the new urban Indian communities, especially, powwows became increasingly important at this time. The concept of the Indian "Princess" also has a very long history in Indian communities, and its modern form also emerged in the 1950s in the post-war period.

The term "Princess" did not come from Indian cultures: use of the term causes some people to think that the "Princess" is a non-Indian idea, adopted from some kind of combination of Girl Scout roles and beauty pageants. The notion of the "Indian Princess," popularized in *Peter Pan*, for example, is certainly not Indian. In the Chicago Indian community, use of the term "Princess" seems to be fairly recent, though the practice itself began at about the same time as the American Indian Center. The first women who represented the Indian Center in the role now called "Princess" were referred to simply as "Miss Indian Chicago." In general, when royalty are introduced at powwows, they are not introduced as "Princess so and so," but, rather, as "Miss." One Chicago elder explained that the term "Princess" was probably adopted when a "Junior Princess" joined "Miss Indian Chicago" sometime in the early 1980s: Serina Yellow Bank may have been the first Junior Princess in 1981–82. The label "Princess" is offensive to some Indians: one member of the Chicago Indian community who responded to a questionnaire suggested that it would be a good idea if the label "Princess" was just dropped. This would avoid confusion with negative stereotypes. While non-Indian pageants, contests, and organizations have certainly influenced Indian practice, the selection of a young woman as a representative of the group and a model for children and for other young women, has a long *Indian* history. The "Princess" label was borrowed, but the Indian tradition remains.

The results of a questionnaire handed out to 100 Indian community members confirm the interpretation of the "Princess" as following a different history and having a different meaning from a beauty pageant. In fact, beauty pageant–type beauty doesn't seem to have much at all to do with the selection of Miss Indian Chicago. Asked what an Indian Center Princess should represent, community members responded with comments such as "role model," "spokesperson," "community volunteer," "represents the idea of a strong proud people and a cohesive community," "stands up for the highest moral life," "awareness of Indian history." There was no mention of the way she looks in a bathing suit or, for that matter, which Girl Scout troop she belongs to! The Princess role was seen as a great opportunity and a great honor for the young woman selected. Through the fundraising efforts of the Princess Selection Committee, the Princess travels around the country, representing the Chicago Indian community in powwows, "ready to dance and be visible" as one respondent remarked.

Traditional military societies on the Plains, where much of powwow tradition comes from, selected a "sister," a virtuous young woman to encourage and to represent them, to remind them of the community they protected and give them courage to do what needed to be done. This young woman was always a virgin, and required to remain a virgin as long as she occupied the role in the military society. She was from a good family and had lived in a good way; she had a good reputation and was an honorable, generous person. She learned the specific traditions of the society and she had an important role in their ceremonies. This was a position of great honor, and *this* is the historical model for the modern-day Princess.

In the 1950s , for various reasons, including the inter-tribal experience during World War II and Relocation, national, inter-tribal organizations began to develop. In particular, the development of the National Congress of American Indians marked an important point in inter-tribal Indian history. At this point, tribes and communities around the country began to think about representing themselves at inter-tribal gatherings and deliberations. This was also the time when the first young woman was selected to travel to other Indian communities and events, representing the Chicago Indian community. This young woman also represented the American Indian community within the city of Chicago itself, raising that awareness of a community that most Chicagoans did not know existed. Large urban Indian communities were also not recognized by the federal government. By sending a representative of Chicago to inter-tribal powwows and gatherings around the country, the Indian people of Chicago established themselves as a community among other Indian communities, not just an accidental grouping of Indian people in an urban area where they were not expected to continue to be *Indian*.

Oral history in the community places the origin of Miss Indian Chicago selection in 1952, at the old building on LaSalle Street. Documentary history confirms this, as BIA records indicate the selection of a young woman representative by the American Indian Club during the Christmas get-together in 1952. At the same get-together, plans for the New Year's powwow were discussed, and the newly chosen representative would presumably have a role in that powwow. Ben Bearskin Sr. is recognized in this document as playing a central role in developing the powwow and associated activities through the Intertribal Council and the American Indian Club, both of which came before the American Indian Center and are part of its history. He was involved in starting a dance troupe through these early associations, and, later, he helped to start a drum group as well. In the late 1940s, it seems that informal social dances were held at a hall on Halsted Street that was rented for that purpose. These dances were primarily opportunities to celebrate and share tribal ways in the urban area: dancers from different tribes demonstrated social dances from their home communities. There is no record of any "Miss Indian Chicago" at these early get-togethers: there is no record of any of the associated activities of contemporary powwows such as Give Aways or Memorials, either, and vendors were apparently not part of the event. Such dances were the beginnings of powwow in Chicago, but they were quite different from powwows today.

Before there was an American Indian Center, the American Indian Club sponsored a very successful powwow on Halloween, 1952. Around Christmastime the same year, members of the American Indian Club, under the leadership of Ben Bearskin, had a get-together at which they planned for the 1953 Halloween event. According to the newsletter of the Chicago office of the Bureau of Indian Affairs, a young woman representative of the community was selected at this meeting, though her role and responsibilities were not described. After the formation of the Indian Center itself, the first public fundraiser event was held in February, 1954. It was described in the newsletter of the Chicago BIA office as a "benefit bazaar." On April 20th of the same year, the first American Indian Center powwow was held in the Oak Park High School. The powwow is also described in the BIA newsletter (vol. I, no. 9), but there is no mention of any "Miss Indian Chicago" in either of these events, although both would have been appropriate venues for her. So, while the "Miss Indian Chicago" or "Princess" notion has been around in the community since the early 1950s, which is about the same time it was emerging elsewhere in the country, there is no clear documentary record of a "Miss American Indian Center" Princess specifically at this time.

The oral history is also somewhat spotty. While there is a strong feeling about and pretty good oral history concerning "Miss Indian Chicago" in the early years, today, community knowledge about Miss American Indian Center in the past fifteen or twenty years is pretty slim. When there is some published record, it is not always accurate according to those who were involved. At some point in the 1980s, probably in response to developments elsewhere in Indian Country (including the Miss Indian World competition), a Junior "Miss Indian Chicago" tradition began, and the "Princess" label became more common. Today, the one "Princess" has become four: there is now a Miss Indian Chicago, a Junior Miss, and two Tiny Tot Princesses.

Today, Paula Murray is Miss Indian Chicago and Sylvia Dane is the Junior Princess. It is likely that there are many members of the community who do not know who their representatives are. My 1995 survey of community members revealed that, of the 100 respondents (representing 23 different tribes, with 66 females and 34 males from various age groups), 45 could not name a single one of the four princesses for that year. Eighteen respondents could name 1; 8 could name 2; 13 could name 3; and only 12 of the 100 knew all four. It is clear that knowledge of the Princess selection and history is lacking. Although I have interviewed many people and searched through the American Indian Center records, it has been virtually impossible even to develop a list of Princesses in the years since 1954. There are bits and pieces of oral history: some remember Norma Jean Bearskin as the second "Miss Indian Chicago," and first runner-up in "Miss Indian World;" some remember Rosemary Cornelius as the 1959–60 Princess, for example, while few remember who served in the 1970s. It is very hard to generate an acceptable list of past representatives. A past director of the Center may have assembled a list of past "Princesses," but no one knows what happened to the list. This all has something to do with what was happening in the community in general in the different time periods; but overall, there is a lack of knowledge about the Princess.

I believe it is important for the Princess history to be known and told, and for community members, especially the young girls, to become more aware of the Princess as a role model and representative. There is no written or photographic record of the girls who served as AIC Princess, and there is no written policy regarding the selection process or oversight of Princess activities during the year of her reign. The lack of such history and guidelines causes problems. For example, when I served as a volunteer on the Indian Center powwow committee in 1994, it became necessary to take disciplinary action in regard to the reigning Princess. I felt uncomfortable about the process because there was no policy and there were no guidelines to help us figure out what to do. The next year, I was asked to be on the selection committee and I still felt unprepared for the responsibility: I did not know what questions to ask or how to give points to the applicants. There were five women on the selection committee that year, but there was no one with any real experience of the process. It seems that the criteria and the questions and the process itself are flexible and change with the different powwow committees. This may well be the best approach, but it makes knowing the history that much more important, so that committee members have a framework to work from. In my own experience, I wished I had been more knowledgeable and that the whole process had been clearer to me.

Additionally, the Princess Committee has a continuing role throughout the year: it is not just about the selection of the Princess. It is up to the women on the committee to chaperone the girls at the various events, to arrange for their appearance at events around the country, and to raise the funds to support their travel to those events. The committee must include at least one elder, because these women are also responsible for educating the girls in the history and traditions of their community, and for helping them to stay on the right path. The committee helps to ensure that the Princess(es) are good role models in the community and good representatives outside of the community.

The Committee and the families of the princesses cooperate in supporting the girls. The families need to understand that their daughters need to be present at many community events and at powwows around the area. They will give away to honor their daughters; they must be ready to travel to support their daughters; they need to prepare their outfits and continue to repair and improve them. They need to instruct their daughters on proper behavior and to teach them about their family and community history. Most importantly, they need to provide moral support and teachings. It is a lot of work, a year of commitment and responsibility for everyone, not just for the girls who are chosen. Like Princess Selection Committees, the families of the girls who run for Princess often are not aware of their roles and responsibilities.

Because "Miss Indian Chicago" represents the community and because the history and knowledge of the position is important in the community, I hope that this article will encourage past Princesses and their families, Selection Committee members, and others who are knowledgeable about the history of the American Indian Center Princess to share what they know so that a history, written, oral or both, can be developed to give some context and direction to present and future Princess selection, oversight and activities. I plan to develop a partial list of Princesses and circulate it in the community for additions and corrections. Where there is disagreement, I will point it out but not make any decision concerning which view is correct.

The American Indian Center Princess, "Miss Indian Chicago," as a representative and as a role model can have a very important influence on the Chicago Indian community, especially on the young women of the community. The Princess attends all Chicago powwows, not just the annual Indian Center powwow: she is present at the smallest fund-raising powwows, the powwows celebrating events or accomplishments of community members, and the powwows at local schools as well as at the large, annual Indian Center powwow. She helps to ensure the success of a powwow, large or small, indoor or outdoor, traditional or competitive. She travels outside of Chicago to powwows around the country, on reservations and in other urban areas: she connects participants in those other powwows to their friends and relatives in Chicago and she carries greetings and good feelings from those powwows back to the city. Traveling between city and reservation, she exemplifies the inter-tribal nature of Indian life today, representing an urban, inter-tribal community, while bringing specific pride to her own family and tribe.

Indians have always honored and respected all women. It is possible that the Princess idea may be a contemporary way for us to express this age-old respect. I feel that urban environments put pressure on tribal traditions and that we need to find appropriate ways to maintain tribal values in the contemporary world. Our children need to learn these values, and the Princess idea might help us to instill in them those good values and teachings, if we handle it well.

Natalia Wilson

The Chicago Indian Village, 1970

"I wonder what President Nixon will say about us with his forked tongue—
and the mayor. I wonder if they will say anything about us."
— Carol Warrington, *The Chicago Daily News*, June 14, 1971

INTRODUCTION

On May 5, 1970, Carol Warrington (Menominee) and her six children
were evicted from their second-floor apartment at 3717 Seminary Avenue
for withholding rent for seven months in protest of the poor condition of
her apartment. A tipi provided by Chicago's American Indian Center was
set up on a tract of land across the street from Carol Warrington's former
apartment, behind Wrigley Field. Soon additional pup tents were set up,
and other Indians moved in. Originally the newspapers called it the "little Alcatraz movement," referring to the Indian occupation of Alcatraz
which began the previous November, but soon the Chicago occupation
would be known by another name, the Chicago Indian Village.

The Village was started in support of Ms. Warrington, but it came to
symbolize something bigger: the need for adequate housing for all American Indians in the city, of which Carol Warrington was but one of the
many in need. Under the leadership of Mike Chosa (Ojibway), the Chicago Indian Village would remain behind Wrigley Field for the next three
months before beginning a journey around Chicago and the suburbs for
the next two years to publicize demands for better housing, education,
training, and jobs for Chicago's Indian community.

Although the story of the Chicago Indian Village (CIV) begins May 5,
1970, behind Wrigley Field, its history begins in the 1950s when the federal government put the policies of Termination and Relocation into
effect. In order to understand the reasons for the CIV's demands, one
must understand the circumstances under which Indians came back to
Chicago in the first place.

POLICIES FOR ASSIMILATION

From the beginning of federal-Indian relations, the federal government has looked for ways to get out of "the Indian Business." During the economic recession and World War II the federal government turned its attention to other matters, and the reform years of John Collier, commissioner of the Bureau of Indian Affairs (BIA), were over. After World War II the federal government moved to take away the trust status of Native American tribes and their land. The first tribes targeted for this "Termination" were those who were judged to be ready to live in white society. On August 1, 1953, congress enacted House Concurrent Resolution 108, which began the process of Termination. At the same time a federal Relocation program, which encouraged Indians to move to urban areas, had already begun.

By 1956 there were already 5,000 Native Americans living in Chicago thanks to Relocation, according to the Chicago *Sun-Times*, coming in at the rate of 100 a month. It announced that:

> Chicago's first inhabitants—the Indians—are moving back. Chippewas, Sioux, Potawatomies and members of some 60 other tribes are migrating here at the rate of 100 a month. A controversial relocation program of the federal government has pushed the city's Indian population to nearly 5000. (Chicago *Sun-Times*, March 22. 1956)

Unfortunately, relocation served to take American Indians from impoverished reservations and situated them in impoverished city neighborhoods. A *Sun-Times* headline on March 22, 1956 reads: "Indians Move Here At U.S. Urging, Slums Rob Many Of Their Dreams." The Indians relocated to the city were not prepared for city life, the jobs they were given were insecure at best—if they could be found—and the housing was deplorable. It is under these circumstances that Native Americans from different tribes joined together to protest the poor situation they had been put in by the federal government.

Fourteen years later, the *Sun-Times* reflected that "The city's Indian population has swelled the last decade as thousands of Indians have come to the city from reservations after promises of jobs and job training, the latter offered by the Bureau of Indian Affairs" (Chicago *Sun-Times*, June 1, 1970). Twenty years after the beginning of relocation we see the effects of the program on the way the Indians were able to survive in the city, and the need to fight the BIA and the city in order to change the situation.

Like other Native Americans around the country, Chicago's Native American residents used political action to publicize their concerns. On March 24, 1970, the Native American Committee (NAC), with consultant Mike Chosa, conducted a sit-in in the Chicago field office of the Bureau of Indian Affairs (BIA). Steven Fastwolf, the committee spokesman, explained that the sit-in was held as "a show of Indian unity" and support for the eleven Indians arrested at the sit-in in BIA offices in Denver, but that the cause goes deeper: "He [Fastwolf] charged that the bureau has failed to provide adequately for Indians living in urban centers, including Chicago's 15,000 Indian population" (Chicago *Tribune*, March 24, 1970). The group made demands for better education, housing, and hiring of Indians in BIA positions. The 23 protesters were arrested when they refused to leave at the end of the business day.

THE CHICAGO INDIAN VILLAGE

The occupation in support of Carol Warrington began under the leadership of Mike Chosa and the NAC. By June 1, 1970, Mike Chosa, his sister Betty Jack, and the rest of the occupants of the encampment had broken off from the NAC, and were still occupying the tract of land behind Wrigley Field. It would not be too long before the newspapers and Chicago accepted the CIV as its own entity,—not just an extension of Alcatraz—and with this the realization would come that the CIV meant business. Although the occupation began on May 5, real press coverage of the CIV did not begin until June 1, 1970, in the *Sun-Times* and *Today*. But once the press coverage began, it did not stop, thanks to the persistence of Mike Chosa.

The encampment remained on Waveland and Seminary Avenues for three months before it was shut down. The group of people who came to support Carol Warrington had in a few months' time become an organization called the Chicago Indian Village (CIV). The CIV was founded by Mike Chosa after breaking away from the NAC over disagreements concerning future political action. The NAC reportedly wanted to travel to other parts of the country in order to present their case and gain support; Mike Chosa on the other hand felt it was important to stay in Chicago, and not to waste time and money elsewhere. Finally Mike Chosa said "all those who want to stay in Chicago follow me back to the Chicago Indian Village"(Leveen, 1978:108), and the CIV was officially born.

Not all of Chicago's Native American residents supported the CIV occupation, as became evident when two women from the St. Augustine Indian Center presented a petition protesting the CIV. "The women said they have collected the signatures of Indians on the petition that says that Village group and others have presented a 'distorted picture of Indian life and Indian needs in Chicago'" (Chicago *Sun-Times*, June 11, 1970). Their main complaint was that other Indians who had come to Chicago had been able to find good homes and jobs in Chicago, therefore the Village did not speak for *all* the Indians in Chicago. The question of who speaks for all the Indians in Chicago would be a reoccurring problem for Mike Chosa throughout the CIV's existence. Although the CIV broke off from the NAC, the NAC and AIC continued to support the same causes as the CIV. On June 11, 1970 the *Tribune* reported in an article that also reported on the Village behind Wrigley Field that the NAC "last week took over a booth at a convention of social workers in the Conrad Hilton hotel and passed out literature critical of the BIA" (Ibid.).

In the CIV's office on Wilson Avenue in Uptown, Mike Chosa continued to work on new plans for the Village, including plans for economic development. Mike Chosa, Betty Jack, and her two children were living in the CIV office and those who were involved with the Village either lived nearby or stayed at the office on occasion. Much of the time in those first months of 1971 was spent in conventional meetings, with by-laws, minutes, and the rest. In addition to being in charge of the CIV, Chosa was also attending the Saul Alinsky Institute, which gave him access to different organizations, leaders, and ideas for the Village. Mike Chosa's primary concern was economic development and community organization: "Community organization would jar loose the funds for economic development as well as other programs, while economic development would provide an autonomous source of support for community organization and other activities" (Leveen, 118).

During this time Mike Chosa was exploring different job contracts that the CIV could take on in order to raise money. On March 22, 1971, the CIV decided on a landscaping job with the National Accelerator Lab (NAL). On March 30, 1971, the *Daily News* reported: "The contract between the Chicago Indian Village and the laboratory represented the first small victory since members of the organization pitched tents a year ago near Wrigley Field to dramatize their demands. . . . The work will be done by the All-Indian Tree Service, the first of five corporations that the Indian Village planed to organize in various fields of business"(Chicago *Daily News*, March 30, 1971).

The CIV also kept busy staging other protests. In March 22, 1971, on the same day they signed with Argonne (NAL), the CIV sat-in at the Fourth Presbyterian Church with a list of demands, including seed money for an Indian school, a long-term mortgage loan to finance a housing development, and $2,500 in emergency funds to house the nine Indian families residing in the Indian Village. Mike Chosa felt that they were justified in asking the church for funds, since they had been collecting donations ostensibly to aid the Indians in the city.

After the sit-in and an agreement to meet the next day, the CIV took over the Ainsle building on Broadway and Ainslie. The Ainslie building was a Chicago Dwelling Association (CDA) building. In December the CDA had sent out eviction notices, and immediately turned off the heat and electricity. At the meeting with the Chicago Presbytery the next day, they demanded to have the heat turned back on. The heat was turned on sporadically. Their stay in the Ainslie building was a hard one; they were plagued by police brutality and by fire. The CIV stayed in the Ainslie building until the fire on the early morning hours of June 14, 1971, which was believed to have been arson. Many reported having been beaten by the police as they were evacuated from the burning building. "We're going to stay here [Belmont Harbor] forever and a day," said Chosa. 'The people (Indians) have no place to stay. They were burnt out. The fire was set deliberately. We can't stand the police harassment any longer. All we ask for is an even chance"(Chicago *Daily News*, June 14, 1971).

A few hours before dawn on June 14, 1971, twenty Native Americans took over the abandoned Nike missile site on Belmont Harbor. Later, the rest of the inhabitants of the Ainslie building showed up in a van and car with supplies. The take-over of the Nike site was their most effective yet, because this site—unlike the others—still belonged to the federal government. The police could take no action without the permission of federal authorities, much to their frustration. "Immediately after the take-over, police Sgt. Raymond Kunkel of the Town Hall District shouted to the Indians: 'Come out! What is your problem?' An Indian man shouted back: 'The white man is our problem. This is federal property. You have no jurisdiction here.' Then a Native youth added, 'Get off my yard!'"(Ibid.) The Belmont Harbor location also had the advantage of visibility. People who knew nothing of the previous CIV occupations knew about this one, because this occupation they saw—every day on their way to work.

The fact that the site was a military base, and had not yet been turned over to the city, was the advantage that the CIV needed. No longer could the police kick them out; now the feds would have to come to them if they wanted the land back. On June 20, 1971, the CIV met with some government officials, including Illinois Attorney General Jim Thompson. As before, the CIV demanded better housing, preferably on district land. As before, their demands were not met: but unlike before, they were able to get the attention of federal officials, which was no small feat.

On July 1, 1971, the Village was evicted from Belmont Harbor. The eviction began when city workmen, protected by police, began to cut sections of the chain link fence surrounding the missile site. "We're simply returning the site to the use of all the people,' said Park Supt. Thomas Berry." The problem was (or should have been) that the lease did not expire until July 19. "Asked if the city's action to remove the fences was taken with the government's knowledge and if the park district had authority to do so, Thompson said, 'No comment.'"(Chicago *Today*, July 1, 1971) After fights with police, and twelve arrests (including Carol Warrington), the members of the Village marched to Fourth Presbyterian, where they were admitted to the basement, and said they would stay until suitable quarters were found. They were evicted from the church the next day.

The day after they were evicted from Belmont Harbor, and then kicked out of the Fourth Presbyterian Church, the Village made its way to Big Bend lake in a local forest preserve, where they were allowed to stay so long as they did not interfere with other people's use of the park. The preserve provided a place to stay, but little controversy, which Mike knew they needed if they were to stay in the public eye. That is why he picked their next location: another Nike site.

On July 30, 1971, the Chicago Indian Village moved to the abandoned Nike site near Argonne National Laboratories in DuPage County. Once again, confusion arose over what to do with the federal land. The site was owned by the Atomic Energy Commission (AEC), but at the time was still under federal control. Sid Beane, who had recently joined the Village, explained their reasons for taking over this site: "Beane said the move to the federal land would dramatize their efforts to invoke government treaties signed in the last century saying that the abandoned land 'is to be turned over to the Indian people'"(Chicago *Daily News*, July 30, 1971). Although the fight was for better housing, the leaders of the CIV were making a larger demand: for the land itself.

The demand for the land by the CIV leader was strategic. They knew that they would never get the land, even if they could prove that it should go to them according to the treaties. Giving the land to CIV, or to any Indian group, would set a precedent that the federal government felt it could not afford, and would never allow. The CIV's leaders knew this, but they also knew that demanding the land would make the request for better housing seem like smaller potatoes.

On August 11, 1971, CIV said they would leave the AEC base, after their demands for housing, training, and jobs were met. On August 19, CIV agreed to leave the Argonne after being offered Chicago Housing Authority (CHA) subsidized apartments in Uptown, and two days later the first four families moved in to their new apartments. This ended the Argonne occupation, but the other people in the Village needed somewhere to stay until apartments were found for all of them by the CHA, and so began the next move for CIV— to Camp Seager.

Camp Seager was a Methodist camp near Naperville, in DuPage county. The Methodists running Camp Seager invited CIV to stay *until* housing could be located for the people occupying the Village. They were informed that it might take at least three weeks to locate apartments for everyone, but Mike Chosa had a longer stay in mind. As usual, Chosa already had the next protest in mind, but this time he had something to lose. The previous moves were all in response to evictions and a lack of concessions, but this time an agreement had been made between CIV and the CHA. Members of the CIV were to apply for the apartments in Uptown, and move back to the city as soon as possible. The CIV promised to keep its end of the bargain, and did not, but neither did the CHA. The families that did apply for apartments had a nearly impossible time getting them—the CHA never seemed to be able to find anything. Unfortunately for the CIV, since so few had applied for apartments, very few had been rejected, therefore they had little to fight about.

The Village stayed at Camp Seager, and had meetings with government officials throughout the fall, but Mike Chosa was often less than cooperative, which lead to a great deal of resentment amongst some of the CIV supporters in DuPage County. Finally, on December 11, 1971, CIV was evicted from Camp Seager. For the next month the Village traveled around; they tried to go back to Argonne, but were quickly ousted; they had sit-ins at the Lion House in Lincoln Park Zoo, claiming that the zoo animals received better funding (and housing) than the Indians; they sat-in outside the gates of Fort Sheridan, (Chicago *Tribune*, January 4, 1972), which lead to an agreement that they could stay at Camp Logan until March 1, 1972.

Camp Logan was one of the more successful occupations of the CIV in terms of outside support, and the reorganization of the Village. For a long time Mike Chosa had wanted to stop the drinking at the Village, and when his sister, Betty Jack (one of the leaders of the CIV), stopped drinking, things started changing. Now that Betty Jack was no longer drinking, some of the members of the CIV began to drift away, and those who had supported CIV, but who did not like the drunkenness, started to return. With this shift in the Village population, Chosa was able to lay down the law about not drinking, which helped to gain outside support. Now that he did not have to worry as much about drunkenness at the Village, Chosa could turn his attention to developing programs for the CIV. An arts and crafts program was created, and later a small shop was opened. The residents of the surrounding communities were impressed by the changes. The governor's office extended the eviction date from March 1 to "whenever alternative accommodations are found" (Leveen, 1978: 447).

The deadline for evacuation was postponed several times while meetings were held, and efforts were made to settle the housing dispute. The Village had gained considerable support from the surrounding community after its reforms. A full page ad in a local paper, signed by 150 organizations and individuals asked that CIV be allowed to stay at Camp Logan. However, the support was not enough. The eviction date was set for June 30, 1972.

Shortly after midnight, the police were sent to the camp, having received reports that the Indians had barricaded the gates with their cars. "Mike using a bullhorn, declared that Camp Logan was Indian country and defied anyone to remove them" (Ibid.) An hour later the police bombed them with tear gas, and the CIV surrendered. thirty-five members of CIV were arrested.

After their release, CIV members dispersed. Some stayed in Chicago and remained active in the Indian community, some joined or formed other organizations, some left Chicago altogether. Yet, the experiences of the participants of CIV outlasted the organization itself. Many of the members of the Village went on to work for Indian communities through other organizations.

CONCLUSION

Although the demands of the Chicago Indian Village were not immediately met, it cannot be considered a failure. Its activism made dominant society in Chicago listen to the grievances of Chicago's Indian population. Without the protests of the Chicago Indian Village, the Relocation and termination programs would have continued unabated. In the 50s and 60s newspapers reported that Native Americans were moving into the cities, as if such an occurrence were unimaginable. They spoke of humble, stoic people, right out of a storybook. The days of newspaper articles that informed the city that there were Indians in town were over. No longer were Indians "very hesitant to ask for help. They'll come only when they're at the end of their rope" (Chicago *Sun-Times*, March 22, 1956). The Indians in Chicago and across the nation had come to the end of their rope, and ask for help they did. But not quietly and stoically—instead they followed the lead of groups such as the Black Panthers, and organized demonstrations. On the West Coast they took Alcatraz, and got the nation's attention. In Minnesota the American Indian Movement was formed, and in Chicago the CIV grew out of a protest over the eviction of Carol Warrington. Chicago's Native American residents were no longer asking for help, they were demanding attention be paid to their concerns and would not stop until they saw results. People were forced to pay attention to Chicago's Native American residents. After a few years they did listen, and began to face the fact that Native Americans would not and could not be terminated by their move to the city.

REFERENCE CITED

Leveen, Deborah Browning: *Hustlers and Heroes: Portrait of the Chicago Indian Village*. Phd dissertatin, Department of Political Science; University of Chicago; Chicago, Illinois. 1978.

PART II
CONTEMPORARY LIFE

SECTION ONE
ORGANIZATIONS

*Native American Organizations
in the Chicago Community*
165

The Chicago American Indian Community
DAVID BECK
167

Challenges and Changes in Indian Child Welfare
INGRID WAGNER
182

*NARA, the Center of Indian Community
in Portland, Oregon*
RICHARD KING
196

The Nation in the City
GRANT P. ARNDT,
WITH INFORMATION PROVIDED BY
DEMETRIO ABANGAN, JENNIFER JONES,
AND JOHN DALL
201

Native American Organizations in the Chicago Community

American Indian Center (AIC)
1630 W. Wilson Ave.
Chicago, IL 60640
Phone: 773-275-5871
Fax: 773-275-5874
Director: Sharon Skolnick

American Indian Economic Development Association
4753 N. Broadway Ste. 1126
Chicago, IL 60640
Phone: 773-784-0808
Fax: 773-784-0981
Director: Jim DeNomie

American Indian Movement
2026 W. Montrose
Chicago, IL 60618
Phone: 888-561-3866
Fax: 773-561-3894
Director : Joe Peralez

Chicago Indian Associates
(Grassroots/Social Justice)
Anawin Center
4750 N. Sheridan Ste. 255
Chicago, IL 60640
Phone: 312-561-6155
Fax: Same
Director: Sister Toni Harris

Audubon Elementary
3500 N. Hoyne
Chicago, IL 60618
Gen Info: 773-534-5470
Direct Phone: 773-534-5742
Fax: 773-534-8244

Career Development Center
c/o Truman College Box 202
1145 W. Wilson Ave.
Chicago, IL 60640
Phone: 773-907-3747
Fax: 773-907-4464
Program Assistant: Hilda Navarro

Chicago Native American Urban Indian Retreat (CNAUIR)
2026 W. Montrose
Chicago, IL 60618
Phone: 773-561-1336
Fax: 773-561-3894
Director: Debbie Valentino

C.I.M.A. – JTPA
1630 W. Wilson
Chicago, IL 60640
Phone: 773-271-2413
Fax: 773-271-3729
Director: Brooks Lockheart

D'Arcy McNickle Center
Newberry Library
60 W. Walton Ave.
Chicago, IL 60610
Phone: 312-943-9090
Fax: 312-255-3513
Director: Craig Howe

Ho-Chunk Language and Art
Director: James Yellowbank
Ho-Chunk Nation Chicago Branch
Office
4941 N. Milwaukee
Chicago, IL 60630
Phone: 773-202-8433
Fax: 773-202-0245
Coordinator: Demitrio Abangan

Indian Child Welfare
Phone: 312-561-8555
Director: Arlene Williams

American Indian Health Service
838 W. Irving Park Rd.
Chicago, IL 60613
Phone: 773-883-9100
Fax: 773-883-0005
Director: Amelia Ortiz
Phone: 773-883-0568

Institute for Native American Development (INAD)
1145 W. Wilson Box 210
Phone: 773-907-4665
Fax: 773-907-4464
Director: Beverly Moeser

Native American Educational Services College (NAES)
2838 W. Peterson
Chicago, IL 60659
Phone: 312-761-5000
Fax: 312-761-3808
President: Faith Smith

Native American Foster Parent Association (NAPA)
1630 W. Wilson
Chicago, IL 60640
Phone: 773-784-9305
Fax: 773-784-9316
Director: Roxy Grignon

Native American Studies
Director: Rene de la Cruz
Title V – Director:
Georgiana King/Ben Scott

Native American Support Program (NASP)
University of Illinois at Chicago
NASP MC/258
1200 W. Harrison
Chicago, IL 60607
Phone: 312-996-4515
Fax: 312-413-8099
Director: Rita Hodge

Prevention Center
Phone: 773-883-0568
Director: Tanya Taylor

St. Augustine's Center
4512 N. Sheridan 2nd Floor
Chicago, IL 60640
Phone: 773-784-1050
Fax: 773-784-1254
Director: Arlene Williams

St. Augustine's "Drop In"
4420 N. Broadway
Chicago, IL 60640
Phone: 773-878-1066
Director: DeAnn Martin

David Beck

The Chicago American Indian Community*

An "Invisible" Minority

You tell all white men "America First." We believe in that. We are the first Americans. We are the only ones, truly, that are 100 percent. We, therefore, ask you while you are teaching school children about America first, teach them truth about the first Americans.

—Memorial of Grand Council Fire of American Indians to Mayor William Hale Thompson of Chicago, December 1, 1927

Today, according to census figures, there are approximately seven thousand American Indians in Chicago, with an additional seven thousand in the surrounding areas.[1] With some seven million people living in the Chicago metropolitan area, American Indians are a small minority. In fact, for cultural, economic, and political reasons beyond their small numbers, American Indians are one of the least visible minority groups in Chicago. Even many lifelong area residents do not realize that American Indians live in the city. The city of Chicago recently demonstrated its official ignorance of the Indian population and its problems when it excluded Indians from the list of minorities whose businesses are eligible to apply for minority set-aside contracts.[2]

Yet American Indians have lived in and passed through the Chicago region far longer than anyone else has, and have maintained a continuous presence for centuries. That presence has been marked by three key features which have come to define both the Indian community's develop-

*. Reprinted from *Beyond Black and White: New Faces and Voices in U.S. Schools*; Maxine Sellerand and Lois Weiss, eds. (State University of New York Press: 1997) with permission of the author and SUNY Press.

ment and its problems: diversity, marginality to the larger society, and maintenance of a separate cultural identity by both individuals and community-based organizations.

The community's diversity has a long history, but it stems largely from (1) Chicago's unique position as an industrial center, and (2) the Bureau of Indian Affairs (BIA)-sponsored program of Relocation, which from the 1950s to the 1970s helped cause the resettlement of Indian people moving from the reservations to cities looking for work. Chicago, designated as a national Relocation center, is in a state without Indian reservations, so all relocatees were from elsewhere. Even before this program began, Chicago's Indian population had been growing rapidly and broadly in the post–World War II years because of booming factory work. Current estimates show that Indian people of over a hundred different tribal backgrounds live in Chicago.

The community's marginality is imposed from the outside and in some ways supported from within the community. America has not yet come to terms with the notion or the legal reality of nations within a nation, and has attempted in various ways to force American Indians to give up their cultural identity and hegemony in exchange for white ways. Though these American attempts have been destructive, they have been unsuccessful. American Indians have stubbornly fought to maintain their cultural traditions, tribal sovereignty, and separate identities even against great odds. This is complicated today by the fact that approximately three fourths of the two million American Indians in the United States live off of federally recognized reservations, in rural areas, in tribal groups unrecognized by the federal government, and in urban areas.[3] American Indians living off of reservations, significantly less than one percent of the nation's population, are nearly invisible in the United States. Yet they are also one of America's most at-risk populations.

Scholarly and media misrepresentation of urban Indian communities like Chicago's have added to their marginality to the larger society. The conditions, problems, and needs of Indian people in Chicago have been shaped by numerous separate but interrelated histories: the tribal and community histories of those Indian people who have made the city their home, either permanently or temporarily, and the distinct history of this urban Indian community. Because of these complexities, urban Indian communities have rarely been studied by scholars, and even less frequently understood. Most studies of urban American Indians focus on the rapid urbanization of the American Indian population in the post–World War II era and dwell on the disruptive forces of the federal Relocation program and migration, or on urban living, using those as a basis to analyze Indian responses and adaptations. As a consequence, these studies emphasize problems, most often of alcoholism and adjustment to city life, instead of either community cultural tradition or development.

Urban American Indians have also sought to remain outside of the mainstream, in part because of this misunderstanding of them by the larger society, but for other significant reasons as well. Historic treatment by federal, state, and local governments, churches and schools, which has been so destructive to many Indian communities and individuals, is one factor. There are few if any Indian people whose families have not been affected negatively by one or more of these influences. These personalized experiences have made individuals understandably reluctant to involve themselves in activities sponsored by these groups.[4]

Urban Indian communities like Chicago are fluid, with individuals and families travelling back and forth between city and reservation on a regular basis. Younger people do this in search of a better-quality environment or education for themselves and their children, while many older community members retire to the reservations to which they or family members have ties. This precludes an integration into the life of the larger community, since for many the city is viewed as a temporary rather than a permanent home.

Community members who remain in the city participate in but to a large extent do not become part of mainstream culture. Even those who do attempt to become part of mainstream culture are marginalized by that culture. One American Indian suburban grade school student recently reported that her teacher in school taught the class that Indians were part of American history, but not part of the current American scene. She was told that there are no Indians alive any more. In addition, for children and even adults the burden of being American Indian is often made more difficult by peers, teachers, coworkers, and others who assume that because the person is American Indian, he or she can answer any questions about any tribe's history or literature or culture.[5] The inability to answer such questions, many of which border on the ridiculous, while understandable, is also demoralizing.

The third feature shaping Chicago's Indian community is its maintenance of cultural identity. This has been done by individual families, by people working in leadership positions within the community, and by community organizations. In fact, this is the primary force defining community development. Beginning with Carlos Montezuma, who moved to Chicago in the late nineteenth century and remained almost until his death in 1923, and continuing with others such as Mrs. Charles Fitzgerald and Scott Henry Peters in the twenties and thirties, and Willard LaMere from the forties through eighties, the community has had forceful leaders working actively to improve conditions for Indian people and to develop community institutions.

Early leaders focused more strongly on pursuing rights for Indian people on reservations back home and on redefining for themselves and the American public the views of Indians as a race, while later leaders focused

more exclusively on problems within Chicago as the Indian population
grew rapidly, but all concentrated their energies on bettering Indian people's lives in ways that were remarkably consistent with their cultural
backgrounds. The founding of the Indian Council Fire in 1923, and the
American Indian Center in 1953, which was followed by the subsequent
proliferation of community organizations in the 1970s, all reflect desires
within the community to serve by helping individuals within the context
of Indian cultural values, for example.

Indian people have maintained a cultural identity because they have
been able to adapt traditional tribal values to their new circumstances.
Despite broadly different cultural and historical situations among tribes,
several fundamental values permeate many Indian cultures including
urban communities. Among those values identified have been maintenance and development of family relationships, responsibility to the community, and reciprocity and generosity, or sharing.[6] Ironically these same
values often prevent Indian people from pursuing or even desiring to pursue the "American dream,' which is based largely on individualism, consumerism, and material possessions.

To understand how this came to be and what all of this means in relation to today's Chicago American Indian community we need to first
understand that community's history.

After Black Hawk's defeat at the hands of the United States Army in
1832, the final treaties ceding Indian lands in Illinois to the United States
were negotiated.[7] This effectively removed all Indian tribes, though not
all Indian individuals, from the state.[8] Indian traders continued to travel
to the city during the nineteenth century bringing fish and berries to sell,
and later in the nineteenth century travelling Wild West shows brought
Indian people into the city. The Great Lakes shipping industry also
employed Indian people who stopped in Chicago when their ships did.

Through the end of the nineteenth and into the twentieth century
American Indian groups continued to stop in Chicago when passing
through, not only traders and working people, but travelers as well.
Because Chicago was a rail hub for the Midwest, and because the nation
lacked a unified rail system, transcontinental travelers switched trains in
the city. Indian delegations from the Midwest and Great Plains often
passed through or spent the night in Chicago while on their way to lobby
Congress or to meet with the President of the United States or the Commissioner of Indian Affairs.[9] Beginning in 1893 and lasting into the 1940s,
American Indians came to Chicago to set up camp for local celebrations.
Individual people from all of these groups sometimes stayed in Chicago,
for short or longer periods of time. All of this was an early basis of both
the community's diversity and its fluidity.

At the encampments, visitors were invited to come see what federal
officials, scholars, and the general public all viewed as the last vestiges of

a dying race, or a reminder of America's past. The Indian Village at the 1893 World's Columbian Exposition, for instance, was a carefully planned part of the ethnology exhibit, which was meant to be an object lesson in the progress of mankind. This display contained both artifacts of past civilizations and living peoples from throughout the world. Following the ideology of Social Darwinism, this combination was intended to illustrate the steps of civilization mankind had undergone. The Indian exhibit was placed at the start of the evolutionary scale.[10] Events like this and their treatment by the press and by organizing officials helped cement the marginal treatment and view of American Indians by the larger society.

The best-known early-twentieth-century Indian resident of Chicago was Dr. Carlos Montezuma, the Yavapai stomach surgeon. He was a nationally acclaimed physician and a national Indian leader, but he also served as a one man social service agency for Indians in Chicago. When Indian delegations passed through the city, en route to Washington, D.C., he graciously met them and made their stay in Chicago pleasant; when Indians became stranded in the city, he interceded with their reservation agencies to help provide the opportunity for them to return home; when Indians came to the city in need of work, he helped them find it. In fact, he informally worked together with the BIA warehouse in Chicago in this latter capacity. In 1904 when a train wrecked in Maywood, Illinois, several Indian members of a travelling Wild West show were injured, some critically. Dr. Montezuma not only treated the Indians as patients, but fought (albeit unsuccessfully) through the BIA system for better compensation on their behalf. These local roles of acting as family and helper for Indian people of all backgrounds in the city, place Montezuma firmly within a tribal cultural tradition in which those tasks were a natural part of leaders' daily activities.[11]

While Dr. Montezuma lived in Chicago the Indian population was so low that it can be considered negligible. The 1910 federal census counted only 188 American Indians in the city, not enough to form much basis of community. Were it not for Montezuma's fame and the occasional encampments held in the city, for which representatives from various local and sometimes distant tribes traveled to Chicago but which were also attended by local tribal members, there would be virtually no documentary record of Indians in Chicago previous to the 1920s.

Nonetheless, in 1919 the Illinois State legislature deemed the Indian presence significant enough to warrant a special holiday. Following the lead of other state legislative bodies, it passed a law proclaiming the fourth Friday in September as American Indian Day, a holiday still celebrated in Chicago's Indian community.

The early celebrations of Indian Day, held from 1920 to 1923, featured encampments at Forest Preserves which tens of thousands of visitors attended in order to catch a glimpse of a way of life considered to be part of the past. These were sponsored by a newly created organization, the Indian Fellowship League (IFL), which consisted of both Indian and white members. These two groups of people unfortunately had conflicting agendas. The white members wanted the Indians to aid in the conservation movement and enjoyed attending pageants which featured Indian cultural events. The Indian members on the other hand, Chicago residents who themselves were of thirty-five different tribal backgrounds, wanted to use the organization to work actively on behalf of Indian tribal rights which were being denied by the federal government.[12] The IFL soon disbanded in disarray, but its conflict represents the marginality of Chicago's Indian population even among non-Indians who wanted to work with them. It also demonstrates the strength of the Indian desires to work on behalf of Indian people in order to protect political and cultural rights that were guaranteed in nineteenth-century treaties.

The death of Carlos Montezuma in 1923, a blow to both Indians in Chicago and to the national Indian leadership, occurred just as a new permanent organization, again of mixed Indian and white membership, came into existence. The Grand Council Fire of American Indians, later known as the Indian Council Fire, exhibited many of the same theoretical conflicts among its leadership as had the IFL. Despite this, for many of its early years it provided both a social and social service outlet to the local Indian population.

The Council Fire's makeup of Indian membership was also diverse, and the Indian leadership among its members represented a new group of Indian people moving to cities: those educated in off-reservation boarding schools. These schools, run both by churches and the BIA, supported with federal money, were notorious for their attempts to obliterate Indian cultures and cultural ways. Like other federal programs aimed at destroying Indian cultures, this too, though destructive in many ways, failed. The leaders who came to Chicago from the boarding schools continued the tradition of leadership brought to the city by Montezuma, by battling for Indian tribal rights and for recognition of the value of Indian culture within the context of American culture, and by acting as family and support to Indian people in need. This happened until the Indian membership lost control of the Council Fire to the white leadership in the late 1930s.[13]

The Indian population in the city of Chicago remained relatively low, officially numbering less than a thousand, until the 1950s. During and after World War II, however, the population grew dramatically. Indians were among the workers who moved to cities for factory jobs during the war. After the war Indian veterans moved to cities like Chicago. As economic conditions on most reservations remained in states of crisis and even worsened, Indian people left to find employment in Chicago and other cities.

At the same time, a federal Indian policy shift, one prong of a broader federal attempt to downscale government, aimed on several fronts to dissolve federal responsibilities to Indians. This shift brought with it one of the most destructive policies ever applied to tribes, Termination, and also brought the Relocation program, established in 1952 to sponsor Indian migration to cities.

Six cities including Chicago were designated as Relocation centers, with offices established to aid newcomers in finding housing and employment. The BIA also hired Relocation officers who worked on reservations to encourage and aid Indian people in moving to the city, providing transportation funds, moral support, and directions to the urban Relocation offices. Of the 122,000 Indians who moved to cities between 1940 and 1960, over 31,000, approximately 25 percent, came under the auspices of the Relocation program.[14] The BIA conducted the Relocation program until 1972. In that time 13,377 Indian people ("units" in BIA terminology) were relocated to Chicago.[15] Nationally as many as 75 percent of Indians moving to cities did not come as part of the Relocation program during this time. In Chicago the estimate stands at 50 percent. In fact, even before Relocation, Indian people chose to move to Chicago because they knew other Indians already lived there.[16]

Chicago was a bewildering place to many of these new residents, for whom the BIA provided little support after the initial contact. The size of the city and its buildings, the crowding of its people, the noise, the streets, and an almost alien way of life were all new to many rural Indian people used to reservation life. Many migrants suffered from loneliness and alienation when they first arrived.[17]

Also alien was the way they were expected to live. Contrary to federal promises, the BIA housed relocatees in temporary housing often near or on skid row. Many were not used to living in the unsanitary conditions in which they found themselves in Chicago. Also, the BIA often housed Indian people far from their places of work or job training. Some returned home immediately, others waited until they had enough money to return, and still others remained. In the later years, some relocatees came through the program a second time, hoping again to find a better life in the city.[18]

The Indian Council Fire, though still in existence, no longer served either social or social service functions for most Indian people in Chicago. Some individuals of course continued to serve these functions through the 1940s and 1950s. One was Willard LaMere, whose family had lived in Chicago since at least the 1920s; another was Anna P. Harris, renowned for her generosity and hospitality toward Indian people of all backgrounds passing through Chicago.[19] Aside from several bars, however, there were few places where Indian people could go to meet each other.

Then in 1953 an initiative from among Indian people in Chicago, with the support of the BIA and local welfare organizations, led to the founding of the All Tribes American Indian Center, the first urban center in the nation. Later "All Tribes" was dropped from the title, but it served as a signal that all Indian people were welcome, that the incipient community's diversity was being recognized in a positive manner.

That diversity expanded rapidly in the 1950s and 1960s. In one typical year, 1957, the BIA placed people of forty-eight different tribal designations in Chicago, including people from the Southwest, California, the Northwest, the Northern Plains, the Southern Plains, the Southeast, and the Midwest. BIA officials sometimes relocated people far from their homes to make it more difficult for them to return. As a result, people of dramatically different cultural backgrounds, sometimes people who were of tribes that were traditional enemies, now lived together. The BIA found jobs for relocatees throughout the city, but found most of the housing in Uptown, a North Side port of entry neighborhood for a wide variety of urban migrants.[20]

Uptown formed the core of the Chicago Indian community for two decades. When the Indian Center purchased a building in the late 1960s, it did so in the heart of Uptown. The center provided both social services and a social outlet for Indian people in Chicago. Numerous cultural clubs founded throughout the years met at the center, including language clubs at which members met to converse in their native languages, recreational clubs including a canoe club and athletic clubs, and programs for youth and community elders. Social services included educational, daily living assistance, counseling, and food programs. In 1954 the center sponsored its first powwow, an annual event that still draws thousands of Indian participants and visitors to Chicago each November.

Although all of these activities helped Indian people adjust to city life and to maintain not only cultural ties but cultural traditions, several factors made this much more difficult. Physical disconnection from home communities made it hard to maintain the language and to take part in ceremonies and community events. Although traditional ceremonies, for instance, occurred in the city, they often did so sporadically or in modified ways.

Another major problem was the disruption of the family system. While not true in every case, generally parts of families, whether individuals or parents and children, migrated to Chicago together. The support system provided by extended families in which grandparents, aunts, uncles, and cousins often played roles as significant as parents and siblings, was left behind. As much as anything, this loss has proven destructive for families in poverty in the city.

By the end of the Relocation era in the early 1970s a host of community based organizations were established, most in Uptown, to meet the increasing needs of the community. These helped in various ways to maintain traditional tribal cultural values in Chicago. People created new "families" in their organizational affiliations, while the organizations took the collective responsibility to work for the betterment of the community, especially its neediest members. These organizations have created a web of support for community members in the areas of health, education, and employment, and have provided spiritual, cultural, and social outlets as well.[21]

The values, though, conflict with those of the larger society, and maintaining them is difficult in a diverse and marginalized community. That difficulty became heightened, ironically, as people's working conditions stabilized and they moved closer to their jobs. The Indian population has now dispersed widely throughout the city and suburbs.[22] People still maintain connections with each other through the organizations and the events they sponsor, such as powwows, but doing so is an increasing hardship.

Despite the positive aspects of community development that have occurred over the past four decades, Indian people still face severe problems in Chicago, due to both their marginality in the larger society and their diversity. Education levels remain low, while unemployment levels remain high, and the poorest segment of the community consists of female-headed single-parent households with children. Underemployment and lack of skill levels for better jobs, both directly related to the education problem, are also significant.

In Chicago less than 15 percent of Indian adults have college degrees, a number higher than the national average for Indian adults of 10.1 percent, and much improved since the early 1970s when only four Indian adults with college degrees could be identified in Chicago. By comparison, however, more than 33 percent of white adults in Chicago have college degrees. More than a quarter of Indian adults in Chicago have never graduated from high school.[23]

Two recent surveys of Indian education in the Chicago public schools found conditions in a state of crisis, and indicate that things are not improving. Native Americans have a higher dropout rate than any other racial or ethnic group within the Chicago Public Schools. In 1986 the dropout rate of American Indians in Chicago Public High Schools stood at 70.8 percent. For white students that number was 41.4 percent; for African American students, 40.5. And of American Indian students entering high school in 1990, 51.4 percent dropped out by their sophomore year, while 65.8 percent had dropped out by the junior year, which indicates that the statistics of the mid-1980s, rather than improving, may actually be worsening. Nationally, the Indian dropout rate is figured at approximately 35 percent, but that number is considered low because it is calculated beginning with the sophomore year, while many students drop out in the freshman year when they reach the legal age of 16.[24]

"*It is clear,*" in the words of a 1992 report, "*that American Indian children in Chicago have all the risk factors associated with poor school achievement.*"

These risk factors include a high incidence of single-parent households, sub-poverty-level incomes, parents lacking high school diplomas and not often being home when the child is, and siblings who have dropped out of school. Of American Indian students who dropped out, 100 percent had already failed two or more courses.[25] The high school dropout rate is high, but many Indian students do not even make it out of junior high. Without support from families, and without extended family to help provide that foundation that children seek to find, many children join street gangs, become delinquent, or move to society's fringes in other ways. Intervention needs to begin therefore at the grade school level or earlier.

A follow-up report, reflecting on the dire situation described in the first report, warned,

> Beyond that, "poor school achievement" is, in and of itself, a "risk factor" for future success. In other words, those dropout statistics we're seeing are apt to be seen as unemployment statistics in the near future, and as today's dropouts begin to raise families, they become "risk factors" in their children's future. As Chicago's Native American population is disproportionately young, the social ramifications are potentially disastrous for a community already under siege . . . . 30% of Chicago's Native American population is under age 18, as compared with 18% under 18 of Chicago's white population.[26]

The diversity and marginality of Chicago's Indian community are often unnoticed by educators, and the community's stubborn insistence on maintaining not only cultural ties but cultural values and tradition often baffles educators.

As an example, the diversity of Chicago's Indian community extends also within the family. Continuing a phenomenon that grew with the mixing of Indian children at boarding schools in the early twentieth century, American Indian men and women from various tribal backgrounds are today raising children in cities like Chicago, and throughout Indian country. The children and even the parents and sometimes grandparents in these families are of mixed tribal backgrounds.

This makes understanding of family and tribal history even more critical in children's understanding of their place in society. A person may be enrolled in one tribe, but identify more strongly with another since he or she may have grown up more in relation to that community. A person may have a family background with two or more tribal affiliations in which the tribes are traditional enemies. This can be a difficult and confusing addition to the other identity crises faced by children entering adolescence, many of whom have to contend as well with additional outside pressures from street gangs, poverty, a weak and uncomfortable educational system, weakened family structures, and a society that virtually ignores them.

Educators therefore need to be aware both of the differences between

American Indian students, and sometimes of the differences within those students' own families. One educator recently said of a thirteen-year-old Chicago Indian boy, "He doesn't know anything about his own history; he doesn't even know about the Trail of Tears."[27] The boy was a Wisconsin Ho-Chunk; his tribe's history has had more than its share of tragic upheaval, including forced Relocations, but the "Trail of Tears" was experienced by the Cherokees who left the southeast for Oklahoma, not the Ho-Chunk who stayed in Wisconsin. Little wonder that he finds his education irrelevant!

Ultimately, as Indian people have learned time and again through painful historical experience, Indian problems must be resolved by Indian people in order for resolution to be effective. That way solutions can be made within a relevant cultural context and within the context of community development within which Indian people are decision makers. In Chicago these educational problems, for example, are now being attacked head-on by community organizations and members, from parent committees to a grade school magnet program to a local Indian-established-and-run college, NAES (Native American Educational Services) College, in a multigenerational context that includes employment and education as part of the solution.

Moneys from Title IV, Part A (now Title V) of the Indian Education Act supported elementary and high school programs for Indian students in Chicago beginning in the 1970s. Those programs closed in the late seventies and in the eighties; however, in 1988, as the result of a program proposed by the Chicago Board of Education, the Audubon Elementary School in the Uptown community began a program in which sixty Indian students were "clustered" in the school, similarly to a magnet school. The curriculum in the school has been reshaped to include teaching of Indian history and culture, both to Indian students alone for a part of the day, and to the entire school. The idea is to affirm the value of Indian culture and history to Indian students and to make non-Indian students aware of the continuing presence of this small minority in American society.

In the meantime, in the mid-1970s, Indian people in the Chicago community founded NAES College to address the problem that even of those American Indians attending college in the United States, fully 90 percent never earned a degree. (The number has not much improved by the mid-1990s, unfortunately.) This was due largely to two factors: the irrelevance of higher education to Indian community needs, and the failure of conventional systems of higher education to account for the cultural problems Indian students encounter in higher education systems. In 1984 NAES earned accreditation from the North Central Association of Colleges and Schools to confer a Bachelor of Arts degree in Community Studies.[28]

NAES College's Chicago campus has been actively involved in the

Audubon School program since its inception, helping design it, and then with support from the State of Illinois, running first a role-model component within the program, and later becoming more actively involved. In the fall of 1994 the college began to develop a Family Education Model at the school that intends to involve youth, parents, community, and teachers in actively working to help the program meet its potential. NAES students are involved at all levels, from active participation in the parent committee, which serves as a program watchdog, to the tutoring program, to teacher training. The Indian teachers who run the program are NAES graduates. No formal assessment of the Audubon Program has yet been made, so its success is undefined. But it does provide a much-needed source of stable development within the community.

Individuals outside of the Indian community must be able to recognize the problems Indian students face if they are to be helpful in the process of problem resolution and community development. They must also be able to both accept and understand the community's diversity, to help eliminate its marginality in those areas in which the community does not desire to remain outside of the larger culture, and to respect the community's maintenance of cultural tradition and values, even when that conflicts with such American values as individualism, material possession, consumerism, and coercive leadership. Educators must take on the responsibilities of learning the historical and cultural conditions of the Indian people they serve, of making non-Indian people aware of those cultures and histories, and of making the educational system relevant to Native American students. Perhaps with such recognition and help Indian communities like Chicago's will be able to move toward a more positive future.

The author presented some of these ideas and text in a paper "How Chicago American Indian Organizations Display Traditional Leadership Characteristics," presented at the American Society for Ethnohistory Conference in Bloomington, Indiana, November 5, 1993. A 1993 National Endowment for the Humanities Summer Seminar under the direction of Roger L. Nichols at the University of Arizona provided an opportunity for some of the background research for this piece, as did work partially supported by the Illinois Humanities Council, NAES (Native American Educational Services), and the University of Illinois at Chicago History Department from 1986 to 1988, which resulted in *The Chicago American Indian Community, 1893–1988: Annotated Bibliography and Guide to Sources in Chicago* (Chicago: NAES College Press, 1988).

Notes

1. *1990 Census of Population and Housing Block Statistics, East North Central Division*, CD90-1 B-4, September 1992.

2. This followed in the wake of the United States Supreme Court's 1989 Richmond v. Croson decision, which requires cities to prove that minority preference contracts go only to minority groups that have been historically discriminated against. City representatives

said they were unable to locate any Indian-owned businesses, which means they failed to look in the city phone book under either American Indian or Native American. The American Indian Economic Development Association, an Indian-run organization in Chicago that works to support Indian-owned businesses, is fighting the city on this issue. The situation was still unremedied in 1994.

3. The 1990 census counted the population of American Indians, Eskimos, and Aleuts at 1,959,234. Of these 437,358 live in American Indian or trust lands, and 1,100,534 are classified as urban. *1990 Census of Population General Population Characteristics, United States* 1990 CP I - 1, table 9, p. 13, and 1990 *Census of Population General Population Characteristics, American Indian and Native Alaska Areas* 1990-CP- I - I A, table 1, p. 1.

4. Several of these factors in relation to Chicago's American Indian community are discussed in Bryan Marozas, *Demographic Profile of Chicago's American Indian Community* (Chicago: NAES College Press, 1984) in relation to undercounting of Indians by federal census takers in the 1980 census.

5. A group of twenty urban, rural, and suburban American Indian children in a Summer Cultural Program at the University of Illinois at Chicago in July 1994, for example, created a long list of stereotypes and racially based problems they face in their everyday lives. One of the things which makes them most angry is being considered ."experts" on Indians simply because they are Indian.

6. For discussion of this, see LaDonna Harris in collaboration with Dr. Jacqueline Wasilewski, *This Is What We Want to Share: Core Cultural Values* (Americans for Indian Opportunity, 1992).

7. The final Illinois treaties reprinted in Charles J. Kappler, ed., *Indian Treaties, 1778-1883* (New York: Interland, 1972 [orig. 1904]) include: Treaty with the Winnebago, 1832, pp. 345-48; Treaty with the Sauk and Foxes, pp. 349-51; Treaty with the Potawatomi, 1832 (October 20), 353-56, Treaty with the Potawatomi, 1832 (October 16), 367-70; Treaty with the Potawatomi, 1832 (October 27), 372-75; Treaty with the Piankeshaw and Wea, 1832, 382-83; Treaty with the Chippewa, Etc., 1833, 402-15. For a discussion of the relation of the war against Black Hawk to the treaties, see Helen Hornbeck Tanner, *Atlas of Great Lakes Indian History* (Norman: University of Oklahoma Press, 1987), 159.

8. Some individual Potawatomi people, for example, received land that is now in Chicago in the treaties they helped negotiate. The Treaty with the Chippewa, Etc., 1829, for example, granted land to Billy Caldwell (Sauganash) and Alexander Robinson (Kappler, 298). See also "Last Pottawatomies Win a 20-Year Fight," *Chicago Times*, September 19, 1941, and a map by Virgil J. Vogel, "Former Indian Reservations" in Cook County Forest Preserves in "Indians, Treaties and Claims" folder, Chicago Historical Society clip-files.

9. These trips are remembered through oral histories and can also be traced through newspapers and other printed sources.

10. Robert W. Rydell, *All the World's a Fair: Visions of Empire at American International Expositions, 1876-1916* (Chicago: University of Chicago Press, 1985), 45; Letter from Brigadier General R. H. Pratt to Franklin K. Lane, Secretary of the Interior, May 21, 1913, in John William Larner, Jr., ed., *The Papers of Carlos Montezuma, M.D., including the Papers of Maria Keller Montezuma Moore and the Papers of Joseph W. Latimer* (Wilmington, Del.: Scholarly Resources, 1983), microfilm reel 3, and *The Historical World's Columbian Exposition and Chicago Guide*, Illustrated from Official Drawings by Horace H. Morgan, LL.D. (St. Louis: James H. Mason & Co., Publishers), 269-70, 294. The latter referred to "the aborigines of this country" as an "almost extinct civilization, if civilization it is to be called." The book urged visitors to see the Indian exhibit, warning that "it is more than probable that the World's Columbian Exposition will furnish the last opportunity for an acquaintance with the 'noble red-man' before he achieves annihilation, or at least loss of identity."

The Indian presence at the 1903 Chicago centennial celebration is described in a variety of sources. See David Beck, *The Chicago American Indian Community*, 47-48, and Chicago newspapers. For example, the *Chicago Daily Tribune* ran at least fourteen articles and cartoons between September 25 and October 1, 1903, relating to the Indian participation in that event.

11. For a biography of Montezuma, see Peter Iverson, *Carlos Montezuma and the Changing World of American Indians* (Albuquerque: University of New Mexico Press, 1982). The three collections of papers on Carlos Montezuma are *Carlos Montezuma Papers, 1892-1937* at the State Historical Society of Wisconsin, also on microfilm; John William Larner, Jr., ed., *The Papers of Carlos Montezuma, M.D.*, microfilm (Wilmington, Del.: Scholarly Resources, 1983); and Montezuma Papers, Ayer Modern Manuscripts (Chicago: Newberry Library). See also David Beck, "American Indians in Chicago Since 1893: Selected Sources," in Terry Straus, ed., *Indians of the Chicago Area*, 2d cd. (Chicago: NAES College Press, 1990), 170-71; David Beck, "The 1904 Train Wreck" *NAES RULE* 35 (September 1987), and Beck, "How Chicago American Indian Organizations . . . .," 4-5.

12. Minutes of Indian Fellowship League meeting, October 15, 1920, handwritten, 20 pages, Indian Fellowship League Folder, Welfare Council of Metropolitan Chicago Box 246, Chicago Historical Society Manuscript Collections, Rosalyn R. LaPier, "'Pipe of Peace Nearly Out at Paleface Feast': Indian Interest Groups in Chicago and the End of Assimilationist Policy in America," master's thesis, DePaul University, draft, pp. 11-28.

13. Reports of Work of the Indian Council Fire, May 1932-February 1933, and May 1933-February 1934, Century of Progress, Indian Council Fire Papers. University of Illinois at Chicago Special Collections, Lapier, "Pipe of Peace Nearly Out," 29-49, 68. For brief biographies of two Indian people who attended Indian boarding schools and then moved to Chicago where they assumed leadership roles in the community, see Rosalyn LaPier, "'We are not savages, but a civilized race.' Scott Henry Peters and His Attempts to Change the Image of Indians," paper presented at the Great Lakes History Conference, October 1992, and Rosalyn LaPier, "Francis M. Cayou: Athlete at Carlisle Indian School," presented at the 1993 Annual Meeting of the American Society of Ethnohistory, at Indiana University, November 4-6, 1993.

14. Kenneth R. Philp, "Stride toward Freedom: The Relocation of Indians to Cities, 1952-1960," *Western Historical Quarterly* 16:2 (April 1985): 179. On federal policy in this period, see Donald L. Fixico, *Termination and Relocation: Federal Indian Policy, 1945-1960* (Albuquerque: University of New Mexico Press, 1986) and Larry W. Burt, *Tribalism in Crisis: Federal Indian Policy, 1953-1961* (Albuquerque: University of New Mexico Press, 1982).

15. Robert V. Dumont, Jr., "Chicago 1973-Notes from a Visit" typed manuscript, NAES College Library, pp. 2-3.

16. Chauncina White Horse, "The Indians of Chicago: A Perspective," typed manuscript, NAES College Library, p. 86; Donald L. Fixico with the assistance of Lucille St. Germaine, ed., "Native Voices in the City: The Chicago American Indian Oral History Project," unpublished manuscript, Community Archives of NAES College, pp. 17-19.

17. Fixico with St. Germaine, pp. 8-21.

18. Others relocated a second time to other cities that they found more to their liking.

19. See Willard LaMere, "History of Indians in Chicago," audiocassette tape of lecture for course of same title, 10-9-79 in NAES College Library, partially transcribed; Chicago Oral History Project Transcript 009, interview of Willard LaMere by Claire Young, January 16, 1983; and Chicago Oral History Project Transcript 016, interview of Susan Power by David R. Miller, September 26, 1983, pp. 5-6. Chicago Oral History Project transcripts are held by both the Newberry Library and the NAES College Library.

20. Dumont, p. 3; David Beck, "Relocation in Chicago," *NAES RULE* 42 (Summer 1993), 5-7; Fixico, *Termination and Relocation*, p. 134. See also Elaine M. Neils, *Reservation to City, Indian Migration and Federal Relocation* (Chicago: University of Chicago Department of Geography Research Paper No. 131, 197 1).

21. See Dumont's discussion of the role of the Native American Committee in the early 1970s, for example.

22. Rosalyn R. LaPier, "Chicago's American Indian Community: A Demographic Report Based on the 1990 Census," unpublished manuscript, 1994, NAES College Library.

23. Calculations made from numbers in 1990 Census Equal Employment Opportunity CD ROM File; 1970s information from Dumont, p. 4.

24. George Cornell, ED349148, *American Indian Education in the Chicago Public Schools: A Review and Analysis of Relevant Data and Issues* (Chicago: NAES College Press, 1992), 36-38; Branda Carl, RC019369, *American Indian Education in the Chicago Public Schools: Another Look* (Chicago: NAES College Student Field Project, May 1993), 13-14. Document available through ERIC, Both studies warn that the small population of Native Americans in the Chicago Public Schools can cause a higher probability of statistical error: Cornell, p. 40; Carl, p. 16.

25. Cornell, pp. 41, 46-47. Emphasis in original. Document available in ERIC.

26. Carl, p. 1.

27. Personal observation.

28. Previous to this NAES granted a bachelor's degree through Antioch College in Yellow Springs, Ohio, which had an outreach program that helped a variety of communities in the United States to develop higher education institutions relevant to their needs. NAES is currently the only remaining private, Indian-operated B.A. college in the United States.

Ingrid Wagner

Challenges and Changes in Indian Child Welfare

INTRODUCTION

In 1978, recognizing that "there is no resource that is more vital to the continued existence and integrity of Indian tribes than their children" (25 USC at 1901(3)), Congress passed the Indian Child Welfare Act (ICWA), in an effort to reverse decades of devastating loss to American Indian families, communities, and tribes through state-facilitated out-adoption of Indian children into non-Indian families. The Act established exclusive tribal jurisdiction over the welfare of Indian children domiciled or residing on their reservations and concurrent but presumptively tribal (state courts being expected to transfer jurisdiction to the appropriate tribe, absent "good cause to the contrary") jurisdiction over Indian children not domiciled on their reservations. Title II of the four-title act established funding for Indian child and family services to support and strengthen existing Indian families.

INDIAN CHILD WELFARE: CRISIS IN CHICAGO

The need for protective legislation such as ICWA is perhaps nowhere as pronounced as in the urban areas of America where today more than 63 percent of Native Americans reside. The issues that brought Indian child welfare to the fore in Congress in the 1970s, and that ICWA is meant to remedy, are wrestled with on a daily basis in America's cities. Sadly, some residents of urban Indian communities would argue that they are still waiting for ICWA to reach them. What's more, the challenges to ICWA that continue to mount in Congress and in the courts pose an overwhelmingly greater threat to Native Americans in cities than to their reservation counterparts because their tribal affiliation is more easily questioned. The city of Chicago provides an excellent example of the troubles that continue to plague urban Indian child welfare systems.

According to the 1990 census, Chicago is home to at least 7,000 Native American people representing more than 100 tribes. Given admitted difficulty in obtaining accurate census counts by the Census Bureau, however, it has been estimated that there are as many as 20,000 Indian people living in the greater Chicago area today. Although it has no real geographic center, the Chicago Indian community has a strong collective self-concept, maintained since pre-Relocation days, and a core institutional network. The numerous and varied institutions are supported by strong social ties similar to traditional extended kinship ties. Joan Weibel-Orlando's explanation of the similarly structured Los Angeles Indian community (Chicago's "sister city" during Relocation) illustrates these social and institutional phenomena well. She writes, "In an urban context characterized by residential dispersion and tribal and factional heterogeneity, regular, consistent, predictable, face-to-face interactions in the context of ethnic institutions are the mechanisms by which Indians in Los Angeles approximate traditional community structures and ethos" (Weibel-Orlando 1991, 83).

While Weibel-Orlando's use of the word "predictable" largely discounts the adaptability that has characterized the Chicago community, and Native American groups as a whole throughout history, her description of the community's component parts is exactly parallel to that of Chicago. People from as far as Wisconsin and Indiana consider themselves to be members of the Chicago Indian community, and come to the institutional core on Chicago's north side on a regular basis to participate in social events, and to receive social services.

Unfortunately, although the strength of the community has increased substantially over time, the availability and management of social services for Indian people by the state has not significantly improved. The legal status of urban Indian residents has remained the same. And while there have been a number of different community service providers over the past fifty years, no one institution has been able to provide consistent service over time. This failure on the part of community institutions is largely due to the rise and fall of a variety of organizations all competing for the same government funding (groups Weibel-Orlando dubs "ad hoc special interest groups") (Weibel-Orlando 1991, 100); very few ending up with enough to sustain valuable services, as will be illustrated later. The organizations that have proven the most successful have been those which maintain either a constant focus—ones that don't fluctuate with the immediacy of a given issue—or those that provide broad community support, as an umbrella for other groups. Lately, however, even these have fallen victim to lack of funding and the fiscal mood of the federal government.

The unreliability of funding and frequent lack of unified community goals is quite apparent in the administration of services for the protection and care of Indian children and their families, both before and after the passage of the Indian Child Welfare Act. This is particularly so regarding the availability of foster care options for Indian families at risk. The community archives housed at the Native American Educational Services College indicate that the need for a community-based foster care program has been a widely discussed issue since well before 1978, as a response to the rampant removal of Indian children from their homes by state social workers and numerous other community social ills. In fact, the issue of Native American foster care in Chicago became a nationally discussed issue in 1972, when an Indian woman who worked as a caseworker for social service referrals at the American Indian Center wrote about her experiences with child abandonment and neglect cases in the national publication *The American Indian Church Woman* (Stealer 1972, 12–14). She recounted the inability of local state agencies, namely the Illinois Department of Children and Family Services, to accommodate voluntary placement of children into foster care. Alarmed by this disregard, the author suggested that there was a definite need for a community-based program, run by Indians for Indians, in order to compensate for lack of cooperation from state agencies. She also saw such a program as a way of instilling pride of heritage in Indian children and adults alike, at a time when being Indian was not a "popular" thing to be.

One of the more noticeable responses to this kind of discussion can be seen elsewhere in the NAES College Archives. A significant section of the Archives' annotated bibliography indicates that from 1976–78, the Department of Children and Family Services and American Indian Health Services of Chicago attempted to co-facilitate a Native American Foster Care program, funded by DCFS. But for reasons undisclosed in the bibliography, within a two year period, correspondences between the two organizations indicate the predicted failure of AIHS at handling such a program, and propose other community organizations through which to run the program (Beck, David, ed., *Chicago Native American Community Annotated Bibliography*, Entries 930-41 [actual archives missing as of 6/97]) However, there is no evidence to suggest that DCFS was successful at reattaching its foster care services to another organization in the community.

The inferred failure of DCFS to continue serving the foster care needs of the Chicago Indian community could easily be attributed to the timing of such an event. The breakdown of relations with American Indian Health Services came in 1978, the same year as the passage of the Indian Child Welfare Act. At a time when the federal government was officially handing out funds to run child welfare programs as mandated by Section II of the four-section act, it is quite possible that the state-run DCFS felt that providing such services to the Indian community was no longer its responsibility.

Ultimately, federal funding for the Indian Child Welfare program in Chicago did not end up in the public sector. Instead, moneys went to St. Augustine's Center for American Indians, a private organization founded by the Episcopal Church to provide counseling and emergency assistance to the Indian community. Today, St. Augustine's receives a small grant of $30,000 with which to run its ICWA program. The bulk of the money goes towards running an after-school tutoring program for at-risk children in the community. Additionally, St. Augustine's has provided an invaluable service by serving as liaison between tribes and state courts in urban child custody cases, and has helped children who were separated from the community by the state child welfare system find their birth parents and reconnect with the community (Straus 1989, 166-7). Unfortunately, the success of these programs is directly influenced by the size and availability of funds. Just this year, St. Augustine's suffered a harsh blow when the federal government announced that it would no longer be providing funds to off-reservation ICWA programs, and asked St. Augustine's to close the program's financial records for good.

Today, almost twenty years after the passage of the act (and much community discussion), there is very little indication that ICWA even exists in the state of Illinois. In fact, a federally funded study conducted in 1988 revealed that in ICWA's first eight years, foster or adoptive placement of Indian children actually went up by 25 percent nationally, making the rate of placement of Indian children 3.6 times greater than that of non-Indian children. In 1997, this rate is still alarmingly high. With regard to the urban community, some of the more relevant social problems identified as causes of this trend include "social isolation in urban environments, poor [read non-standard middle class] child-rearing skills, and drug and alcohol abuse." (Mannes 1990, 11 [Note: While non-standard white middle-class parenting skills were often dubbed "poor" by social scientists and service workers, there is an alternative explanation. Many of the Indian children who were placed in Indian boarding schools spent their lives in an environment devoid of family structure. When those children matured, and had families of their own, their unfamiliarity with family structure often fostered "non-traditional" relations between parents and children, typically viewed by case workers as problematic.]) The results of the 1988 study clearly demonstrate that solving the Indian child welfare problem calls for a holistic community remedy that addresses the entire Indian family, not just the children. Attempts to address these problems in Chicago, however, have been sporadic at best.

Many of these problems persist due to the blatant absence of ICWA protection in the city of Chicago. The reasons for this absence are twofold. Simply put, within the framework of ICWA policy, the problems stem from general ignorance of Section I of the act on the part of the state, and general lack of resources to effectively implement Section II of the act on the part of the Indian community. Although the special legal status of Indians in Chicago denies them federally-provided social services away from the reservation, Indian social welfare cases are most often taken up by the state as part of its responsibility to the well-being of its citizens as generic entities. While state policies and procedures for addressing Indian cases have existed in writing at the Department of Children and Family Services (DCFS) since 1978, they are rarely enacted, and the meager training that state social workers receive on such issues is seldom remembered. As one DCFS administrator notes, there has never been any coherent initiative or special attention for how the Indian population is being served (anonymous interview, Illinois Department of Children and Family Services, July 2, 1997). Part of this lack of attention is attributed to the absence of an Indian land base in Illinois (noting that the only "significant" population is in the city of Chicago), and part is attributed to lack of resources afforded to DCFS for such group-specific attention. Within the larger scope of the entire city and state, the Native American population is a minute part of the DCFS caseload. The current estimate of Indian children in substitute care is about 200, compared with 53,000 non-Indian cases statewide (anonymous interview, Illinois Department of Children and Family Services, July 2, 1997).

In the most general sense, this lack of attention and training on the part of DCFS leads to a high rate of misidentification of Indian children by state social workers. There are provisions for identifying Indian children once they are in the state welfare system, but such a passive process is misplaced. Indian children must be identified as such in the first visit by the caseworker in order for ICWA to be correctly and completely enforced. Currently, no instruction exists for such procedures in the field. In a recent study conducted by DCFS and prompted by the Native American Foster Parents Association, 100 social workers known to be handling Indian cases were surveyed. Of the thirty surveys returned, already twenty-seven of those children had been fully adopted into non-Indian homes. This kind of caseworker ignorance, not to mention illegal practice, has been perpetuated since 1978, and only today is the state beginning to admit its negligence.

Sadly, the ramifications of this misinformation are many. It has allowed the practice of forcefully removing Indian children from their homes, putting them in danger of cultural separation, to continue as it did in the days before ICWA. Most often, social workers either do not know the appropriate questions to ask in order to establish the child's ethnic identity, or they are somewhat aware, and only think of families on the most generic level, neglecting special procedures accidentally. Occasionally, workers rely on appearance to indicate whether the child is of Indian ancestry. But identification based on the stereotypical image of the "red man" alone has proven utterly insufficient. Often Indian children look as much Caucasian or African American as they do Indian (anonymous interview, Illinois Department of Children and Family Services, July 2, 1997).

In turn, when the right questions are not asked, frequently Indian parents are not made aware of their rights under ICWA to have their children placed in culturally specific care. There is an obvious need for community education on the act. Akin to this community ignorance is the widespread problem of "unenrollable" Indian children. With the increasing frequency of cross-racial and cross-tribal marriage that is inevitable in an inter-tribal urban community, fewer children are able to meet both tribal and federal blood quantum requirements for recognized Indian status. While these children are recognized as Indian in their own community, they are not eligible for federal or tribal support (interview with Mary Jacobs, NAFPA board member, July 7, 1997). This problem of enrollability and "official" Indian identity could prove particularly harmful if the changes to the ICWA definition of "Indian child" suggested in the Pryce bill are ever implemented. Consequently, the sort of domino effect that this multi-tiered ignorance produces overwhelmingly leaves the children entangled in bureaucratic red tape (often in culturally unsuitable holding shelters) while the family or community and the state hash out what went wrong retro-actively.

The other major obstacle to proper implementation of ICWA is a general lack of resources in the community for appropriate social service administration, mandated by Section II of the act. Such services are intended to be preventative, aimed at the preservation of the Indian family, as well as supportive of children in foster or adoptive care. Perhaps the most important of these services, and the most lacking, is the availability of licensed Native American foster homes. With more than 200 known Indian child welfare cases in Illinois, and approximately twenty-five foster families, the need far outweighs the supply.

Although Native American foster parents are not required to be licensed by the state under ICWA, they must be in order to receive state funding for the support of the child. Unfortunately, the state licensing process is long. Not surprisingly, the part of this process devoted to Indian cases is brief to non-existent. One currently licensed Indian foster parent noted that the attitude of DCFS toward foster parent training on ICWA was overly dismissive, as if to say, "this is a law for Native Americans, but we don't deal with Native American cases very often, so we don't have to worry about it too seriously" (interview with Roxy Grignon, NAFPA Executive Director and foster parent, July 2, 1997).

Other social services, which are required under ICWA for the preservation of Indian families, are equally lacking. Some of these services include drug and alcohol treatment centers, day care facilities, psychiatric counseling for parents and children, and emergency shelters. While the state does offer some of these, and they are free to the public, they are not

adequately equipped to handle the special needs of the Indian community. By and large, the major reasons for Indian children entering the child
welfare system are no different than those of any other race or ethnic
group. Drug and alcohol abuse and domestic violence are prevalent problems throughout the city. But the underlying issues that lead to these
symptoms are often culturally-related ones that need to be addressed
specifically in an Indian setting by someone who understands their origin.

In all of these scenarios, it is ultimately the children who suffer. In the
event of violent relationships, mothers often abuse drugs and alcohol to
escape their problems. The physical abuse and fetal chemical dependency filters down to the children quite readily in many instances. In cases
where the mother has been ostracized because of her association with an
outsider, there is still a feeling of responsibility towards the children on
the part of the community. But acculturating/educating those children
into the culture is often difficult because of the label their mothers carry.
Without proper community social services to handle these important cultural issues, and awareness by the state of their culturally specific nature,
children will continue to be taken from their families on the basis of neglect. Furthermore, poor understanding of extended family placement
options by the state leads to continued thinning of future generations for
the entire Indian community.

SOLUTIONS FROM WITHIN: NAFPA

It is clear that the Chicago Indian community has had a long history of
trying to achieve an equal and reliable distribution between culturally sensitive placement options and competent preventative care in order for
ICWA to be adequately implemented in the urban environment. Historically, the extent of Bureau of Indian Affairs funding has been placement-
oriented, providing a sort of bandaging effect, but no possibility for
addressing the community issues at the heart of the placement problems.
As a result, such dependency on the federal government for already scarce
funds has caused child welfare programs to battle each other on an annual basis, leaving the fate of all organizations in limbo, and making the con-
sistency of services an almost impossible concept (Mannes 1990, 12–13).
This is equally true for the rest of the country as it is for Chicago.

As past studies of Indian child welfare have indicated, in the long run,
it is next to impossible to help troubled at-risk youth without sincere
attempts to transform entire dysfunctional families into working commu-
nicative entities through consistent social service (Mannes 1990, 15 refers
to the 1988 study by M.C. Plantz, et al. entitled *Indian Child Welfare: A
Status Report*). While the state offers some of these necessary services, it
has been shown that finding "Indian friendly" and culturally sensitive
services is extremely difficult. Most often, those services, which manifest

themselves in the removal of Indian children on the basis of cultural mis-understanding or ignorance, are part of the problem, rather than just part of an inadequate solution.

The logical response to the unacceptability of the current Indian child welfare situation, with respect to proper enforcement of ICWA, cultural preservation, and Indian rights in general, would seem to be a response that comes from the heart of the community, where the issues are actual-ly lived on a daily basis. As Weibel-Orlando notes, "An institution whose existence is dependent on policy decision-making processes far removed from the institution's influence and control is particularly vulnerable and unstable. Continuity of traditional institutions independent of supralocal control is a stabilizing factor in an otherwise fairly unstable system" (Weibel-Orlando 1991, 124–5).

THE NATIVE AMERICAN FOSTER PARENTS ASSOCIATION

The Native American Foster Parents Association is the newest organiza-tion in the Chicago Indian Community, truly a grassroots organization in that it began in the home of one person, Roxy Grignon, almost three years ago. (The factual information presented in the remainder of this chapter, unless otherwise cited, is taken from a series of three interviews with Roxy Grignon, an anonymous DCFS administrator, and a second member of the NAFPA board of directors who is also an assistant researcher for DCFS.) It started with no money, no staff, no policy or procedures, and no real clout as a legitimate organization either inside or outside the Indi-an community. As support from community members grew, and Grignon became aware of an increasing number of families at risk, the variety of services she provided from her home increased in turn. She was constantly reminding state social workers that under ICWA, potential foster homes must be evaluated in the least restrictive, and most culturally inclusive framework possible. She educated potential foster parents on their rights in the licensing process and kept a list of those who volunteered. She directed at-risk families to places in the community where they could receive food, clothing, and emergency shelter. She provided transporta-tion to and from court for custody hearings, and sought the help of the resident psychologist at American Indian Health Services to provide fam-ily counseling. In short, she was doing by herself what neither the state nor the Indian community had been able to do for decades.

In December of 1996, a small but important event took place that dras-tically altered DCFS's passive attitude toward NAFPA and the Indian community as a whole. A young Native American woman called Grignon's home (still NAFPA headquarters at the time) in hysterics, say-ing that a state social worker had just taken her five children away from her. She said that she had heard of the services that Grignon was providing and hoped that she could do something to help her get her children back. Grignon told her to call that social worker and tell her that she was an enrolled tribal member, that she and her children had certain rights under ICWA, and that she should call Grignon right away in order to find proper placement for those children. The social worker did call Grignon and said that if she could find enough homes for these five children, she could take them. Within hours, Grignon found homes in the Indian community for all five children and the social worker dropped off the children that evening to meet their new foster parents. As a result of that evening's events, Grignon demonstrated that her organization had the capacity for fast and legal action for the well-being of the community's children. Just a month later, in January of 1997, NAFPA was officially incorporated with an established all Indian board of directors, including Roxy Grignon as the executive director.

The ultimate aim of NAFPA is to create the kind of community safety net which keeps Indian children in their community, providing them with the cultural environment necessary to thrive and be proud of their identities. Likewise, the preservation of the Indian community depends upon the protection and support of the parents. Family reunification and preservation are two of NAFPA's main goals. The referral services that NAFPA provides for at-risk parents are equally important to the process of cultural preservation, with the aim of someday reuniting healed parents and culturally secure children. While parent cooperation is sometimes hard to achieve because of substance abuse or domestic violence–related problems, already NAFPA has successfully placed six children, recruited twenty-one new foster families, and returned two children to their mother and tribe.

Sadly, NAFPA has a long way to go before it can fully compensate for the continuing ignorance of social workers and out-adoption of Indian children into non-Indian homes in the state of Illinois. There are still those twenty-seven Indian children identified by the DCFS survey who were illegally adopted into non-Indian homes even since NAFPA's inception in January of 1997. And the numbers are growing. There is some hope that through NAFPA's relationship with DCFS, those families can be identified and persuaded to undergo cultural sensitivity training themselves, and perhaps bring those children into the community for special programs and events so that they can develop a sense cultural identity.

UNTO THE NEXT GENERATION

"Outside the formal structure of Indian affairs there remain a number of Indian constituencies—urban Indians, sub-tribal groups, and single-issue organizations—whose demands have not been met. Despite federal government efforts to discredit or disorganize some of these groups, and to place tribal governments between itself and them, many retain political capacities of their own, particularly in the areas of litigation and political protest" (Cornell 1984, 55). Although NAFPA's agenda could not be categorized as political protest, NAFPA does participate in a sort of active resistance to illegal practices that easily qualifies it as one of these groups.

LOCAL COMMUNITY POLITICS

The fact that NAFPA began as a truly grassroots organization with no staff, no funding, and relatively few assumptions has proven to be an important factor in its success as a community institution. The history of the Chicago Indian community shows that the success or failure of a social institution is often directly related to availability of funds, and that when funding is made the first concern, institutions are not above battling each other to keep their own programs alive. The community relations which ensue are antagonistic and factionalized, preventing the kind of united front necessary to bring about long-term change for the betterment of the whole community.

Because the achievement of NAFPA's goals is not entirely contingent upon the meager funding that many of the other community institutions vie for, it has the opportunity to change the way that institutional politics operate in the Indian community from beyond the fray. By setting an example of how to interact strictly on an organization-to-organization basis, NAFPA can move the focus of discussion from the relationships of the individual parties involved to the achievement of a universally understood goal–in this case, the protection of the community's children and the preservation of Indian culture and identity.

URBAN POSSIBILITIES

The more specific model that NAFPA creates is equally promising for improved ICWA enforcement in other urban Indian communities with similar problems. At the 1997 ICWA conference in Reno, Nevada—a conference that generally addresses issues of reservation ICWA enforcement and tribal jurisdiction, discounting the problematic status of the urban community—NAFPA representatives got a standing ovation after they addressed the conference about the work they are doing and the success they are having. Requests for program information came pouring in from other urban child welfare organizations, a fact Roxy Grignon largely attributes to NAFPA's ability to address a singular issue and achieve visible stability with relative speed and little money (Roxy Grignon interview, July 2, 1997).

While the idea of a foster parent registry is not a totally unique idea in urban Indian communities, NAFPA's relationship with the state of Illinois via DCFS, and their positive approach to sensitive jurisdictional issues, is something that other urban ICWA related community-based programs have been unable to achieve. Broken into its component parts, NAFPA has been able to build a strong, productive relationship with the state for two basic reasons. First, by approaching the reform process from an improved training standpoint, rather than as a tug of war over children as a preemptive measure to the state's authority, NAFPA is continuing to allow the state to do its job as child welfare administrator, while making sure that the Indian community has a hand in how that job is done. According to Kalven's model, "the powers that be" (in this case the state child welfare system) often act out of concern for doing their job, while their actions fail to serve the interests of their beneficiaries, and instead serve the interest of larger external players (Kalven 1997, 9). NAFPA's approach to improved child welfare administration serves to counter that model.

Similarly, by providing DCFS with a registry of foster parent names from which to work, NAFPA bypasses a major legal issue that has served as a road-block for other urban groups with similar registries and goals. In Rapid City, South Dakota, for example, a group called the Brown Stone Woman Project is trying to build the same kind of registry with similar emergency placement facilities. The group has likewise tried to establish a working relationship with the state of South Dakota (a state with a significantly larger Indian population than Illinois). But their approach has been one which requires the state police and child welfare authorities to notify the organization immediately whenever they encounter a child at risk. In turn, the use of the registry for proper substitute placement is held exclusively by the Project itself. The inevitable problem with such an approach is one of confidentiality. The state of South Dakota is bound by law to keep the names of any families entering the system confidential. Only in the event that the court assigns the case to another agency can that kind of information be released (Porterfield 1997, 1,3). By providing a registry for the state's direct use, rather than keeping one as a preemptive measure, NAFPA has been able to override the state's confidentiality provisions as a quasi-contracted service provider, without stepping on any state toes.

In regard to funding issues, NAFPA has taken effective and legal action on things they could do without funding. But what NAFPA does demonstrate is that the perception that progress equals capital "induces a sort of paralysis," to borrow from Kalven (Kalven 1997, 5). To allow this paralysis to enter the body of an organization is to say that the agenda of that body will only be accomplished on the terms of the people who possess the capital. This in itself is not a new concept. But the prevention of this paralysis is something that few groups have been able to grasp. By focusing on the reclamation of resources that do not require capital, such as abandoned, neglected, or misplaced Indian children, and Native American foster parents, much of task at hand can be accomplished before funding even becomes an issue. In turn, suggests Kalven, this kind of reclamation and commitment to progress attracts capital from outside (Kalven 1997, 10), as has been the case between NAFPA and DCFS.

FEDERAL IMPLICATIONS: A NEW DEFINITION

Although the implications of NAFPA as a model for reform on the federal level are not as immediately visible as those on the local and inter-urban level, they are perhaps the most significant in the overall scope of federal Indian law and policy. As a model for other urban Indian communities, NAFPA represents a demographic region that encompasses well over half of the Native American population in this country. The political leverage that NAFPA has already claimed on behalf of the entire Chicago Indian community in its dealings with the state of Illinois suggests that the time has come for redefining the relationship of the federal government to urban Indian communities in general. The Chicago Indian community and other urban communities like it should not be viewed as haphazard extensions of tribal governments and reservation communities, but as separate intertribal communities with agendas and political power of their own. NAFPA's success in Chicago only expedites this inevitable political realization. And while NAFPA is content to deal with one community issue at a time, the issue it has chosen and the tactics it has used have been extremely important in paving the way for the new urban Indian politics nationwide. ("The New Indian Politics" was a term coined by Stephen Cornell in his 1984 article by the same name as a way of describing the political climate in federal–Indian relations since the beginning of the era of self-determination in the early 1960s.)

As has already been discussed, the political status of Indians in cities is unique. In many cases, ties to reservation communities are strong due to extended family contact, ceremonial practices and tribal enrollment. In other cases, urban residents are not enrolled tribal members at all, but their Indian ancestry is widely acknowledged by the urban community. It has also been shown that because of this unique status, the urban community has its own set of social and political issues that remain unaddressed by the government that has vowed to protect them under the federal trust relationship. The problems, such as lack of adequate social service administration, have been primarily handed down to the tribes in a misguided attempt at honoring tribal sovereignty. But the tribes are as far removed from the sources of the problems as the federal government, and frequently have their hands tied by state jurisdiction. ICWA is the first legitimate legislative attempt at addressing the relationship between federal, tribal, and state government, but again urban populations are left in limbo, as shown above.

In demonstrating how NAFPA serves as a model for a new urban Indian politics, an important distinction must be made. That distinction is the nature of the urban community's collective self-concept, as it compares to that of tribes. Stephen Cornell writes that the evolution of Indian groups took place historically along two related but distinct paths— the conceptual and the political or organizational—and that today, multi-faceted ethnic self-concept has been greatly subordinated to the political group organization that was imposed by white society through the formation of tribes (Cornell 1988, 27, 42). Indeed, the category of "tribe" has been the basic political unit upon which federal-Indian relations have been based for centuries, carrying with it the tribal name as the imposing society's nod to cultural autonomy. But in urban areas like Chicago, where there is no defining land base or uniformity of dress or domicile, collective self-concept is hidden. As a result, there has been no attempt at imposed political organization. Nevertheless, the political concerns of the people are just as real, and just as culturally specific as are their rights as Indians.

In light of this organizational discrepancy, NAFPA is attempting to enter the political arena, as a sort of self-imposed organization in the Cornellian sense, by actively pursuing better ICWA enforcement from other political groups. Through its relationship with the state, NAFPA is proclaiming that the community's social and political concerns are equal to those of other political bodies. In turn, NAFPA's reclamation of Indian children for the Indian community helps reinforce the continuity of community self-concept and make it visible and viable to other political entities.

This is not to say that urban Indian communities should occupy the same status as tribes. To give every urban Indian community the status of sovereign would be redundant. What NAFPA is demanding is a voice for the urban community in the determination of its own affairs—a voice that has long been misplaced in the throat of a polity unfamiliar with the issues at hand. By actively reclaiming control over the protection of local Indian children under the auspices of ICWA, NAFPA is not only claiming control over the future of the Chicago community, it is also preparing the ground for the Chicago Indian community's participation on the urban, state, and national political stages in the future.

As Jamie Kalven so eloquently put it, "It is not a matter of seizing power, or courting power, but of generating power in the sphere of everyday life, the domain in which we, after all, live out our lives" (Kalven 1997, 31). Such is the case with NAFPA. One child, one issue, one day at a time, the new urban Indian politics will come to the fore.

BIBLIOGRAPHY

Beck, David, ed. *Chicago Native American Community Annotated Bibliography*. Entries 930-4
1. (actual archives missing as of 6/97).

Cornell, Stephen. "Crisis and Response in Indian-White Relations: 1960-1984" In *Social Problems*, Vol. 32, no.1, 1984:55.

Cornell, Stephen. "The Transformations of Tribe: Organization and Self-Concept in Native American Ethnicities," 1988: 27,42.

Mannes, Marc, ed. *Family Preservation and Indian Child Welfare*, 1990: 11.

Porterfield, K. Marie. "ICWA Registry Plan Slowed by Privacy Rules." *Indian Country Today*, 1997: Section C: page 1,3.

Stealer, Norma. "Indian Children Need Indian Homes." *The American Indian Church Woman*, vol. 38, no. 2, 1972: 12-14. In the Community Archives of NAES College.

Straus, Terry (1989).: *Indians of the Chicago Area* (1st ed.) Chicago; NAES College Press. 166-7.

Weibel-Orlando, Joan. Indian Country, L.A., 1991: 83

Richard King

NARA, the Center of Indian Community in Portland, Oregon
A Possible Model for Chicago

NARA, the Native American Rehabilitation Association of the North West, Inc., was started in the early 1970s as a halfway house for alcoholic American Indians who were in need of a clean and sober living space. NARA has evolved throughout the years as the center of community for the urban Indian population of the city of Portland, Oregon. This evolution did not happen overnight; it was a slow but steady process.

In Portland, as in most large cities, there is a relatively large and diverse Indian population. Some Indians came to Portland to work; they are often employed by the federal government (in the Indian Health Service and the Bureau of Indian Affairs, both of which have area offices in Portland, and in other federal agencies such as the Veterans Administration, the US Postal Service, Housing and Urban Development), or by tribal and non-profit organizations such as NARA, the Selitz Tribe, the Portland Area Indian Health Board, and last but not least, the Intertribal Fisheries Office. Indians who are enrolled members of the various tribes located in Oregon sometimes choose to live in Portland even if they do not work in the community: these Indians are members of the Warm Springs tribes of the Warm Springs Indian Reservation, the Klamath tribe, and the smaller coastal tribes such as the Grande Rhonde and Selitz tribes. The fourth and catch-all group are Indians who arrived in Portland through Relocation, and other ways. The BIA Relocation effort brought many Indians to Portland and also a number of people relocated here to work for the war effort during World War II. As with all Indian urban groups, the Portland Indian community is as diverse as Indians themselves; they are from many different Nations and tribes throughout the US. The categories I have outlined are just that, categories for definition purposes only. Indian people tend to float from group to group, but I believe it would be safe to say that my categories are much intact for community definition purposes. NARA throughout its many years of existence has evolved as the primary center of Indian community in the greater Portland metropolitan area, also including the Vancouver, Washington metro area.

NARA was originally a halfway house for recovering alcoholics that was formed primarily by recovering alcoholics who were Indian and had no "Indian" place to go after getting out of treatment or in many situations out of the Oregon state penal system. The first "NARA House," as it was originally called and is sometimes still called today, was located on the east side of the Willamette River just across Powell Boulevard downtown. The original site is now a place for fast food restaurants. NARA moved from Powell Boulevard to the area east of the Willamette across the river from downtown on Division Street. The facility on Division Street is presently the outpatient alcohol/drug program. It had served as an inpatient treatment center for many years and as the need and concept of NARA expanded it was eventually converted into an outpatient treatment program as well as an outpatient medical clinic for clients who were in treatment at NARA.

NARA, through its many years of expanding, obtained a lease on an older rest home that was located in Gresham, a small town that the city of Portland has literally consumed. This facility was large and had ample room for the needs of NARA and its treatment mission. This facility had room for at least 75 client beds if it were used to full capacity. NARA usually averaged about 50 clients at maximum including men, women and small children of clients who were in inpatient treatment. The Gresham facility had a day-care center for the client's children, a GED program sponsored by a local junior college, and a sweat lodge for clients in inpatient treatment. NARA was one of the first Indian programs in the U.S. to integrate culture and use culture as one of the components in their treatment program. Culture is one of the main, if not the main, aspects of treatment and recovery in the NARA treatment model. NARA's treatment program is a combination of the twelve steps of recovery as originally outlined by Alcoholics Anonymous and Indian (primarily Lakota) cultural attributes such as the sweat lodge and sundance ceremonies.

Because NARA has become very successful at treating both men and women clients, NARA also has incorporated the treatment of families as well as adding a day care center for the families involved in inpatient treatment. The day care center is only available to the children of clients who are in inpatient treatment and these clients are primarily women. Being a non-profit Indian organization, NARA usually networks with other Indian and non-Indian service organizations and agencies in the city of Portland to assist their clients in their recovery journey. Clients at NARA are then able to obtain services available to everyone in the Portland metro area such as being eligible for the food stamp program, county health services, and also access to halfway houses and sober living situations when they eventually leave in-patient treatment. One of the many reasons for NARA's high success rate for treatment is that the required stay for inpatient treatment is between 45 and 60 days. The national average stay in inpatient today is usually 21 days. NARA has a very positive reputation among recovered alcoholics/drug addicts and counselors in the field of chemical dependency treatment in the Northwest, and is generally thought of as the primary Indian treatment program in the Northwest (although, this point is debatable with other Indian treatment programs in the Northwest and with people who relapse and have not successfully completed in patient treatment). It would be politically correct to say that NARA is the premier Indian treatment program in the state of Oregon for families and adults.

In the 1980s several Indian programs and Indian centers throughout the U.S. closed their doors due to the "Reagan Revolution" and "Reaganomics." Portland, Oregon, also closed their Indian Center due to the effects of Reaganomics, the mismanagement of funds, and to embezzlement by the director. This situation shifted some of the potential Indian Center clients to NARA, but realistically it never had a significant impact on NARA. The majority of the potential Indian Center clients with chemical dependency issues did not acknowledge that they had a need for chemical dependency treatment.

One important thing: NARA did not get into the human services business, other than chemical dependency treatment, until the 1990s. Even though NARA did have an office for placing clients in housing, assisting them in obtaining employment and performing these types of services were primarily for their clients. Their focus remained on their clients only and not the Portland Indian community at large. NARA's board of directors did not utilize their clout as leaders of the Indian community until 1993, when a local Indian organization with an Indian Health Service (IHS) contract to operate an Indian health clinic lost their contract with IHS. NARA did operate a small health clinic for its active inpatient and outpatient clients. This clinic was located in the outpatient building and was operated by the county and staffed by a nurse practitioner and a registered nurse. NARA's board of directors was approached by IHS to oversee the health clinic on an interim basis and, after board action, agreed to oversee the clinic as a service to the Indian community of Portland. Eventually, NARA accepted the Portland Indian Health clinic under their organization on a permanent basis.

So, today, NARA has evolved from a halfway house for male alcoholics in the early 1970s to the center of Indian community in Portland in the late 1990s. How did NARA evolve from a halfway house initially called "NARA House" to the center of Indian community in about a 25-year period? The answer to this question is really quite simple and logical.

Over the years, NARA has produced literally hundreds of alumni and for-mer employees who live in the Northwest and are recovering people: this writer is an example. Many of the former NARAee's have remained and settled in the Portland metro area and in the Northwest in general. These former NARAees have obtained employment in most all, if not all, the Indian organizations in Portland as well as many of the non Indian organ-izations. These former NARAees have had a positive influence on the Indian community as a whole and in general have had a recovering effect on the Indian population of Portland.

Not all of the Indian population in Portland is in recovery, but a sig-nificant number is and they have a positive, "move forward," attitude. This "move forward" attitude in the Indian community has replaced the negative "Indian crab bucket" attitude for Indians in Portland. (The story of the Indian crab bucket is as follows: "There was a bucket of Indian crabs and each time one of the crabs would get to the top of the bucket, all the other crabs would pull it back down. In essence, all the other crabs would not allow the one crab to get out of the bucket or get ahead.")

To illustrate my point that former NARAees have made a positive impact on Portland, I will use the annual Delta Park powwow as an exam-ple. The Delta Park powwow is held in conjunction with the famous Rose Festival, an annual event held each year in the city of Portland. This is the largest summer powwow held in Portland and it is held in June of each year. The committee for the Delta Park powwow is usually made up of several NARAees who play an important part in the powwow's protocol. The Delta Park powwow promotes a non-drinking or drugging policy at this community event and this is a direct link to NARA's recovery mission. NARA usually sponsors a large powwow during the Christmas and New Year holidays. This powwow usually attracts former NARAees who have been a part of NARA at one time or another as well as Indian people from the Portland metro area. The vast majority of people attracted to this hol-iday event are in recovery and are clean and sober. This is also somewhat like a family reunion for the huge NARA family scattered throughout the Northwest. NARA with its positive attitude and with its mission of sobri-ety and wellness in its existence, has become and remains the center of Indian community in Portland, Oregon.

NARA recently obtained a new complex which is located outside of the city of Portland in Scapoose. This complex was originally built as a Chris-tian school for a Christian church-related organization. This complex was sold to a large national chain of chemical dependency treatment centers that sprang up nationwide in the 1970s and 80s. This treatment organiza-tion remodeled the school into a first-class treatment center. They remod-eled the school building into a inpatient unit and left the gymnasium and ball field intact for client recreational purposes. The only real improvement NARA had to add on to this magnificent complex was a sweat lodge. NARA now has a very beautiful treatment campus located out in the evergreen forest of Oregon. This is a tremendous move from a run down rest home to this very beautiful complex. As NARA continues to treat chemically dependent Indians, this beautiful complex will only influence the clients to feel better about themselves in this wonderful surrounding.

NARA has steadily maintained its primary treatment goal of providing chemical dependency treatment to the Indian communities of the Northwest in both Portland and the reservations located in the BIA and IHS administrative areas. Did NARA become the center of the Indian community because its primary focus is on chemical dependency treatment? I would argue that once a community treats its primary problem of addiction it will become healthier in all areas of its life. Just like when a person becomes chemical free, almost always their life will improve in all areas. I argue that it is not only true for individuals but also this is true for communities. Communities are like individuals: if you treat the disease in a community, such as chemical dependency, the community will eventually get better and recover. NARA did and will remain the center of Indian community in Portland. This is due to the fact that NARA is doing something about the number one problem of the American Indian, if not the entire U.S., treating chemical dependency and its related issues, and showing positive results.

My father is a traditional Assiniboine and my mother was a Chippewa-Cree, both from Montana. In my lifetime and in my recovery journey as an Indian, I have had the privilege to live in large urban areas where there are numerous Indians from all over. I lived in Portland, Oregon, for a number of years. I also had the privilege of living in Chicago at two different times in my life, as a young sailor at the height of the Vietnam War and as a graduate student in 1996–97 at the University of Chicago. I realistically believe that the recovery movement in Portland, Oregon, can be adapted in Chicago and can be utilized by the Indians living in this great city. This article represents a model for any Indians to utilize to begin recovering from all the terrible aspects of the disease of alcoholism that affects us all. I have never met an Indian person who has not been directly affected by alcoholism and its terrible effects. The success of NARA has to lie in the fact that the focus of their program was treating chemical dependency and its effects. NARA did not focus on social services: it focused only on addiction and recovery. When we focus on social services, we tend to forget about addiction. This is what worked for NARA. I believe a similar type of treatment program could work in Chicago, but it will take time to get started. Chicago has all sorts of resources available to get such a program started, numerous positive and recovering Indians to set something up very similar to NARA, social services, and funding. Even though alcohol has taken a terrible toll on Native peoples, when we focus on recovery, healing takes place. I can see the idea of NARA taking place in Chicago to the benefit of all Native people.

Grant P. Arndt

WITH INFORMATION PROVIDED BY

Demetrio Abangan, Jennifer Jones, and John Dall

The Nation in the City

*The Ho-Chunk Nation's Chicago
Branch Office and the Ho-Chunk
People of Chicago*

Observers of Native American movement to cities like Chicago once believed that urbanization would mean the end of tribal identity, as "pan-Indianism" paved the way for total assimilation. That view is changing. Based on their extended observation and participation in Chicago's Native American community, Terry Straus and Debra Valentino (Oneida/Menominee) have recently suggested (1996) that the "detribalized" sense of Indian identity fostered by intertribal urban organizations is being countered by a trend towards "retribalization." To explain this new and unanticipated development, they cite changing demographic profiles that now place the majority of enrolled Native Americans in urban areas, combined with a recent surge in economic and political development among a number of Native American tribes. Such trends have led Native Americans living in cities to assert their connection to their tribal communities, and tribal communities and governments to reach out to their urban members.

The Ho-Chunk people of Wisconsin are at the forefront of the retribalization of Native American life in Chicago. In October of 1993, the Ho-Chunk Nation (then known as the Wisconsin Winnebago Tribe) opened an office in Chicago. In doing so, the Ho-Chunk people became one of the few American Indian tribes in the country to create an official governmental presence in a city. The experience of the Ho-Chunk people provides insight into what it means to be a part of a Native American nation while living in the city.

History of the Ho-Chunk Nation

According to their traditions, the Ho-Chunk people originated at a place on the shores of Lake Michigan, north of Green Bay (Lurie 1978). It was probably nearby that they first encountered Europeans. Ho-Chunk villages spread across Wisconsin throughout the next centuries until, in the early nineteenth century the United States attempted to forcibly remove them across the Mississippi after a series of treaties and land cessions (Lurie 1978). Though many tribal members adapted to life on a series of reservations in Iowa, Minnesota, South Dakota, and ultimately Nebraska (now home of the Winnebago Tribe of Nebraska), a large number of the Ho-Chunk people rejected attempts to make them leave Wisconsin. These Ho-Chunk people continued to live on the land in the tall pine forests of south-central Wisconsin. Together with those who returned from the forced Relocation throughout the nineteenth century, they constitute the ancestors of the present day Ho-Chunk Nation (Lurie 1978). After petitioning the government, the Ho-Chunk people eventually received allotments of individual homesteads in a number of clusters throughout the central Wisconsin area. In these communities, they kept their culture and language alive and resisted the encroachment of European-American society all around them, surviving as a people. With the passage of the Indian Reorganization Act in 1934 the Ho-Chunk began to discuss reconstituting a formal government. In 1963, they adopted a constitution and became officially recognized as the Wisconsin Winnebago Tribe (Gudinas 1974). By that time, a significant number of Ho-Chunk people spent at least a portion of the year outside their homestead areas, many working in cities across the country.

Ho-Chunk Life in Chicago

Native Americans from tribes across the country began moving to Chicago during and after World War II. A number of Ho-Chunk individuals from both Wisconsin and Nebraska were already living in the city, and joined with newer arrivals to become leading participants in Chicago Native American life. They helped found and lead several important early intertribal community organizations, including the Indian Council Fire (most active in the period between 1923–1954), the North American Indian Mission (1947–8) and the All-Tribes American Indian Center (1953–present). In 1956, a number of Ho-Chunk people active in Chicago's Native American community at the American Indian Center formed the Chicago Winnebago Club as an organization to encourage socialization and cultural exchange among the Ho-Chunk people in Chicago (Snowball 1986, 16). According to Brenda Snowball's research and her interview with Benjamin Bearskin Sr., (Carley 1986, 16):

The meetings consisted of bringing food to share, listening to tribal songs, dancing, gathering and exchanging information .... It offered an opportunity to speak their native language as opposed to the day-to-day use of English (Snowball 1986, 16).

Willard LaMere, an important leader in Chicago Native American organizations, described the club as a way for younger tribal members being raised in the city to be "educated in regard to cultural exchange, the language, tribal politics, folk art and folk traditions unique to the Winnebago" (Snowball 1986, 17).

THE HO-CHUNK TRIBAL OFFICE

In the early 1990s, members of the Ho-Chunk Nation became concerned that members living outside of the immediate area should share in the services the tribal government offered to members living near the tribal lands in Wisconsin. The tribal government decided to open branch offices in several midwestern cities. In addition to offices in La Crosse, Madison, and Milwaukee, Wisconsin and St. Paul, Minnesota, the Ho-Chunk Nation opened an office in Chicago.

Because urban tribal offices are an unprecedented institution for the Ho-Chunk people and a unique development for Native American governments more generally, the office went through a period of experimentation as its staff and tribal members tried to determine what the office would do. At the core of the office's mission, according to Demetrio Abangan, former director of the Chicago office, was helping tribal members living in Illinois obtain the same benefits as those enjoyed by Ho-Chunk people living on tribal land in Wisconsin. That has been the office's major function since. Office staff provide Ho-Chunk Nation members with help in obtaining tribal loans for education and housing, At-Large health and social services, as well as general problem-solving and assistance with paperwork. Ho-Chunk people can also walk in for more individualized services, such as funds for a trip home to Wisconsin in case of special need. The office staff also act as advocates for Ho-Chunk and other Native peoples living in Chicago in their lives in the city, as well as attempting to aid Native Americans from other tribes who stop in. In 1997, the office also arranged for the Ho-Chunk Nation to purchase ancestral land in Utica, Illinois, near Starved Rock State Park, where the office holds an annual powwow. According to Jennifer Jones, current head of the office, the Starved Rock land may be used as a site for the sale of NA arts or the construction of housing for Ho-Chunk elders.

While its main concern is linking Ho-Chunk people in Chicago with the tribal community in Wisconsin, the Chicago Branch Office has also established connections to its urban community. During his time as office director, Mr. Abangan sat on the local chamber of commerce and also worked with branches of the Metropolitan government, in one case offering office space for a local advocate from the mayor's offices. Such activities form important parts of the Office's role as a public representative of the Ho-Chunk people. The office has also attempted to support and cooperate with other local Native American organizations, and tries to assist other Native Americans who stop in.

THE CHICAGO AREA LEGISLATIVE MEETING

Following the increase in government programming and services by the Ho-Chunk Nation in the early 1990s, Ho-Chunk residents of Chicago began to hold meetings to provide a forum for obtaining proper recognition and input for Ho-Chunk people living in Chicago. The creation of a new tribal government with the 1994 adoption of the constitution for the Ho-Chunk Nation gave the Chicago area meeting a new level of connection to government decision making. The new government includes a legislative branch composed of representatives from five districts. Legislative Area Five represents all "At-Large" Ho-Chunk tribal members outside the fourteen counties in Wisconsin containing the main Ho-Chunk tribal land. A census of tribal members taken by the Ho-Chunk Nation in 1995 shows that there are substantial numbers of Ho-Chunk tribal members living in urban areas like Chicago, Minneapolis/St, Paul, Milwaukee, and in many other states, including Colorado and California, and that over half of all the 5,500 tribal members live in Area Five.

The new tribal constitution provided a new function for the revived Winnebago Club, which was transformed into the monthly Chicago Legislative Meeting. Ten to twenty tribal members meet once a month in a conference room at the branch office, decorated with a large flag of the Ho-Chunk Nation in the background. After an opening communal meal and prayer, the group discusses tribal matters, including both recent and pending government actions and local area plans. Conducted according to the forms of Robert's Rules of Order, the meetings are tape recorded so that minutes can be handed out at the next meeting. After reviewing the minutes for the previous meeting, tribal members can introduce new topics for discussion. The monthly meetings also often provide a chance to interact with legislators and other representatives of the Ho-Chunk National Government. Legislators attend the monthly meetings in Chicago and at the other branches to discuss recent issues of governance with their constituents. Participants in the monthly meetings can voice area concerns to their legislative representatives, so that the representatives can take the concerns back to the full Ho-Chunk legislature and seek appropriate action. The Chicago Branch office, like the branch offices in other cities, is used as a polling place for at-large members in all Ho-Chunk Nation elections.

The Ho-Chunk Nation's government and Ho-Chunk Nation tribal members in Chicago are now actively exploring what it means to establish official governmental functions for tribal members in cities off tribal lands. Because the representation of non-local tribal members is a new and unprecedented governmental challenge, the ongoing events in Chicago will determine the future role of urban members of the Ho-Chunk Nation in their tribal government and the collective life of the Ho-Chunk people.

CONCLUSION

The connection of Chicago's Ho-Chunk residents to their national community in Wisconsin has taken on a new form with the creation of the Ho-Chunk Nation Urban Branch Office, but the underlying connection itself has existed ever since Ho-Chunk people first moved to Chicago. Ho-Chunk people living in Chicago have traveled home to Wisconsin and Nebraska on an annual basis ever since first moving to the city. By making urban Ho-Chunk people part of their national government, the Ho-Chunk Nation exemplifies the increasing importance of tribal governments and communities in urban Native American life. This "retribalization" of urban life not only reinforces tribal identities among Native Americans living in cities, but also underscores the foundational importance of tribal identities and communities to Native American peoples, wherever they live.

BIBLIOGRAPHY

Gudinas, Ruth. 1974. "Wisconsin Winnebago Political Organization: Structure/Culture Incompatibility and Organization Effectiveness." Ph.D Dissertation. Department of Political Science. The University of Chciago.

Lurie, Nancy O. 1978 "Winnebego." in Handbook of North American Indian, Volume 15: Northeast. ed. Bruce Trigger. Washington D.C.: Smithsonian Institution Press.

Snowball, Brenda. 1986. "The Chicago Winnebgo Club." Bachelor's thesis. NAES College.

Straus, Terry and Debra Valentino. 1996. "Retribalization in Urban Indian Communities." Paper presented at the American Anthropological Association Annual Meeting, November 1996. San Francisco, CA.

PART II
CONTEMPORARY LIFE

SECTION TWO
HERITAGE AND HISTORY

Coming Home: The Return of the Ancestors
CLARE FARRELL
209

The Schingoethe Center of Native American Cultures
DONNA BACHMAN
219

Clare Farrell

Coming Home

The Return of the Ancestors

The historic settlement of the area we call Chicago today began over two hundred years ago with the trading post of Jean Baptiste du Sable in 1779. Long before its recorded development, however, this area was home to many Native nations, including the Illiniwek, Miami, Sauk, Meskwaki, Potawatomi, Ottawa, Ojibwe, Mascouten, and Ho-Chunk, besides the peoples of early prerecorded time. Over this period of thousands of years, there is a history of life and death that has left innumerable unmarked grave sites. According to the spiritual ways of North American Native peoples in general, death is the passage from life in one world to life in the next—a journey that must not be interrupted. Burial rites took many forms depending on the individual Nation's practices, but one code was universal: the ancestors must not be disturbed in their final resting place.

The Potawatomi Way of Respect for the Dead

The following is from an interview with Potawatomie Elder Billy Daniels (Forest County Band), head of the cultural program *Mnoknomagewen* (Good Teaching), which works to preserve the traditional culture:

* * *

As Indians, we come from heaven—from God—in the first place, and when we die, we go out west to a spiritual place that non-Indians call "spirit land." This is our "Indian heaven," which is a different place than the non-Indians heaven.

When one of our people die, we have a ceremony to send them on their journey. We can't talk about what happens at this time, unless we're at a funeral. It is not good to talk about this at other times. Some tribes will, but we have to follow our own traditions. Four days after the burial, we build a small house on top of the grave. This is what has always been done, and our people still do this on our own tribal burial grounds. It's like having a tombstone, but we don't write anything on the houses.

Once our people are buried, they should not be disturbed. The reason we have a funeral is to leave them there to rest. They are on a journey to the west, and we don't know how long it takes—only God knows. Our people don't feel good about our ancestors' graves being dug up, and their remains being studied and stored in museums. I always ask non-Indians the question: "How would you like it if someone dug you up and put you in a case?" They always say they wouldn't like it. We as Indians have a lot of feeling toward nature, and believe that everything should be left alone as it was meant to be.

When our graves are disturbed, we offer tobacco and ask our ancestors' forgiveness. Tobacco is our leader, like the non-Indian has the Bible. We pray that we, the descendants, are kept safe, because our ancestors are angry when they are disturbed, and we don't want their anger to come back on us.

There are only a few people on the reservation who know how to do a reburial ceremony the right way, and these are the only people who will do it. Otherwise, it's too dangerous. Those that are still in the ground should stay there—all colors of people should know that. I'm not very old and I know that. I know that we should follow our traditions. We often address our ancestors in prayers, and offer them food, asking their help. We don't forget them, because we're all connected.

* * * *

After the invasion of the Americas in 1492, disrespect for the Native American life way extended to the desecration and destruction of burial sites across the country. In Illinois, there was no legal protection for unmarked burials until 1989, and Indian burials were either removed or swept aside to make way for the burgeoning population. In keeping with the policy across the country, Native ancestral remains, along with their associated burial goods that were kept for study, were stored in institutions across and outside the U.S.A. Native self-awareness and self-esteem in the 1970s gave birth to the demand for repatriation: the return of ancestral remains, burial goods, and cultural items to their respective nations.

The history of the repatriation movement in North America spans only a short term in the last quarter of the twentieth century. The desecration of Native American graves, on the other hand, began with the landing of the Pilgrims at Plymouth Rock in 1620. The journal of their voyage records that the very first Pilgrim exploring party had dug up a grave and robbed it of its burial goods. Since that time, wanton disrespect for Native American dead and the sacred traditions that support reverence for the ancestors has continued unabated (Dwight B. Heath, *Mourt's Relation: A Journal of the Pilgrims at Plymouth*, 27-28, 1986).

The initial protest to the continued excavation, display and storage of Native American ancestral remains rode on the wave of the civil rights movement. These activities were recognized as symbols of oppression and racism against the Native community. In 1974, a group called American Indians Against Desecration (AIAD) formed with the intent of influencing legislation to bring about the return and reburial of Native American remains. Then in 1986, several Northern Cheyenne leaders discovered that almost 18,500 ancestral remains were warehoused in the Smithsonian Institution. This catalyzed a national effort by Indian organizations to obtain proper repatriation laws. The first piece of legislation that dealt with the issue was the National Museum of the American Indian Act in 1989, directed specifically at repatriation efforts within the Smithsonian Institution. Then in 1990, Senator John McCain (R-AZ), Senator Daniel Inouye (D-HI), Representative Morris Udall (D-AZ), and Representative Charles Bennett (D-FL) all introduced bills that culminated in the creation of the Native American Graves Protection and Repatriation Act (NAGPRA).

A long grisly history of abuse preceded this enlightened legislation. Up to two million Native American remains are currently held in museums, government agencies, and private collections—nearly as many as the population of Native people alive today. (No accurate national census of these dead has yet been done. Various estimates are compiled in David J. Harris, *Respect for the Living and Respect for the Dead: Return of Indian and Other Native American Burial Remains*, 39 Wash. U. J. Urb. & Contemp. L. 195 n.3, *supra* note 4, 1991, including Haas (100,000-150,000), Moore (300,000-600,000 in US alone), National Congress of American Indians (more than 1.5 million) and Deloria (2 million).) These had been obtained by soldiers, government agents, pothunters, private citizens, museum collecting crews, and scientists in the name of profit, entertainment, science, or development. The systematic collection of body parts began before the Civil War, with Dr. Samuel Morton collecting large numbers of Indian crania in the 1840s. He intended to scientifically prove, through skull measurements, that the American Indian was racially inferior, thereby establishing the "Vanishing Red man" theory. This study became the scientific justification used by the government to relocate tribes, take tribal land, and establish policies of genocide (Robert E. Bieder, *A Brief Historical Survey of the Expropriation of American Indian Remains, supra* note 13, 1990, i.e., The Bieder Report).

The taking of Indian body parts became official federal policy with the Surgeon General's Order of 1868. The policy directed army personnel to procure Indian crania and other body parts for the Army Medical Museum (Reproduced in full in the Bieder Report, supra note 13, at 36-37). Over several decades, more than 4000 heads were taken from battlefields, burial grounds, POW camps, hospitals, fresh graves, and burial scaffolds across the country. Government head hunters even decapitated Natives who had never been buried—Pawnee warriors from a Kansas battlefield, Cheyenne and Arapaho victims of the Sand Creek Massacre, and Modoc leaders who had been hung. Collection crews from museums also competed for remains to furbish their newfounded institutions (Entries in accession records for the Army Medical Museum, Anatomical Section: A.M.M., nos. 8-12 from W. H. Forwood, Assistant Surgeon, US Army, Ft. Riley, Kansas, January 20, 1867).

The glaring contradiction behind these practices is shown in the universal code that early American society and its governance was based on. In common law jurisprudence, which the U.S. inherited from England, respect for the dead was considered a mark of humanity. A British Prime Minister, William E. Gladstone, once wrote:

> Show me the manner in which a nation or a community cares for its dead, and I will measure with mathematical exactness the tender sympathies of its people, their respect for the laws of the land, and their loyalty to high ideals.

This same value system arrived with the early settlers, with the understanding that the normal treatment of a body, once buried, is to let it lie. Over the ensuing centuries, U.S. law has developed strict cemetery regulations that protect grave sites in perpetuity, and make it a crime to disturb a grave in any way. Yet none of these considerations were applied regarding Native American burials, reflecting the racist attitudes of the invading nations, for it was not until 1879 that a federal court ruled that an Indian was a "person" by federal standards (United States *ex rel.* Standing Bear v. Crook, 25 F. Cas. 695 (C.C.D. Neb. 1879)(No. 14, 891). This, and the fact that Indians were not granted citizenship until 1924, made any successful legal protest an impossibility.

Besides NAGPRA of 1990, which has limited ability to protect burials on federally-owned land, forty-three states have passed unmarked burial protection laws in recent years, including Illinois and all the midwestern states. Most, however, do not protect as fully as necessary. Removal of human remains is allowed for everything from highway expansion to golf course and recreation areas, but with the benefit of repatriation to the descendants.

The extent of trauma to the Indian nations as a whole due to the centuries of grave site desecration is beyond estimation. Native Americans recognize a continuity between yesterday, today, and tomorrow, with a resulting harmony that is central to the health of the entire land. To

Native American nations, Native Hawaiians and Native Alaskans, it is the common belief that if the dead or their burial goods are disturbed, the spirit itself is disturbed and will wander—a tragedy that can bring ill effects on the living as well. To assist in the reparation of past abuses, and provide for respectful treatment today and in the future, NAGPRA has four provisions:

1. To increase protection for Native American graves and provide for the disposition of culturally affiliated remains inadvertently discovered on tribal and federal lands.

2. To prohibit traffic in Native American ancestral remains.

3. To require federal museums and institutions to inventory their collections of Native American remains and burial goods within five years and repatriate them to culturally affiliated tribes upon request.

4. To require museums to provide summaries of their collections of Native American sacred objects and cultural patrimony within three years and repatriate them if it is demonstrated that the museum does not have right of possession.

The deadline for inventory completion of ancestral remains was November of 1995. Many institutions, and most notably, the federal agencies such at the National Forestry Service, the Bureau of Land Management, and the Army Corps of Engineers, did not meet the deadline. While there are civil penalties, effective as of February 12, 1997, for museums and all federally-funded universities and institutions that have failed to comply, only public demand can force compliance of the federal agencies. However, repatriation of affiliated remains and burial goods—those that can be traced to an historic, federally-recognized nation—has already begun, with regulations in place for return to descendants and/or their nations upon request and proven identity. Much work is left, however, in the proper return and reburial of unaffiliated ancestral remains. Two draft forms dealing with this complex issue of how, to whom, and where to rebury the tens of thousands of unidentified remains, have already proven unacceptable to the combined Native nations.

The outcome of this struggle is a victory on many fundamental levels. It heralds the renewed voice of indigenous peoples that demands self-determination, control of one's own cultural heritage, and recognition as a people in the greater family of humanity. It is a statement of the current global efforts toward decolonization that marks the activity of indigenous peoples around the world. It is the expression of an earth that strains toward her own survival as she calls longingly for her people to return home to her ravaged lands.

Only when the descendants of this country's colonizers no longer claim domination over Native American peoples—both living and dead—can balance be restored for the benefit of all.

Burial Site Protection in Illinois: The Beginnings

An era of nearly seven decades of desecration in Illinois ended with the closing of the burial exhibit at Dickson Mounds Museum on April 3, 1992. Its legacy of abuse began in 1927 when chiropractor and land owner, Don F. Dickson, began the systematic uncovering of 248 Native American remains, which he left intact and exposed to view. This became a highly-publicized "tourist attraction" that brought, at its peak, 80,000 visitors a year. Native Americans began to challenge the right of museums to display human remains for public viewing, and Dickson Mounds became a symbol of the widespread disregard for Native rights. After repeated demonstrations and negative press coverage beginning in 1990, the museum finally agreed to place cedar planks over the burial chamber as a form of reburial, found acceptable to some and incomplete to others. The ancestors' remains were, however, successfully removed from public view.

The trail of abuse continued with a permit given in 1993 to excavate an ancient village and burial site at New Lenox, Illinois, approximately 30 miles southwest of Chicago, in order to build a golf course. This village was part of a more expansive complex spread across 230 acres, on land occupied for over 11,000 years, and it was later shown to be a unique site dating to the 1640's, with features unlike any in the midwest. Without consultation with the Native Nations whose cultural patrimony and ancestors were involved, a direct breach of federal guidelines, the New Lenox Park District obtained permission to excavate five acres of the site for a parking lot, as well as the graves of three ancestors, later determined to be of the Miami nation. Though regulations governing the Illinois Human Skeletal Remains Protection Act of 1989 state that permits shall be denied when "in the case of economic development or construction, there are reasonable and feasible alternatives to removal of human remains" (Illinois Administrative Code, Title 17, Chapter VI, Sec. 4170.310 d) the grave was disturbed in order to build an entrance road, which ultimately was not used when the layout was altered. At that time, the Repatriation Committee of the American Indian Movement (AIM) of Illinois, headquartered in Chicago, worked to prevent further destruction of the village area and other possible burial sites. Joseph Standing Bear Schranz, Ojibwe, established the Honor Guard, a dedicated group of Natives and non-Natives, who stood at the entrance to the site in honor of the ancestors' spirits, to watch for looters during the continuing authorized excavation, and to educate passersby in the traditions of Native Americans, in order to foster respect.

The episode at the New Lenox site catalyzed the formation of the Native-based, non-profit organization, Midwest Save Our Ancestors' Remains & Resources Indigenous Network Group (Midwest SOAR-

RING) in 1994. With its headquarters immediately west of Chicago in Oak Park, its mission is to facilitate the repatriation of Native American ancestral remains and burial goods, to work for the preservation of the burial, cultural, and sacred sites in Illinois and the Midwestern states, and to protect and conserve the natural environment. Midwest SOARRING seeks to be a facilitator and liaison for the Nations that had previously occupied this state, to provide for the reburial of all the ancestors still held in museums, government agencies, and private collections.

Through extensive communication with representatives of the Native Nations and statewide Native organizations, as well as ongoing contact with U.S. government agencies, Midwest SOARRING has achieved a close working relationship with individuals and organizations alike, with the following early achievements:

• challenged the legality of the Memorandum of Agreement for the New Lenox site, where three of the ancestors' remains were removed to construct a golf course, in light of Federal Regulation 106, in 1994

• established ongoing communication with the Illinois Historic Preservation Agency (IHPA), the Army Corps of Engineers, and the Advisory Council on Historic Preservation (ACHP) in Washington, D.C.

• supported the effort to defeat IL HB484 in 1995 which would have removed archeological survey requirements from all privately-owned land

• nominated the New Lenox site for the National Register of Historic Places (NRHP), becoming the first Native American organization in the state to seek such national recognition for a Native site, now listed as eligible and formally nominated for the NRHP

• met in council with representatives of the Illinois State Museum, the IHPA, and other Native Americans regarding repatriation of over 6,000 relatives still held at the museum

• works with the American Indian Council of Illinois (AICI) for repatriation and burial, sacred and cultural site preservation

• monitors the permitting process prior to development, which will track sites in Chicago as well as the surrounding areas where Native grave sites are threatened with removal

DESECRATION AT THE DUNNING CEMETERY IN CHICAGO

On a Thursday in August of 1995, two houselots were bulldozed in preparation for construction. By Sunday of the same week, police had come to stop the project and cordon off the area due to reports of human bone upturned in the soil. When all the facts were in, the site was recognized as the old Dunning Cemetery, a pauper's graveyard located on the northwest side of Chicago, and over one hundred remains had been dug up and dumped in a landfill before the work was stopped. The Attorney General's office was notified, and both criminal and civil penalties were assessed within a year's time.

This was a known, recorded cemetery, and the remains were not unseen by the workmen. A stringent penalty was needed to prevent repeated desecration, yet the fine of only $9000 is relatively small for a housing developer. While no dollar amount can reflect the magnitude of this crime, economic loss is a primary deterrent for repeated violations. It is very questionable whether others will see this as a valid warning or as a clear signal that the price is not too high to try it again.

Indeed, a nearly identical occurrence took place in Beardstown, Illinois, approximately 50 miles northwest of Springfield. Up to 40 graves were bulldozed during ground preparation for an apartment complex in August of 1997, again in a section of an historic cemetery. A permit had been granted for the development, though records indicated that graves from the late 1800s were probably present. After the damage was done, the project was allowed to continue without fines or recognition of the crime committed.

The destruction of a cemetery in the name of development is a vivid statement on the absence of a working moral code for the dead in modern America. As long as respect for the ancestors is absent from the national conscience, *all* burial sites are endangered.

THAT YOU MAY CONTINUE YOUR JOURNEY

A grassroots effort must often precede any governmental intervention in a given issue, therefore Midwest SOARRING works with individual agencies and people to effect repatriation and burial site protection. Since private landholders in Illinois may legally choose to have graves removed from their land, it is necessary to deal with each case individually in an attempt to either prevent excavation, or assure that the removal is completed with prayer so that the ancestors can continue their journey in peace.

In November of 1996, as a first-time cooperative effort among an archeologist, private landholder, and Native people, Midwest SOARRING gained permission to enter land slated for a new subdivision in Lake Barrington, where a cemetery with graves 1,000 to 5,000 years old had been found. Maria Pearson, a Yankton-Sioux elder who serves as advisor to the board, led the prayer for the 23 ancestors who were forced to leave their intended final resting place.

> In the mud of the newly-racked landscape, we stood in silent honor of the ancient ones. Facing the west, our elder built an altar with the eagles attending. As the four directions song split the cold air, the spirits joined us, fusing

today and yesterday as one. Smudge burned strong and steady as four hawks circled. Sacred food was fed to the ancestors and to the descendants who represented all peoples. As our common journeys continued, we built a four-color bond, and in the power of unity, forged the path toward a new day of respect.

As another example, in the following May of 1997, members of the boards of Midwest SOARRING, the American Indian Council of Illinois (AICI), and the Quad-Cities Native American League, met with members of the Meskwaki Nation and representatives of the John Deere Corporation. A horse farm owned for many years by members of the John Deere family was to be developed into a professional golf course on the western side of Illinois. Many sacred sites were known to exist along the bluffs, and initial surface survey work showed nearly fifty sites ranging from simple campsites to burial mounds.

In an historic agreement among all parties concerned, no pathway, roadway or other unnatural disturbances were planned on the sacred sites, and the anonymity of the burial areas would be preserved. Since five of the mounds had suffered from looting many years in the past, they needed to be repaired. The Meskwaki Nation allowed members of the Honor Guard and Midwest SOARRING to restore the mounds to their original level, thereby mending a serious breach in the natural order.

The magnitude of this event can be summed up in the symbol of the circle: the Native ancestors buried their dead, non-Native individuals disturbed the burial sites, and both Native and non-Native people, working together, restored the mounds, thus completing the circle with unity.

MOVING FORWARD

On May 2, 1998, National Day of Prayer, Midwest SOARRING sponsored a Prayer Vigil at the Capitol Building in Springfield, Illinois. After years of futile attempts to negotiate with state officials, approximately 200 people marched from the Illinois State Museum to the west steps of the Capitol in order to hear representatives from many Native nations present their common concerns to the Creator. There are approximately 12,000 ancestral remains that had been taken from Illinois, but there is no land for reburial. While over 33,000 Native Americans live within the state boundaries, there are no reservations, land base or representation in the government. The object of the vigil was to promote dialogue between the state of Illinois and the original Native nations to achieve two goals:

• Establishment of a Burial Board with Native American representation to monitor inadvertent discovery of unmarked burial sites during land development

• Provision of land for reburial of repatriated ancestral remains and burial goods

The first goal is clearly within reach. It would provide a Native representative to contact upon discovery of a grave, not just the coroner and state archeologist, as currently legislated. This arrangement has worked well in other states, and will offer the opportunity for the proper handling of Native remains during construction in Illinois. The second goal should be equally available since the government owns lands throughout the state. Meetings for consultation will need to be scheduled, so that the traditional requirements of each nation will be met.

As urgent speeches as well as prayers in many languages were presented this day, the power born of united effort brought us many steps closer to our goals.

* * * *

These isolated incidents are major victories, for the huge gap between Western and Native culture, as well as traditional and modern attitudes, cannot be easily or quickly bridged. The lack of awareness of the sacredness of Native burials pervades a society whose ancestors lie buried and often forgotten in other lands, and the disturbance of grave sites will occur again and again while the law permits. It will be the work of continued cooperation among individuals focused on respect that will bring us continually closer to harmony among all peoples.

Donna Bachman

The Schingoethe Center of Native American Cultures

A Contemporary Educational Institution

The ongoing challenge facing the professional museum staff of the Schingoethe Center for Native American Cultures in Aurora, Illinois, since opening to the public in 1990, has been to transform a personal, amateur collection into a contemporary, relevant museum.

The Schingoethe Center for Native American Cultures is one of many educational components of Aurora University. Opened to the public in 1990, the Schingoethe Center was created as a museum to preserve and curate a collection of some two thousand objects relating to Native American cultures across the Americas; the collection has since doubled in size. The donors of this collection were Herbert and Martha Schingoethe of Aurora, Illinois. They continue to be active collectors on the museum's behalf.

The mission of the Schingoethe Center for Native American Cultures is to encourage understanding and appreciation for the historic and contemporary diversity and artistry of Native American cultures through exhibitions, outreach programming, and research.

Like other such collections, the scope of Herbert and Martha Schingoethe's Native American materials has been formed from a childhood arrowhead collection, on-site collecting, and visits to numerous auction houses. While Southwestern material culture is the abiding core of the collection, exemplified by an outstanding collection of blackware, Navajo textiles, and Kachinas, the Schingoethes have conscientiously sought examples of objects from all North American Native American culture areas. In giving their collection to Aurora University, the Schingoethes anticipated not a traditional museum but a center vitalized by changing exhibitions, programming, research, and sponsorship of the annual pow-wow on Memorial Day weekend.

The four thousand plus objects in the Schingoethe Center reflect the personal taste of the donors and range from the incidental to the impor-

At the 8th Annual Aurora powwow May 23-24, 1998. Sponsored by Aurora University's Schingoethe Center for Native American Cultures.

tant, the commercial to the significant, and include both historical and contemporary objects. The preponderance of contemporary objects has brought with it a positive aspect. Objects created by living native artists have helped the staff in presenting Native American cultures as *living cultures*. The works of living Native American artists are exhibited along side historical works throughout the museum. The bead work of Charles Chief Eagle Jr. is displayed next to a bag from the nineteenth century. A jingle dress from last year's powwow is placed next to an historic buckskin dress.

As part of the Schingoethe Center's public programming, a Blackfoot storyteller reminds children and adults that the legends collected in the museum library's books are *living history*. Making presentations to some 5,000 school children annually, the Center staff works to dispel the all-to-common notion of Indians as a dead people and to celebrate the living cultures of native North America.

Exhibitions are displayed in a Main Gallery of some 1,500 square feet and an Education Gallery of 884 square feet. Major change-outs occur every two years with the two galleries on alternating years. The Education Gallery often features traveling exhibitions, which have ranged from a prehistoric exhibition on Midwest mammoth hunters to an art exhibition by nationally known Flathead artist Jaune Quick-To-See-Smith. Travel-

Schingoethe Center, Aurora University.

ing exhibits circulated by the Center include three framed poster sets: "Native American Cultures," "Contemporary Native Americans," and "Women of Hope: Native American/Hawaiian." In addition to the poster sets, exhibitions are tailored for school and library galleries. Depending on security levels, artifacts are included in these traveling exhibitions.

A major commitment of staff time and energy involves assuring compliance with the federally mandated NAGPRA (Native American Graves Protection and Repatriation Act) legislation passed by the U.S. Congress in 1990. The act requires that all federally funded museums inventory their collections of Native American human remains and cultural objects and notify all culturally affiliated tribes, Alaska Native villages, and Native Hawaiians of these holdings.

While the Schingoethe Center for Native American Cultures holds no human remains and by policy will not accept human remains in the future, it does, of course, contain a rich and valuable collection of cultural objects, some of which may be discussed in terms of the "sacred" and "objects of cultural patrimony" categories that are a part of the NAGPRA legislation.

Between 1996 and 1997, the Schingoethe Center was visited by representatives of three native nations. These face-to-face consultations were educational for all involved. The museum learned more about the context of their artifacts as well as much information that had been lost in the his-

Schingoethe Center for Native American Cultures at Aurora University. Bonnie Whitlock, a Museum Advisory Board Member, is shown giving a tour.

tory of an object's transmittal across the years. Tribal representatives and museum staff have had the opportunity to discuss cultural affiliation, the meaning and importance of artifacts, and how best and respectfully to care for artifacts. In some instances, the museum adopted new methods of cura-

At the 8th Annual Aurora Powwow May 23-24, 1998. Sponsored by Aurora University's Schingoethe Center for Native American Cultures. Photo by Michael Sawdey.

tion that speak to both conservation standards and cultural sensitivity.

Museums like the Schingoethe Center that have had the opportunity to participate in these consultations have grown in wisdom concerning the objects they hold in trust and native peoples have been given a closer look into the care their objects have received. The NAGPRA consultations are an ongoing part of the Schingoethe Center's responsibilities. Better and increased communication with native nations will enable the museum to better document and interpret the Native American cultures for its many constituencies.

In addition to exhibition and curation, the Schingoethe Center's mission includes outreach through educational public programming. The contemporary emphasis in exhibitions is reinforced by an extensive Discovery Box program. Twenty-five subjects, from stone tools to weaving, from the Illinois Indians to the Indian Boarding School Experience, from the Southeast to the Arctic peoples, are covered in hands-on and curriculum material in these Discovery Boxes. Designed for checking out by schools and youth organizations, the boxes contain contemporary Native American-made examples of traditional crafts, information on the context and lifeways that produced these materials, articles on current practices and practitioners, and information on native nations, yesterday and today. Additional resources for the educator are found in the museum's resource library of 1,500 books, publications, and audio-visual materials. The library is catalogued and may be referenced through Aurora University's web site, www.aurora.com.

Reinforcing the Discovery Boxes are public presentations by Native American speakers, artists, and organizations. The largest public program is the Aurora powwow, held annually since 1991, which brings some 150 native dancers, drums, and performers from across Indian country to a two-day celebration of native cultures for all people. Special features at recent powwows have included performances by hoop dancers and a clown. More than $14,000 is awarded in the dance competition. The powwow welcomes over 5,000 attendees each year who come for reasons ranging from participating to watching and from eating fry bread to shopping the fifty-some vendors of native crafts and arts.

The Schingoethe Center for Native American Cultures is a public museum operated under the auspices of Aurora University. The museum is closed on Mondays, Saturdays, University holidays, and the month of January. There are limited hours in December. Please call for specific hours: 630-844-5402. There is no charge. Regular days and hours are:

Tuesdays: 10:00 A.M.–8:00 P.M.

Wednesdays–Fridays: 10:00 A.M.–4:00 P.M.

Sundays: 1:00 P.M.–4:00 P.M.

PART II
CONTEMPORARY LIFE

SECTION THREE
HEALTH

The Healing Circle
SARA BOSKOWITZ
227

American Indian Cultures Deteriorating From Within
TIM VERMILLION
235

Sara Boskowitz

The Healing Circle

An Urban Community Program for Native Americans with Type II Diabetes and Their Families

INTRODUCTION

The American Indian Health Service (AIHS) is a small community health center serving the primary health care needs of Native Americans and their families in the city of Chicago. The agency was incorporated as a not-for-profit in 1974 for Native Americans by Native Americans and their families in the city of Chicago. AIHS is one of 32 Urban Indian Health Service Programs throughout the U.S. Funding is primarily through Title V of PL 637, the Indian Health Care Improvement Act of 1976. Approximately 14,000 Native Americans live in the Metropolitan area of Chicago (Census, 1990). In response to this increase in the Native American population the AIHS was founded. Today more than 103 different tribes are represented among the clinic's clients, with the largest number from the Ojibway (or Chippewa), Sioux, Menominee, and Ho-Chunk (or Winnebago) tribes. Poverty, lack of educational attainment, and differing values and beliefs put the Native Americans at risk for poor health, and compared with the rest of the U.S. population, they have greater rates of diabetes, hypertension, renal failure, tuberculosis, and hepatitis. Community area 3 in Uptown neighborhood on the north side of Chicago, the neighborhood in which most of the Native American community lives, has been designated a medically under-served area with high rates of tuberculosis, infant mortality, homelessness, and joblessness. Many of the clients the AIHS serves are the "working poor" and remain uninsured.

SIGNIFICANCE OF TYPE II DIABETES IN THE NATIVE AMERICAN POPULATION

Type II diabetes mellitus, also known as non-insulin dependent (NIDDM) or adult onset diabetes, has become a health problem of catastrophic proportions in the Native American population. What was once described as a benign disease is now a leading cause of morbidity and mortality in this population (West 1974; Stein, West, & Roby 1965). This grim outcome prevails because self-management is often inadequately taught to Native Americans with diabetes. If early assessment of clients' knowledge of diabetes mellitus were made regularly, Native Americans could self-manage diabetic symptoms and forestall and even prevent morbidity, mortality, and other complications (Rubin, Peyrot, & Saudek 1989).

DIABETES AS A HEALTH PROBLEM
AMONG NATIVE AMERICANS

Ninety percent of diabetes cases for all races are Type II, and it is estimated that for every diagnosed case there is one undiagnosed. The Indian Health Service (IHS) reports an age-adjusted prevalence rate of diabetes in 1992 as "69/1000, or 2.8 times the U.S. rate" (Public Health Service [PHS] 1995, 5). Great tribal variation in the prevalence exists with "rates ranging from 15.3/1000 in Alaska to 119.2/1000 in southern Arizona" (Valway et al. 1993, 271).

The mortality rate for Native Americans with diabetes is almost three times the rate in the total U.S. population. The IHS reports a diabetes mellitus death rate for 1990–92 as 30.0/100,000 versus 11.8/100,000 for the total U.S. population (PHS 1995). Native Americans develop diabetes at younger ages and suffer a high rate of complications such as amputations and end-stage renal disease (Newman, De Stefano, Valway, German, & Muenta 1993). For example, "between 1983 and 1986, diabetic nephropathy resulting in end-stage renal disease occurred in Native Americans at almost six times the rate seen among the U.S. white population" (Gohdes, Kaufman, & Valway 1993, 241).

Sixty-one percent of Native Americans live in urban areas, yet because most IHS studies have been done among reservation tribes (notably the Pima in the Southwest), very little is known about the extent of diabetes and its consequences among urban Native Americans. We do know that great disparities between the health of American Indians and whites living in urban areas. The gap appears across almost all age groups and most causes of death. A 1988 report based on a random chart review of 3,306 visits by Native Americans served at two urban clinics, in Oklahoma City, Oklahoma, and Wichita, Kansas, reported 16.97% of female visits and 20.73% of male visits, respectively, for diabetes (Taylor 1988). Grossman et. al. (1994) reported in 1994 a combined urban American Indian and Alaskan Native mortality rate for diabetes of 19/100,000 compared with a white population rate of 8/100,000. A 1991 study conducted in Chicago, which used a convenience sample (Lipton, Fruh, Allen, & Casillas 1994), found a 14% prevalence rate of Type II diabetes in Native American self-respondents.

The total direct and indirect cost of diabetes in the United States is estimated at $92 billion (Centers for Disease Control [CDC] Diabetes Home Page, November, 1995). Direct medical costs, which include only the costs directly attributable to diabetes, rather than all health care costs of individuals with diabetes, are estimated at $45 billion. Indirect costs are estimated at $47 billion, and include disability, work loss, and premature mortality (CDC Diabetes Home Page, 1995). It is difficult to estimate the financial burden of diabetes to the Native American community nationwide due to a number of factors. Native Americans have a significantly lower socio-economic standing, a disproportionate rate of prevalence of diabetes and its complications, and there is significant underreporting of the population. Newman, et. al. (1993) estimated that "Native American heritage is underreported by 65% on death certificates" (1993, 297). However, one measure of the impact of diabetes has been calculated for Native Americans. Years of Potential Life Lost (YPLL) is a useful index of premature mortality that gives more weight to deaths among younger people (National Association of County Health Officials 1991). It measures the years of life "lost" by individuals who die prematurely (i.e., between the ages of 1 and 65). Overall, the rate of YPLL for Native Americans has been calculated at 114/1,000 compared to the U. S. total population rate of 61/1,000 (U. S. Department of Health and Human Services [DHHS], Indian Health Conditions, 1990; Young 1994).

Possible risk factors for the increased incidence of NIDDM among Native Americans include genetic predisposition (the thrifty genotype theory) that involves an altered ability of the body to maintain fat stores (Knowler, Pettitt, Bennett & Williams 1983); metabolic factors (lower plasma insulin levels, increased insulin resistance, and overprotection of insulin by the liver (Bogardus 1993); obesity; diet; and inadequate physical activity (Knowler et al. 1983).

BARRIERS TO SELF-MANAGEMENT IN THE NATIVE AMERICAN POPULATION

Environmental and cultural factors precipitating Native Americans' development of NIDDM (Hosey, Freeman, Straqualursi, & Gohdes 1986) include socioeconomic factors such as younger average age, lower incomes, less education and some Native American values and beliefs. The Native American population residing in IHS service areas, again, according to the 1990 census, is younger than the general U.S. population. Thirty-four percent of IHS clients were younger than 15 years and 6 percent were older than 64. For the general U.S. population, the corresponding values were 22% and 13% respectively. The Native American median age was 24.2 years compared with 32.9 years for the general U.S. population. Native Americans are significantly poorer than most ethnic groups in the United States. In 1989, Native Americans residing in the current Reservation States had a median household income of $19,897 compared with $30,056 for the general U.S. population. During this time period, 31.6 percent of Native Americans lived below the poverty level in contrast to 13.1 percent for the general U.S. population (PHS, Trends in Indian Health, 1995). In Chicago alone the high school drop-out rate was 75 percent in 1992 (Board of Health).

The impact of culture on communication, values, and beliefs, including a 600-year history of cultural oppression (Lang 1989; Huttlinger et. al. 1992; Hagey 1984) have influenced the health of Native Americans. When health care workers from the general population interact with Native Americans, they represent the part of society that has often undercut Native American values and defined to what extent Native Americans could interact with the rest of American society, and, by extension, with the U.S. health system.

Many authors (Hagey 1989; Huttlinger et. al. 1992; Ross 1992; Scollon & Wong-Scollon 1986; O'Neil 1990; Carreses & Rhodes 1995) have discussed the significance of differences in cross-cultural communication patterns, in particular, between practitioners and patients. Among Native Americans active communication can include refraining from response or inquiry out of respect for another's relative state of readiness for discourse as well as their own. Their values of silence, non-interference and respect, and the belief that the "time must be right" all influence patterns of communication (Ross 1992). Hagey noted in her study with the Ojibway and Cree that the use of silence is attributed to the "deeply-rooted ideal of non-interference . . . any direct questioning is thought to violate the dignity of the other person" (1989, 30). Hagey (1983) emphasized that "a fundamental difference in beliefs" (30) is a significant barrier to health education. Huttlinger, et. al. (1992) found in their study group of 20 Dine (Navajo) informants that communication barriers are a large problem: "discrepancies occur more often in cross-cultural settings when the patient's verbal and nonverbal communication patterns may be different from those of the provider" (707). The Dine describe diabetes as being the "white man's disease" that has come upon them (Native Americans) in recent times. Many believe that diabetes disrupts the internal balance of well-being. Treatment regimes must therefore address the whole being, and may include the use of traditional healing practices.

The Indian Health Research Program, sponsored by IHS, has identified diabetes as one of eight current priority research areas for Indian health (Nutting, Helgerson, Welty, & Jackson 1990). Also, the national health objectives for the year 2000 identified the American Indian population as one of five special populations targeted for the reduction of the incidence of diabetes (Public Health Service 1991).

COMMUNITY HEALTH ASSESSMENT

The first community health needs assessment of the Chicago Indian community was conducted in 1992 by AIHS using key informants, a needs survey, and a review of clinic charts. The health issues most frequently identified were alcoholism, diabetes, childhood immunizations, and access to care. The primary stressors identified by the participants were: chronic disease, disrupted families, decreased access to health care and medications, unemployment, lack of affordable housing and a high drop-out rate from high school. In review of medical charts it was found that 40 percent of the patients had been diagnosed with Type II diabetes while 60 percent of the Elders had diabetes. The two major strengths identified by the community were traditional values and beliefs and the family support structure. A plan was developed in conjunction with the advice of Elders and traditional people within the community. This plan included a decision to provide support for traditional values and beliefs by the agency through the use of the medicine wheel framework. The medicine wheel as conceived by this program consists of the four directions, and includes the well-being of the whole person, his spirit, his body, his mind, and his heart.

CONCEPTUAL FRAMEWORK OF THE HEALING CIRCLE

The philosophy of the *Healing Circle* is to provide holistic diabetes care and education within the traditional framework of the medicine wheel. The program has been developing at AIHS since 1991. A traditional framework is used, in that the four quadrants of the medicine wheel are represented in the program through the integration of activities addressing the spirit, mind, body, and heart. The way of the medicine wheel helps patients visualize the path one takes with diabetes and how one can best learn through sharing this path.

Some activities that have helped us foster the spiritual side have been health care provider awareness of values and beliefs, involvement of a spiritual leader, increased access to traditional ceremonies, and increased involvement of the Elders. Many of the providers do not share the same cultural background as our patients. These providers are introduced to the values and beliefs of the Native American community and how these beliefs affect health. The health providers are introduced to some traditional values and beliefs such as:

- non-interference
- the notion that the time must be right
- the traditional Indian view of life is to approach it in terms of the amount of living one can expect to experience in the span of one day

- respect
- the value of reticence
- the acceptance of obligations
- avoidance of open, face-to-face conflict as a matter of respect (Ross 1992)

The following poem by Black Elk (1932) is an example of the traditional feeling that the path of spirituality is taken with every step we make and every breath we take.

> "With visible breath I am walking.
> A voice I am sending as I walk.
> In a sacred manner I am walking.
> With visible tracks I am walking.
> In a sacred manner I walk."

This poem is shared with our western providers to help them understand the power of spirituality in the life of Native Americans.

The variety of tribes and bands represented in our clinic can cause potential conflicts of beliefs and traditions. An Ojibway spiritual leader from Northern Minnesota visits us about four times a year. He has helped us in learning more about ceremonies, and how to incorporate spirituality in an urban center. He has also taught us about incorporating the use of the four sacred herbs, tobacco, sage, cedar, and sweet grass. We burn sage in the clinic and smudge frequently. We teach and encourage clients to use smudging to help us pray and resolve problems. We participate in ceremonies, such as the pipe ceremony or the inipi, each according to his or her own traditions, and help to make this ceremony available to clients. The inipi (sweat lodge) is a traditional ceremony we help bring to the people. The sweat lodge ceremony was chosen because the sweat lodge is the ceremony most common to North American Indian tribes. At our summer camps for diabetes a sweat lodge is constructed by our spiritual leader and the children. We also have a sweat lodge available close to the city for use at other times.

As part of the program we have renewed our commitment to our Elders and their wisdom and teaching. Through senior luncheons that we hold twice a month, we honor the Elders and encourage their participation in the Healing Circle.

Through primary care, nutrition, exercise, and home visits to follow up on primary care we strengthen the body. At all of our programs we provide food that is both nutritional and appetizing. We have "taste tests," where participants can chose from a number of fat-free or lowered fat items to "try out" before purchasing them at the grocery store. Our exercise programs are integrated into patients' daily life, such as the "500 mile walk." In this program patients track the number of miles they walk over a period of 2-3 months, at the end, a feast honors all of those who finish the program. Our spiritual leader makes home visits with our community health nurse to pro-vide traditional healing practices side by side with western remedies.

Health education improves the knowledge and understanding about diabetes that is necessary to self-management. Our nutritionist works with the traditional cooks in the community to find healthy ways of eat-ing favorite foods, such as fry bread. Health education about nutrition emphasizes how to use traditional foods such as berries, rice, and venison in healthy proportions. Other projects include, awareness programs for community agencies, a diabetes registry, a summer camp for Native Americans with diabetes and their families, a monthly support group, exercise and weight reduction programs, and health education.

Having a community person as the co-director of the program decreas-es the gap between cultures and improves the communication and under-standing by clients of diabetes. Outreach, screening, referrals, case man-agement are provided throughout the community by a community health nurse and a community health worker.

Conclusion

Although it is fairly easy to evaluate long-term physiological indicators of the control of diabetes, evaluation of the effectiveness of the program is very difficult. It combines scientific research and community program development and implementation in a collaborative relationship that has never before existed. Additionally, outcomes such as quality of life and improved self-care are difficult to measure cross-culturally. Personal nar-ratives have been the most effective way of evaluating the program to date. These show that home visits shared by the spiritual leader and the com-munity health nurse are welcomed and people reported that participation in the talking circle and sweat lodge have had a significant impact in their lives. Tradition does not allow us to discuss the comments made by our clients within the confines of the talking circle or the sweat lodge but this program shows the value of increasing Western health care providers' awareness of the strength of spirituality in healing to the Native Ameri-can and the importance of using traditional means of spirituality in what-ever way we can in a medical clinic.

References

Bogardus, C. (1993). Insulin resistance in the pathogenesis of NIDDM in Pima Indians. *Diabetes Care*, 16(1), 228-231.

Carries, JA & Rhodes, LA (1995). Western bioethics on the Navaho reservation: benefit or harm? *Journal of the American Medical Association*, 274, (10), 826-829.

Centers for Disease Control Diabetes Home Page (November, 1995). Diabetes Update. Available: Internet.

Gohdes, D., Kaufman, S., & Valway, S. (1993). Diabetes in American Indians: an overview. *Diabetes Care*. 16 (Supp. 1), 239-243.

Grossman, D.C., Kreiger, J.W., Sugarman, J.R., & Forquera. (1994). Health status of urban Native American Indians and Alaska Native. *Journal of the American Medical Association*, 271 (11), 845-850.

Hagey, R. (1984). The phenomenon, the explanations and the responses: metaphors surrounding diabetes in urban Canadian Indians. *Social Science and Medicine*, vol. 18 (3), 265-272.

Hagey, R. (1989). The Native Diabetes Program: rhetorical process & praxis. *Medical Anthropology*, 12, 7-33.

Huttlinger, K., Krefting, L., Drevdahl, D., Tree, P., Baca, E., & Benally, A. (1992). "Doing battle": A metaphorical analysis of diabetes mellitus among Navaho people. *The American Journal of Occupational Therapy*, vol. 8, 706-712.

Knowler, W.C., Pettitt, D.J., Bennett, P.H., & Williams, R.C. (1983). Diabetes mellitus in the Pima Indians: genetic and evolutionary considerations. *American Journal of Physical Anthropology*, 62, 107- 114.

Lang, G.C. (1989). "Making sense" about diabetes: Dakota narratives of illness. *Medical Anthropology*, 11 (3), 305-27.

Lipton, R., Fruh, S., Allen, P., & Casillas, S. (1994). Health behaviors and diabetes risk factors among American Indians in an urban setting. *The IHS Provider*, December, 192-195.

National Association of County Health Officials (March, 1991). *APEXPH: Assessment protocol for excellence in public health*. Washington, DC: Author.

Neihardt, J.G.(1972). *Black Elk Speaks*. NY:Simon and Schuster.

Newman, J.M., De Stefano, F., Valway, S.E., German, R.R., & Muenta, B. (1993). Diabetes-related mortality in Native Americans. *Diabetes Care*. 16(S. 1), 297-299.

Nutting, P.A., Helgerson, S.D., Welty, M.J., & Jackson, M.Y. (1990). A research agenda for Indian Health. *The IHS Provider*, May, 29-37.

O'Neil, J.D. (1990). The cultural and political context of patient dissatisfaction in cross-cultural clinical encounters: a Canadian Inuit study. *Medical Anthropology Quarterly*. 3: 325-344.

Public Health Service (1991). *Healthy people 2000: National health promotions and disease prevention objectives (summary report)*. (DHHS Publication No. S/N 017-001-00473-1). Washington: U.S. Government Printing Office.

Public Health Service, Office of Minority Health. (1993*). Toward equality of well-being: strategies for improving minority health*. (DHHS Publication). Washington: U.S. Government Printing Office.

Public Health Service, Indian Health Services. (1991*). Indian Health Service, regional differences in Indian health*. (DHHS Publication). Washington: U.S. Government Printing Office.

Ross, R. (1992). *Dancing with a ghost*. Canada: Reed Books.

Rubin, R.R., Peyrot, M., & Sadek, C.D. (1989). Effect of diabetes education of self-care, metabolic control, and emotional well-being. *Diabetes Care*, 12, 673-79.

Scollon, R. & Wong-Scollon, S. (1986). In K. Young (Ed.), *Interethnic communication*. Newberry Park: Sage Publications.

Stein, H.G., West, K.M., Roby, J.M. (1965). The high prevalence of abnormal glucose tolerance in Cherokee Indians of North Carolina. *Archives of Internal Medicine*, 116, 842-45.

Taylor, T. (1988). Health problems and use of services at two urban American Indian clinics. *Public Health Reports*, 103 (1), 88-95.

Valway, S.E., Linkins, R.W., & Gohdes, D. (1993). Epidemiology of lower-extremity amputations in the Indian Health Service, 1982-1987. *Diabetes Care*, 16, suppl 1, 349-353.

West, K.M. (1974). Diabetes in American Indians and other Native populations of the New World. *Diabetes*, 23 (10), 841 -855.

Young, T. K. (1994*). The health of Native Americans: towards a biocultural epidemiology*. New York: Oxford University Press.

Tim Vermillion

American Indian Cultures Deteriorating From Within

The deterioration of the American Indian culture began as the Europeans accidentally landed on this continent. Thinking that they had landed in India, they called the original inhabitants Indians. Realizing they were wrong, the Europeans for hundreds of years have not made an effort to correct that mistake. The discovery of America—the New World—was a secular replay of the Garden of Eden, another chance to create the kingdom of God on earth. The belief that America was God's promised land is still current today. President Ronald Reagan once stated, "I have always believed that this anointed land was set apart in an uncommon way, that a divine plan placed this great continent here between the oceans to be found by people from every corner of the earth who had a special love of faith and freedom."

This country was new to the European, but there is this matter of its original inhabitants. The Puritans viewed the aboriginals as part of their divine mission: they were heathens to be alternatively exterminated in the fashion of Old Testament dogma, or protected and converted with New Testament love. Since their promised land was already occupied by Indians, the Puritans (as they called themselves) had to locate them in their Biblical script. At times, they dealt with us the way the Israelites dealt with the Canaanites, violently. But many American Indian tribes clung to their traditional way of life, and for two and a half centuries more of God's people would have to right the heathen as they tried to impose their way of life.

Relentless efforts to acculturate American Indians into the European culture began with the first missionaries who sought to "civilize" in order to Christianize. Education was an important part of that process: schools for centuries have drilled into our minds the traditions and concepts of the non-Indian culture. In missionary and government boarding schools, tribal languages were tyrannically condemned; American Indians were forbidden to speak their own languages. This was the real beginning of the most devastating avenue of the attempts to acculturate the American Indian. It was not the killing off of the buffalo, the livelihood of the American Indian, especially on the Great Plains; nor was it the burning down of virgin forests, just because it was home to certain tribes that had taken refuge there; nor the attempt at germ warfare, when smallpox was introduced to the American Indian, through contaminated blankets. It was, instead, the destruction of *mentacide*, a conditioning that creates a mutual position of distorted thinking, promulgated by Hollywood, advertisements, and logos.

American Indian cultures today are fading because we are becoming more influenced by our own mentally distorted images of what we think culture should be. People have called it commercialized, staging our sacred ceremonies for public view; these sacred traditional practices are viewed by people, Indian and non-Indian alike, who don't understand the American Indian culture, and therefore interpret the practices as primitive, barbaric, bestial, and supernatural. Some of us are now willing to disgrace our sacred ceremonies, for the sake of recognition and money.

Today there are many individuals who are passing themselves off as medicine men, medicine women, healers, and pipe carriers, people who are American Indian, and especially the non-Indian who goes, book in hand, setting up ceremonies. I have often wondered what would happen if I took a Bible, and began performing like a priest, and began carrying out the rituals of the non-Indians, sacred religious ceremonies.

It is dramatized because Hollywood and the media have significantly influenced us with their non-Indian conceptualization of a homogeneous Indian culture. The Hollywood message through movies that the American Indian was always killing innocent people even convinced us, the American Indian. I can remember when, as a child, I sat in the front row of the theater rooting for the U.S. Calvary as they chased off the Indians.

We may accept the changes that have occurred in our culture as a healthy growth from primitive to civilized culture. We as American Indians may call it many things. But the fact is that a great many American Indians are lost when it comes to tradition and culture, and it is usually because people who are concerned about their culture are becoming fewer. The elders who have the knowledge and are willing to pass this wisdom on to their younger generations, no one listens to, and except for a very few, there would be a language barrier.

Today, when cultural awareness becomes an issue, we either consult a non-Indian or a book, or begin to play a guessing game, guessing at what is original and accurate about our customs. We are influenced by and rely on books too much, even books that portray our ceremonial practices as primitive and supernatural. These statements influence our conceptual image of being Indian, and Indian people actually feel shame, ashamed of Indian customs.

Conceptual interference has developed in the self- and community-images of Indian people. Indians, especially those who are able to speak their tribal language, find it very difficult to explain Indian culture and traditions to non-Indian people. Since culture plays a great part in shaping the personality, cognition, and perceptions of individuals, it is very difficult for us to explain, particularly in a different language, our own customs and beliefs. This accounts for considerable misinterpretation. The American Indians' everyday way of life, which was walking in harmony with the Great Mystery and all His creation, today is interpreted as religion, and not spirituality as we understand it. Religion and spirituality have always been spoken about synonymously. The American Indian believes that spirituality is a natural instinct, a need to understand the meaning of Where do we come from? Why we were put here on this earth? Where does the journey lead? And did someone plan your whole life? This is the reason our title for God is the Great Mystery. Religion, on the other hand, seems to be a devotion to an acknowledged ultimate reality or deity.

Today American Indians are rapidly becoming victims of *mentacide*, a systematic extermination of an entire people's way of conception, and one of the primary reasons is because many American Indians cannot speak their own tribal language, nor can they understand it.

My understanding of the dynamics of Mentacide was vague until I had an experience that shocked me into reality. When I attended a conference on alcoholism in Minnesota, I spotted an American Indian at a reception following one of the workshops. I was glad to see another Indian, and I approached him, saying, "Hello, I'm sure glad to see another Indian here, how are you doing, and where are you from?" The gentlemen turned and greeted me, but then to my astonishment he said, "How did you know I was Indian?" I was silent for a minute waiting for the punch line, or to acknowledge his statement as a joke, but he was dead serious. I started to get angry, but sadness replaced it, as I realized what had happened to this man. As I walked away, I then saw a man in a three-piece suit, a briefcase, and his hair done up in a beauty salon permanent.

This man had his own distorted image of himself: he believed that he blended in with the dominant non-Indian crowd. This reminded me of when government officials in Washington dressed some American Indians up like Abraham Lincoln and told them that they were now civilized.

I hope people don't misunderstand my attempt to create the scenario of events that have led us toward mentacide. Adapting to the ways of the dominating society, in order to meet your responsibilities, marrying outside your nationality, dressing, talking, acting like, living like the non-Indian, there is nothing wrong with that. My message is don't be ignorant of your own culture and tradition. If you have a way to learn your tribal language, do it. Everyone has a cultural heritage; find out what it is and be proud of it; don't fall into ignorant shame, to the point where you begin condemning your own people.

The devastating dynamics of mentacide have been mentioned. We now have to talk about a dynamic called alcoholism, a threat much greater. Talking about alcoholism is like trying to decide which came first, the disease or the symptoms. There is debate about whether the American Indian people were constitutionally predisposed to alcoholism or whether the American Indian, because of the oppressed conditions of reservation life, learned to function only at a sub-level and not to their full capabilities. Whichever is the truth, for the American Indian, even more than acculturation, alcoholism appears to be their chosen source of extinction.

On most American Indian reservations, there now exist two types of cultures: the rapidly becoming obsolete American Indian culture, and the rapidly dominating alcoholism culture. Earlier I stated that culture plays a great part in shaping the personality, cognition, and perception of its members. Alcoholism culture has the same dynamics to influence its members.

Alcoholism culture affects its members even more thoroughly than the traditional culture of a society.

Alcoholism and alcohol use affect individuals in all three major areas, physiological, psychological, and sociological, and causes these areas of functioning to deteriorate. Alcoholism and drug addition are so pervasive and rampant among the American Indian society that the ramifications caused by the disease have become so tolerated . . . the disease goes on almost unnoticed.

Today, because of the pervasiveness of alcohol use in American Indian communities, an individual cannot help but be born into an environment where alcohol use and alcoholic behavior is accepted in the immediate family, the extended family, and the whole community.

Children born into a society of alcohol users do not have role models to look up to and model themselves after. These children will almost certainly become problem drinkers because the model they patterned themselves after was in most cases an alcoholic.

An alcoholic eventually becomes a social parasite. The alcoholic usually does not have a steady work history when he/she works. This person usually lives off relatives, friends, welfare, and social service programs. Sociologically, the individual is characterized by: wanting something for nothing, inability to hold a job, consistently being on welfare, staying in trouble most of the time, and developing their own list of enablers.

Enablers are people who don't understand alcoholism, and therefore do things like getting the alcoholic out of jail, feeding the alcoholic, housing the alcoholic, getting and buying the alcoholic clothes. If they are related to the alcoholic, they usually end up fighting with other relatives over the alcoholic. In many cases the enabler is the spouse of the alcoholic, who although she may not be drinking herself, may end up sicker than the alcoholic, because the enabler ends up doing things the alcoholic wouldn't even dare do.

A child born to an alcoholic mother who was actively drinking while carrying the child will be born with a tolerance for alcohol, meaning the child will be able to drink a lot more alcohol whenever he takes a drink than the child whose mother did not drink alcohol while carrying her child. This child will have a physical dependence on alcohol. This disease will lay dormant until activated by the first drink of alcohol. Some people may understand this as heredity but many professionals, people who are children of alcoholics, alcohol users, and enablers may find this statement offending. This is recognized as becoming an instant alcoholic, meaning upon initial introduction to alcohol, this individual will be able to drink large quantities and maintain functions; this person will also experience withdrawals after discontinuation of alcohol consumption. Psychologically, this person will develop a dependent personality having a need to keep up with his peers, and will form the habit of wanting to experience the euphoria caused by alcohol, giving him false courage, to be the life of the party, and do things he wouldn't ordinarily do sober. It becomes a crutch to overcome shyness. An individual using alcohol may or may not develop physical problems that are noticeable early, and when these deteriorating effects come about, the addiction for some is so strong that they totally ignore doctors' warnings and continue to drink. In some cases individuals have stopped drinking but the majority have a relapse, because the disease wasn't treated. The family with an alcoholic member typifies the saying that you can pick your friends, but you're stuck with relatives. No amount of wishing will make this member seek treatment. We are unable to confront this relative because we were introduced to our relatives at an early age, and from then on it is hard to see them as people.

What happens so often is that family members get stuck with roles and this role takes over your whole life. This type of family system makes it almost impossible to meet and work as people, because relatives frequently blackmail each other in the name of relationships. Many times you would hear things like, "you have to do this because you're my mother," or "I'm your daughter." Alcoholic members use this to change negotiations to help them gain control: the alcoholic takes over.

The family with an alcoholic member may be living together, but they are all functioning separately, because they all suffer from alcoholic characteristics, self-centeredness, self-importance, and in reality the family is fragmented with no leadership, no plan, no goals, no objectives, just a day-by-day existence.

In an American Indian extended family today, a family is actually composed of at least three generations, all related somehow, and affecting each of the other generations. The family with an alcoholic member/members may in a sense believe that they are living in their traditional extended family system, but may in fact be living together to manipulate each other. The American Indian extended family system that is supposed to be rich and stable, becomes a complete chaotic system when it tries to function within an alcoholism culture.

Alcoholism culture has overpowered our American Indian culture; many people actually believe that they have become acculturated, but in reality they are living in the Alcoholism culture.

There are a lot of pros and cons when it comes to talking about the usefulness of American Indian reservations. Was it in the long run a serious detriment to the American Indian to place him on the reservation, and provide for his livelihood? Has reservation life created dependence among American Indians to a point where they are now capable of functioning only up to the ego level?

From this point of view I maintain that American Indians have become perfect candidates for the Alcoholism culture. We have come to a point when we are stereotyping ourselves: if you don't drink, you're not Indian.

There are at least 8,068 American Indians in the Chicago and Metropolitan area and at least 90% of these people have felt the ramifications caused by alcoholism and drug addiction. A great many of these suffering people do not realize that they are affected by alcoholism and many times, it's just by not having a complete understanding of the disease.

There are approximately 16,000 American Indian people in the state of Illinois and it is not known whether these people have a need for:

1) proper health care,

2) awareness that there is a need for treatment and resources,

3) awareness that there are prevention intervention resources available.

There are approximately 45 to 50, male and female, American Indian people in various correctional institutions in the state of Illinois who may be there as a result of alcohol/drugs, and in need of American Indian community support during their incarceration, i.e. someone to visit and perform spiritual ceremonies, to train them in how to practice traditional values and understanding traditional values and beliefs would help them recognizing their American Indian identity.

The American Indian began coming into the urban area as the Relocation Act came into effect during the 1950s. The American Indians were given an opportunity, all expenses paid, until you found a job, to relocate into the urban areas of the United States, to find employment, and a better way of life. As a result the population of American Indians in Chicago, as in many other large cites, increased, to approximately 20,000. This number began to decline in the early 1960s as the American Indian people began to migrate back to their reservations for various reasons, mainly because the Relocation Act was not as successful as expected. The

American Indians' return to their reservations had many reasons, but primarily it was because the American Indian people being uprooted by the Bureau of Indian Affairs (BIA) and taken away from their homeland to face a totally strange world without any type of preparation, and had no forewarning of this fact, had a very devastating effect on the people. The sudden change in environment, the responsibilities of everyday survival, which was based on material gain and money, was something strange and new to American Indian people. The BIA had no foresight that this would happen. The only, and probably the main concern of the BIA was acculturation of American Indian people into a mixture of mainstream cultures.

Two other major reasons for why the Relocation Act failed are: 1) Many of the American Indians who came to the urban area were suffering from alcoholism and or drugs addiction before they were relocated, and brought their problem with them, 2) Opportunities to get alcohol, and drugs were greater in the cities, and the pain of being uprooted and taken away from their homes had such an adverse effect on these people, that their alcohol and drug use increased to rampant proportions.

Since 1972 more than 133 American Indian people in Chicago have died on the "street," were murdered, or just simply died in flophouse cubicles, abandoned buildings, emergency rooms, or in apartments without anyone there to turn to for help. In 1953 alcoholism and drug addiction was labeled a disease. Alcohol is a socially tolerated chemical, and therefore regardless of racial, ethnic, or cultural background, many people do not accept the fact that it is the cause of many problems. Since the 1600s American Indian people have suffered from the serious problems that alcoholism and drug addiction created, yet from that point of time and until today American Indian people have been resistant toward any positive method of prevention, intervention, treatment, and many do not have any awareness of any kind of recovery process.

The non-Indian's efforts to acculturate us have failed: we now live in the Alcoholism culture.

PART II
CONTEMPORARY LIFE

SECTION FOUR
VISUAL AND VERBAL ART

Eugene Pine, Artist
TERRY STRAUS
245

First Voice
AIEDA
248

Red Path Theater
ED TWO RIVERS
250

Poems and Drawings
JEANNE LA TRAILLE
252

Friends, Kings, and Princess • *Chicago Streets* •
The Last Kiss
MARK LA ROQUE
260

The Clown's Dance
ALICE AZURE
262

Saturday Night Special
ED TWO RIVERS
272

Terry Straus

Eugene Pine, Artist

The cover of *Native Chicago*, reproduced here, was created by Chicago Indian artist Eugene Pine. It represents the Chicago Indian Village near Wrigley Field, the Cubs baseball stadium (see Wilson article, Part I, section 3). The tipi village by Wrigley Field was part of a 1970 political demonstration by Chicago Indians to protest the lack of adequate affordable housing in the city, a protest Mr. Pine himself remembers.

Some readers will surely also recognize the scene from their own experience; others will recognize it from community oral history. Even those unfamiliar with the housing protest, however, will be able to see in the cover illustration the symbols of Chicago, of urban life and of Indian residence, Indian family, Indian traditions, and Indian participation in the contemporary world.

Mr. Pine has work hanging at Truman College, now home to the Beacon Street Gallery with which he has a continuing connection. This fall, as for the last four years, his painted tipi will be set up in the Federal Building downtown. A portrait of Mr. Pine hangs in the Chicago Cultural Center as part of the "Chicago Portraits" exhibit.

Mr. Pine submitted the following statements about himself and his work:

About the Artist

Eugene Pine is a gay Native American (two-spirited) artist living with AIDS. He was born in Minneapolis in 1951, his mother was Winnebago and his father was Chippewa. They moved to Chicago when Eugene was two years old. He has lived and worked in Texas, California, Wisconsin, and Colorado. He has been awarded numerous grants from the NEA as well as other foundations. His work has appeared in solo and group shows

Painting © 1998 Eugene Pine.

around the country. He has served on the Public Arts Committee. He has been a board member of the Colorado Gay & Lesbian Community Center, a founding member of the Colorado Gay & Lesbian Native American Support Group and founding member of the Eugene Pine Native Arts Collection at Hull House here in Chicago. He has spoken at Cornell, the FAA, HUD and a number of corporations, schools, and seminars on the topics of Public Arts, Cultural Plurality, AIDS and discrimination. He currently lives in Chicago and is glad he is home.

* * * *

When I was three years old, I found out I was an Indian. It wasn't a secret. I had been surrounded by Indians all my life. It was when I found out I was an Indian, like the ones on TV, a bad guy, a blood-thirsty monster, like the statue in front of the Chicago Historical Society. The statue was of a crazed Indian man standing over a pioneer woman and children, ready to commit mayhem.

It wasn't until I was in high school in the '60s that I became aware of the Civil Rights Movement. Over the past 30 years, I have studied all I could about the cause and effects of bigotry. I learned that I could do little to change the world, but I could change my view of it.

I am a painter and I paint images of Indians in all kinds of situations. Many of the images are similar to those of the ones I saw growing up, but painted in a new light, a new color. It makes me feel like I'm capable of spiritual and heroic things, and I am capable of being human with all the failings and vulnerabilities that that entails.

I also know that, as a human being entering a new millenium, it is going to take a lot more than the bounds of bigotry allow, to save us from ourselves.

AIEDA

First Voice

The Artists' Registry

The 1990s have been a decade of increasing interest in Native American visual, performance, and fine arts in Indian communities and in the larger society. In the Chicago Indian community, fine arts from sewing and beadwork to painting and doll-making have been displayed, exchanged, and sold. Poetry performance and storytelling have become part of most community gatherings, and certain local experts have become recognized. Red Path Theater has become the first Native American theater group in the state, presenting an annual season of plays by Native American writers with Native American actors and technical crew under Native American direction. Film and video, once barely evident within the community, have been encouraged by the annual Chicago Native American Film and Video Festival.

Outside the community, interest in Native American arts has not been lost on local galleries and museums. Several Chicago museums have developed and/or continued exhibits and other public programs on American Indian arts. In this, the post-NMAI (National Museum of the American Indian Act [1989]) and post-NAGPRA (Native American Graves Protection and Repatriation Act [1990]) era, museum personnel regularly seek consultation and cooperation of American Indian people in the development of public programs on Indian arts and culture. In Chicago, the Native American Cultural Center collaborated with the Field Museum and the Chicago Historical Society on several projects, placing American Indian interns in those organizations for the dual purposes of providing museum training to the intern and assuring "First Voice" in the development of programs and exhibits. Insistence on "First Voice" was the primary motive behind the development of the Artists' Registry, a project of the Native American Cultural Committee of Chicago, under the direction of the American Indian Economic Development Association (AIEDA).

The essential idea of "First Voice" is that all public presentations about Native Americans ought to acknowledge and incorporate the perspectives of contemporary Native American people, not simply to co-opt and continue as usual, but to re-orient and re-direct educational efforts in accordance with Native American perspectives. In the past, museum personnel readily accepted the concept of "First Voice," but rarely acted upon it, protesting that they could not afford long-distance consultants and it was too difficult to find local people to work with. The Artists' Registry has removed these barriers/excuses.

Pam Alfonso (Menominee) and Ed Two Rivers (Anishinabe) began developing the Artists' Registry in 1993. Today, under the direction of Carlos Peynetsa (Zuni), Community Ventures Coordinator at AIEDA, the Registry contains the names, tribal affiliations, and resumes (photographs, slides, tapes, or descriptive material) of more than 200 Native American artists in music, film, performance/visual arts, crafts, oratory, storytelling, poetry, and acting. Through the Registry, Native American artists find opportunities for employment and local institutions and individuals gain access to "First Voice." AIEDA's own logo (see below), designed by artist Leonard White, came through the Artists' Registry, for example, as did the contract with Eugene Pine for the cover of this book. The Artists' Registry has provided over 182 such opportunities during the past six months, and continues to register artists and provide referrals. Mr. Peynetsa also provides assistance and advice to local Native American artists currently developing resumes and portfolios.

Art and economic development were once thought of as distant if not mutually exclusive endeavors. Recently, however, the idea of art as economic development has emerged. In Chicago, a 1992–3 survey of American Indian–owned businesses in the area conducted by AIEDA provided a wake up call: of 102 businesses identified as Native American, 36, or slightly more than one-third, were arts and culture related entrepreneurs in the community.

The Artists' Registry thus follows the twin objectives of ensuring "First Voice" in public programming and expanding the potential of visual, performing, and fine arts as sources of individual and community revenue.

Ed Two Rivers

Red Path Theater

The connection between theater and the stories of Native America is a natural one. Through all the generations of our existence, our culture and our history have been passed down through the act of storytelling. Storytelling is also the business of theater, and Native American playwrights are finding new audiences in the ancient arts of the theater.

Red Path Theater Company, the only Native American theater company in Illinois, produces plays which are relevant, educational and entertaining. Mandated by a mission statement to produce the works of Native American playwrights, we seek plays that are area and/or culturally based. Red Path Theater is primarily a developmental theater concentrating on work by new and emerging Native American playwrights. The company includes and encourages involvement of Indian youth in writing, acting and technical management of the stage. With the help and encouragement of Victory Gardens Theater and the Theater Department of Truman College, Red Path works to develop a pool of trained, Indian Theater professionals from which other theater groups may draw.

Red Path Theater Company, from very modest beginnings, in an Uptown basement to its current status as theater-in-residence at Truman College, has remained rooted in the Indian community. As a community based organization, its members and its primary audience (from teenagers to elders) come out of the Chicago Indian community. Past presentations have included folk-tales from reservations, the work place and the streets of urban America. To date, the following new works have been performed: *Old Indian Trick, Sunka Chisle, Shattered Dreams, A Stray Dog, Forked Tongues, Ishi and the Wood Ducks, Chili Corn, To Leonard (Poetry and Dance Performance)*. The Company's most recent project is Baba Cooper's *The Gathering*, which features an all female cast.

Red Path has performed in various locations in the Midwest, but every production is also performed in Uptown, the very heart of the urban Indian community in which many of the stories are set. These are stories of a more realistic and internally generated view of issues such as domestic violence, substance abuse, gang recruitment and racism. In a very real sense, these are their own stories, memories and experiences woven into the script.

Overall, casts usually consist of an ethnic mixture of talent that reflect the surroundings and thus enhance authenticity, which is so vital to the relevancy of the story. The mixture, we've found, enhances the production value of the show even more in that each group teaches the other important elements necessary to the successful development of the show. Red Path Theater Company has become an important part of our community. For many, the company represents a symbol of hope, a demonstration of the remarkable creativity and resilience of Indian people. Its presentations echo and reflect daily Native lives, contain humorous and educational messages, but *always suggest* positive alternatives for change. Red Path Theater places a priority on connecting with the youth in the community, offering alternative outlets and modes of expression to those of urban street life. Red Path Theater strives to broaden, strengthen and enrich literary and theatrical experience in the Chicago Indian community, supporting and performing stage plays in a first voice. Every component of our program is organized with service to our community in mind. We are dedicated to encouraging the Native American community to recognize the importance of their unique histories and cultural heritages by creating on-going theatrical dramas that enlighten, ennoble and empower.

To my dear friend Juliet
Read... enjoy! Jeanne

Jeanne La Traille

Poems and Drawings

Aware

I wonder how many people are aware
There still Indians surviving out there?
You'll see us walking down the street
We may be the next person you meet
Don't stereotype us with buckskin and feather
You won't see us dressed in buckskin or leather
Oh, you've whitewashed and changed us to
      some degree
But, our inside Indianess you do not see
At pow-wows you adore us
You are filled with admiration
It's such a shame this is only a momentary
      sensation
So, you may see us Indians anywhere
We're not all gone, we are not rare
We are still out there everywhere
      LOOK OUT!
I see one now.

J. Jeanne La Traille

Chicago Dream

Is it real
or am I living a dream
in this great metropolis, Chicago?
I am amazed, I am humbled
by the awesome beauty of the city,
beauty even in the ugly.
It's so complex:
beauty in architectural structures,
ugliness in the decay of once proud buildings.

As I stroll in the Loop
I see such contrast—
the wealthy, the middle class, the homeless
on State Street, Michigan Avenue—
a woman in her sable fur,
the battered woman pushing a grocery cart filled with her
   worldly possessions,
wearing two or three dresses, several jackets
and a tattered coat,
shoes old and several sizes too large.
Now, look over there at Buckingham Fountain—
isn't it beautiful?
Travel north to the endless beaches
of Lake Michigan.
Now look back . . .
ah, the beauty of the skyline,
skyscrapers overwhelm the sky
piercing low-lying clouds
with tenderness.
Michigan Avenue, the million-dollar mile,
the Gold Coast, Lake Shore Drive,
home of the privileged wealthy.
Travel south to Maxwell Street,
the poor man's Marshall Field's.
Cottage Grove, decaying brownstone buildings,
tenements, housing projects.
Look east: Chicago Art Institute, Soldiers Field,
Field Museum, Shedd Aquarium,
Museum of Science and Industry, Navy Pier.
The sun shines on the multitude of
swimmers, sunbathers,
all shapes, all sizes, all colors,
gorgeous tans, brick-red sunburns.
In winter, harsh winds blowing away

whiteheaded waves,
assaulting the beach with fury.
As I walk down the street I play
a game with myself.
I walk with my head down.
I look at people's feet.
I guess, I try to imagine what they look like above.
I'm a people watcher.
There are so many ethnic groups here,
marvelous faces portraying life,
the masks of tragedy and comedy
reflected in the faces of the masses.
I see many that could have been me:
the successful person alive within himself,
or the pushcart lady alone with fears and doubts.
Which is me or am I a little of both,
as we are all a part of everyone.
Chicago holds all the pieces of human life.
If I feel depressed, sad or lonely,
I only have to look at the skyline of Chicago.
It overwhelms me, it embraces my soul with hope.
Yes, I'm living in a dream, my dream
here in Chicago!

Memory of an Elk (Elkskin Dress)

He was proud and stately
This elk of majestic manner
He roamed the land
He wore his freedom as a rightful banner
He was awesome
A king in his domain
With wisdom and dignity he did reign
He was proud and stately
A vision to behold
His head held high in summer
and in the winter's cold
His time has passed but he lives on
For his spirit still dwells there but,
It also dwells within the Elkskin
dress I wear
He hears the beat of the drum
Yes, his spirit dances with me
His spirit dances proud and free
I'm honored to wear the Elkskin dress
As proud as I can be
As I dance his Spirit dances with me
As I don the dress I feel a change
A change you cannot see
In a different role I'm cast
No longer in the present
But in the distant past
I'm all the Indian Women
Who used to be
For I have the Elk-Spirit dancing
with me.

MIGWETCH, ELK SPIRIT!

My City

I see my city rising in the mist
This is over-the-rainbow splendor
I claim you for my own
I realize I must share you
Your beauty is awesome
Your charisma is overwhelming
You are bountiful in your gifts
You give us
universities
colleges
marvelous varied architecture
uniquely your own
miles and miles of lakefront
miles of beaches
a multitude of parks
you are a sports town
football
baseball
you offer us music in all forms
opera
classical
jazz
blues
country
ethnic
you tickle our fancy with
many forms of dance
ballet
modern
ethnic
meringe
You give us people, all kinds of people
White
Black
Red
Yellow

Rich
Poor
Young
Old
Happy
Sad
Ill
Healthy
You give us beauty
You give us life
You are my city
I love you CHICAGO!

Push Cart Lady

I saw her sitting there
Alone, surrounded by bundles
She was huddled against
a comforting building
The hard, cold bricks and
        cement her cushion
Her body was quivering
spasmodic with cold and fear
She was there yet, she wasn't
        She exists in the now
But she lives in the past
She lives with her memories,
In those memories she wasn't
a bedraggled, tattered woman
The object of curiosity and scorn
Her world is the world of yesteryear
She cares not for today's world

So she lives in her memory world
    of the past
I still see her sitting there
Alone, surrounded by bundles!
Little Push Cart Lady.

Mark LaRoque

Watching children in a Chicago playground . . .

friends,
kings and princess

Old friend I fought you
King of the mountain
to see who would marry the princess

Angels flying in the snow bank
and the princess said we would be
snow falls on mountain tops
hats for trees

As the clouds moved on
so did we

chicago streets

Happy lady in a stocking cap
age frozen like your smile
changes to see other times
in fresh grown rain puddles
times gone by
where are your memories tomorrow . . .
will they be of sitting in a drizzling rain
umbrella at your side
looking into pasts
reflections in the rain.

The Last Kiss

When I first moved to Chicago, I met a woman who loved me. A friend had given her a picture of me that she used to carry with her.

I know this because she used to show it to me knowing I would try to get it back. It also happens she lived with her father on his social security and sometimes hit me up to buy a pack of cigarettes.

On Fridays a lot of Indians would go to the Indian bar. It wasn't really an Indian bar because it was in Uptown which is home to the world's poor no matter the color.

No matter the bar is gone now, so is the woman.

She used to come in the bar, hair combed, wearing the brightest red lipstick on ample lips. She would come through the door pointing her lips like radar seeking me out. I would hide but her radar acted like sonar capturing my heartbeat distinct from the crowd.

It got so I would put out my cheek without a fight, giving up to the inevitable. I know now she missed the chase and I should have kept up the game.

I went to her father's funeral quite accidentally. I went into the Indian Center to see why all the people were outside smoking. It's tradition to smoke at an Indian funeral or pass out cigarettes to those that didn't smoke.

It seems proper to laugh outside and blow out smoke to carry to the Creator adding laughter to our thoughts of those gone on.

Anyway, it seems awhile went by before seeing her again. She wasn't the same anymore. Not only did she lose the one that took care of her or her home, she lost her lipstick.

It happened during winter she was homeless and cold. I heard they found her bundled up in an alley, I know she didn't really die from pneumonia.

I still remember her
and write this for her.

The Passing

She didn't feel the cold
as she took her last breath
only that she held him
in her arms
and it was warm.

Alice Azure

The Clown's Dance

"Old lady witch! Old lady witch!" the laughing children shrieked at the raggedly costumed woman waiting to enter the dance arena. Reaching into an old, stretched-out sports sock, the ugly, smiling-masked "witch" drew out a fistful of candy and threw it at the children.

Behind the latex mask, Celestine had been adjusting her breathing, trying to get used to the ninety-degree heat and humidity before joining the other dancers in the opening Intertribal. Bystanders chuckled as the children kept swarming around her for more candy. Some tourist-types even took a few pictures of her. Pretty soon, she felt ready to enter the dance circle.

Startled by the ugly face suddenly bobbing up and down beside them, the lady buckskin dancers momentarily lost their rhythm. Celestine laughed while mimicking their swaying style with grandiose bends and dips. Taking devious delight in their quizzical stares, she shuffled a few fast steps to catch up with her friend, Faye, who was wearing the Plains-style dress Celestine had made for her.

"What do you think about this mask?" she loudly whispered above the drumming, into Faye's ears.

Immediately recognizing her friend, Faye's eyeballs rolled up as she covered a broad grin with her fan. "Oh, Celestine! What are you up to, now?"

"Princess Hot Legs is the name," Celestine answered, pointing to the name on the sash crisscrossing her misshapen moosehide cape.

"You never told me about—about—this!" Faye stammered, as they danced together.

"Geez, Faye. You used to dance in feathers! Why are you surprised?"

"I didn't expect this from you. That's all." Faye withdrew, concentrating on the song.

Shrugging off Faye's reaction, Celestine Gunnville, a.k.a. Princess Hot Legs, went off to join some of the jingle dancers, who were at the side of the dance circle. The drum was really taking off, as Smokey Town was singing.

Norene Sylliboy grinned from ear to ear while Colleen Blue tried to ignore Hot Leg's crooked coup stick that jutted into the air at the honor beats. The other jingle dancers did their best to keep beat with the drum while Hot Legs shuffled her size twenty four moccasins in unison with them, all the time moving up and down in front and to the back of their line. Reaching one end, she started "scrubbing," her thin stick legs in those outrageous moccasins keeping a crazy exultant beat with the drum.

"Dang it," Isidore, her husband, seethed, watching all this in the crowd's shadows around the speaker's stand. "What's got into her?" He looked down at the ground, trying hard to stifle the unwanted laughter pushing at his chest. His right hand slipped into a front pocket, fingering the little bottle of nitroglycerin pills he kept for emergencies. "No sense making things worse," he reasoned, so he continued to look anywhere but at the jingle dancers. The choking laughter calmed down.

Off to the side, Isidore caught part of conversation between the Dreadful thunders, who were new to the community. "Who does that White woman think she is," harrumphed Rita Dreadfulthunder, "making fun of Indians?"

Shifting his weight, Isidore hooked his thumbs into his back pockets. He wanted to tell those people that the clown was an Indian, his wife. Instead, he tolerated their too-easy assumptions, silently saying, "She's only having fun, not making fun."

Still, he knew something had gotten into her. "Permission or no permission, she's still acting too crazy." He'd never seen her quite like this before, in public, too.

There's More to Clowns than Mimicry

He remembered the night when she had first paraded the princess up and down their living room. "Boy oh boy, did I laugh," he smiled in recollection. "Even took some pictures of her." Actually, he loved her craziness. "Most of the time," he added, watching her wave expansively to the spectators outside the arena fence.

"What do you think about Princess Hot Legs making an appearance at the Indian Center's powwow up north?" she had asked him that night.

Coyote had been all ears at the innocent question.

Isidore, on the other hand, had been caught off-guard. "What?" he half protested, backing away from her. He didn't like situations like that, lots of attention-getting antics. Not that he was shy. Coming from a long line of fast, fiddle-playing Turtle Mountain Chippewas, he had no trouble being up front, as long as he felt the territory familiar. Celestine dressed like a clown was okay in the privacy of their living room, but in a powwow arena, another thing. "Anyway, women aren't supposed to dabble in stuff like that," he tried to assure himself, "at least, as long as I've ever known."

Indians mimicking Indians was nothing new to Isidore. Jay Bird, the Kiowa-Apache guy, who called himself Crazy Legs, used to do that when he danced with the Sac and Fox at Black Hawk State Park during their annual Labor Day homecoming. Crazy Leg's dancing was a real show-stopper, and that ugly, big-nosed mask with the long braids and grim expression even made the dignified Sac and Fox dancers crack some smiles. "In fact, I bet she got the idea from Crazy Legs," Isidore thought about Celestine's outfit.

"Do you think you should do something like that?" he had responded gravely to Celestine, while hitching his left hand into his back pocket and rubbing his chin with the other hand. He avoided the woman issue, not wanting to get her going on that subject. Ignoring his question, she had smiled up at him, "Will you come with me, Sweetheart?"

"Good going, Sweetie!" Coyote had cheered. "Pour it on! Men love that sort of stuff!"

"Please, Isidore," he remembered her pleading, while hugging him just so.

"Well, okay," he had sighed. Hugs like that were hard for him to ignore. "Let's see what they think."

IN ANOTHER WORLD

Coyote breathed a sigh of relief. He was beginning to think Chicago was becoming as boring as the Northwest, where Indian folks knew Him very well.

Actually, Celestine knew Him quite well, too. Ever since a long time ago, when He was told to go and "lighten" her up a little, He always found her to be quite obliging. Even though she lived in the Midwest, Coyote looked forward to those "lightening up" visits with her. This time, besides the fact He was bored, what had caught His eye was her "Princess Hot Legs" outfit. He sniffed fun.

WHEN A LITTLE KNOWLEDGE IS A DANGEROUS THING

Isidore had helped Celestine pack Hot Legs into a bag, in case the pow-wow committee wanted to look at the outfit. When they arrived at the American Indian Center, Joe Muin, the chairman, had already started the meeting. Isidore and Celestine sat down at the back of the room.

Tip Verde, the arena director, was finishing his presentation about

arrangements for security. Choo-Choo Ricehill, in charge of dancer registration, along with Fose Good Bear, the master of ceremonies, each gave
their reports.

Then it was Celestine's turn to talk. As she had telephoned Joe ahead
of time, he had a little knowledge about what she was going to ask.

"I simply would like your permission to be Princess Hot Legs at the
powwow," she started, holding up the bag. "Now that I'm no longer
young, I find it easier to laugh and poke fun at myself and even act ridiculous—like wearing this Halloween outfit in front of a crowd."

Other things she mentioned were the seriousness of her youth, not
being able to try new things, like blowing a trumpet—for fear of being
ridiculed. "I couldn't even look people straight in their faces unless I
crossed my eyes," she said. That surprised Isidore, who, on more occasions than he wanted to remember, had to confront her uncrossed, very
piercing stare.

"Hot Legs doesn't always do things right," Celestine continued, "and
will probably act a little inappropriate and embarrass a few dancers. I'm
not trying to imitate a Heyoka, either—a sacred clown. That's pretty serious business, requiring lots of training and responsibility. On the contrary,
what I have here is a simple Halloween outfit."

Coyote hid a smile with His paw.

"You know," Joe Muin interrupted, "we Native people always had our
clowns. And, of course, they served a purpose beyond simple amusement.
They had special knowledge—passed down from ancestor to ancestor
over hundreds of years. This knowledge helped the people understand
things best learned through humor. Years ago, at Black Hawk State Park,
I remember an Apache guy—Jay Bird. He called himself Crazy Legs when
he danced."

A little startled, Isidore hadn't realized Joe knew Crazy Legs. "Why
was Joe talking about Crazy Legs?" he wondered.

Joe continued. "If you watched carefully, it was obvious he knew the
songs, even though he wasn't Sac or Fox. Every step he took was attuned
to the drum. Yet, through exaggeration, he appeared to be the opposite of
the serious, traditional dancers. Crazy Legs became a bridge between the
audience and these dancers. This probably was as welcome for the dancers
as it was for the spectators, for in those days, the all-White powwow
committee focused more on money and control than on the special ties
these dancers had to their original homeland, old Saukenuk."

Joe paused. People remained quiet, not sure if he was through.

"Isn't all of that just what I want to do?" Celestine said to herself.
"Crazy Legs wasn't any Heyoka. Just someone with a bent for making
people laugh."

Joe wasn't through. "You know, don't you, that Saukenuk was one of
the largest Native communities on this Turtle Island just before the Euro-

peans came? Anyhow, the audience loved Crazy Legs, and laughed with him. The little children reached out to touch him. Year after year, he visited with us at the Black Hawk powwow over there in Rock Island. Everyone had a good time with the way he made us laugh."

It stayed real quiet for a long time. Being an elder in the Chicago Indian community, people respected Joe that way. After a little longer, Joe smiled at Celestine, "Well, maybe I'll see you Saturday at Lake County Fairgrounds." The meeting was over.

Tip Verde shook Isidore's hand. "Take care, now," he smiled while lightly touching the brim of his summer-style western hat.

"I can't wait to see that outfit again," laughed Choo-Choo Ricehill. She had been at the Indian Center's Halloween party where Celestine had won the prize for best costume.

Celestine gathered up her purse and bundle of Princess Hot Leg's things. "Joe certainly was helpful, wasn't he?" she mused.

Not sure if Joe's comments meant "Yes" or "No," Isidore rubbed his chin, feeling a draft of wind whoosh by towards the door.

Clown's Dance Resumed

"Yep. That's where I went wrong, letting her ask that powwow group for permission to dress like that," Isidore sighed, smoothing his hair back while tilting his cap up and backwards. He headed off to find Ruthie Sam's buffalo burger stand.

After a few more dances, Celestine knew she had better quit. The heat was weakening her, and the salty sweat inside the mask felt miserable. Slipping out of the arena, she headed for her car and drank a quart of bottled water before going to the dressing rooms to change.

Coyote breathed a sigh of relief, as He hadn't counted on all her energy. "Almost needed those nitroglycerines myself," He panted, "after that Crow Hop went on and on!"

The Banished Mask

Arriving home that night, they left the mask and other paraphernalia in the back seat of the car. Celestine reversed the mask, however, to air out the inside. Isidore's nice Pendleton jacket was left in the front seat. The rear back window they left slightly ajar, as the heat was intense, even then.

Booming music over shouts, laughter, and beer smells came out of the downstairs neighbor's open door and windows as they walked up the back alley stairs to their second-story apartment.

A heavy, humid heat greeted Isidore the next morning. As usual, he was up early, and was watching "Sunday Morning" with Charles Kuralt when Celestine finally walked into the living room.

"Good morning, Sweetheart," she yawned. "I must have been tired to sleep like this. Guess I'd better hurry so we can get back up to Lake County."

She started down the back stairs, intending to get the mask so she could clean off the previous day's salt and sweat.

Opening the car door, she immediately saw the mask wasn't where she had placed it. Quickly, Celestine pushed aside the duffel bag holding the rest of the outfit. Nothing. Isidore's jacket was still in the front seat. Feeling under the car seats, nothing again, except a map book and snow scraper.

"Maybe I forgot and put it in the trunk." Nothing was there.

She repeated every motion, only faster—bags, jacket, map book, newspapers—everything was turned up and over and inside out. Hot Legs' items were pulled from the black duffel bag. No mask.

Remembering the party, Celestine went back through the alley, thinking someone might have wanted to use the mask, so stole it, borrowed it—what not—from the car. Celestine poked around in a few garbage barrels, overloaded with beer bottles and pizza boxes. No mask.

Circling around the block, street curbs and bushes were examined, ending up with a half-hearted examination of the big trash bin by their back alley stairs. No luck.

Back at the car, she went through the back and front seats and the trunk all over again. Really into it by now, she ran back through the alley and took the stairs two at a time.

"Did you take the mask out of the car?" she cried at Isidore.

"What are you talking about?" he replied evenly, not being one to get overly excited.

"The mask! It's not in the car, and no one would go after that instead of your jacket!"

"You're still not making sense," he answered, again ignoring her accusation.

"Isidore! I'm trying to tell you! The mask is not in the car, where I left it last night! Who would want to steal an old face mask instead of your good Pendleton jacket?"

"Let's go down and look," he suggested. Together, the two of them sorted through everything in the car.

Isidore bunched his shoulders up in apparent resignation, saying "Well, I don't know. Maybe someone got it through the open window there."

"Isidore," she protested, "that window was open just a crack! How in the world could someone have done that?"

"Just stop getting so worked up, will you? I don't know what to say, just what's done is done. Now can we go get some breakfast? I got hungry waiting for you to wake up."

The vanished mask kept gnawing at Celestine's day. Did Isidore dispose of it? Why? The thought that she might have embarrassed him crossed her mind. Immediately, an oozing sense of chagrin invaded her mind, sickening her with its thought that her actions might have caused such a strong reaction on his part. If only he had said something! She wouldn't have hurt Isidore for all the world.

Then she replayed his denial. That didn't help, either, as there was no sense to be made of a mask that vanished from a locked car. She felt the ooze settle deep inside.

Two Worlds Collide

Back up at the powwow, Celestine went over to where Fose Good Bear was haranguing the dancers to get ready for the Grand Entry. "Princess Hot Legs won't be making an appearance today," she tersely announced.

"Serious stuff, huh?" Fose replied, his tone somewhere between matter-of-fact and inquisitiveness.

"What do you mean?" she shot back at him.

"Nothing. Nothing. How come no Hot Legs today?" he asked teasingly.

"Her mask was stolen."

He whistled low. "Well, now. That could be serious," he replied. "You be real careful."

Wanting to pursue this warning, but seeing his attention shift to the assembling dancers, she left Fose to look for Isidore. "What in the world was that Fose Good Bear talking about, anyway?" The day seemed ruined.

The Grand Entry began. It was going to take a long time, as the dancers were double the number from yesterday. The singers started the Entry Song, and in procession the dancers came, feet in perfect rhythm with the drum, defying the enervating dog-day heat, Eagle Staff, flag bearers, all the princesses; old male traditional dancers, then the young men; grass dancers, fancy dancers; female buckskins; lady cloth traditionals, followed by jingle dancers; all the young girls—on and on they came, eventually forming multiple, packed hoops of joyful, pulsing colors around the drums.

All the spectators were standing, marveling at this display of dance improvisation and high-spirited self-confidence.

For all its glory and grandeur, nothing in the great Chicago Art Institute could come close to matching the designs, palettes, symbolism, technical skill, or sheer beauty borne by these living, very contemporary, tribal people.

Isidore became impatient with the long standing. "Dang heat," he fretted, surreptitiously slipping a pill under his tongue.

After the offering of prayers for a good day, Fose announced the Veteran's Dance would be four cycles of songs—one for each branch of the

Armed Services. Milwaukee Bucks—a Winnebago drum group—began the first song.

Thankful for the chance to move, Isidore stepped into the arena after the flag bearers completed a circuit, motioning for Celestine to follow.

"Please, Isidore," Celestine pleaded. "You don't have to dance."

"I'll go around just once," he answered, holding up his right index finger to her, "then you go on for me. Okay?"

It was useless to try to dissuade him from dancing in the Veteran's Dance. He wouldn't just walk the dance, either. Stubbornly, he insisted on stomping. "A matter of honor," she guessed.

When they got back to where they started, Isidore resumed his place next to their lawn chairs, removing his glasses to wipe away the sweat. Celestine kept dancing, holding her shawl loose and open at her waist, hoping to capture any stray breezes.

Even though some of the younger dancers had dropped out during this dance, other people intermittently came into the arena, mostly relatives, to honor all their family warriors living and departed.

Isidore saw the Dreadfulthunders step into the circle behind where Celestine should have been.

"Where in the world did she go?" he wondered, searching for her purple shawl. "What the. . .," he gasped, catching a glimpse of Hot Leg's grotesque, smiling mask, bobbing alongside Rita Dreadfulthunder.

A lightheadedness suddenly lifted him between the worlds. Waves of heat and salt sweat dribbled down his eyes as an invisible weight pushed needle-pointed stabs of pain deep into his chest. Through the surrounding, sunlit haze, a forest of columns emerged slow-motion out of the earth. Then the columns began to change into people, all beautifully clothed in white, brightly beaded buckskin garments. Instinctively, he recognized his relatives from time immemorial.

Grouped around ancient campfires, the misty, gossamer spirit-beings gently waved at him. "Come. Come," they beckoned with the wispy ribbons of slow-climbing, twisting smoke, smiling for him to join them. Sunlight, dappled by the humid haze and smoke, sparkled against the azure sky, like thousands of glittering Christmas tree balls.

Shuffling in and out of this smoking, magical world, Hot Legs stomped in time to the new song, now honoring Navy veterans, such as Isidore.

Fighting to make his increasingly rebellious spirit stay awhile longer, he managed to lower himself into the lawn chair and get his glasses back on. Fumbling in his right pocket, he found the little bottle of nitroglycerin pills.

Coyote panicked when He saw the visiting Grandfather and Grandmother spirit-beings. This was not the way He planned things!

Then He heard Rita Dreadfulthunder snarl, "Get out! Get out! You have no right to mock us!" while digging her fingernails hard into His paw.

Celestine, not realizing that the comments were directed to Princess

Hot Legs, jerked her arm away. "Maybe the poor woman is mad from heat exhaustion," she thought.

That thought snapped Coyote back into action. He knew what He had to do to get Celestine to Isidore's side.

Rita Dreadfulthunder's knees gave way, and her round mass collapsed in the mix of invisible and visible beings.

Fose saw the dancer fall and immediately was at her side, with helpers and first aid.

Sudden spurts of cool, insistent breezes pushed Celestine around the circle, after she knew the dancer would be okay. Then she saw Isidore sitting in the lawn chair, with his chin lowered onto his chest.

"I'm all right," he quietly said, when she frantically dropped to her knees beside him. "The pills are working, now."

She knew better than to say anything more. To do so only would have agitated him. They had been through this type of scene many, many times. No one around them sensed anything, as more than a few elders in the crowd stayed seated during this particularly long cycle of veterans' honor songs.

Lifting his head, Isidore could see his relatives were gone. "Only for awhile," he thought, as the faint smell of campfire smoke hovered around, tugging at his spirit.

AWRY POWER DISSIPATED

Back in the apartment that evening, Isidore watched Celestine maintain an agitated, sad silence. Putting his arm around her shoulder, he gently asked, "Still thinking about Princess Hot Legs?"

"It's just so strange," she answered in exasperation.

"What are you going to do with the rest of her outfit?" he asked, squeezing her shoulder a little.

"Probably throw it in the dumpster. Nothing would be right again without her mask."

Hugging her a little more, Isidore continued, "Well, then, let's put an end to this thing. We'll smudge the car and her other things. Then burn the bundle."

And that's what they did. After Isidore fanned the sage smoke all over the car's interior and trunk, Celestine carried the little bundle of Princess Hot Legs' items into their alley, under the lighted post. Isidore lit a match to the smudged bundle, and they watched the flames begin to devour the contents.

"I'll finish this up, Sweetheart," Isidore said. "Why don't you start some coffee for us, now?"

"Okay," she sighed, "that sounds good. There's still some blueberry

pie, too." Placing a light kiss on the bridge of his nose, she turned and went up the stairs.

When she was out of sight, Isidore went over to the garbage bin, slowly stooped down and pulled a wadded-up bundle from behind its corner. After carefully placing it on the fire, he added a handful of cedar and tobacco.

In the vicinity of the nearby El tracks, a dog yipped plaintively, probably having lost His bone, and headed towards Interstate 90, back to where He came from, the Northwest.

Ed Two Rivers

Saturday Night Special

(ain't good for nothin but killin...)

Joe Tension was born and raised in Chicago. A modern day warrior . . . an urban Indian . . . a dog soldier schooled on city streets. His friends in the community were worried because in recent months he'd taken up with a bad element. Rick Cartier was a part of that "bad element." His was a totally different story . . . in spite of similarities in backgrounds. Joe was political; Rick was criminal . . . a small-time drug dealer.

They sat in Rick's kitchen. A small Emerson radio stood on the table near an egg-stained dish. An ashtray and a bag of marijuana occupied the other end. Rick turned down the radio, then handed Joe a beer.

"Whatever made you think this a Hollywood picture show? Ain't no fantasy here."

Joe sipped the beer, not answering. Rick continued.

"You best wake up before it's too late bro."

"Why?"

"I got news. Hot off the press." Rick pushed his hair back.

"You got the wrong message. You think you're Brad Pitt or something? You live in hotels and take your rags to the Oriental woman with a gold tooth. That don't make you righteous . . . makes her rich."

A full-blooded Indian, Rick had been raised in foster homes. By age twenty-one he'd served a total of six years. He was bitter . . . danger-ous . . . extremely deadly.

He watched Rick relight the joint. The guy looks big, he thought, like that Leroy Brown character in the song, " . . . the baddest dude on the bad side of town." Rick handed him the joint. Got to be careful, Joe thought. Got to do this right.

"Some good shit ennit?" Rick asked.

Joe coughed, nodded his head in reply, and handed it back to Rick.

Rick laughed and held the joint at arm's length admiring his new tat-too. "This is where it's at."

"You gonna die before your time is due." Joe sang and clapped his hands to the music. The Animals. It was her favorite song before his girlfriend was killed. Her death had devastated him.

"Right!" Rick snapped his fingers, not noticing as Joe pulled a revolver out of his back pocket.

"Yo Rick, look up man."

Rick's eyes widened.

"Put the gun down. Jesus Christ man!"

Rick believed in the philosophy that if you pulled a gun, you'd better damned well be ready, willing, and able to use it. Joe was. He swung the pistol with all his might. He heard the clunk, felt the impact and knew that he'd connected good. Rick grabbed his head and held it for a short while. He put his hands out in front of his face. He watched blood ooze between his fingers and run in small rivulets down his forearm. His own pistol lay on the floor in the next room . . . empty. Rick felt a sense of nakedness.

"Man, I'm bleeding."

"You don't think you're a Saturday night special now . . . do you?"

"What are you talking about?"

"Mary Lou!" Joe's voice became hard. "You told her you were a regular Saturday night special. 'No good for nothin but killin.' Just like that rock and roll song says. Like my pistol."

Rick's eyes widened. The fan ticked.

Joe saw Rick gasp for breath. It was just for a brief second. He pushed the pistol closer . . . until it touched his eyelid.

Rick stared . . . transfixed. Joe saw him blink.

"You freaking out on the dope? I got some downers. You want a couple V's? I got some tens." Desperation colored Rick's words.

Joe saw Rick's face change. Muscles twitching. He pushed a little harder. Oh yeah, the man is scared, he thought. A cockroach scampered out from under the refrigerator.

"Look down the Goddamned barrel. Just like you made Mary Lou do."

Joe swung his pistol again. He saw blood leap from the gash just above Rick's left eye. He ain't all that bad now is he? This guy's just big. You just tall and that's all, Joe thought.

"I don't know no Mary Lou. I swear on a stack of bibles."

"That's right. You never know the women, do you? You just pick at random." He saw Rick's facial features alter again. The fear was becoming desperation. Now, he thought, is the time to be careful.

"I loved that girl since eighth grade . . . Veteran's Pow-wow. I fell in love . . . head over heels. Ever fall in love like that?" Joe questioned.

"No."

"That's right. You don't like women do you?" He swung the pistol again but missed.

273

"I didn't . . . "

Like a hunter waiting for the perfect shot Joe had taken his time . . . it paid off. He'd done what the cops couldn't. It had taken him three years but he'd put it all together. All he wanted or needed to do is hear the man confess.

"I swear."

"You had to be in Thunder Bay on June 29th, three years ago."

"I was here in Chicago. At a party. I can prove it. Hell, that much, I can prove beyond a doubt."

"How?"

"Because I did a woman here in Chicago on June 29th three years ago. Hell yeah, I can remember it clearly. I killed a bitch . . . "

Joe swung. Rick yelped. His eyes began watering. Shoot him now, Joe thought. He didn't. He needed to hear him say it.

"I never hurt your woman. Never went to Thunder Bay."

"How do I know I can believe you?"

Rick didn't answer. He sat; calculating risks. Another pistol slap and his mind was made up.

"I can tell you details."

Joe nodded.

"I was at this party. There was this Indian girl from out West. Didn't look like she wanted to be there. Her girlfriend wanted to party. I offered a lift to her neighborhood. She just wanted to get home."

"Look down the barrel. I'll know you're telling the truth. That's fair, right?"

"If I do will you believe?"

Joe nodded again.

"Okay. Point it at my right eye. Yeah, there."

He reached for the weapon to direct the barrel, hesitated, then changed his mind.

"How'd you do it?"

"What? Man come on. You said . . . "

"You said details. So how did you kill her?"

He leaned closer. Rick cringed and ducked. Joe didn't swing the gun.

Rick noticed a cobweb above the door. Keep talking, he thought. Maybe the bastard will get careless. He was becoming even more desperate.

"Well I didn't figure to kill her . . . not at first." The fan ticked. After a moment longer Rick continued, "But later on I knew that I was going to do it."

"Why?"

"Because she was Indian, I guess. She looked it too."

A fly buzzed around the room. The fan ticked louder. Rick's insides were twisting. The same cockroach scampered from under the refrigerator again, turned and dashed away. Joe waited.

"I pulled a gun and told her to get on the floor of my truck. She was crying and begging me to let her go. Of course I couldn't do that even if I wanted to."

"What happened then?"

"Took her to my apartment. Had some fun with her."

"Had some fun?"

"You know? I screwed her real good then tortured her."

"Tortured?"

"I like that the best." Rick licked his lips.

"Look down the barrel." Joe drew back the hammer.

"Don't let that hammer slip."

"You started torturing her?"

When Joe pushed the pistol closer, Rick nodded. Nausea washed over him.

"Do you have any idea what I went through?"

Rick focused on the pistol.

Joe shook his head. "Tell me."

"It was because she left me. She wanted freedom. I was a burden. She just split."

"So? That happens to all kinds of kids. They don't kill people like you do."

"I was molested by people who swore that they would protect me."

"So why Indian women?"

"Because of her." He paused, collected his thoughts, then continued. "I twist their heads until their necks break. Sometimes I cut off their nipples. Sometimes I just smash them up real good."

Joe felt his neck hairs bristle. Can I do this? he wondered.

Sweat glistened on Rick's forehead. His hands shook. "I didn't kill no Mary Lou in Thunder Bay . . . I killed a girl in Chicago!"

"Now you're telling the truth."

Rick began breathing easier. "Okay! Put the gun up now."

"Not just yet."

"You promised."

"You remember her name?"

"Margo or something. Mitchell?"

"That's right! You're sharp! She hated it." A tear rolled down Joe's cheek. It slowed at his chin, hovered for a moment then fell with a silent splash to his chest. "You know what she called herself?"

Rick felt dizzy. Breathing became an effort again. He knew the answer.

"Mary Lou," Joe said.

"Joe please."

"I got you now Rick. Right? Don't I got you?"

THE END

PART II
CONTEMPORARY LIFE

SECTION FIVE
PEOPLE

Chicago Native American Demographic Profile
AIEDA
279

*The Contested Minority Status of
American Indians in Chicago*
MARISA WESTERVELDT
286

Indian or Not?: Ethnic Identity Among Biracial Indians
LISA ORTIZ
294

*Culturally Intact Heroines:
A Pro-Activist View of Native American Womanists*
KAREN STRONG
300

Canadian Islanders in Chicago
AGNES WAGOSH
305

Coming Around Again
MARY JACOBS
311

Dr. Robert Beck: Reconnecting
TERRY STRAUS
318

AIEDA

Chicago Native American Demographic Profile
Conclusion

The demographic data summarized in this profile allow certain generalizations about the Chicago area Native American population and related implications for community service.

Overall, there has been a significant increase in the American Indian population in the city and in the state. The Indian population of Chicago has been increasing since 1900 and continues to do so. The 1990 census documents, for the first time, the contribution of Hispanic Indians to that increase: almost a third of those identifying as American Indians, Eskimo, or Aleut on that census also claimed Hispanic ethnicity.

The Indian population is dispersed, with residents in virtually every neighborhood in the city. Certain neighborhoods, especially Uptown-Edgewater, have consistently had a higher concentration of Indian residents. Within the past decade, however, there has been a pronounced tendency for Indian people to leave those neighborhoods, moving north and west in the city, away from the area generally recognized as the "center" of the Indian population. This pattern is consistent with Indian population movement in other urban communities such as Detroit and Minneapolis.

In part, this shift in residence has probably been due to job availability: people move to where the jobs are, even if it means moving out of the city. Employment statistics from the 1990 census show a wide spread of occupations among American Indian people in Chicago, with some variance by gender. The most common occupations for Indian men were truck driver, janitor, security guard, and laborer; the most common for Indian women were cashiers, secretaries, and elementary school teachers. The largest growth in a particular kind of employment was in service occupations, but this growth has not been complemented by increasing pro-

1990 Chicago Community Area Profile
COMMUNITY AREAS WITH THE HIGHEST CONCENTRATIONS OF NATIVE AMERICANS

Area No.:	3	24	6	77	4	22	1	30	14	2	5	16	23
Total:	63,839	87,703	91,031	60,703	44,891	82,605	60,378	81,155	49,501	65,374	33,010	50,159	67,573

Total Persons: 2,783,726

	3 Uptown	24 West Town	6 Lakeview	77 Edgewate	4 Lincoln Square	22 Logan Square	1 Rogers Park	30 South Lawndale	14 Albany Park	2 West Ridge	5 North Center	16 Irving Park	23 Humboldt Park
Total N.A. Population:	652	464	368	316	310	304	280	267	249	207	204	201	197
Ages													
< 1	10	7	4	5	5	4	5	5	8	2	6	2	3
1-2	26	20	11	12	17	11	10	9	14	9	7	9	13
3-4	20	17	8	6	15	17	10	12	12	6	8	9	9
5	10	14	3	5	5	4	7	6	7	3	7	7	4
6	13	13	7	4	6	9	4	4	3	4	1	0	5
7-9	32	29	12	10	16	13	14	12	12	11	4	16	10
10-11	24	23	9	3	11	8	6	7	11	4	8	5	8
12-13	28	20	5	9	5	14	8	5	13	7	7	5	7
14	7	3	3	1	4	7	5	2	5	3	7	3	7
15	10	10	2	5	6	4	2	4	5	1	3	3	9
16	9	9	4	3	4	4	3	0	4	1	1	2	2
17	7	8	4	6	6	4	4	2	4	2	1	4	3
18	7	14	6	5	4	7	3	4	4	4	6	2	6
19	18	4	6	4	3	8	5	8	2	1	1	8	5
20	11	7	5	3	6	3	10	3	5	3	5	4	4
21	8	6	11	4	7	3	5	4	7	4	5	6	3
22-24	27	34	23	28	21	20	19	28	11	15	6	8	15
25-29	41	49	46	32	33	39	31	43	17	27	24	20	15
30-34	56	47	44	36	30	26	33	35	13	19	21	31	16
35-39	50	45	26	33	19	21	40	20	25	26	20	9	14
40-44	57	20	31	22	14	16	18	17	24	17	13	11	5
45-49	43	16	32	19	16	18	11	8	16	9	11	12	9
50-54	44	8	16	16	15	11	6	8	10	10	9	13	10
55-59	32	7	13	11	11	8	4	8	7	8	5	5	5
60-61	6	4	5	5	7	1	2	1	1	1	4	2	3
62-64	16	6	12	8	8	6	0	2	3	2	6	2	1
65-69	19	16	11	8	4	10	6	5	3	1	5	2	2
70-74	11	5	7	5	5	4	3	2	1	3	1	1	1
75-79	7	2	2	4	4	0	3	0	1	1	0	0	1
80-84	3	0	0	1	3	1.	1	2	1	1	1	0	0
> 85	0	1	0	3	0	3	2	1	0	2	1	0	2

U.S. Bureau of the Census, 1990 STF1A, Illinois

fessionalization or movement into higher paying, higher-status occupations reported by the census.

Employment is a major reason for population shift; schools, housing, and safety concerns are other such reasons. Although the Audubon School Native American Center has provided a fortunate alternative at the elementary school level, there is no such "Receiving Center" at the high school level in Chicago. Chicago public high schools are considered threatening and insensitive by many American Indian families. Failure and drop-out statistics on American Indian students buttress these suspicions. While a steadily increasing number of Indian people attend college, Indian college students tend to be older, returning students, not recent high school graduates.

Whatever the reasons for the population shift, it may be generating areas of entrenched poverty in the Indian population. As those with better personal and financial resources leave the less desirable areas, those with few means or no resources remain. Social service agencies in Uptown

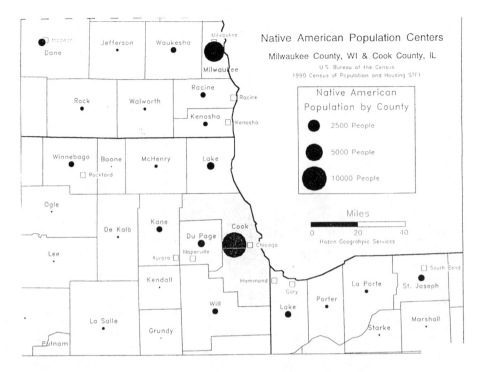

report an increase in clientele over the past decade, in spite of the declining population. Apparently, those remaining in the area have large families and are in greater need of services than was the case ten years ago.

This shift in residence pattern suggests a need for improved and expanded services to Uptown residents, rather than a decrease in services that might be indicated by the significant drop in the population.

The Indian population of Chicago is very diverse. This is clearly demonstrated in the statistical data. There are many different tribes represented in Chicago and no single tribe or tribes dominate in terms of numbers or influence. The organizational structure of the community is not controlled by any single tribe: indeed, the directors of the different community organizations reflect some of the tribal diversity (Chippewa, Lakota Sioux, Mesquakie, Navajo, Ojibwa, Menominee).

In terms of socioeconomic characteristics, although the aggregate statistics still look grim (Indians are the second poorest group in the city), the median income of $20,899 is up from that of 1980 and there are certainly individual success stories as revealed in the survey of Indian-owned businesses and in the shift in residential pattern. There is considerable socioeconomic diversity in the Chicago American Indian population. In the words of LaDonna Harris: "You don't have to be poor to be Indian," and in Chicago there are a growing number of middle-class Indian people who

6 COUNTY METRO AREA 1990 - SOCIOECONOMIC CHARACTERISTICS BY RACE & HISPANIC ORIGIN

Variable	6 Metro	Percent	White	Percent	African-Amer	Percent	Latino	Percent	Native Amer	Percent	Asian	Percent
Median HH Income	40,755		40,755		22,511		28,556		29,143		40,581	
HH w/inc. < $15,000	491,782	18.7%	281,466	14.3%	169,904	36.8%	47,347	23.1%	1265	26.2%	11,714	16.2%
$15,000 - 34,999	761,884	29.0%	548,055	27.9%	147,931	32.0%	79,556	38.9%	1,548	32.0%	19,385	26.7%
$34,999 - 49,999	506,027	19.5%	400,705	20.4%	69,069	15.0%	40,777	20.0%	996	20.6%	13,867	19.1%
> $50,000	855,716	32.8%	736,294	37.4%	74,567	16.2%	36,752	18.0%	1,024	21.2%	27,551	38.0%
	2,615,409		1,966,520		461,471		204,432		4,833		72,517	
Persons in Pov	808,401	11.3%	274,605	5.5%	408,833	29.4%	160,742	19.9%	2,394	17.0%	2,399	9.7%
Children in Pov	315,914	17.0%	77,702	6.6%	184,989	41.4%	74,234	25.0%	782	21.0%	6,379	8.9%
Families in Pov												
Marr w/ child. < 5 yrs	6,384	3.9%	3,078	2.3%	958	7.0%	2,585	12.9%	40	12.7%	715	9.3%
child. 5-17 years	14,851	3.9%	6,008	2.1%	4,698	9.6%	4,587	10.4%	42	6.0%	1,084	5.3%
child <5 and 5-17 yrs	12,583	7.6%	5,181	4.4%	3,277	15.2%	5,695	18.0%	59	14.2%	588	8.7%
No children	16,188	2.4%	9,740	1.6%	3,858	6.1%	2,070	7.0%	27	3.1%	1,359	8.6%
Total Married family	50,006		24,007		12,791		14,937		168		3,746	
Fem HH w/ child. < 5 yrs	1,831	19.6%	541	11.6%	773	29.0%	685	24.2%	9	14.3%	20	8.4%
child. 5-17 years	3,049	12.9%	1,077	8.4%	1,485	20.5%	787	17.0%	0	0.0%	84	13.2%
child <5 and 5-17 yrs	1,906	27.8%	522	21.3%	890	32.7%	721	31.3%	14	50.0%	27	22.1%
No children	3,342	6.3%	1,147	3.1%	1,564	15.8%	593	7.7%	20	20.0%	209	10.6%
Total Fem HH family	10,128		3,287		4,712		2,786		43		340	
Male HH w/ child. < 5 yrs	14,606	45.2%	3,656	31.4%	9,342	52.4%	2,173	55.5%	78	60.9%	54	17.6%
child. 5-17 years	41,811	32.2%	9,162	16.9%	28,308	43.6%	5,841	42.8%	80	22.9%	388	18.3%
child <5 and 5-17 yrs	31,393	62.2%	5,124	49.1%	23,338	65.6%	4,307	66.3%	109	70.8%	131	41.9%
No children	10,244	8.0%	3,395	4.0%	5,957	15.9%	1,013	14.7%	0	0.0%	315	13.2%
Total Male HH family	98,054		21,337		66,945		13,334		267		888	
Total Families in Pov	159,188		48,631		84,448		31,057		478		4,974	
Child Labor Force Partic.	3,791,437	68.3%	2,809,018	69.4%	624,908	61.8%	397,592	73.2%	7,971	72.8%	133,242	71.4%
Unemployment rate	256,000	6.8%	117,136	4.2%	107,325	17.2%	41,134	10.4%	938	11.8%	6,378	4.8%
Youth Unempl. rate	37,901	18.4%	16,314	11.5%	15,628	41.0%	37,901	18.4%	184	30.8%	808	13.3%
High School Compl. rate	3,550,896	76.6%	2,809,156	81.1%	528,804	65.9%	173,307	44.0%	6,269	72.7%	127,880	83.6%
Coll. Compl. rate	1,136,775	24.5%	955,206	27.6%	94,743	11.8%	30,526	7.8%	1,386	16.0%	75,213	49.2%
Home Ownership rate	1,595,050	60.9%	1,343,490	68.2%	174,067	37.5%	77,387	38.2%	1,877	39.1%	38,200	54.0%

U.S. Bureau of the Census, 1990 STF3A, Illinois

live above the poverty line. Socioeconomic diversity in the Indian population has increased over time. The greatest number of Indian people living in poverty (as defined by the Census Bureau) is in the city itself rather than in the surrounding six county areas or the state more generally.

As is common in groups with a high rate of poverty, many of American Indian families are single-parent families, and most of those single-parent families are female-headed households. These statistics are consistent with the observations of community service personnel and carry at least one important implication in regard to community services: In order not to sustain the feminization of poverty, to allow women the opportunity for education and steady employment, good child care services must be developed in the community. Such development of child care services would support both personal and community development. Presently, there is no one organization committed to establishing adequate child care in the community, although several organizations have subsidiary programs that include child care.

The Native American population in Chicago is very young. A very high percent (29.8%) of Native Americans in Chicago are youth (under 18), much higher than that of the general population. This is also true throughout the state, though it is more extreme in the city itself. Some explanations have been suggested in this book. The youthfulness of the In-

POPULATION COUNTS AND PERCENTAGES BY RACE AND HISPANIC ORIGIN: 1990

	Total Population	White	Percent	Black	Percent	Native American	Percent	Asian	Percent	Other	Percent	Hispanic Origin (any race)	Percent
Illinois	11,430,602	8,952,978	78.3%	1,694,273	14.8%	21,836	0.2%	285,311	2.5%	476,204	4.2%	904,446	7.9%
6 County Metro*	6,903,863	4,819,088	69.8%	1,386,696	20.1%	13,368	0.2%	246,554	3.6%	438,157	6.3%	816,932	11.8%
Cook County	5,105,067	3,204,947	62.8%	1,317,147	25.8%	10,289	0.2%	188,565	3.7%	384,119	7.5%	694,194	13.6%
Chicago	2,783,726	1,263,524	45.4%	1,087,711	39.1%	7,064	0.3%	104,118	3.7%	321,309	11.5%	545,852	19.6%
Uptown	63,839	29,948	46.9%	15,735	24.6%	652	1.0%	9,263	14.5%	8,241	12.9%	14,398	22.6%

*Includes Cook, DuPage, Kane, Lake, McHenry & Will Counties

U.S. Bureau of the Census, 1990 CP-1-15, Illinois

CITY OF CHICAGO 1990 - SOCIOECONOMIC CHARACTERISTICS BY RACE & HISPANIC ORIGIN

Variable	Citywide	Percent	White	Percent	African-Amer	Percent	Latino	Percent	Native Ame	Percent	Asian	Percent
Median HH Income	26,301		31,460		19,899		24,857		20,899		28,587	
HH w/Inc. < $15,000	303,242	29.6%	122,918	22.5%	147,518	41.2%	38,411	28.2%	871	38.3%	8,821	26.5%
$15,000 - 34,999	340,762	33.4%	181,803	33.2%	114,064	31.9%	54,759	40.3%	749	33.0%	11,140	33.5%
$34,999 - 49,999	169,045	16.7%	100,658	18.4%	48,185	13.5%	24,282	17.9%	332	14.6%	5,954	17.9%
> $50,000	207,862	20.3%	142,554	25.9%	48,397	13.4%	18,443	13.6%	321	14.1%	7,313	22.1%
	1,020,911		547,933		358,164		135,895		2,273		33,228	
Persons in Pov	592,298	21.6%	137,021	11.0%	354,194	33.2%	128,580	24.2%	1,559	22.1%	17,759	17.4%
Children in Pov	240,968	33.9%	38,249	16.7%	158,691	47.3%	60,031	30.6%	532	30.6%	4,815	19.8%
Families in Pov												
Marr w/ child. < 5 yrs	3,953	9.1%	1,363	5.7%	767	9.2%	1,914	16.1%	17	15.2%	552	16.1%
child. 5-17 years	10,222	10.0%	2,949	6.3%	3,922	12.2%	3,873	13.7%	30	13.2%	734	12.8%
child <5 and 5-17 yrs	8,609	16.8%	2,657	11.9%	2,600	18.6%	4,473	21.8%	42	32.3%	471	19.9%
No children	9,244	4.7%	3,978	3.0%	3,265	6.9%	1,772	10.0%	6	1.9%	979	12.7%
Total Married family	32,088		10,945		10,554		12,032		95		2,736	
Fem HH w/ child. < 5 yrs	1,279	25.7%	302	18.5%	577	31.0%	551	27.0%	4	15.4%	10	9.2%
child. 5-17 years	2,245	19.6%	594	15.8%	1,255	23.7%	656	20.1%	0	0.0%	57	17.1%
child <5 and 5-17 yrs	1,523	35.2%	349	33.9%	782	38.1%	581	33.6%	14		24	26.1%
No children	2,584	9.8%	696	5.2%	1,440	17.2%	436	8.6%	0	0.0%	155	11.5%
Total Fem HH family	7,631		1,941		4,054		2,204		18		246	
Male HH w/ child. < 5 yrs	11,165	53.7%	1,794	43.4%	8,013	55.6%	1,829	59.4%	57	68.7%	48	23.3%
child. 5-17 years	32,600	44.2%	4,032	28.2%	24,938	48.3%	4,965	48.1%	56	29.8%	300	26.8%
child <5 and 5-17 yrs	25,225	67.9%	2,549	61.9%	20,171	68.7%	3,692	70.8%	72	70.6%	118	51.1%
No children	7,876	12.0%	1,722	5.8%	5,401	17.1%	945	18.3%	0	0.0%	196	13.7%
Total Male HH family	76,926		10,097		58,523		11,431		185		662	
Total Families in Pov	116,645		22,983		73,131		25,662		298		3,644	
Child Labor Force Partic.	1,361,339	63.7%	693,145	65.6%	458,968	58.7%	250,677	70.3%	3,440	66.9%	56,448	68.5%
Unemployment rate	154,231	11.3%	42,126	11.3%	89,236	19.4%	29,381	11.7%	550	16.0%	3,701	6.6%
Youth Unempl. rate	21,443	30.3%	4,573	16.6%	12,391	45.8%	5,451	26.7%	110	45.3%	472	19.4%
High School Compl. rate	1,153,871	66.0%	645,262	72.2%	391,426	63.1%	105,871	40.8%	2,564	64.2%	51,156	76.7%
Coll. Compl. rate	339,862	19.5%	240,654	26.6%	65,121	10.5%	17,187	6.6%	639	16.0%	26,650	40.0%
Home Ownership rate	425,411	41.5%	267,992	48.8%	122,084	33.8%	42,739	31.4%	570	25.8%	11,258	34.5%

U.S. Bureau of the Census, 1990 STF3A, Illinois

dian population is likely to persist as the youth of today become parents, have larger than usual families, and themselves ultimately move out of the city, perhaps even retire to a home reservation, and die at an earlier-than-average age. The young age of the Chicago Indian population is important to consider in the establishment of community priorities and organizational programs. Youth services are and will be needed within the community. The point needs to be made in developing programs and writing proposals that the services needs of the Indian community are different from most other communities in this regard, that there is an inordinate proportion of young people in the population, and not enough programs aimed at them.

Throughout the United States, the number of Indian people in cities exceeds that on reservations. In Chicago, the Indian population has been increasing throughout this century. The time has come to address the special issues of Indian people living in cities.

Marisa Westerveldt

The Contested Minority Status of American Indians in Chicago

Since 1990, Chicago city law has included an ordinance that was expressly designed to help local minority- and women-owned businesses obtain city contracts. This legislation incorporates the following definitions of official Chicago "minority groups":

> i) African-Americans or Blacks (persons having origins in any of the Black racial groups of Africa);
> ii) Hispanics (persons of Spanish culture with origins in Mexico, South or Central America, or the Caribbean Islands, regardless of race);
> iii) Asian-Americans (persons having origins in any of the original peoples of East Asia, Southeast Asia, the Indian subcontinent, or the Pacific Islands);
> iv) Other groups, or other individuals, found by the board to be socially and economically disadvantaged and to have suffered actual racial or ethnic discrimination and decreased opportunities to compete in Chicago area markets or to do business with the city.
> (Article IV 2-92-420)

The juxtaposition of racial designations and cultural distinctions reveal, a real confusion on the part of the City Council as to what properly constitutes a Chicago minority group. The inclusion of some geographic terms like "the Indian subcontinent" and "Africa" lends an illusion of specificity to what is actually a very vague listing of general origins and allegiances. This apparent elaboration of three categories also serves to deflect attention from the fact that a sizable portion of Chicago minority (i.e., non-Caucasian or EuroAmerican, depending upon whether racial or ethnic distinctions are used) inhabitants are lumped under the homogenizing term of "Other." People who ally themselves with unmentioned groups like the Chicago American Indian community are rendered so fragmented and invisible by such legislation that Article IV appears to be more of a disadvantage than an offer of assistance.

The tortured language of this city ordinance and its evasive attitude towards American Indian and other "Other" claims seem less surprising when the circumstances surrounding the formation and passage of this legislation are revealed. The Chicago City Council acted in response to many facets of the American sociocultural climate in the late 1980s and early 1990s. Perhaps the most significant of these influences was the U.S. Supreme Court ruling in *Richmond v. Croson*, a decision that was a reflection as well as an extension of popular support for the dismantling of minority set-asides and other affirmative action programs. An examination of the complicated history that lies behind the passage of the legal minority definitions detailed in Article IV reveals the deep conceptual juncture that exists between pre- and post-Croson minority rights programs. The eventual denial of automatic recognition for the minority status of Chicago's American Indian residents has precipitated results that demonstrate the continuing necessity for affirmative action programs in a world where the concept of minority groups is becoming increasingly ambiguous and controversial.

The ideas that would be eventually codified in Article IV have obvious origins in the Civil Rights Movement and social activism of the 1960s and other previous decades. Chicago and other American cities have long experimented with a variety of both voluntary and mandatory minority rights programs. However, the most direct forerunner of the Chicago "Minority-Owned and Women-Owned Business Enterprise Procurement Program" was a declaration issued by Mayor Harold Washington in April 1985. The strongly worded Executive Order 85-2 asserted that

> Whereas . . . the practice of racial, ethnic and sexual discrimination was, in the recent history of the United States, authorized and, in some instances, mandated by law . . . such practice is repugnant to the principles of liberty and equality embodied in the Constitution of the United States and . . . of the State of Illinois . . . legal prohibitions against such practice have eradicated neither discriminatory practices nor their effects... past discriminatory practices have placed women and racial and ethnic minorities in a position of social and economic disadvantage.

The city of Chicago would therefore seek to ameliorate these abuses through additional remedial legislation. The implementation of institutional action was apparently given additional impetus by the publication of the Lowry Report the month before, in March 1985. This report, which had been commissioned by Mayor Washington and the city in 1984, was intended to be a documentation of historical city discrimination against minorities. The Lowry Report determined that, despite the intervention of city-wide endeavors like the voluntary Chicago Plan of

1970 (Blue Ribbon 45-48) there was a continued discrepancy between minority and majority opportunities in Chicago. One of the most striking differences was discerned in the distribution of lucrative city contracts. Although ostensible minorities constituted about 60% of the Chicago population by the mid-1980s, minority businesses continued to handle less than 10% of yearly city contracts (Blue Ribbon 1990, 31). Definite "long standing social and economic barriers impairing . . . minorities" could be seen in these patterns, and such impediments to "both the social progress and the economic development of the City of Chicago" could be removed only through an official city commitment to the promotion of "a sense of economic equality among its citizens and its contractors" (Executive Order 85-2, 1-3). A minority set-aside program for city contract awards was viewed as an eminently viable solution to the problem of ongoing economic disadvantage. The minorities that were subsequently singled out for attention were those groups that were currently recognized by the federal government's Equal Employment Opportunity Commission: "Blacks; Hispanics, regardless of race; Asian-Americans and Pacific Islanders; American Indians and Alaskan Natives" (Executive Order 85-2, 3). National conceptions of local minority groups also owed much to particular popular sociocultural attitudes and movements. The incorporation of these national categories into the local laws of Chicago and other cities eventually caused a variety of problems in the increasingly conservative political climate of 1980s America.

As was mentioned above, the major catalyst for a general reconsideration of local minority categorizations was the 1989 U.S. Supreme Court decision in the case *City of Richmond v. J.A. Croson Co* (488 U.S. 469). In 1983 the predominantly black city council of Richmond, Virginia, had created and affirmed a "Minority Business Utilization Plan," which made use of federal EEOC categories for its definition of affected local minority groups. Like the later Chicago Executive Order 85-2, this plan sought to encourage the participation of minority-owned businesses in city-contracted projects. Non-minority prime contractors who had been awarded Richmond city construction contracts were henceforth required to subcontract at least 30% of the contract's dollar amount to one or more qualified Minority Business Enterprises. These "MBEs" were defined as businesses owned by "Blacks, Spanish-speakers, Orientals, Indians, Eskimos, or Aleuts" (Croson 477-78). There was a waiver provision in the legislation that allowed prime contractors to sidestep this requirement, but the council made it clear that

> To justify a waiver, it must be shown that every feasible attempt has been made to comply [with the requirement], and it must be demonstrated that sufficient, relevant, qualified MBEs . . . are unavailable or unwilling to participate in the contract to enable meeting the 30% MBE goal. (Croson 478-79)

Such a stringent ordinance was clearly meant to be an active and definitive response to a recent study that had shown that only 0.67% of Richmond prime construction contracts awarded in the period 1978–1983 had gone to MBEs, despite the fact that the city population was fully 50% Black (Croson 553). Yet even its basis in concrete historical evidence could not protect the Richmond Minority Business Utilization Plan from the controversy that was then building around the validity of minority demands for aid and relief.

The Richmond Plan was challenged soon after its implementation. The J.A. Croson Company, a non-minority owned mechanical plumbing and heating contractor, bid on and won a plumbing project contract with the Richmond City Jail in September 1983. Regional manager Eugene Bonn attempted to comply with the Minority Business Utilization Plan, but he could locate only one qualified MBE that was willing to work with Croson. The non-negotiable fees demanded by this MBE pushed the project $7,000 over its prospective budget. Bonn proceeded to ask the city to rebudget the project, but his proposal was declined. The city also declined his request for a waiver, though Bonn went to some lengths to demonstrate his unsuccessful search for interested MBEs. The J.A. Croson Company was later informed that Richmond had dissolved their agreement with Croson and had offered the plumbing project to a rival contractor (Croson 481-83). Croson responded by bringing action against Richmond in Federal District Court.

The legitimacy of the Richmond Minority Business Utilization Plan was upheld in the Federal Court of the District of Eastern Virginia (Croson 1, 779 F. 2d. 181, 1985). Croson then took the case to the Fourth Circuit Court of Appeals, which initially affirmed the Richmond Plan only to reverse its decision upon remand. The 1987 Circuit Court decision declared that the Richmond City Council's ordinance displayed "more of a political than a remedial basis for the [institution of] racial preference" (Croson II, 822 F. 2d. 1355, CA4). The Supreme Court displayed a similar approach when they affirmed this Circuit Court decision in 1989. The Court took issue with the forum chosen for the redress of minority disadvantages as well as the constitution of those minority groups at local levels. Pointing out that "There is absolutely no evidence of past discrimination against Spanish speaking, Oriental, Indian, Eskimo, or Aleut persons in any aspect of the Richmond construction industry" (Croson 506), the Court asserted that State or City legislative bodies are restricted to the enactment of only those laws that are oriented toward the prevention of minority discrimination in its specific local forms and current extent. The unexplained, unsupported inclusion of all federal minority groups and the seemingly arbitrary, unrepresentative selection of an unvarying 30% minority quota rendered the Richmond Plan politically suspicious and hence invalid in the eyes of the Court. Those justices who voiced majority opinions claimed that local affirmative action legislation would be acceptable if and only if the groups in question had suffered demonstrable discrimination within that area and the laws enacted were specifically "tailored" responses to those recorded incidents. Broad, sweeping ordinances like the Richmond Plan were inherently unacceptable within an increasingly parsimonious sociocultural climate.

This federal decision in *Richmond v. Croson* had a predictable effect upon all the localities that had enacted affirmative action ordinances or executive orders similar to the Richmond Plan. Other cities, fearful of the potential for costly court challenges, began to alter or eradicate such laws. When Richard M. Daley assumed the office of Mayor in Chicago, he issued a 1989 Executive Order (Executive Order 89-7) that was identical in content to 85-2; however, he also convened a Blue Ribbon Panel of lawyers and social scientists to explore the possibility of more viable alternatives. The Report of this Blue Ribbon Panel was issued in March 1990, and it recommended that the city of Chicago use federal minority categories only for affirmative action programs that involved projects receiving federal funding (Blue Ribbon 1990, 150). For purchases and projects receiving only city money or funds from sources without mandated minority set-asides, the Panel recommended that the city orient its affirmative action program around the concerns of "those business enterprises that are owned by persons of a class that has suffered discrimination in the Chicago area" (Blue Ribbon 1990, 151). Using sources like the Lowry Report, the Panel was able to report ample evidence for Chicago-area discrimination against African-Americans, Hispanics, Asian-Americans, and women (Blue Ribbon 1990, 151). It claimed "insufficient testimonial or statistical data" for the demonstration of a similar city-wide bias against American Indians (Blue Ribbon 1990, 152). This federally-recognized minority group could not qualify for local assistance to enhance participation in a solely city-funded project or endeavor unless an individual business could prove that it had suffered "actual discrimination and decreased opportunities to compete in Chicago markets or to do business with the City of Chicago" (Blue Ribbon 1990, 152). Chicago-area Indians were thus relegated to the vague and dubious Article IV category of "Other".

More recent debacles over affirmative action laws like the removal of mandatory minority set-asides for California state institutions may make the concern over Chicago's denial of automatic city minority status to local Indians seem like the proverbial tempest in a teapot. After all, the conditions mandated by the Croson decision did not negate the federal minority status of American Indians, and Article IV provides a continual means for Chicago area Indians to receive situation-specific remedial preferences. Yet this official city refusal to recognize Indians as a local minority has resulted in some questionable outcomes. Evidence gathered by groups like the American Indian Economic Development Association (AIEDA) demonstrates that requiring Indians to comply with what dissenting Supreme Court Justice Thurgood Marshall described as the "onerous documentary obligations" (Croson 548) of proven discrimination can actually constitute a new and additional opportunity for potential discrimination. Since placement on the city MBE directory can help a fledgling business attract the attention of private as well as public firms, exclusion from the list means that a majority of struggling Chicago-area Indian businesses remain obscure and unable to participate in local contract bids (Sundman 1992, 10). There are already many documented cases of Indians being denied bank loans and other financial assistance in the Chicago area (Sundman 1992, 10; Marvin Tahmahkera's struggles to obtain startup funding for his successful Comanche Steel Company are detailed in *MBE: Minority Business Entrepreneur Magazine*, May/June 1985, 9-12). An assertion of suffering at the hands of discrimination is already a highly difficult and often costly statement to make in the current American sociopolitical climate; and when solvency is at stake, most small business owners lack the time and extra resources that are needed to chronicle and pursue instances of perceived discrimination. Even more insidious is the often-overlooked fact that the denial of automatic minority status has repercussions outside of the business community. The categories used in Article IV can be used to render Chicago-area Indians ineligible for other affirmative action-apportioned jobs as well as the minority quotas for locally funded endeavors like city colleges and scholarships. It is therefore clear that automatic recognition is a powerful component for the potential success of Indian groups and individuals, and that the denial of unchallenged city minority status is a definite disadvantage.

The ramifications of Article IV seem all the more dangerous and discriminatory when the justification for the removal of Indians from the list of "official" Chicago minorities is investigated. The 1990 Blue Ribbon Panel declared that "Minorities other than African-Americans, Hispanics, and Asian-Americans make up roughly 0.3% of the Chicago-area small business community" (Blue Ribbon 1990, 76), too statistically small a group to analyze in the context of the study. Although they were willing to concede that "Native Americans are the most common members of this very diverse group [of Others] (Blue Ribbon 1990, 76), the Blue Ribbon Panel claimed to have found only two Indian-owned businesses in Chicago. In contrast, a separate and independently-funded 1992 study conducted by AIEDA located over 137 potentially Indian-affiliated businesses in the Chicago area (Sundman 1992, 10). The existence of such blatantly contradictory evidence throws great doubt on the assumptions that underscored the construction of the Blue Ribbon Panel report. There seems to have been an immediate and a priori belief that Indians were a marginal component of the Chicago population and an even more marginal part of the city business community. This belief was apparently so pervasive that any other possibilities were left unchecked; further investigations into Indian businesses were curtailed, and even the potential Indian affiliations of Chicago Hispanics and the other recognized minorities were overlooked in favor of different racial, geographic, and cultural allegiances. The overly complicated categories of Article IV do not in fact display a heightened sensitivity to the construction of minority identity; instead, they reflect and reify old sociocultural stereotypes. One of the stereotypes that seems to have been incorporated into the deliberations of the Blue Ribbon Panel and even the scientific investigations of the Lowry Report is the long-standing idea of the "vanishing Indian," a primitive, rural person destined to disappear or seamlessly assimilate under the pressure of superior Western culture and its urban-suburban lifestyles (Berkhofer 1978, 240). Indian businesses and even Indian residents are not looked for because they are presumed to be largely non-existent in a twentieth century American city. A denial of city minority status for American Indians constitutes an official, institutionalized denial of the possibility for a sizable and distinctively Indian presence in modern Chicago.

It is indeed apparent that minority-status recognition could play an instrumental role in the continued survival and success of Indians living in the city of Chicago. In the years since the Blue Ribbon Panel published its report and Article IV was codified, both interested individuals and groups like AIEDA have worked hard to promote the visibility of Indians in the city and the city's business community. For instance, in 1992 AIEDA Executive Director Yvonne Murry-Ramos and Program Director Pam Alfonso organized a Native American Business Breakfast for Indian owners of Chicago-area businesses. The success of this event and a demand for subsequent meetings were interpreted as solid indications of a perceived need for extended contacts both inside and outside Chicago Indian communities. Accordingly, a city Native American Business Directory was created to fill the void left by exclusion from general Chicago MBE lists. By the end of 1990, 87 Indian-owned businesses were listed for the city of Chicago (AIEDA 1990, 70). Subsidiary city departments like Water and Parks Service were lobbied and eventually convinced to add American Indians to their hiring categories of presumptive local minorities. To date these additions have not been challenged by the city, state, or federal governments, and so they continue to provide hope that Indians will eventually be recognized as an official minority for all Chicago city affirmative-action programs.

In closing, it should be noted that Chicago's Article IV is not a unique city ordinance. The fallout of the Croson decision has endangered the legal minority status of Indians in many other American cities. The fact that such restrictions could exist even in regions with large Indian populations is further proof that harmful stereotypes like the "vanishing Indian" have not yet been eradicated from the popular consciousness. It is evident that citydwelling American Indians must continue to combat this stereotype through public assertions of their presence within the city population; the "lists and lobbying" type of publicity that was used by AIEDA in Chicago may be put to effective use in other areas. Concrete evidence for the persistence of American Indian ethnicity within city structures will hopefully help lay the myth of the "vanishing Indian" to rest and promote a greater American acceptance of the idea of a modern, urban Indian.

References

American Indian Economic Development Association. *Chicago Native American Demographic Profile*. Chicago: AIEDA, 1990.

Berkhofer, R.F. *The White Man's Indian: Images of the American Indian from Columbus to the Present*. New York: Alfred A. Knopf, 1978.

Blue Ribbon Panel. *Report of The Blue Ribbon Panel to the Honorable Richard M. Daley, Mayor of the City of Chicago*. Chicago: City of Chicago, 1990.

"Comanche Steel Company." *MBE: Minority Business Entrepreneur*. May /June 1985: 9-12.

Sundman, Helena. "City Pushed to Include Indians in Set-Asides." *Chicago Reporter*. July 1992: 10.

Executive Orders, Ordinances, and Legal Cases

Article IV 2-92-420, City of Chicago Legal Code, 1996 version.

Executive Order 85-2, Mayor's Office, City of Chicago, 1985.

Executive Order 89-7, Mayor's Office, City of Chicago, 1989.

779 F. 2d. 181, Croson 1, 1985.

822 F. 2d. 1355, CA4, Croson 11, 1987.

488 U.S. 469, City of Richmond v. J.A. Croson Co, 1989.

Lisa Ortiz

Indian or Not?

Ethnic Identity Among Biracial Native Americans

World War II and the Federal Relocation Program contributed to a large movement of Indians from rural reservations to urban areas. Like members of other ethnic groups, Native Americans eventually married and had children with people of other ethnic groups, producing children of mixed ethnic identity. Chicago Indian organizations have observed a sharp increase in children of mixed heritage.

My research project addresses the question: Is the Native American mixed-race individual still accepted and identified as Indian by other Native Americans living in Chicago? My hypothesis was that mixed-heritage peoples are accepted by the Chicago Native American community as Indian.

To evaluate my hypothesis, I asked 20 Chicago Native Americans to participate in a structured interview. Of the 17 who participated, 8 were self-identified as mixed-blood and 9 "full-blood." The research instrument used as a questionnaire containing 12 questions, in face-to-face interviews that allowed the researcher to observe the participants' facial and body language.

---

1. Being enrolled is when an individual is legally a member of a federally recognized tribe of the United States or Canada. Individuals must submit an application to their prospective tribe citing ancestral background, usually grandfathers or grandmothers. Once this is done, the tribal council (government) of the tribe approves the application, provided everything is in order, and informs the individual that they are a member of the tribe entitled to receive full benefits. The full benefits of a tribe may include voting privileges, use of tribal services, such as health clinics, social services and others, employment with the tribe, and in some cases, receiving money from tribal casinos.

COMBINED PARTICIPANT ANALYSIS

When the data from all the participants was combined, ten participants, over half of the total number of participants, stated that blood was important in Indian identity. Four respondents stated that how an individual presented him-or herself was important, while at the same time four respondents stated that having or showing respect was important. Two participants stated the Indian identity was a feeling in the heart while another said that he or she was not really sure what determined Indian identity.

Where skin color or tone was addressed, ten respondents stated that skin color did not play a determining role in whether an individual was identified as Indian while three stated that skin color was sometimes used to determine identity. Two participants stated that skin color did play a part in their assessment of an individual's identity while two participants said that it should not but it does. Physical appearances including skin color, hair color, and eye color were not important in determining Indian identity for seven of the participants, while another seven stated that appearances somewhat determined Indian identity. Three participants stated that physical appearances were important in Indian identity.

Asked whether mixed-race children should be considered Indian or not, twelve respondents stated that yes, they should, while three stated that if the children were of one-quarter Indian blood, then they should be considered Indian. Two participants said that it was up to the children whether they wanted to be Indian.

MIXED-BLOOD ANALYSIS

Of the eight mixed-race individuals interviewed, five stated that possessing Indian blood was part of the Native American identity, while two stated that how a person presents him-or herself to others is part of the identification. Three participants stated that respect was part of Indian identity, but two respondents expressed respect toward others, while one respondent stated that respect for being Native American was important. One respondent out of the seven stated that knowing where one comes from and something about his or her culture was important while another respondent expressed that it was a feeling from the heart when he or she stated, "I don't think it should be left up to just blood quantum. I think that's a part of it yeah, and you can't get away from it 'cause I don't think anyone's willing to. . . . but, I think it's more of in your heart, who you are. . ." Another respondent stated that following Indian traditions was important to Indian identification when he said, "I believe in all the traditions that I've been taught, and I've followed a lot of my tribal doings back home which I carry with me." Only one participant out of seven stated that he or she was not really sure what qualities determined an individual as Indian. If taken in the order of importance, possessing Indian blood was deemed the most important factor. Showing respect for others and how well individuals presented themselves to others both ranked second in order of importance. Having respect for being Native American, knowing something about your culture and where you come from, having a feeling from the heart, and knowing your cultural traditions were considered important to only one participant each.

Where skin color or tone was addressed, five of the seven participants stated that skin color was not important in determining whether an individual was identified as being Native American. The two participants who said yes, skin color determines whether an individual is Native American, followed up their answers by stating that skin color should not matter in identification, but it does and that is just how things are.

With respect to determining whether mixed-raced children should be considered Indian or not, five of the seven mixed-race participants said yes, while one stated that it depended upon whether the children wanted to be viewed as Indian. This participant also stated that "if the children want to learn about their Indian heritage, they should be encouraged to do so and should be able to live as an Indian without any problems." The last participant stated that mixed-blood children should be considered Indian if at least one of the birth parents was known to be Indian. He or she also stated that the child or children would have a difficult time growing up, but that knowing that one of the birth parents was Indian would help in accepting mixed-blood children.

The question regarding whether physical appearances determined an individual as being Indian or not was answered no by five of the seven respondents. Some participants' statements to back up their answers ranged from, "It doesn't depend on what they look like physically. With so many mixed-blood Indians nowadays, it's hard to say who's Indian and who's not. I try to give the people the benefit of the doubt. If they are Indian and they know about their culture, then they will be able to talk about it in such a way that other people will know they are Indian." to "It's kind of innocent until proven guilty. I don't think . . . . I'm not that concerned about someone having to call themselves Native American or whatever even if they don't look like a supposed Native American, whatever they're supposed to look like" to "Well, I have many of those come up to me and tell me that they have Native American blood, and I believe them . . . . because there are a lot of those people that I even went to school with that do not look Native, but they are. They do have a strain of Native Indian blood, so if someone came up to me and said well I'm a Native American same as you are, the I'll go ahead and believe them. There would be no doubt in my mind." Other participants who answered no to physical appearances playing a part in Indian identity talked about mistaken racial identity and Native Americans being all colors when he or she stated, "People ask me if I'm Indian because they think I'm Filipino or Mexican, but I think a lot of people just ask, well what tribe, where are you from, what reservation and then . . . . I don't . . . it's kind of a hard question. But, Native Americans are all colors, it's kind of a hard thing." and "I don't use physical appearances a lot because I don't look Native American myself. It's good to be Indian now." Two participants stated that physical appearances sometimes played a part in Native American determination, but that they did not use it a lot when they stated, "I would ask them where their background is. Well, it wouldn't determine whether it was yes or no immediately, there would definitely be a question first" as well as "Sometimes it does. Some people come up to me and say stuff like that and I just look at them sometimes, and when they walk away, I just laugh a little bit. But, I've just got to remember that I've got cousins that have blond hair and blue eyes and they're Indian."

FULL-BLOOD ANALYSIS

Nine full-blood Native Americans were interviewed: five females and four males. Five of the nine participants stated that in order to be considered Indian, individuals had to be able to prove their Indian blood. Whether this was to be done through status cards or through other means was not addressed. Two participants stated that how a person presented and carried him-or herself is what determined an American Indian, but one of these participants was also one who said proof of Indian blood was needed. Some of the other identifiers for the full-bloods included "a feeling of being Indian in your heart," doing things the "Indian way," taking someone's word that they are Indian, and respecting elders. The order of importance is seen as having proof of Indian blood, followed by how a person presents and carries him-or herself, with a feeling in the heart, doing things the Indian way, respecting elders, and taking a person's word that they're Indian deemed important to one full-blood participant each.

When asked whether skin color or skin tone determined Indian identity, five of the nine participants stated that skin color did not play a big part in their determination of Indian identity. Two said that skin color played a part to a certain extent, and their determination of identity depended upon how the person presented him-or herself to others to not being sure at first glance if the individual was Indian because they could not be sure about someone with light skin color anymore. One of the remaining participants stated that skin color should not play a part in determining identity while another stated that yes, skin color played a big part in identity because "Indians were brown not pale or dark-skinned."

When the question of should Native American mixed-race children be considered Indian, five participants stated that if the children possessed at least one-quarter Native American blood then they should be considered Indian. The last participant said that it depended upon the children, that if they chose to live as Indian, they should be considered Indian. Interestingly, one of the participants stated that although he or she approved of mixed-breed children being considered Native American, he or she disapproved of Indians marrying outside the Indian race.

When the question of whether physical characteristics pre-determined respondents' views of individuals who claimed to be Indian was asked, four respondents stated that their view depended upon whether the persons claiming Indian blood could answer questions as to what tribe he or she belonged to, where their Indian blood came from, where he or she was from, and where he or she was enrolled.[1] The participants also stated that if the person being questioned is telling the truth, they could answer each question with some degree of truth, and if the truth was being spoken it was easily recognizable by the respondents. One participant expressed that physical characteristics played no part in his or her opinion of someone claiming to be Indian, while another stated that he or she was a little more compassionate toward those with physical characteristics that did not look Indian. The seventh respondent said that he or she was taught to never make those with White or other race characteristics feel not Indian because it is not their fault that they are mixed, while the eighth said that his or her view depended totally upon physical characteristics "because Indians do not have blue eyes, at least none that I've seen," and that an individual who had blond hair and blue eyes did not "seem Indian" to him or her. The last participant did not answer the question, but had a tendency to sound a lot like the eighth respondent when he or she stated, "I know in my heart that we were here first. The real Native Americans were here in the beginning, with their brown color, we have brown eyes, we have brown hair. . . . our actions are a little bit different from the Caucasians."

CONCLUSION

If the survey were generalized in the Native American community, half of the Indian community would not let physical appearances determine Indian identity. One possible explanation for physical characteristics not playing a determining role in Indian identity may be due to that fact that many Indians have lived in the city for a long time, and because of having lived in the city for such a long time may have made them more tolerant of Indians who look different due to the mixing of Indians with people of other races. The other part of the community said that physical appearances played a role somewhat in Indian identity, but that if individuals could truthfully answer questions of who they are, where they came from, where they got their Indian blood from, and where they are enrolled, then physical appearances did not matter any longer. When asked about how an Indian would know if an individual was telling the truth about having Indian blood, many said "that watching body language and watching the eyes of the person would tell if that person was lying or telling the truth."

Karen Strong

Culturally Intact Heroines

A Pro-Activist View of Native American Womanists

FOR YOUNG NATIVE AMERICAN WOMEN

"Prepare yourself and be patient. If you cannot be patient, then be careful."

—Karen Strong

Culturally intact Native American heroines are mature women who live within the cultural norms and traditions of their native communities. They are the grandmothers, elders, aunts, sisters and friends within the community: they have listened to those around them, and responded to questions and requests without compromising who they are. They are teachers, in the community and beyond it: the strength of their teaching is "grounded in cultural knowledge" (Katz 1995, 15). They are literate: in some cases, they have overcome barriers to literacy such as abuse, teen pregnancy, and persistent teacher racism (Bowker 1993). Carrie Dann (Shoshone) had to teach herself to read well in order to continue the land rights case that she and her sister Mary took all the way to the Supreme Court! Such women are dedicated to preserving and protecting their culture for the next generation, which will, according to prophesy, lead the people back to their traditions (Johnson 1994, 6-7). They are *womanists*, not feminists: they work for their communities as a whole and they understand the critical role of women in those communities. They are pro-active, working towards a future that they expect to see develop, and their work is part of that future.

Bilingual, bicultural literacy has been enhanced by the longest running women's theater group in this country. The Spiderwoman Theater has been performing on stage together, seperately and with other theater groups since 1975. (Actually, they performed together as children in their father's circus snake oil show long before Spiderwoman Theater was formed.) They have performed several times in Chicago, most recently

(May 1998) in an adaptation for stage of Louise Erdrich's *Love Medicine;* they also did a successful and much appreciated residency in the Chicago Indian community co-sponsored by AIEDA and Randolph Street Gallery in 1993. They are urban Indian women, and they communicate the strength of urban Indian communities as well as the value of their own particular traditions. The oldest sister chose the stage name Lisa Mayo when she began acting professionally. She joined her sisters, Gloria and Muriel Miguel, for what was planned to be a short period, but the three have grown into a successful theater company that has traveled to China, Russia, Europe, and Canada as well as throughout the United States. They begin every show by stating that they, as Kuna/Rappahonnock womanists, perform to make the audience aware of Native American issues, both feminist and community-oriented.

Lisa Mayo, the robust Native American woman, unafraid of her large body frame, remarked in an interview with Elizabeth Theobald (1994, 161),

> I auditioned for native roles but I never got them because I didn't look like a casting director's idea of an Indian, and if I was in another play, I'd have to fit myself in. Then I realized—I'm not an ordinary Indian. I was brought up in Brooklyn, trained in musical tradition and converted to Judaism. I have to tap into my own resources. With Spiderwoman, I could find my own voice.

On a 1994 tour in Santa Fe, New Mexico, the Spiderwoman Theater curtain closed to the sound of four Oklahoma Native American men trilling the Spiderwomen as though they were native warriors going into battle. This is high, honored praise from Native American male scholars. I was awed by the ribald portrayal of Native American women's issues. They can speak out, be heard, and remembered.

Another warrior woman in the arts is Charlene Teeters (Spokane), one of the founders of the Coalition on Racism in Sports and the Media. The news media refers to Char as a "radical" or an "activist," not as a Native womanist protecting her Native American culture, showing a double standard in regard to recognizing heroines. Char has been producing art installations nationwide against Indian mascots in sports. She began these installations against racist stereotypes that are accepted by the American public as sports mascots while a graduate student at the University of Illinois (Champaign), protesting Chief Illiniwek. Her installations against Indian mascots have been shown in New York City, at Bradley University in Peoria, Illinois, at the Institute of American Indian Arts Museum in Santa Fe, and in Spokane, Washington. Char knows sports mascots can hurt Native American children, especially if these stereotypes are the only mainstream exposure for the American public. The self-esteem and dignity of Native American children and all Native Americans can be damaged by the misappropriation of Native American culture in the name of entertainment. The PBS film, "In Whose Honor?" (1996) by Jay Rosenstein brings to full light those who want to pick, choose, and appropriate the Native American culture for the sports arena without any Native American input about this supposed honor.

Nobel Laureate Rigoberto Menchu is a heroine to many Chicagoans. She renounced marriage and motherhood to join the Church, where she was able to become educated. She learned four languages: Spanish and the Indian languages Mam, Cakchiquel, and Tzutuhil. Then she not only taught the people how to read, she offered lessons about organizing politically. Once a political purpose for reading is established, then learning to read well becomes a goal. Young Native American girls need to know why they need to read, leaving no argument unturned. They need to participate in a discussion from as many views as possible. Political reasoning has been the most effective argument. In Canada, uneducated Native women learned to read well when they understood that reading about their disenfranchisement by the Canadian government would help them to plan and organize Canadian Natives towards regaining their tribal citizenship (Silva 1988).

Powerful Native American women's words on stage, in print and in film can bring one who feels alienated and depressed into another state of mind. Native American women need to read about the unsung heroines who have persevered. These women need to seek out caring people who will encourage them to praise in their efforts to resolve age-old problems within the span of their own lives.

Most Native American women who have influenced the political arena have done so quietly and harmoniously. Like treelines in the fog, they do their work behind the public scenes of most political action. These strong women think openly and publicly share their thoughts. Debbie Valentino, for example, was one of the founders of a storefront program that focuses on families rather than individuals, and which includes a strong literacy component. Some of these women do eventually become recognized for serving their communities selflessly over a long period of time. For example, the Chicago Indian Community recently recognized Vonda Gluck for her years of service as a board member of Native American Educational Services (NAES) College (1996). Vonda was able to become culturally literate by returning to her reservation and seeking knowledgeable elders. Her work at the Field Museum led her to begin crafts work, especially doll-making, at home, in order to surround her terminally ill husband with wonderful items. She encouraged cultural literacy and social connection by inviting a group of women to join her and thus inspired others to reconnect with traditional crafts as well.

Jeanne LaTraille, an Oneida womanist, was one of the woman who met at Vonda's home to share craftmaking knowledge and stories. She came to

Chicago to go to the Art Institute, but it was during the World War II, and she was encouraged to support the war effort by becoming a draftsman, taking training at the Illinois Institute of Technology. She has just completed her BA degree at NAES College in Chicago. Jeanne was always a reader, even when she was operating the forklift or guarding prisoners from the guard tower; she always wrote and illustrated stories for her grandchildren. She reads everything from grocery-store tabloids to the Great Books. At NAES, however, under the tutelage of Dr. Lola Hill (Chippewa), she discovered poetry and she has been writing, reading, and teaching poetry in the Chicago area for several years now. She writes poetry to express her own life experiences, to share them with others, and to teach about the Indian community in Chicago. At 75, Jeanne LaTraille considers that her recent literary experience is a second chance to live life fully.

Family illness or crisis, or a conflict situation may cause culturally intact women to seek literacy. Clovia Malatare managed to temper her youthful wandering by spending time reading in the local Chicago libraries. As a Catholic school runaway, this young Lakota womanist protected herself from streetlife by learning to love reading. To this day, she and her children are avid readers of diverse genres of literature.

Becoming literate involves choosing a more public role than most Native American women want. This open choice of independence also provides an open path for the learning process. The myriad of choices for the further development of a community practicing social consciousness is not clear to young Native Americans. In this day and age, how does one decide which way to go, and still be recognizable as a Native American? Native American womanists show possible and plausible ways through life histories about themselves that can be used and reused as many times as needed. Telling their stories offers the wisdom that many young Native Americans and other interested parties may be willing to hear and read.

The proactivist view of the Native American womanists has been integrally connected to the survival and perpetuation of Native cultures. Within contemporary society, becoming literate both in mainstream society and traditional culture has become paramount to the breath of life. The bicultural experience will offer flexibility of thinking essential for the development of acceptable solutions to world as well as community problems. The challenge for today's youth is to use the thought process with the historical reflection of inclusion of all that has come before us for future issues. Remember the Native American womanists of the past, and those presently around you, and move forward, proactively, as they have done.

BIBLIOGRAPHY

Bowker, Ardy. *Sisters in the Blood: The Education of Women in Native America.* Montana: Montana State University, 1993.

Cheromiah, Emily. Telephone interview. September 26, 1997.

Emery Dye, Eva. National Women's Suffrage Association, 1905.

Freire, Paulo. *Pedagogy of the Oppressed*. New York: Continuum, 1996.

Gunn Allen, Paula. *The Sacred Hoop: Recovering the Feminine in American Indian Traditions*. Boston: Beacon Press, 1992.

Huff, Delores. *To Live Heroically*. Albany: SUNY, 1997.

I, Rigoberta Menchu': An Indian Woman in Guatemala. Elizabeth Burgos-DeBray, ed. London, 1992.

"In Whose Honor?" Jay Rosenstein. PBS, 1996.

Indian Roots of American Democracy. J. Barreiro, ed. *Northeast Indian Quarterly*, 1998.

Johnson, Sandy. *The Book of Elders: The Life Stories & Wisdom of Great American Indians*. San Francisco: Harper, 1994.

Katz, Jane. *Messengers of the Wind: Native American Women Tell Their Life Stories*. New York: Ballantine Books, 1995.

Mankiller, Wilma and Michael Wallis. *Wilma Mankiller: A Chief and Her People*. New York: St. Martin's Press, 1993.

Orr, Vanessa. *The Legacy of Elizabeth Peratrovich Lives On. Capital City Weekly*. February, 1997.

Roberts Strong, Karen. *Finding the Native American Woman's Voice: On Becoming Literate*. Ph.D. diss. University of Illinois, Urbana-Champaign, 1997.

Silva, Janet. *Enough is Enough: Aboriginal Women Speak Out*. Toronto: The Women's Press, 1988.

Theobold, Elizabeth. *Beyond the Images: Native Voices and Visions in New York Theater*. Native American Expressive Culture, 1994.

Wallis, Velma. *Two Old Women*. New York: Harper Perennial, 1993.

"Wiping Away the Tears." Gary Rhine. Kifuru Productions, 1991.

Agnes Wagosh

Canadian Islanders in Chicago

During and after World War II, many Anishinabe people from Manitoulin Island, Ontario, came to Chicago. Most came because of the job opportunities in the city, and pretty much all of them were successful in finding work. Chicago became their second home, but they continued to travel back and forth to the island and most seemed to return to Manitoulin when they retire. On Manitoulin, jobs were pretty scarce: about the only industry that existed was cutting pulpwood and some farming. Many islanders were skilled lumberjacks, but could not find work on the island and crossed the border to cut pulp in Michigan. Others decided to look beyond the forests for employment and move into urban areas where jobs were more plentiful.

The Relocation Program in the United States did not cover Canadian natives. Although there was some relocation assistance within Canada, job opportunities seemed better in the States. Jobs were hard to find in Sudbury and Toronto, and even in Detroit. In Chicago, everyone found work within a week or so. Chicago was considered a good place to be: there were jobs and places to live. Often, the men would come first, secure a job and a stable income, and then send for their families. Sometimes, however, women came on their own to find work. Band members in Chicago let their friends and relatives back home know about opportunities for work and residence and eventually a small community of Canadian Anishinabe developed in the city.

Canadian natives in Chicago did not receive U.S. state or federal social services: they were pretty much on their own. These were hard-working family men who were not big on partying or drinking. They developed good relations with their co-workers, remained in their jobs for many years, and generally did well in Chicago, providing for themselves and their families, earning enough to be able to travel regularly to the reserve and even to develop some savings.

The first to arrive in Chicago became role models for those who followed. Jacob and Alex Jacko, among the earliest to arrive, came during World War II, to work in war related industry in the city. Jacob Jacko had left home at an early age. His father did not approve of the girl he planned to marry, and told him to leave town. Like many Ontario Anishinabe, he ended up in Michigan, cutting pulp. One day in 1941, he left Michigan and boarded a bus heading for Chicago. He enjoyed the bus ride, especially looking at the flowers and green grass when he had been used to northern forest. Jacob was 31 years old; he knew no one in the city. On his own, he found a job and a place to stay. Like many Indian people who came into cities to find work, he moved in and out of it regularly. After his successful move to Chicago, he moved back to the reserve, married Bessie Gaiashk, and started a family. Together, they moved back to Chicago, where Bessie worked at Motorola. They both worked for many years in Chicago and eventually returned to the reservation when they retired. After he retired, Jacob still wanted to be productive: he could not just not sit and do nothing. He built a house for his family and indulged in his hobby of sawing logs. At age 86, he still drives, goes to church on Sundays, and visits Chicago periodically, especially to see the children who remained here when he returned home. His Chicago relatives also travel to the reserve to visit them.

Jacob's brother Alex said it was twenty below zero when he left home. At that time, everyone was talking about the "War Effort," so he went to work in Detroit. He worked in a big warehouse for the U.S. Army, but he was not happy there. He tried to enlist in the army, but was rejected and so went back to Wikwemikong (on Manitoulin) where he worked in farming with another brother, Gabriel. Jake, successful in Chicago, wrote to Alex in Wikwemikong, encouraging him to come to Chicago, and Alex decided to follow the suggestion. Like his brother, Alex came to Chicago speaking very little English, but he was not afraid to go out and try something new, even in a language not familiar to him. Jacob also encouraged other friends and relatives from "Rabbit Island" to come to Chicago.

I will mention four other Anishinabe families from Wikwemikong who came to Chicago somewhat later. Richard and Mabel Roy came to Chicago about 35 years ago. They came with just a few dollars, and Mabel was pregnant. Richard went to work while Mabel stayed home and raised three boys, Richard, Dale, and Chris. Two of those boys are now married and the third is still looking. Richard decided to buy a house as it was difficult to find people who would rent to a family with three boys: they stayed in this house until the boys grew up. Richard believed that the boys should be on their own, earning their own way when they became adults, and all of them have done so. Richard continues to work for the city of Chicago as a cement finisher and he created a patio behind his second house where his family and other Anishinabe people gather to visit. Mabel later worked part-time at Clare Inc., a company that manufactures electronic relays. She got her job through the recommendation of Agnes Wagosh, another Manitoulin Islander already working there. When Clare closed, she took a job that required her to commute quite a distance every day. Richard plans to retire in 1998, and they plan to move back to Manitoulin.

There are a lot of Roys in Chicago: another Roy family, not directly related to Richard and Mabel, came from West Bay reserve. One of the early West Bay Roys, Theodore Roy, or "Ted," arrived in Chicago in the 1950s, even before Richard and Mabel. Ted is retired now, but he worked as a painter for many years. Since his retirement, Ted splits his time between Chicago and West Bay. His wife and teenage son live in Chicago. After Ted arrived, his brother Mike and his sister both followed him to Chicago, in much the same way as Alex followed Jake Jacko. Mike's wife, Georgina, also from West Bay, works in day care with children in the Chicago community.

Florence Roy Richmand is another old-timer from the island: she is also from West Bay. She and her husband, Vince, came to Chicago at about the same time as Richard and Mabel. They also were able to buy their own home and raise their children here. At one point, Florence sold her home in Chicago and moved back to the island; but her stay was brief and not much later, she moved her family back to Chicago. Vince, her husband, is now retired and her children are grown up. Like Richard and Mabel, they bought a second home after their children left. Florence still works at the post office in the city, commuting to work every day from their home in the suburbs.

Lillian Peltier is somewhat unusual among the Anishinabe to arrive in Chicago from Manitoulin Island, because she did not come to join someone already here. She arrived here by car with another islander, but she really came alone from Wikwemikong. Like the others who came around the same time (about thirty years ago), she did quite well here. Lillian is a white collar worker. She bought a condo for her home and she travels during vacations to visit her family in the "cedar swamps" of Wikwemikong. Lillian's family was quite musical and her son from Wikwemikong joined her in Chicago for a while after studying music in Toronto.

The Kitchkeg boys, Clement and John, are from South Bay Mouth. They came to Chicago together as young adults, and they both married here. They are now men and they continue to live in the city, but visit their homeland frequently. They are not as regular a part of the island group in Chicago, because they have other family responsibilities here through their wives. The other islanders continue to be aware of them, however, follow what they are doing, and they welcome them when they are able to participate in gatherings and celebrations of the group.

Now I have to mention Virginia Debassige. Her story is unique. She came to live in Chicago about forty years ago with one of her children, escaping a very difficult situation at home. She worked and saved some money in order to leave, and she had to be very inventive in order to get away. She came to Chicago because she knew people who were here and because she believed she would be able to find work. Her first job was babysitting, which allowed her to keep her own child with her. Her other children followed her to Chicago when they were able to. Virginia did not speak English, nor could she read or write. One day, her son, Levi, went with her to go job hunting. Advance Transformer hired her. Levi told them that she did not speak English and was not literate; but they said that she would make it, and they were right. She remained at that company for more than thirty years. Gradually, with the help of her coworkers, Virginia began to pick up English. By this time, most of her children had moved to Chicago to be with her.

Virginia is a planner. Before she retired from Advanced Transformer, she bought a house on the reserve. She was preparing for her old age. When she reached the age of 65, she retired and moved into her home in West Bay. Virginia was illiterate but that did not stop her from making a living and thinking about her future. Along the way, she quit drinking but she still enjoys bingo. She commutes often to Chicago to visit her children who are still living here. Most of her children have done well enough to own their own homes in the city. Her daughter, Georgina, is married to Mike Roy (see above): islanders seem to prefer to marry other islanders whenever that works out, even in Chicago.

David Fox arrived in Chicago right after World War II. His father, Wilfred Fox, had been employed in the war effort in Michigan, where he caught pneumonia and passed away in 1947. Wilfred's brother, John, became a kind of second father to David and his siblings. David lived with a foster family in the town of Spanish, Ontario, during high school. There he got to know an Ojibwe man named Bova Granier, who was working in Spanish. Bova and his family moved to Chicago, where he worked at Bastion-Blessing Construction on Peterson Avenue. Bova encouraged David to come to Chicago and stay with his family on Winthrop Avenue, which he did. David found work right away and began to a attend a lot of American Indian Center activities after he had been there for awhile. David is married to Josephine, who lives now in Indiana, but continues to be involved with the American Indian Center and to be a respected elder in the Indian community in Chicago.

David encouraged his friends and relatives in Manitoulin to come to Chicago. He specially encouraged his "brother," Dominic Wagosh: Dominic was the son of David's uncle, John, who had taken David and his siblings as his own children when their father died, and therefore was like a brother to David. David gave Dominic a piece of paper with his phone number and address in Chicago on it, and encouraged him to come. Dominic wanted to leave Wikwemikong for personal reasons, and he also wanted to see a new place, so he got on a bus one October day, in fact, the day of Canadian Thanksgiving. He arrived, as it turned out, on the day before Bova and David moved from the address he had written on the paper: Dominic almost missed them. He arrived in his lumberjack clothes with only $2 in his pocket, and that was $2 Canadian! He was very lucky to find David before he moved, because he didn't know where else to go.

Dominic didn't get a job right away, but he obviously needed money, so he worked for a daily pay office to help pay the rent and buy food. Eventually, with the help of another Chicago Anishinabe, he got a job at a factory on Ashland Avenue. He saved enough money to pay half the rent on an apartment with David. By Christmas, he felt secure enough to write to his Wikwemikong friend, Agnes, and ask her to join him.

Agnes came by herself and right away found a job at Children's Memorial Hospital with the help of Maggie Murry, another Islander. The job was within walking distance, which was very important, since she did not have a car. She moved in with Maggie when Dominic decided to go back on a riverdrive in the Canadian bush.

Actually, there is an interesting double Chicago connection that brought Dominic back to Chicago. He developed an infection on his legs from the brush on the riverdrive, and went to the doctor in Espanola. As he walked back from Espanola, he passed through Manitowanig, where he happened to run into David Fox who was there on vacation with his good friend from the American Indian Center, Willard LaMere (Winnebago). David asked them "When are you guys going home?" and they told him they were on the way, so he said "I'm going with you" and he got in the car and returned to Chicago.

After he got settled in a two-room apartment at 1033 W. Belmont Avenue in Chicago, Dominic sent for his brother and sister who both came to stay with him. Their mother also visited from time to time. The building where they lived was almost like a commune of islanders: several Manitoulin families lived there in separate apartments, everyone helping each other out. Agnes lived there too, in a separate apartment, and her son, Jerry, had joined her as well. It was never lonely in that building and everyone watched out for each other. Agnes finally went to work for Clare, Inc., after she lost her job at Children's and she stayed at Clare for 35 years, making some very good friends there. She still participates in Clare reunions whenever they happen: Clare itself closed several years ago. Agnes and Dominic married, eventually, and both continued working until two years ago when Dominic retired. They had built up good retirement benefits and now distribute their time between the reserve, Kincheloe, Michigan, and Barefoot Bay, Florida. They visit Chicago often, participating in Indian community events, and staying with their old friend/relative, Josephine Fox, in Indiana.

These are some of the Anishinabe elders who made Chicago their home for a good portion of their lives. Many are now elders in the community. They are indeed role models for the next generations of Indian people, both on their reserves and in Chicago. They were hardworking, responsible, and friendly people. They were good providers and good parents. They owned their own homes and saved money for their retirement: they did not rely on government services or support. They were courageous, often leaving home with little money and poor English skills. Their greatest resource was their own dreams, and the other Anishinabe people who had come to Chicago before them. They enjoyed each other's company and socialized a lot together, but were not tremendously active in the larger American Indian Center or other Indian community organizations until more recently. Between work, family, church, and traveling back and forth to Canada, there was little time for serious community involvement. The early islanders in Chicago were strong Catholics and religion was a big part of their lives, but they also respected traditional Anishinabe ways. They were fluent in Ojibwe and all continued to speak Ojibwe at home in Chicago as well as in Canada: their language was an important link to their home and their culture. Like other American Indians in Chicago, the Manitoulin Island Anishinabe were and are people of *two* homes: Chicago and the reserve. In most cases, even those who spent their entire adult, working lives in Chicago, spent time each year "up north" and either have already or plan to move "home" when they retire.

Mary Jacobs

Coming Around Again

On Christmas day in 1952 my parents, Willard Cummings and Lora Neil Brooks, were married in Dillon, South Carolina. On the next day, my parents left Robeson County to make Chicago their new home. As a child I never thought about the courage or sense of self that that my parents must have had to complete that seemingly simple act of moving away from home for the first time. They had come from very simple beginnings. My dad was 22 when he married my mom. He was the third child of Newton Cummings and Flora Ann Lowry. My father's parents were share-croppers moving up from a one-mule farm to a two-mule farm. Finally my grandparents were able to realize a dream and bought their own 100-acre farm in the Prospect community. They had fourteen children; seven girls and seven boys. All but one of my father's siblings (a brother) would live to adulthood.

My mother was 18 when she married my father. She was the second-youngest child of Andrew Worth Brooks and Mary Jane Locklear. My mother's father operated a crane, and he helped build highways across several states, including Oklahoma and Virginia. My grandmother, my mom's mother, stayed in Pembroke raising their twelve children; only nine would survive to adulthood.

My parents were born during the Depression and their schooling took place in segregated schools. Everyone was poor and few people had the opportunity to better themselves through higher education. During my parents' school years there were the three school buses that rode through Pembroke: one for whites, one for blacks, and one for Indians. My father had attended both of the local high schools for Indians in Robeson County, Pembroke and Prospect High School, but never completed the degree. My mother did graduate from Pembroke High School and even attended a semester of college at Pembroke State University.

Now re-named the University of North Carolina at Pembroke (UNCP), UNCP has the distinction of being the only state-supported college created for the education of Indians. UNCP was established in 1887. It was called the Croatan Normal School. Croatan was one of many names by which the state recognized Robeson County Indians. The legislation that created the Normal school stated that Lumbee people had to purchase the land and erect a building for their school; both of which were completed within the legislative two-year deadline (Oppelt, 1990).

While my parents were growing up, Pembroke State represented the only chance for higher education for Lumbees in North Carolina. The college was a school for teachers and teaching represented one of the few career paths open to Lumbees at that time; the career options were preaching and farming. For those Lumbee men without the required education, the military offered a good alternative.

My father went into the army during the Korean War. He served one term (three and a half years), during which he wrote to my mother. He had had dreams of being a veterinarian and during the war he served as a medic. Going to medical school was not in his future since no school in North Carolina would accept him and he did not have the money to go out of the state. After the war he returned to Robeson County and began working doing carpentry work. Today carpentry work (hanging sheet rock and finishing work) is still a popular area for young men with little education in Robeson County. The work was and is seasonal and sporadic at best.

While working, my father heard about a school in Chicago from Peter Dial, a young Indian man from the Prospect area who had attended there. The school was the Allied Institute of Technology, a trade school, on Michigan Avenue. Peter also gave my father the address of a boarding house were he had lived while he had attended the school. So my parents left Robeson County with the address of the school and the name and address for a place to live.

My mother said that she recalled feeling very apprehensive about moving to Chicago. She had never lived outside Robeson County and wondered if she and my father would be accepted by their neighbors, because Indians were not accepted by whites in and around Robeson County at that time.

They spent New Year's weekend with my great uncle Coolidge Mack Cummings (my father's paternal uncle), his wife Van, and their children in Louisville, Kentucky. Coolidge was a pastor in a "white" church there. It would be several years before he would return to Robeson County to pastor a Indian church. Over the years in Chicago, my parents would visit Uncle Coolidge in Kentucky often.

On the last day of 1952 my parents drove into Chicago. They had an address for an apartment house that Peter Dial had given them; it was 1418

West Jackson. My father said that the woman who ran the apartment house just happened to have an available apartment. They signed the lease. That same week my father went to the Allied Institute to sign up for classes. Since he had not contacted the school earlier, he did not know that the school term had already started and he would have to wait one term before he could enroll. Meanwhile, both he and my mother looked for work.

First Jobs

My father's first job in Chicago was at a plant that made coils for bedsprings. The plant was on Pulaski, but since my parents had a car he was able to get from their apartment to work until he was in an accident. My father recalled that a "drunk" ran into him and the car was totaled. After that he found job closer to their apartment. That job was in a tool and die shop on Madison, at about the 1200 block west.

My mother worked for a catalog company, the Alden catalog, across the street from the apartment. She was able to do the work, but felt that the management was too overbearing. None of the workers in the shop were allowed to speak to each other and all of their breaks were timed. She felt as though every minute was regulated. She left the first job and then went to a small company that printed bank certificates and hunting licenses. She proofread the materials after they were printed. But after getting pregnant, she stopped working because the fumes from the ink made her ill. She would not work again until all of her children were in school.

About a month after moving to the city, my father began attending school at the Allied Institute. He was able to use his GI benefits to pay for school and completed his A.A. degree in Industrial Engineering. Immediately after completing the degree, he got a job with Scully-Jones, a family owned company that designed and made tools for other industries. Later Scully-Jones became a part of Bendix Corporation. My father would stay with the company for twenty-four years before leaving that job to move back to Robeson County.

Keeping in touch with home

Mom said that most of their neighbors in Chicago were poor whites from the south: Kentucky, Tennessee, and Mississippi. She recalled that poor southern whites were most of the people that they met, but whenever they heard about another Lumbee person in the city they would make an effort to meet them and visit with them. My mother said that both her parents and my dad's parents would write them and let them know about other Indians (Lumbees) from home living in or traveling through Chicago.

My mother recalled visiting H. B. Jacobs (she could not remember his full name), a Lumbee man who had served in World War II and married

Lora Neil Brooks. Photo courtesy of Mary Jacobs.

a woman he met in Germany. The Jacobs lived on Adams, near my parents' apartment. There was also Morrison and Odessa Maynor, who lived just north of Kimball Avenue. Then in 1958, my mother's nephew Samuel Brooks came to Oak Park to attend college at Emais Bible College, a brethren college located in that suburb (my mother's family attended the brethren church in Pembroke). My mother's elder brother, Venus Brooks, was pastor of the brethren church in Pembroke and he had wanted his son, Sam, to attend a brethren school. Samuel would marry a white woman from Oak Park and live in that suburb for most of his life.

My parents were able to meet a lot of Lumbee people moving to De-

Willard Cummings. Photo courtesy of Mary Jacobs.

troit or living in Chicago for brief periods who were there for work. While my parents knew of Indians from other tribes living in the city, they did not make much effort to seek them out. My parents grew up in a generation of Lumbee that did not consider themselves "real Indians" because "real Indians like the ones in the movies wore feathers and lived on reservations in the west."

Before there was a real movement among the Lumbee to recover lost traditions and consider themselves a tribe, the people relied on familial ties for identity. That is, your family group (large groupings of families descended from some major figure) determined your identity as an Indian.

My father recalled that few people asked him about his race, but when they did he said he was a Cherokee Indian from Robeson County. He recalled "that's what they told us we were." Cherokee Indians of Robeson County was one of the many names that Lumbees had to use until the state and federal government would allow Lumbees to name themselves in 1956.

But my parents did not rely on a tribal identity to know who was Lumbee; rather people were known only by "who their people were." At that time (and to an extent this is still true), when Lumbee people first met they introduced themselves by telling who their parents and grandparents (and sometimes other relatives who might have been well known in the county) were. Knowing who another Indian's "people" were placed that person in their proper context. With that information you knew where they probably lived in the county, went to school, and which familial church they attended. It also gave information about what kind of work they probably did and, to an extent, the familial reputation (being smart or other personal characteristics) that might extend to that individual as well. That was the way that my parents were able to keep in touch with events and people from "home" that they might not have known otherwise.

But my parents did return to Robeson County after moving to Chicago. For all of the twenty-five years that they lived in Chicago and later Maywood, they returned "home" almost every summer. I remember well leaving home at 2 or 3 A.M. to begin the trip to Pembroke. It would usually take us 18 or more hours of driving and we would not stop until we reached "home." To all Lumbees of my parents' generation and to most today, Robeson County is always called "home." When I return there people usually ask "How long will you be home this time?" And my parents and in-laws usually want to know "when are you coming home?" They are referring to our family home in Pembroke, but they are also referring to Robeson County as a larger home for Indian (Lumbee) people.

My Return to Chicago

My parents had eight children. I was their last child; the youngest or "baby" of the family. I was born in Chicago, like all my brothers and sisters, but considered Pembroke my home. My parents moved back to Robeson County when I was thirteen years old and I attended junior high, high school, and college in North Carolina. I met my husband (another Lumbee person) there and we were married in my mother-in-law's living room.

I decided to move to Chicago after being accepted into the doctoral program in Social Work at the University of Chicago. I really had mixed feelings about moving here. After my husband and I were married we moved to Southern California and had been living there for six years. I did not know a lot about the U. of Chicago before moving here and I was not sure that I would like it. I did know that Chicago had an Indian community, but I did not know of any Lumbee people here except my sister.

My sister, Stephana, was the third eldest child in our family and she never moved to Robeson County with the family. She was already married to a white man she had met at church, and they stayed in Illinois after we moved. All of my other siblings and family were living in Robeson County (and still are).

However, after moving here, I did meet other Indian people, but my sister and I are the only Lumbee people here that we know. My first cousin Samuel Brooks passed away in the mid-1980s and his widow and children still live near Oak Park. My sister and I do visit with them. In addition to school, I work with a group in the Indian community in Chicago who are trying to create more Indian foster parent homes for Indian children, the Native American Foster Parent Association (NAFPA).

I, unlike my parents, grew up during a period of great traditional recovery in Robeson county. Lumbees were more in touch and aware of themselves as a tribal group and were a growing political force in national tribal politics as well. Although Lumbees are still not federally recognized, we do have a national reputation because of all the work that individual Lumbee people do at a national level with various Indian communities and in Washington, D. C. Upon moving to Chicago, I told people here in the Indian community I was Lumbee; they recognized my tribe and I felt very welcomed by the Indian community here.

Today, my parents do not come to Chicago often, but do visit here with my sister and me and our families on occasion. I think their hope is that we will finally return to Robeson County to live permanently, but they understand that returning is not always possible. There are still rather limited employment opportunities in Robeson and the surrounding counties. In addition, the jobs there do not pay well and there are still a lot of racial tensions in the community, especially between whites and Indians.

I hope that I will return to Robeson County or at least the state of North Carolina someday, but for now I am happy to be living and attending school in Chicago. I, like my parents, consider Chicago a temporary stop on the way back home.

Terry Straus

Dr. Robert Beck

Reconnecting

Robert N. Beck, Professor of Radiology, Center for Imaging Science, is an elder of Comanche descent who has occupied a position of great importance and high status at the University of Chicago Hospitals. He is not well known in the Chicago Indian community, but he will be. He has begun that process slowly and appropriately, connecting quietly, offering his knowledge and his experience in support of community goals, especially in health and education. His life history demonstrates that Indian identity is not a static state, but a lifelong process: it is textured, variant, and has its own history in each life.

Dr. Beck's Comanche heritage is through his maternal grandmother, Ophelia LaBarre, an enrolled member of the Comanche Tribe who lived on the reservation in the Indian Territory of Oklahoma. Her husband, James Nason, was a white man who grew up in Indian Territory near Anadarko, spoke the Comanche language, served as a translator for itinerant missionaries, and participated in Comanche culture. Mr. Nason stands in silent testimony that acculturation is not a one-way street. Decades ago, most social scientists believed that Indian identity was seriously threatened by marriage to a non-Indian, especially a white person. Fortunately, today we have the impressive and convincing work of scholars like Brenda K. Manuelito (Navajo), past director of the D'Arcy McNickle Center at the Newberry Library, to confirm what most Indian people already knew intuitively: acculturation works both ways. White people marrying into close-knit Indian communities are at least as likely to adopt Indian cultures as their Indian spouses are to relinquish them. In Dr. Beck's family, his grandparents' marriage was interracial and decidedly Comanche.

> "When my grandfather developed a serious respiratory ailment, the family moved from Oklahoma to San Angelo, Texas, and later to a ranch in West

Texas (near Arden, Texas). This occurred when my mother was in her teens. And although my mother made regular trips to Oklahoma, to lease her land and visit her Comanche relatives and friends, the move to Texas severed all daily ties to the Comanche community, which my mother's parents and the children experienced as a major loss, and as a threat to their identity as Comanches. As a result, they continued to cling to all the symbols and artifacts of their Comanche heritage (beaded leather moccasins and purses, bows and arrows, and the like).

As a child, I was told many stories of what life in the Indian Territory of Oklahoma was like, particularly by my grandmother (who lived on the ranch, where, in my early teen years, I spent as much time as possible). Her childhood memories included raids by soldiers and groups of settlers, an epidemic of typhoid fever, etc. From her, by example, I learned of the Indian sense of respect and reverence for everything in the natural world; one takes only what is needed, and lives in harmony with the natural world.

My mother married Otto Beck (then a meat cutter in San Angelo, of German immigrant heritage) when she was 17. They had three children, I being the youngest, with two older sisters, who still live in San Angelo. Thus, from birth, I was exposed to two quite different cultures, each with its own set of traditions, beliefs, and values. As a child, I found this confusing; however, as long as she lived (she died of cancer at 44, when I was 22), my mother always encouraged me to think for myself, to follow my curiosity and interests, to explore the world, to raise questions, and to resolve the culture-conflict issues in my own way. (by e-mail, April 27, 1998)

"While I regret that I have not succeeded in maintaining regular contact with the Native American community, I feel that my Native American heritage is reflected in the values I have tried to live by.

I'm from San Angelo, a quiet oasis at the edge of the desert in West Texas, where the major activities are sheep ranching and oil production. It was a great place to grow up. In particular, the night sky in that area is truly awe inspiring. It excited my curiosity and stimulated adolescent thoughts about all the large questions—How do we really 'know' anything? What is the meaning and purpose of life on Earth? And, how should I spend my life? As a result, I developed a passionate interest in science at an early age and, in the event that I survived military service, looked forward to spending my life doing physics, which seemed especially appealing.

I graduated from high school in 1945, just before the atomic bomb was dropped on Hiroshima. I was delighted that the war was over, but I was also deeply disturbed by the fact that physicists were responsible for the development of such destructive weapons. It simply didn't fit well with my image of physicists, or the way I wanted to spend my life, and it set off a sequence of 'detours' in my education and career path. I needed time to explore other alternatives—history, biology, psychology, anthropology, philosophy, mathematics—each of which might provide answers to questions that interested me. (Free Press, Nov. 1996, p. 19)"

"For as long as I can remember, it has been clear to me that I needed to know more about how people come to believe whatever it is they believe (including which parts made sense to me and which did not!), and to develop an integrated view of myself and the most reliable knowledge of everything around me. My interests in mathematics, the physical, biological, and social sciences, the liberal arts, and education have grown out of this need. Very fortunately for me, the University of Chicago, with its diverse community of scholars, has provided the opportunity to pursue these interests in my own way, and to make some meaningful contributions to academic life along that way.

I have maintained respect and a sense of reverence for the natural world, which I have always found awe-inspiring in the complexity of all its aspects, and believe that it is essential to the long-term prospects for human survival to live in harmony with that world. [I must say that I have been very pleasantly surprised by the growing shift that I have observed during my lifetime, away from exploitation of natural resources, simply for monetary gain (the major focus of my generation, which grew up during the 'Great Depression'), toward greater value being placed on conservation and renewal of these resources. And while it is relatively easy to get people emotionally involved in 'saving the whales' (which I applaud!), it is still much more difficult to get them equally involved in 'saving the plankton'!]

Although the University of Chicago is seen by many as a very competitive environment, I have tried to avoid direct engagement in competitive relationships. By maintaining a focus on academic interests and goals that I share with others, and by placing high value on cooperation and collaboration, rather than on competition, I have generally found it possible to participate in (and/or to build) multidisciplinary teams of people who are dedicated to worthy goals. In particular, my interests in understanding why we behave the way we do (at the genetic, gender, and cultural levels) has resulted in a passionate interest in developing better methods for brain research. I have pursued this interest since the 1950s, and participated in the team-development of:

• improved imaging methods (e.g., positron emission tomography, PET systems, for studying the effects on brain metabolism of normal stimuli and legitimate drugs, as well as drugs of abuse);

• the development of imaging facilities (e.g., magnetic resonance imaging, MRI, for the study of brain structure);

• the development of the Frank Center for Image Analysis, focused on the brain imaging research (which was established with funds from the Clint Frank family, a founder of the Brain Research Foundation);

Doctor Robert Beck

• and in the development of the Center of Imaging Science (CIS), a joint venture with Argonne National Laboratory, with the goal of establishing collaborative relationships to conduct research on imaging problems that would benefit from a multidisciplinary team effort, whether the problems involve microscopy, astronomical, or medical imaging.

In recent years I have become increasingly interested in contributing to public education, because I believe the new knowledge produced through the application of imaging methods in the sciences and medicine should be passed on to the community-at-large. This interest has led to:

• the proposal to develop an imaging exhibit at the Museum of Science and Industry, called IMAGING: The Tools of Science (which won the prize for the best science exhibit to open in 1993!);

• the development of an undergraduate course, Perspectives on Imaging, which I've taught with Barbara Stafford, Professor of Art History, parts of which are published on the CIS Web Site;

• a collaboration with IBM and the North Central Regional Educational Laboratory, in Oak Brook, to implement EduPort, a digital broadcast technology for 'distance learning' on a very broad (ultimately global) scale. Although our proposal did not succeed in being funded, this collaboration will continue with a focus on getting schools equipped with networked computer facilities.

Now that I have formally retired (on March 25, 1998, in my 50th year at the University of Chicago!), and have no administrative responsibilities, I plan to continue to pursue, with greater intensity, projects involving public education in general, and the Native American community, in particular. To that end, I have begun to explore ways to become more directly involved with the Native American community in Chicago. I have attended meetings at NAES College and in Washington, focused on prospects for getting more Indians informed about opportunities for becoming directly involved in federally funded research projects to improve health care delivery to the Native American community, particularly in the sensitive areas of breast and prostate cancer, alcohol and drug abuse—areas in which my experience and contacts with a broad range of scientists may be of value" (by e-mail April 27, 1998).

Growing up with a Comanche mother and grandmother in Texas and Oklahoma, Bob Beck lived by what he considers to be Indian values throughout his very productive professional life. In this way, he honored and expressed his Indian ancestry while following a remarkable and successful career in mainstream medical science. His work has improved the quality of life for myriad cancer patients and drug addicts, and contributed significantly to both research and development in medical imaging. Retired, now, after 50 years at the University of Chicago, he looks forward to a more focused involvement in Indian communities, issues, and activities—the continuing life history of his Comanche heritage and Indian identity.